INSIDE THE RED BOX

CONTEMPORARY ASIA IN THE WORLD
David C. Kang and Victor D. Cha, Editors

This series aims to address a gap in the public-policy and scholarly discussion of Asia. It seeks to promote books and studies that are on the cutting edge of their respective disciplines or in the promotion of multidisciplinary or interdisciplinary research but that are also accessible to a wider readership. The editors seek to showcase the best scholarly and public-policy arguments on Asia from any field, including politics, history, economics, and cultural studies.

INSIDE THE RED BOX

NORTH KOREA'S POST-TOTALITARIAN POLITICS

PATRICK MCEACHERN

COLUMBIA UNIVERSITY PRESS   NEW YORK

Columbia University Press

Publishers Since 1893

New York   Chichester, West Sussex

Copyright © 2010 Columbia University Press

Library of Congress Cataloging-in-Publication Data

McEachern, Patrick, 1980–

Inside the red box : North Korea's post-totalitarian politics / Patrick McEachern.

p. cm. — (Contemporary Asia in the world)

Includes bibliogrqaphical references and index.

ISBN 978-0-231-15322-5 (cloth : alk. paper) — ISBN 978-0-231-52680-7 (e-book)

1. Korea (North)—Politics and government—1994– 2. Korea (North)—Foreign
relations. 3. Kim, Chong-il, 1942– I. Title. II. Series.

DS935.774.M44   2010

951.9305′1—dc22   2010017046

Columbia University Press books are printed on permanent
and durable acid-free paper.

This book is printed on paper with recycled content.

Printed in the United States of America

c 10 9 8 7 6 5 4 3 2 1

TO JACLYN

Contents

Contents

Figures and Tables

Acknowledgments

This book simply would not have been possible without the hard work of many people. First and foremost, I thank Mark Gasiorowski whose thoughtful critique, clear direction, and warm encouragement shepherded the book from conception to realization. He consistently challenged me to think deeper and consider another angle, and he provided clear and incredibly timely advice on issues large and small. I also owe a debt of gratitude to Bill Clark, Wonik Kim, and David Sobek for helpful comments on the manuscript and for helping lay the foundations for this project. Bill Clark first exposed me to regime types and encouraged my interest in concepts like totalitarianism; Wonik Kim provided valuable insights into the state/society-relations perspective and helped me explore East Asian history; and David Sobek helped me place this project in wider perspective for the discipline.

I also thank a number of my colleagues at the State Department and elsewhere in the federal government, think tanks, and other academic institutions. John Merrill, Brian Kux, Allison Hooker, the rest of INR's Team Korea, my many colleagues on the Korea desk, and others have taught and continue to teach me a great deal. I also appreciate the opportunities I have had to discuss and debate issues with my friends and colleagues. The views expressed here are mine alone and do not necessarily represent those of the U.S. Department of State or the U.S. the government.

I am constantly amazed at the generosity of scholars willing to read part of all of a manuscript like this one. I benefited from productive exchanges with Andrew Scobell, Victor Cha, Steven Kim, Stephan Haggard, Jim Hoare, Susan Pares, Rüdiger Frank, Patrick Köllner, Johannes Gerschewski, Bruce Cumings, Kirk Larsen, Alexandre Mansourov, Alexandre Vorontsov, and many others whom I am inevitably leaving off this list. One should not assume, of course, that these helpful discussants agreed with my argument, making me all the more grateful that they were willing to engage on this topic. I also owe a special thank you to Anne Routon, the editors of this series, and all those at Columbia University Press who made the entire publishing process as smooth as humanly possible.

Last but certainly not least, I single out my loving wife, Jaclyn, for all of her support through this long process. She put up with my moods and my demands for rather obsessive and prolonged focus that only seem unreasonable in retrospect. I certainly could not have completed this without her love, affection, and constant support, so it is only fitting that I dedicate this book to her.

INSIDE THE RED BOX

CHAPTER ONE

Introduction

North Korea is a country that has a very vertically oriented governing
structure to be sure . . . but at the same time it is [a] place for politics.
And so I think it is fair to say that there are people in North Korea
who really are not with the program here, [who would] really rather
continue to be producing this plutonium for whatever reason.

—Chris Hill, U.S. Assistant Secretary of
State for East Asia and Pacific Affairs. March 25, 2008

Kim Jong Il, chairman of the National Defense Commission and general
secretary of the Korean Worker's Party, hosted President Kim Dae Jung of
South Korea in Pyongyang for a historic summit in June 2000. One of the
long-standing issues under discussion was the presences of American troops
on the Korean peninsula. The DPRK ostensibly existed to protect Koreans
and their special, moral, socialist way of life from the violent, greedy, and
uncivilized imperialists and puppet counterparts south of the DMZ.

Party Secretary Kim Yong-sun of the DPRK told the South Korean president that the U.S. military must remove all its troops from the peninsula. Kim Jong Il reportedly interrupted, "What problem would there be
if the U.S. military remained?" Seeming surprised, Kim Yong-sun began
presenting the party line. The U.S. military threatened North Korea and
impaired national reunification. The long-held North Korean position was
simple: the United States must withdraw.

The North Korean party secretary did not get his whole sentence out.
Kim Jong Il again interrupted, "Secretary Yong-sun, stop that. Even though
I try to do something, people under me oppose it like this. Perhaps the
military, too, must have the same view of the U.S. military as Secretary
Yong-sun. The U.S. military should not attack us. But, in President Kim's

explanation, there are some aspects I concur with. [The U.S. military] need not withdraw now. It will be good for the U.S. military to remain to maintain peace even after reunification."[1]

Kim Jong Il was either making history or playing tactical games. This incident could easily have been staged. However, he also may have been expressing genuine conflict within his regime. Groups within North Korea may reveal preferences, and Kim may have to balance and placate these groups. My theory of North Korean politics holds out the possibility that events like this one are not staged. North Korea's highest-level defector, Hwang Jang Yop, has described Kim as one who often publicly castigates senior officials on a whim.[2] Political psychologists note that he is prone to impulsive remarks and policy stands.[3] It is possible that this display actually reflected different bureaucratic positions within the state that Kim seeks to control. Kim is not a captive of his subordinates. He can make decisions and pursue initiatives solely on his own accord, but this is an incomplete understanding of the state's operations. The core argument of this book is that Kim is critically important but so are North Korea's political institutions.

It is not uncommon for North Korea specialists, especially in government circles, to assert that Kim is the only important node in North Korean politics. However, Kim cannot rule by fiat; individuals and institutions below him matter. At the very least, they inform and execute strategic-level decisions and make operational decisions based on their understanding of Kim's wishes. An important goal for any analyst of North Korean politics is to understand how this internal politics works. Whether recognized or not, assumptions about the North Korean political system shape one's view of how it reacts to the external environment. A poor understanding of North Korean politics will inevitably lead one to call the products of that political system (its policy choices) "surprising" or "perplexing."

Existing models of North Korean politics do not sufficiently explain the regime's political process. North Korean actions are continually labeled surprising precisely because of this inadequate view of its political operations. This book seeks to explain—and to a lesser extent predict—North Korea's policy choices based on a revised understanding of its basic functions.

In this specific incident, Kim Jong Il may have decided to shift course given this changed external environment, but what explains the stop-and-go nature of important policies and strategic changes in course? In the economic realm, for example, why suffer the costs of loosened administrative control over the economy to foster economic efficiency if the state is simply going to reverse these gains the following year? How can the regime pursue contradictory policies simultaneously, and why do some senior leaders cautiously voice opposition to decided policy if all policy choices originate from Kim, the "nerve center"? The various monolithic ideal types I describe are useful starting points but are ultimately inadequate for describing and predicting North Korean political choices. Incorporating North Korea's institutional politics into a model of the regime's functions that includes Kim's central role goes a long way toward aiding our understanding of Pyongyang's policy choices and beyond.

Additionally, the summit statement reminds analysts that establishing the meaning and authenticity of statements remains challenging. Are North Korean statements merely tactical efforts to deceive the outside world, or do they also serve as a conduit for internal communication? Pyongyang's focus on information security leads it to try to deceive hostile states even more than most governments. However, concerns about internal threats to Kim's power lead the state to stovepipe information or compartmentalize access to data in such a way as to restrict cross-institutional collaboration and communication. Demand for cross-institutional communication prompts leaders to debate strategic policy choices in the North Korean press, where central leadership can keep a close eye on these communications. Systematically analyzing these data in context can help the outside observer see the interaction between various interests inside North Korea.

Views of the Regime

The popular view that only one man matters in North Korea quickly breaks down upon investigation. One may hypothesize that policy reversals are a function of a dictator ultimately unsure of his own decisions and second-guessing himself. Of course, this does not square well with either the popular or the scholarly image of the dictator. Instead, Kim may be playing tactical games merely to sustain a regime lacking any existential purpose. This, too, inadequately explains a host of specific policy programs and general goals, such as reunification and anti-imperialism. Indeed, one may even label this cartoonish view of the North Korean state as a straw man;

much more sophisticated views of the North Korean state exist that still present the state as some type of monolith.

A number of excellent accounts have been written about U.S.–North Korean negotiations. These explain in great detail the bureaucratic conflict within the U.S. government during these negotiations but rarely refer to any substate actors in North Korea.[4] While these thoughtful authors recognize that some internal dynamic must operate in North Korea, they admit that this process is unknown. Unknown does not imply unknowable.

Partisans in the debate over whether to engage the North question whether the state has or can uphold any of its international commitments. Both sides can select data to bolster their argument, but this selection often does not serve a fruitful analytical purpose. It does not help explain why North Korea upholds its international commitments sometimes and breaks them at other times. Nor does it explain, for example, why the opaque state pursues a risky economic policy of marketization simply to change course later.

I argue that Pyongyang's divergent policy choices reflect, in part, different views and interests within the state. Kim must react to domestic as well as international stimuli. One must first recognize that internal politics matters and then address specifically how North Korean internal politics functions to produce different policy outputs. Such a project has utility for comparative theorists and for policy analysts concerned with how the state functions. The project focuses on the question of how, because a consistently demonstrated pattern of North Korean politics inherently refutes the argument that sub-Kim domestic politics does not matter.

Diverse Institutional Views

The three primary political institutions in North Korea are the Korean Workers' Party (the party), the Korean People's Army (the military), and the cabinet (the government). Chapters 5 to 7 detail the policy positions these institutions express in the official media and how these institutions carefully expose diverse policy preferences to an internal audience, recognizing that foreign observers and the top leadership may read their articles. This exercise exposes a number of specific and general debates, including budget fights over the relative merits of allocating funding to agriculture and consumer goods versus the military and heavy industry. It shows high-level cabinet members attending ceremonies committing rail and road connections across the DMZ and hosting South Korean trade delegations at the same time that party and military officials speak of insulating the state from foreign pressures and engaging in deadly interactions with South Korea.

Specific institutions regularly and openly claim revealed policy preferences as their own and even question policy directions sanctioned by Kim. For example, in 1998 a senior military official said, "The Korean People's Army expected nothing from the agreement [Agreed Framework] and had no interest in dialogue and negotiation through diplomatic channels. Now, the United States, throwing away the mask of 'appeasement' and 'engagement' . . . prove[s] that the KPA's [Korean People's Army] judgment and stand were completely correct."[5] It is only human to want to express to one's colleagues when one's policy preferences should be implemented or to claim victory by being "right." More important, it is common to rational modes of policy creation to use the information resources available in different parts of the system. Communications between working-level and senior-level officials below Kim and his inner circle are necessary for rational rule.

Economic Policy

This more-divided political system has allowed greater discussions on several important issues. The cabinet, party, and military have expressed distinct views on the strategic direction of the North Korean economy. Increased marketization has waxed and waned over the time under analysis as the regime's three institutions have argued for and against allowing the societally driven economic changes to continue. Though party and military officials favor greater socialist orthodoxy in the North's economy, market economics plays a greater role under Kim Jong Il's system than under Kim Il Sung's regime. North Korea still maintains significant elements of a command economy, and the state has not made any irreversible decisions to comprehensively reform the economy. But the scale of the command economy has shrunk in the last fifteen years.

All three institutions and Kim openly recognize the need for economic revitalization, but they differ on how to achieve this goal. The cabinet has been at the forefront of advocating a greater role for markets, decentralized enterprise management, and other mechanisms to increase the efficiency of the North Korean economy. The party rejects a platform they label "reform and opening," warning that the cabinet's policy platform risks bringing down the regime as happened in Eastern Europe. They present a nationalistic argument for the regime to pursue its own Korean way of enhancing economic fortunes through socialism. This often amounts to calls to redouble worker efforts, control cabinet "functionaries," prioritize certain industries, and emphasize work campaigns. The military likewise takes exception to the cabinet's economic policy but has a more limited set of institutional interests to protect. It argues that opening undermines its specific mission to provide security. It opposes inter-Korean economic projects and nonstate actors engaging in commercial activities that undermine their security objective and reduce the prestige of military officers in favor of the "new rich" class of entrepreneurs.

U.S. Policy

Kim Jong Il's North Korea has also demonstrated that its system functions according to a different model in the critical areas of anti-imperialism and reunification policy. The concrete manifestations of these two areas are Pyongyang's foreign policy toward the United States and its policy toward South Korea. The party's main source of input into policy decisions is ideological guidance. As such, it consistently presents the case against accommodating the American "imperialists" in diplomatic forums. It seizes on unfavorable news, presents historical narratives, and makes pure ideological claims that undermine the Foreign Ministry's efforts to engage Washington. The party takes great pride in the high-profile ballistic missile and nuclear programs, touting them as accomplishments of its science and technology leadership. For the party, North Korea did not sacrifice to develop these technologies, which it views as too important not only to national defense but also to national pride to simply trade away for paper commitments from inherently untrustworthy imperialists.

The military also opposes negotiating with the Americans. Its view is that Washington seeks to limit North Korea's coercive potential, particularly in the missile and nuclear areas. The Korean People's Army objects to limitations that a foreign power seeks to place on its ability to defend the state. This insertion of the military institution into politics takes a limited but pragmatic strategic vision. The military objects to negotiations because such diplomatic activity hinders its ability to provide for the state's military-based security. The KPA does not see nuclear weapons as a bargaining chip to extract diplomatic concessions. Rather the weapons are an important element of national security that deter a superior fighting force from pursuing a regime-change strategy. Consequently, the military attempts to operationalize these generic preferences at specific turns.

The cabinet's Foreign Ministry is the only institution that consistently presents the benefits of engaging with the Americans. As the lead organization in each of the different sets of talks during this period, the Foreign Ministry has presented the value of negotiating on missile and nuclear issues by highlighting the concessions the other side provided. It presents North Korea's positions to its foreign counterparts fiercely and has not shied away from ultimatums. But when relations soured, the cabinet often simply went silent while the party and military presented reasons why such an engagement was never productive or worthwhile. This cabinet's strategic interests conflict with the military's and party's interests and platforms; it presents a strikingly different future for the North Korean state, with American security guarantees and economic revitalization.

Inter-Korean Policy

The party, the military, and the cabinet likewise demonstrate three internally consistent agendas on inter-Korean policy. Though all three groups support eventual reunification, they advocate different policies to achieve this end. The party presents a 1950s-style reunification path. That position is so nostalgic that some analysts question whether the party still genuinely maintains a desire to reunify the state through force. South Korea is now a successful democracy with a military likely capable of defeating the North even without American assistance.[6] When Kim Il Sung's forces crossed the thirty-eighth parallel in 1950, the North enjoyed military superiority over the South, and Seoul's antidemocratic tendencies at the time weakened its claim to legitimate rule. Pyongyang also enjoyed support from a much wider group of leftists among the South Korean populace that opposed the

South's rightist government in the early years of the inter-Korean competition compared to today. Seoul's superpower ally continued to demobilize its military forces after World War II, especially in Asia and even more so in Korea. Kim Il Sung enjoyed Soviet political support that brought reluctant Chinese support well in advance of Beijing's actually committing 3 million "volunteers" to the Korean War. Pyongyang had a much better chance of forcing reunification on the North's terms in 1950 than today.

The party maintains that, eventually, conditions will be ripe for a 1950s-style reunification drive again. The "great patriotic war" is immortalized in North Korean lore despite its recognized role in leveling the whole of North Korea and much of the South. The United States is not demobilizing, but it may—someday—withdraw from Asia or at least might decide not to get involved in a long and bloody second Korean war, especially if it ran the risk of nuclear escalation. The Soviet Union is gone, but Pyongyang could conceivably enjoy Russian or Chinese political support in international organizations like the UN Security Council to preserve peninsular stability and limit U.S. presence on the Asian mainland. China's commitment to the North explicitly rules out assistance if Pyongyang initiates a conflict, and it is highly questionable whether Beijing will defend Pyongyang as its legacy treaty commitments promise in case of internal collapse or even foreign invasion. South Korea still has a leftist social element, but it has been much weakened since democratization and is not likely to violently rise up in a militarily significant way against its democratic government in face of a North Korean advance.

Nevertheless, the party takes the long view and prefers to prepare for the day when the North may reunify the Korean nation under one flag. When it is weighed against its alternative and incorporates the individual self-interest of elites, the party's position is more understandable. North Korea is not a state with favorable options. Reforming and opening up bring their own risks, especially to regime elites. If the state reforms in the way of Eastern Europe, revolutionary aims would be lost, decades of sacrifice and family efforts would be for naught, and the physical security of regime elites might be put in jeopardy. Even if the North is integrated into South Korean society under the most favorable of conditions for these elites, they would lose much of their privilege. In short, it is not irrational for this group to want to extend the current system as long as possible rather than take the short-term risks of regime collapse and loss of social

TABLE 1.1 Institutional Policy Preferences			
	CABINET	MILITARY	PARTY
Inter-Korean policy	Favors inter-Korean dialogue and trade as means to reunification.	Reunification struggle requires militant position. Advocates rational contributions to strengthen the military.	Favors forcing reunification on the North's terms in the Kim Il Sung model (Korean War). Ideology strengthens the military.
U.S. policy	Imperialists threaten the state, but the revolution is strong enough to combat long-term security risks associated with a declining material base.	Imperialism can only be defeated militarily. Opposes opening that would undermine the state's security interests.	Confrontation with imperialists fundamentally defines this group's identity. Opposes accommodation on principle.
Economic policy	Is a proponent of economic reform.	Opposes economic reform for pragmatic reasons.	Is ideologically opposed to economic reform.

positions—and possibly the loss of their lives. In practice, this means the party rejects increased economic contacts with the South and stresses military strength.[7]

The military's inter-Korean position is similar in practice to the party's. The military uses fewer explicit justifications for its actions, but it, too, takes exception to the cabinet's inter-Korean economic projects that allow greater cross-border rail and road traffic. It presents military security as a nonnegotiable goal; other issues should not interfere with the KPA's ability to provide for the state's security. The military continually notes in the North Korean media that it stands ready to reunify the state by force. Tactical advances and the motivation of KPA soldiers can assure victory, the military leaders confidently argue. Whether they actually believe they can force the South into a protracted war and avoid American intervention is not knowable. Koreans have a long history of fiercely defending their independence against all odds, and those who gambled and won in North

Korea two generations ago put themselves and their families in positions of power for a long time in a system that otherwise makes climbing the social ladder extremely difficult. More importantly, military leaders must prepare to carry out orders to go to war, so it is natural that these leaders try to position resources most effectively for such a contingency. The fortress state means prioritized resource allocation to the military, sealed northern and southern borders, and developing all available weapons systems, including nuclear weapons and their means of delivery.

The cabinet's inter-Korean policy is the most distinct. It does not reject reunification but does not mention it much either. Inter-Korean policy for the cabinet is wrapped up in a different view of the future of the state. The cabinet has a more difficult time articulating a strategic vision for a unified peninsula under the North's control as a by-product of its advocacy. Instead, it aims at more immediate economic goals and a long-term vision of a more sustainable economy. Foreign investment, special economic zones, development assistance, and humanitarian aid provide economic and social benefits. The special economic zones especially provide foreign investment with fewer immediate risks since they are fairly well insulated from the wider society. The cabinet's efforts to attract more foreign investment, development assistance, and humanitarian aid, especially from South Korean government sources, require improved North-South ties. The cabinet manages this relationship with an emphasis on the economic benefits it provides, but its policy does not logically end with reunification. As such, the cabinet opens itself to criticism from party and military quarters that such policies abandon a core, emotionally and rationally held goal of Koreans.

These debates reflect how North Korea's institutions embody the competing goals the regime must manage. There is a role for ideology but also for pragmatism. The party is an important institution but only one of three peer institutions that compete for influence. The nature and functions of North Korean politics have changed. North Korea has undergone an evolution, not a revolution. North Korea did not reshape its politics from scratch, but how the regime functions remains a key question for any student of North Korea.

These policy differences are puzzling if one subscribes to a monolithic view of the North Korean government. Why does Kim permit this dissent? Is the dissent genuine? If not, what is its purpose? Why would the regime attempt to demonstrate its absolute control to both internal and external audiences yet allow evidence of disunity? How can one make sense of this political system that consistently defies conventional expectations? It is my contention that North Korea's bureaucracies work at crosscurrents; recognizing that the river flows in different directions simultaneously is an important first step in crafting an effective navigation strategy. Kim is still the most important part of the North Korean system, but he is only one part. Recognizing where the others fit into the puzzle of North Korean politics helps build a better understanding of the regime's political choices.

Toward a New Model

Understanding how the state functions, crafts policy, and conducts politics is the critical first step in explaining and even predicting policy choices. Continually surprising and perplexing outcomes suggest that existing models of North Korean politics may be outdated or wrong. Despite this demand for understanding, few have attempted in recent years to comprehensively model the North Korea political system. This book is intended to fill this void.

There is demand for scholarship on the North Korean state among both comparativists and foreign-policy practitioners, but the supply of methodologically rigorous scholarship is low. A review of the two major comparative-politics journals and the three general political-science journals yields only one article on the state since its founding.[8] Likewise, some area specialists recognize that the state is poorly understood in both policy and academic circles. This problem has not been resolved. The small amount of area-studies literature broadly related to this topic does not speak to the comparative literature and usually has little or no explicit theoretical discussion. Area specialists have largely avoided studying the state's domestic politics altogether or have applied the same limited data points on the North's internal functions. This scholarly chasm has hampered our collective understanding. I attempt to bridge this gap by building on the strong theoretical tradition of comparative politics, the rich empirical work of area studies, and my own contribution to these areas.

One reason for the dearth of scholarship is the required refrain that North Korea is a data-poor country. While this is true, it is often overstated and perhaps discourages new researchers before they even begin. The lack

of empirical research on North Korea is a great opportunity to make significant statements and expose substantial "new" data that have been largely
overlooked. There are more untapped scholarly resources available on this
state than most others. Furthermore, North Korea's controlled media is a
useful window into the state's function precisely because it is controlled.
Dismissing this information as thoughtless propaganda loses an opportunity to look inside this controlled regime's operations. New data and pat-
terns can be discerned when the state is studied systematically.

North Korea suffered a confluence of crises in the 1990s. The state's
founder and national hero died in 1994, and his son took power. China and
Russia established diplomatic relations with South Korea, and the United
States came precariously close to war with North Korea during the first
nuclear crisis in 1993–94. Pyongyang lost its Soviet benefactor in 1991,
notably losing energy and food aid. The state suffered extreme economic
hardship, and decades of poor agricultural policy choices, along with North
Korea's periodic intense flooding, plunged the state into famine in the late
1990s.[9] Multiple analysts argued that the regime's days were numbered,
suggesting the state would not survive the decade.[10] While the state did not
collapse, these forces did alter it. North Korea's political evolution rapidly
accelerated, dislodging some elements, retaining others. The assumption
that North Korea's government functions in much the same way as it did
under Kim Il Sung is highly questionable.

The centralized narratives generally hold that both Kims relied on a
small set of inner circle advisers to craft national policy. Some of these
individuals command large bureaucracies, but most do not. They are powerful because of their relationship with Kim not their relationship with the
bureaucracies they command. Power flows from the top: Kim uses car-
rots (gifts) and sticks (purges and threats) to control this group. Kim may
direct policy through a favored institution, such as the military or the party,
but policy innovation comes from the center. The major bureaucracies
are composed of functionaries. In Stalin's terms, these are "transmission
belts" to implement small-group decisions. When policy fails, functionaries are necessarily to blame for failing to properly implement sage policy.
Both power and authority are centralized.

This centralized narrative comes in various forms with varying degrees
of state dynamism built into the explanation. The state is Stalinist, post-
Stalinist, personalist, neosocialist corporatist, an eroding totalitarian state,

or an eroding socialist state.[11] Kim rules as an absolute monarch through the military,[12] the party,[13] or an inner circle of advisers and kin.[14] Some of these models suggest that there is movement away from Kim Il Sung's more thorough power and authority, but Kim Jong Il does not radically depart from his father's mode of rule. While I expand upon the meaning and arguments of these characterizations, I ultimately find them lacking. I argue that these monolithic ideal types fail to capture the pluralism that helps distinguish the younger Kim's rule from his father's. My central thesis is that while Kim Il Sung's rule can be described as totalitarian, Kim Jong Il rules through a more decentralized, post-totalitarian, institutionally plural state.

Pluralism is often associated with democracy, so I should be clear that I am not suggesting that North Korea is democratizing. Quite the contrary, I argue that the state has stabilized as a type of autocratic government but that not all autocratic regimes are alike, and teasing out North Korea's specific variety has utility.

In this type of state, interests are more diffuse, and institutional preferences are debated cautiously but publicly.[15] Debates are not first and foremost personal; they are primarily institutional. Important policy differences are not mainly formed by individuals closely tied to Kim but by large bureaucracies with consistent interests and the capacity to produce detailed knowledge.[16] National policy outcomes are determined by the interaction of three second-echelon institutions: cabinet, military, and party.[17] Much of the policy innovation comes from below. In these cases, Kim and his inner circle make the final decision, but the three institutions present policy papers and options. Authority is centralized, but power is diffuse.

Not all policy innovation originates with the nerve center, but it is an overstatement to suggest that none of it does. With his centralized authority, Kim has the ability to accept or reject advice. His institutions can present three distinct options, any of which he may accept. Or he can reject them all and go with his own fourth option. He is not simply a passive broker of low-level bureaucrats, and he enjoys access to additional sources of information that most of his subordinates simply never see. On questions of high politics such as the missile and nuclear issues, Kim can centralize and micromanage the process more thoroughly than on issues of low politics. Personally micromanaging economic policy would prove much more difficult, given the large number of lower-level decisions and transactions required. But even on the nuclear question, Kim relies on subordinates to negotiate with foreign powers, including the United States. He allows discussion and debate on these issues in the official press and acts upon distinct lines of policy advice from subordinates. Issues of high politics are more centralized than issues of low politics, but they still follow the general outline provided by the model I present.

If this hypothesis is empirically correct, then this mode of rule produces different expectations than the previous understandings of North Korea's modus operandi. North Korea is not a simple organizational unit with one man making core decisions. The state processes foreign actions through a rigid and predictable political apparatus and returns reactive policy choices based on the external and internal considerations. Treating North Korea as a black box overlooks the critical internal political calculations that often modify policy choices. Anticipating North Korea's responses to foreign actions is not always intuitive, but this theory should improve our predictions.

The Stakes

North Korea is of great interest to foreign-policy practitioners and scholars alike. It is the world's poorest state with a nuclear weapon and has demonstrated its willingness and ability to transfer its nuclear know-how and equipment to the Middle East. It has the largest military conscription rate in the world, develops and exports ballistic missiles, and continually threatens its neighbors. Humanitarian catastrophes and a fundamental denial of human rights are chronic problems. It is the only communist state to weather a hereditary succession, and one of the few remaining one-party communist states to survive the end of the Cold War. The state has been linked to counterfeiting foreign currency, drug running, and terrorist incidents.

North Korea shares a land or sea border with the second-, third-, and thirteenth-largest economies in the world. Though economic numbers are imprecise, the CIA's *World Factbook* lists it as the ninety-fifth largest economy in the world—just behind Cameroon. In 2007 only three national economies in the world suffered a worse growth rate than North Korea, though this seems to have moderated in 2008.[18] It has commanded roughly half of China's annual development assistance in recent years and requires food and energy aid from its neighbors, its primary adversary (the United States), and the international community. It has experimented with limited market reforms only to backtrack later. North Korea rightfully commands the world's interest, but it is poorly understood.

The common element in these issues is the North Korean regime. Understanding the North's internal processes helps with attempts to gauge its reaction to policy choices made in Washington, Seoul, Beijing, Tokyo, and other interested capitals. I am, at the outset of this study, agnostic on the normative question of selecting between policy options toward North Korea ranging from accommodation to pressure strategies. I do seek to assist analysts interested in predicting North Korean reactions to these policies based on an informed understanding of the state's decision-making structure.

Understanding how North Korea's political system functions offers critical insight into a wider group of authoritarian regimes. North Korea is arguably the most centralized authoritarian state in existence today. It has been described as simultaneously fitting the mold of the totalitarian, personalist, and corporatist models. Theories and typologies of authoritarian states are comparative in nature; thus understanding North Korea's domestic politics has useful applications for the wider study of authoritarian regimes. And if the state that comes closest to the proposed ideal type departs significantly from theoretical expectations, this may suggest that important revisions are needed for these typologies.

While many of the former Soviet satellite states in Europe transitioned toward democracy, many regimes in the Middle East, Africa, Latin America, and Asia arguably share some common characteristics of a post-totalitarian state. An updated and revised view of North Korean politics has direct relevance for explaining a wider group of states that do not seem to be moving toward democracy. In this way, I hope this book will be relevant to readers interested in how this general group of states' craft policy, sustain themselves in the face of challenges, evolve, and react to regional and global foreign actions.

Finally, the universe of communist states that weathered the Soviet collapse is small. North Korea is the least reformed of the remaining communist governments. I trace the process by which North Korea evolved politically and prevented its own collapse through economic crisis, famine, international pressure, and its first and only leadership transition.

Explanation requires theory, and well-crafted theory may be exportable to other countries. Authoritarian resilience is the other side of the coin of the well-researched question of democratic transitions and has bearing on this research program. The evolution and resiliency of North Korea's government informs both the question of how post-totalitarian regimes operate and the dynamic process of postcommunist (non-)transitions.

Road Map

Chapter 2 reviews the competing theories of North Korean politics, including the totalitarian, post-totalitarian, personalist, and corporatist models. I lay out my theoretical model, explaining why the state evolved from its totalitarian origins and how the system consequently functions today. I conclude the theoretical section with a research design and describe my data sources and means of evaluating this theoretical model.

Chapter 3 documents the historical evolution of North Korean politics under Kim Il Sung, while chapter 4 discusses the modified institutional structure of Kim Jong Il's rule. The younger Kim did not accept wholesale his father's mode of rule, nor did he re-create the state from scratch. Chapter 3 describes the founding national institutions, ideology, and mode of rule. It shows how these gradually evolved under Kim Il Sung's watchful eye, including formal constitutional revisions and a general decline of the Juche ideology. (Juche, the official national ideology of North Korea, is discussed more fully in chapter 3.) The second part of the chapter acknowledges several shocks to the system in the mid-1990s that accelerated the state's transformation. The collapse of its Soviet benefactor, nuclear crises, the death of the state's founder and national hero, and famine jeopardized the existence of the state. The younger Kim had to adapt to deal with the existing realities. The state's "emergency management" and response to social pressures from the famine altered North Korea's politics. Chapter 4 focuses on the resulting political order, providing relevant background on North Korea's constitutional institutions not included in the general historical narrative.

Chapters 5 through 7, which constitute the empirical tests of this model, contextualize North Korean policy debates observed in the press and provided by foreign interlocutors. The model is dynamic. In these chapters I explain how the state processes specific examples of foreign actions and produces policy responses. I go inside the red box to construct this narrative rather than making blind assumptions about internal dynamics. I document what the key North Korean institutional leaders said in commentaries, articles, and major speeches and show how these positions are consistent for the leaders of a particular institution with variation between institutions. I evaluate how these leaders communicate their institution's preferences to other institutional leaders and in some cases how they even resist high-level policy choices. Strategic positions by institution are remarkably consistent, responding in the same general frame to specific challenges. However, national policy varies. These chapters evaluate how these debates frame the discussion internally and explain otherwise perplexing national policy choices.

Chapter 8 concludes with three important issues. First, does my model fit the data better than competing models reviewed in chapter 2 (and, in turn, what are downstream consequences of the model)? Second, I evaluate the effect of this model on our general understanding of authoritarian regimes. Does this revised understanding of North Korea's politics offer lessons for other states in the post-totalitarian world? Finally, I analyze general lessons for foreign-policy practitioners. Policy choices will remain normative, political decisions, but understanding North Korea's political system can aid a balanced view of the concrete and predictable trade-offs involved in these choices.

CHAPTER TWO

Post-totalitarian Institutionalism

This chapter provides a conceptual basis on which to evaluate North Korean domestic politics and puts forth my theory of the system's functions. I argue that North Korea under Kim Il Sung approximated the totalitarian ideal type, but North Korea today is better understood as a centralized polity in which second-echelon institutions play an important role. Kim Jong Il's government is highly centralized, but it is less centralized than his father's. North Korean politics comprises the interaction of the military, party, and cabinet with "oversight" by the security apparatus. (See chapter 4 for a discussion of these institutional actors.) These institutions enjoy limited autonomy in an effort to productively leverage their expertise while Kim Jong Il retains generalist political control over them. Kim and his inner circle of advisers have final authority, and Kim can intervene arbitrarily at any stage in the political process. Kim has a proclivity for micromanagement, but he is also constrained by the inherent limits of the twenty-four-hour day. His greater reliance on rational inputs, compared with his father's preference for more ideologically guided decision making, means Kim Jong Il must rely on a larger set of experts. Kim is by no means absent from the model, but on the majority of issues, institutional inputs set the decision-making stage and shape most policies' implementation.

These semiautonomous groups have opportunity and cause to interact in the policy formation and execution process, creating room to discuss pluralist politics in North Korea. Kim Jong Il's focus on political survival and emergency management over ideology as a guiding force makes today's North Korean government more rational than in the past, but it does not suggest that ideology is irrelevant. Bureaucratic winners and losers are defined on an issue by issue basis. In short, institutional politics—in conjunction with Kim Jong Il's critical role—helps explain political outcomes. I first evaluate existing theories of nondemocratic rule that have been applied to North Korea.

Existing Models of North Korean Politics

This section synthesizes the main typologies used to describe North Korean politics and shows where they have failed to account for contemporary elements of the North Korean system. Many studies describe North Korea as some type of a monolithic state. Kim has "almost total power,"[1] the system is marked by a "hybrid of modern Stalinism and traditional Korean authoritarianism . . . [and a lack] of interest group participation."[2] It is "post-Stalinist,"[3] "an eroding totalitarian regime . . . [where] an absolute dictator still rules,"[4] and the "application of a 'bureaucratic model' to North Korea is premature."[5] Other area specialists have recognized the conflicting roles for the cabinet, military, and party in limited circumstances and noted the increasingly visible roles of the military and state "though under the guidance and directions of the party," but no study has attempted to apply this to North Korean politics generally or build a model of institutional interaction.[6]

The area studies literature is strong on empirics and relatively weak on theory. The comparative literature in this case is the reverse. Both miss an opportunity. I attempt to help bridge this gap. I argue that certain elements of the ideal types apply to North Korea. Explicitly incorporating the comparative literature builds on previous theoretical advances and allows a more sophisticated model as a fruit of knowledge accumulation. No case fits these ideal types perfectly, but the North Korean case is sufficiently different that it merits a different typology.

Partisans in the comparative debates have accused one another of erecting straw man arguments around the usage of terms like totalitarianism, monism, pluralism, interest groups, and corporatism. This has delayed theoretical progress in previous debates and is a stark warning to proceed cautiously. However, if one is to understand North Korea as another state that fits into a comparative framework, it must be defined in comparative terms. The danger of conceptual stretching and emotional connections to certain terms comes into conflict with the desire to integrate the presumed uniqueness of this state into a comparative framework. Every state is unique at some level, and North Korea's label as a "rogue state" demonstrated the continued view that this state is particularly different. Nonetheless, this does not suggest that it cannot or should not be studied comparatively. One explicit theoretical purpose of this study is to bring this presumed outlier into the comparative tradition to explain it and help develop a better understanding of some category of nondemocratic states more generally.

Given the importance of studying this state comparatively, the remainder of this section shows the inadequacy of current comparative ideal types in explaining North Korea's policy inputs. Policy choices (outputs) that continually surprise and puzzle observers further motivate this theoretical reevaluation. To be productive, a comparative study should be able to assess the validity of applying these previous models to a given case, provide a better alternative to current theories, and note the possibility of other states falling within the theoretical outline.

Totalitarianism

Totalitarian states isolate individuals and replace previous private social networks with state organization. Totalitarian leaders are revolutionaries, intensely committed to destroying the old order and building a utopian political order based on an all-encompassing ideology. Monopolizing information sources and propagandizing provide purpose to the atomized masses for the radical changes. The state, which does not tolerate pluralism or opposition, regularly purges officials to pursue its revolutionary aims. The party and secret police use terror and arbitrary coercion to instill fear and anxiety in the population.[7] Antiregime organizing is not a matter of calculated risk as under authoritarian regimes; people are deterred from extrastate organization that has the potential to be viewed as antiregime.[8]

Totalitarianism regimes are short lived. Since the state's goals are utopian, they are unreachable. The revolutionary euphoria that helped singular leaders or parties come to power subsides; the elite that benefit from this dictatorial rule face a cognitive dilemma: the system as it exists does not promote its stated ideals, but the elite have an incentive to maintain their privileged place in society and avoid punishment by opposing regime change.[9] Consequently, the state loses much of its utopian motivation, bureaucratizes, and makes routine the normal state functions.

Ideology may remain as a propaganda tool for the masses and the shrinking group of true believers, but for many who employ it, it is particularly hollow. Ideology becomes primarily a tool and a constraint on state actions, but it ceases to be a motivating force for the increasingly disenchanted and educated elite. Those in power are no longer a band of revolutionaries working against the system. They *are* the system, and it behooves them to protect its interests. From this newfound conservative position, limited plurality emerges from the natural tendency to bureaucratize.

This pattern can be found in multiple historical examples. Almost a century ago, Max Weber recognized this general movement from revolution to bureaucratization.[10] Nor is the pattern alien to Korean culture or its core benefactors. The young neo-Confucian scholars that perpetrated the literati purges in the early Choson Dynasty on strong ideological grounds ultimately lost their revolutionary euphoria, bureaucratized their rule, and protected their privileged place in society.[11] In the Soviet Union, this rise of limited pluralism followed the death of Stalin.[12] Likewise, North Korea has evolved from approximating the totalitarian ideal type under Kim Il Sung to a more plural polity under Kim Jong Il. But this is not simply the story of a state growing more rational or a pragmatic state replacing an ideological one. The developments in North Korea require greater refinement to capture the state's functions in a way that helps the observer understand, explain, and even predict its policy choices.

Post-totalitarianism

Post-totalitarianism is best understood as an umbrella term that recognizes the unique attributes of states that emerge from the breakdown of revolutionary totalitarianism. The evolved states emerge gradually and retain main attributes of the prior totalitarian regime rather than radically departing from the totalitarian model with a wholesale acceptance of a new form of rule. The emphasis on evolution rather than revolution makes understanding the state's political history even more important for explaining the way the state currently operates.

Of course, recognizing that states evolve from a similar starting point in no way suggests that they evolve in the same way or on the same trajectory. They can move in very different directions. In an early attempt to categorize regimes emerging from Soviet domination in the 1990s, Juan Linz and Alfred Stepan presented their views on the emergence of a certain class of these post-totalitarian states. They argued in part that the decay of ideology in the Soviet bloc created space for democratic opposition—particularly in Central and Eastern Europe. Technocratic employment became a real alternative to party careers as citizens withdrew into private life and the state increasingly tolerated private activity. When ideologues dominate politics, administrative competence declines. Absent policy inputs from outside the state, politics stagnates if specialists from below do not push new concrete ideas up to the long-entrenched generalists at the top. In a participatory bureaucracy, ideas flow up and down. Experts provide original ideas, which are moderated by bargaining. Without a permanent purge, specialists can develop expertise and send new ideas up to the leadership. Likewise, an expert bureaucracy can modify—wittingly or not—orders of superiors according to developed professional standards.[13]

Combined with these developments, the loss of ideological purpose creates room for rational policy. Absent a revolutionary ideological lens through which to prescribe policy choices, the state looks to rational data. Technocrats and a diversity of ideologies—new and old alike—help define the universe of policy choices. This evolution of the polity comes in stages. In the early phase, the leadership is divided, coercion is used less, and contact with the outside world is less restricted. Terror is no longer arbitrary; the state learns to deal with dissent outside of the state structure for the first time. The fusion of state and society slowly begins to separate, disheartening some while providing opportunity for others. Crackdowns on dissent freeze the post-totalitarian system into a purposeless, unmoving state with an increasingly relevant civil society opposition that makes it susceptible to collapse.[14]

This band of states evolved in a similar direction, because after World War II they had similar starting points and common pressures; they looked to one another as political development models. There would still be diversity among even those states that came to join European institutions like the EU and NATO, but one could draw effective generalizations about the transition process and their political outcomes. However, states farther east like Belarus and the Central Asian republics looked substantially different. China, Cuba, and several states in the Middle East and other parts of Asia likewise evolved from a totalitarian or semitotalitarian existence but not on the same generalized path as the European post-totalitarian states. North Korea too evolved from this common starting point, but it was subject to important social forces and evolved into something different.

Put differently, if one accepts the argument that Kim Il Sung approached the totalitarian ideal type and his son's state looks substantially different, then North Korea meets the most general definition of the post-totalitarian model. This does not suggest that it follows the specific trajectory that Linz and Stepan outline for the states of Central and Eastern Europe. North Korea certainly looks very different from the European post-totalitarian states that lacked a leader as strong as Kim and where the nature of state-society relations is fundamentally different.[15] Indeed, there is reason to believe they are on distinctly different trajectories. Consequently, I develop a new post-totalitarian model that incorporates elements from each of the characterizations in this section as well as new theoretical components relevant to the North Korean state. Before doing so, however, it is useful to review the remaining ideal type characterizations that inform the new model.

Personalism

Personalistic rulers use coercion and fear like totalitarian regimes but govern not by tradition or ideology but by personal, arbitrary rules. Tradition and ideology constrain totalitarian leaders, but not personalistic rulers. They employ power for private ends, using national resources to extract private wealth and private wealth to maintain power. This is increasingly difficult when mass organizations are prevalent as in many industrial states. Personalistic states are simple and unstable because cutting off the head of the monster kills the beast.[16]

North Korea resembles this model in several ways, and this model comes closest to the popular description of North Korea as a state governed by "one man rule." But this model does not explain the remaining ideological constraints and power-wielding elite that continue to trumpet totalitarian rule. Personalism explains policy reversals and contradictions only as a function of the leader's changing motives or psychology. It has a difficult time explaining recurring policy contradictions and cross-purposes evident in North Korea. The model also predicts an unstable state, yet North Korea has weathered the collapse of its Soviet benefactor, severe economic decline, nuclear crises, a hereditary power transition, and a famine.

State efforts to propagandize and promote ideology remain puzzling under this characterization of personalist rule. Efforts to modify the ideal type to include an all-encompassing ideology or a mass party remove much of the model's explanatory power and produce expectations more in line with other ideal types. Further, Kim and his colleagues have enriched themselves at the expense of their populace, but private gains do not explain broad national goals like reunification, macroeconomic improvements, and broad anti-imperialism. Elite privilege is common to nondemocracies and a single man tops even totalitarian states, but the personalistic ideal type leaves puzzles that other analytical tools help bridge. I incorporate the relevant attributes of this ideal type into my model of North Korean politics, but it is insufficient to simply place the North Korean state under this ideal type characterization.

Corporatism

Corporatism is an elastic concept.[17] North Korea's specific variety, "neosocialist corporatism" in Bruce Cumings' characterization, departs somewhat from what most political scientists mean by the term. Cumings sees the North Korean body politic as a noncompetitive, united entity in which disharmony is harmful. Kim and his familial-based inner circle regularize policy relations between different interests in this top-down, hierarchal model. Mixing metaphors, the state is a family with the father directing affairs out of his paternal wisdom—an element shared by the personalist model. The personality cult emphasizes that through wisdom, Kim promotes virtue, love, and benevolence, and expects loyalty in return. Policy radiates from the nerve center (Kim). Innovation does not come from below.[18]

Cumings sees little change between the two Kims' reigns and finds the organic metaphor applies to both regimes. He tests his theoretical expectations by reference to the same core evidence found in this study: the North Korean media and public statements as well as perspectives from some political insiders. North Korean propaganda states that policy (and all wisdom) radiates from Kim. North Korea's press continually repeats that both Kims are benevolent father figures "sagaciously" guiding their flock. Cumings takes this oft-repeated propaganda line as evidence of how the state actually functions. Policy begins with Kim; those below Kim implement policy.[19]

I argue he overstates this case and miscategorizes Kim's normative demands for absolute loyalty as an empirical reality. It leaves open the question of why one should believe the official characterization of the state. This model has some very useful elements that help develop a theory of how Kim and his core inner circle group of about two dozen advisers make final decisions. However, the model does not give enough attention to formative elements of policy. Neosocialist corporatism is more useful in the study of high politics such as nuclear diplomacy, where policy inputs and execution can be more easily centralized, than in the case of broader social and economic questions. But systemic studies must take into account the types of information Kim and the inner circle use to form decisions and processes to implement those decisions. Further, the model does not discuss the downstream consequences of the particular version of corporatism, leaving a further opening for theoretical improvements.

The corporatist characterization alone has a difficult time explaining North Korean actions. This model cannot explain open policy disagreement in the media and evidence of institutional elements working at cross-purposes. It does not explain bureaucratic resistance to central decisions or in-fighting. The more conflict rather than regularized bureaucratic interaction shapes policy decisions and implementation, the more one must conclude that pluralism is at work. The evidence I present suggests my model should be used instead of the corporatism model, at least in a contemporary context, as it more completely captures the state's policy process of both high and low politics and moves beyond an analysis of Kim and his relations with his core advisers.

The most productive difference between neosocialist corporatism and my formulation of North Korean politics is the role of institutional bargaining as a form of policy moderation. The institutional pluralist state makes the most extreme policy choices more difficult. Institutional opponents argue against their competitors' extreme policy choices, encouraging bargained policy compromises that sit closer to the center of the political spectrum. These choices are moderate not by a global standard but by a domestic standard. They more fully capture the interests advocated by differing segments of the state's policy experts. All North Korean institutions share a strong anti-imperialist sentiment that most Americans would consider extreme, but the cabinet's relatively moderate advocacy of negotiations tame the party's advocacy for a second Korean War in response to the perceived American threat, for example. However, international observers should not take this as welcome news per se: a dynamic presupposes an imbedded, influential group of elites in Pyongyang actively argues against proposing, negotiating, agreeing to, and respecting certain international agreements and economic reform policies. Consequently, while ultimate authority remains in the hands of one man, power is more diffuse. Pluralist models dispute that all power is defined at the top and radiates downward.

Institutional Pluralism

Institutional pluralism grew out of challenges to the totalitarian framework, emphasizing how groups of individuals cluster together to pursue specific or general policy goals. These groups, which are not sanctioned or explicitly created by the state, have multiple, conflicting, and overlapping ideas and preferences. These groups engage policy only on issues in which they have an interest, which may or may not encompass the entire corpus of policy decisions. Institutional pluralism does not engage the totalitarian model so much as it presents an argument about how a specific totalitarian state, the Soviet Union, evolved. The model disputed the continued applicability of two core components of the totalitarian ideal type: that the state "atomizes" the individual from an otherwise natural social reality and that the state is monolithic.

Gordon Skilling and Jerry Hough were at the forefront of this post-Stalinist model of Soviet politics, disputing the argument that the post-

Stalinist Soviet Union completely "atomized," or psychologically isolated, the individual. Instead, groups develop within elite circles with counterparts among the masses that try to influence certain segments of policy. Any polity that takes on greater roles and powers produces greater incentives for interested social groups to try to influence that state's policy decisions. The Soviet state was an extreme example of this type of "big government," encouraging individuals with shared attitudes and interests to cluster together to influence policy in any way they could. Access to the halls of power in the Kremlin or local governments in the Soviet Union looked different from lobbyists working in a democratic state, but the basic incentive structure was similar. As post-Stalinist Soviet repression eased, interested individuals had greater opportunity to organize and then exert influence on the state.

Advocates of the institutional pluralist model did not doubt that the top leadership could intervene arbitrarily in lower-level policy making. Rather these authors sought to progress beyond this level of understanding. In most cases, limits on senior leadership's time and capacities required delegation. Since the top leadership had been much more extensively studied, these scholars decided to devote most of their attention to describing the second-order groups that transgressed state and society. Groups with common preferences coalesced around government decisions at the local, regional, and national/imperial levels. Groups bridged the elite/masses divide and influenced decisions outside the top leadership's purview. The system was less monolithic and less centralized than the totalitarian ideal type suggested.

The totalitarian model could point to Carl Friedrich and Zbigniew Brzezinski's *Totalitarian Dictatorship and Autocracy* as elucidating the core tenets of the applied totalitarian model, while the institutional pluralism model was a relatively diffuse set of theories that evolved with the Soviet state. Institutional pluralism does not have a conveniently laid out core canon that synthesizes and directs the larger model. Skilling and Franklin's *Interest Groups in Soviet Politics* contains different views on the functioning of the Soviet state. Even the coeditors disagreed over the nature of the state's diffused power and wrote separate concluding chapters.

Yet it is still valuable to attempt to distill the main components with lasting relevance to this project. The two most prominent concepts in this research area—interest groups and pluralism—are plagued with multiple meanings that have led to a great deal of confusion and criticism. Clarifying them is a critical first step. Debate around these two terms focuses on two core questions: What is the nature of these groups? And how do they affect policy decisions? In other words, who are the actors and how do they act?

Groups Defined

Skilling borrowed from David Truman and Arthur Bentley's democratic definition of "interest groups" to elucidate his theoretical definition of a group. Interest groups are "any group that, on the basis of one or more shared attitudes, makes certain claims upon other groups in the society for the establishment, maintenance, or enhancement of forms of behavior that are implied by shared attitudes."[20] But proponents of the institutional pluralism thesis recognized that their version of interest groups looks little like the democratic variety and have functionally defined it very differently. Interest groups cannot block a dictator's initiative by reference to public opinion, the courts, or supporting alternative candidates in popular elections as Bentley and Truman describe. Interest groups in a democratic context are societal-based actors pressuring—or presenting interests to—government officials (the state). In the communist context, state and society are much more tightly fused and an external society is not acting upon a separate state. Democratic interest groups use and try to shape public opinion, parties, and elections to influence lawmakers, while communist leaders seek legitimacy (authority) and power from different sources and cannot seek influence in this same democratic manner. Truman and Bentley show how formal lines of legal control are only part of the story, but their story is fundamentally a democratic one.

Skilling and Hough try to build on this democratic concept and describe interest groups more generally as "informal clusterings that articulate distinctive interests." The theory applies to more than state institutions that are permanent, structurally separate from the leadership, and provide services that the regime values with a stable and consistent pattern of interaction. Skilling claims evaluating these bureaucratic groups alone is an incomplete reading of the relevant political forces, concluding that professional and occupational categories outside the state have a discernible influence on policy direction. He includes groups such as "professionals" and other vaguely defined "clusterings."[21]

The empirical chapters in Skilling and Griffith's volume largely focus on the more easily identifiable state institutions such as the party, the military, and the judiciary. In North Korea, indigenous societal-based actors are as close to nonexistent as one can imagine, but three main institutions interact at the top of the system: the cabinet, the military, and the party. I find these types of groups that somehow transgress the elite/masses divide in an unobservable manner inappropriate for describing the North Korean political system. But the concept of interested, institutional groups as second-echelon actors in conflict with one another has real bearing on my model. The value is more apparent in the more difficult area of theorizing how such groups interact with each other and a state's supreme authority (e.g., Kim Jong Il).

Group's Influence

Under the institutional pluralist model, multiple groups under Kim interact to help shape policy direction. Institutional pluralist advocates never argue that the state is a passive broker of these groups' interests, nor do groups necessarily have a systematic influence on policy decisions: "Interest groups are but one of the many elements involved in policy making; they are not necessarily decisive, and may sometimes be marginal in their impact . . . hampered and sometimes blocked by other factors, in particular the power of political leaders and authoritative organs of government and the party."[22] The point is that power is more diffuse than totalitarianism suggests and there is another element at play in regular policy-making decisions—especially those decisions that do not reach the highest echelons of the state. Skilling shows how interest groups are compatible with authoritarianism.

These groups with diverse interests attempt to exert influence in certain areas. Not all clusterings have an interest in every issue, nor does a single individual belong to only one group. These shifting and overlapping group identities make the theory more plausible but complicates systematic testing. Much of the research program relied upon case studies of parochial issues in Soviet politics where the researcher had limited access to selected interviewees or read selected portions of the official press to analyze how they may interact. Skilling argued that this research revealed only the tip of the iceberg of state-suppressed preferences—a plausible but ultimately unverifiable claim. With proper organization and opportunity, he argued, such dissident preferences could explode on the scene like the Solidarity movement in Poland and Charter 77 in Czechoslovakia.[23]

Critics charged this was not a theory at all. The totalitarian ideal type still stood strong, although even the Soviet case did not meet the ideal type fully. Critics of institutional pluralism noted the power diffusion idea was obvious and not particularly useful: "Power is diffuse even in concentration camps. . . . The major question . . . is *how* power is diffused." Alexander Groth showed how traces of pluralism could be seen even in Stalin's Soviet Union and Hitler's Germany, while William Odom repeatedly noted that "it is indeed a misconception to believe that all power in the USSR was ever wholly in the dictator's hands. Sophisticated users of the totalitarian model never really treated the matter so unambiguously. The key question has always been how power is dispersed, not *whether* it is dispersed" (emphasis in original).[24] These later advocates of the explanatory power of the totalitarian model argued that the institutional pluralism thesis erected a straw man, distracted attention from the core of the totalitarian system, and focused on the trivial at the expense of explaining how the state functioned fundamentally. They claimed institutional pluralism was not a new model at all and represented, at best, a misguided attempt to correct totalitarianism.[25]

The debate became one of degree. How diffuse is power in the system, what is the nature of different power holders, and how do these power holders influence policy? These are very similar tasks that the institutional pluralism thesis started out with, revealing that partisans in this debate actually held substantial common ground.

While I borrow from the theoretical debates over institutional pluralism in forming my views of North Korean politics, the hodgepodge nature of this theory makes disputing or supporting its wholesale applicability to North Korea less fruitful. I take a more positive approach with regard to this research program and incorporate its thought into my own theory.

The Emergence of Post-totalitarian Institutionalism

Totalitarian regimes are extreme. They must maintain a mantle of revolution to motivate the high collective energy required to keep the state in a constant state of readiness to repulse foreign imperialists and control internal enemies. Such intensity is difficult to maintain. It is justified by arguing that times are special. The uniqueness of a threat or opportunity encourages individuals to accept extreme hardship with the promise of a better future. Over time, the call to work especially hard loses its significance. Special times become normal, and promises of utopia are not realized. Intensity naturally fades, and the state must take great pains to motivate an increasingly skeptical and exhausted populace. Time is totalitarianism's natural enemy, especially as economic returns flatten or turn negative.

New Dilemmas, New Solutions

Nevertheless, this type of state has several tools at its disposal to encourage the masses and elites to follow the party line and to discourage unwanted behavior. North Korea under Kim Il Sung approximated the totalitarian ideal type on all five of these core areas.

1. A single, all-encompassing ideology predominated.
2. The Korean Worker's Party controlled the government and military bureaucracies.
3. The state used arbitrary terror to atomize individuals and maintain obedience.
4. The state monopolized the media.
5. The state planned a command economy.

On every one of these counts, North Korea moved away from its totalitarian past. The question remains: why? Contrary to popular belief, the totalitarian state promises its citizens and elites something in return for their buying into the system. Totalitarian states are not built on the relatively weak platform of simple repression. Pyongyang promised its citizens a powerful country in terms of ideology and international security and a prosperous nation. And it was rapidly losing its ability to produce on both of these pledges due to forces that the regime could not manage.

The North Korean state, despite its continued emphasis on self-reliance, was notably and increasingly reliant on external benefactors throughout the later decades of the Cold War. A state must draw on additional resources to shape and constrain a citizenry and group of elites that grows increasingly skeptical of revolutionary ideals and requires different sources of motivation. These groups must be convinced of the continued threat to their way of life by outside forces and that this way of life is worth protecting. Otherwise, the state must utilize scarce resources to materially entice support or to effectively compel groups to act in the desired way.

At the very least, the state must provide the basic material needs of the population (food, water, shelter) to maintain legitimacy. In North Korea's case, shelter would include energy for heating that prevent citizens from freezing in the country's cold winters. Without these essentials, the masses and elites alike can conclude that the revolution is simply unsustainable. It is impossible to convince a starving citizen that he or she is not hungry. In this case the state must remind the population of the horrors of the Korean War and note that the current difficulties are better than the alternative— the risk of a war-torn peninsula and an immoral, exploitative polity.

Domestic and international forces that threaten the regime's ability to provide these requisite needs undermine its ability to sustain itself. Some forces are rather straightforward while others may be initially counterintuitive. For example, greater international insecurity bolsters the state's role as protector. Viewed in a linear frame, greater international insecurity represents failure in the regime's stated mission to protect its citizens and system. However, this amorphous sense of insecurity that may arise from new actions or outright fabrications compels the population and bureaucracy to support easily identifiable means of addressing this insecurity, most notably by prioritizing military needs. This reinforces the spiral effect of the security dilemma, producing more insecurity that must be countered. Efforts that may actually undermine the state's security like missile and nuclear developments can be presented to a mass or elite audience as actually increasing security due to the amorphous nature of the concept. Both success and failure in providing security can be framed to pursue the same policy end.

Bread-and-butter issues are quite different. Threats that can be concretely experienced such as hunger, force a more results-oriented approach. People know if they have enough food to eat. Basic economic questions cannot be theoretically interpreted without reference to reality with the same ease as some questions of high politics. In some areas, the state does not need to move away from its ideologically guided thinking, while other areas more clearly demand results. If issues were not linked or did not inter-act, the state would not face a dilemma. It could pursue a results-oriented economic policy to provide for the basic needs of its population and main-tain a highly militarized polity, providing for the defense of the country. Indeed, the structural realities of the DPRK's first twenty-five years allowed Kim Il Sung to achieve enough success in both of these goals—economic and ideological advancement—to maintain a popular regime. Kim Jong Il faces a more difficult situation with tough trade-offs between maintaining ideological correctness/revolutionary politics and meeting his population's basic human needs.

Both Kims had to address the gradual erosion of the state's power to maintain their rule, but challenges under the younger Kim became acute. Neither Kim wanted to loosen control, but in the 1990s the younger Kim had to respond to three events outside his immediate control: the death of the country's founder and national hero (his father), the collapse of its main benefactor, and the famine. North Korea had to cope or collapse. Certain political and economic changes risked bringing down the whole system. Over time, doing nothing posed the same risk. With everything to lose, Kim proceeded to partially rationalize the state's governance struc-ture to exert greater efficiency while keeping his most important link to legitimacy—his hereditary claim to his father's revolutionary history. Kim's efforts to stave off national collapse produced a political order that looks and acts in ways that are substantially different from what the totalitarian model predicts.

In short, Kim maintained much of the old system and changed only what he thought he must in order to address the changing internal and external situation and avert collapse. I do not suggest that Kim had a pre-conceived idea of what a new North Korea might look like, and I do not consider him a committed economic reformer. His changes to the political and economic structure have been fragmented and partial but have left an indelible mark on the regime's functions.

Greater Pluralism

Certain regularities have emerged and a general direction of the state's pol-itics and economics can be identified. Kim belatedly shifted emphasis away from revolutionary politics to partially address the dire social situation and institute new checks and balances on the system to complement his own ruling style. While his father was a charismatic revolutionary, the younger Kim was a more detail-oriented micromanager who could more effectively divide and conquer the state rather than dominate a unified system as his father had. He lacked his father's gravitas and compelling personal narrative and tried to make up for it with even more Machiavellian cunning. But Kim Jong Il's move to a more divided political system would be very difficult to reverse, creating a certain stability to the new arrangement. The cabinet, military, and party emerged as peer organizations that provided a certain type of internal governmental checks and balances. Kim faced real resistance in the military and cabinet if he tried to resubmit their authority to the party, creating a stable expectation of continued institutional jostling and pluralism.

This development eroded the preeminent position of the party. The decline of ideology as the fundamentally guiding policy and the decline of the Communist Party are analytically distinct ideas, but they go hand in hand in practice. As the state recognizes a need for more rational decision making, the type of information required changes. Party ideologues continue to provide some input, but they lack the skills to make technical or expert statements. Instead of retraining these aging ideologues in specific disciplines like economics or foreign affairs or massively migrating existing technical expertise into the party apparatus, technocrats housed in the government ministries find themselves with more influence on policy making.

Experts are valued for their limited but deep expertise. Only in the aggregate can experts touch on all or most issues that afflict society. Experts exert a type of power that is necessarily diffuse in contrast to the ideological generalist. Experts' work does not offer a one-size-fits-all answer to questions in the way ideological correctness promises. Nevertheless, the government's work, no longer constrained to the same degree by ideological minders, continues to run into opposition by those previously in a place to squelch ideologically incorrect lines of research. However, the cabinet is no longer an institution subordinate to the party. It is a peer competitor.

A similar process occurs in the military. The military, previously under the party's domination, has a continued importance as the defender against imperialist aggressors. Since the removal of the Soviet benefactor set in motion a set of crises that intensified economic and security concerns, the state has renewed interest in military-directed security strategies. The ideological correctness of military doctrine too became less important. The military genuinely needed to provide for the state's security without the possibility of superpower backing. However, change here proved least significant. Security is a relatively amorphous concept without objective benchmarks of success. The military could continue to argue that more defense spending buys more security, although competing interests as they grew more powerful could argue that effective diplomacy and economic contacts offered another route to national security.

With these three institutional actors participating in policy deliberations, central leadership relies more on competing proposals that put in sharp relief the costs and benefits of strategic choices. Kim still retained the option of pursuing his own initiative, but new ideas articulated from below took on a greater role in policy making. For example, economic and social control goals came into conflict in North Korea. The country cannot supply the food needs of the populace, and North Korea's self-isolation and autarky are a particularly heavy burden on the state's economy. But the state's ideology and security are fundamentally rooted in keeping out foreign ideas and influences. Competing interests and those who articulated those interests clashed. The predominance of ideological correctness became a luxury that foreign benefactors (or the lack thereof) no longer demanded, providing greater opportunity for pragmatists to advocate economic opening.

Maintaining political stability becomes a precarious balancing act. The state must accept the need for radical changes in certain areas in order to provide basic services while not forfeiting the entire game by undermining security. This is particularly true in the economic arena as the command economy's returns level off and eventually turn negative. In North Korea's case, the plan's economic returns leveled off in the 1970s and turned negative in the 1990s. After the Soviet collapse, North Korea's economic maladies became acute and chronic. Avoiding the impending risks of continued economic decline required loosening control to allow more efficient economic operations and international trade. This, however, requires accepting the security risks of new ideas flowing into the country and takes some assets and liabilities off the state's power balance sheet. The state's roles shrink, and it becomes an open question whether that causes its power to increase or decrease. The state attempts to replace one risk with another.

The state must re-create itself not in the likeness of a Stalinist protector that encouraged many new regimes in the early part of the Cold War
to follow Stalin's totalitarian model but in a way that maintains as much
of the familiar, old system as possible and attempts to minimize necessary changes. Change by its very nature is destabilizing. One can imagine
how concern about change would be particularly acute in a state predicated
on strong control and micromanaging people's lives. In the post-totalitarian phase, maintaining political stability is not a simple, straightforward
endeavor. Paradoxically, the state may have to loosen control in order to
maintain it.

This transition is not a process of optimizing the state's ability to
function for its citizens. Kim remained on top and elite families generally retained their status. These people have private and public interests.
While motives are impossible to observe, it is an oversimplification to
claim these elites only serve their own private interests. Kim uses gifts and
prestigious awards to motivate and purges and punishments to compel,
yet divergent normative ideas about how the regime should operate are
routinely expressed in the state media. Money and status are not the only
objectives that motivate human action. Leaders of institutions highlight the
importance of their institution's mission and advocate both its institutional
interests and policy choices consistent with that worldview. Personal interest cannot explain this. This combination of private and public interest is
not unique to the North Korean government but neither is it the exclusive
domain of democratic entities.

In face of genuine domestic opposition vying for power and failure to
provide for the basic needs of its population, an opposition could eventually pressure the regime to change radically. Poland and Czechoslovakia
provide examples of the power of indigenous opposition groups within
a communist state. However, North Korea currently lacks real opposition
within the country. The population does not have a clear alternative to
the status quo. And were there an alternative, the people lack meaningful
forms of civil society organization to pursue it due to continual purges and
extensive repression. This does not mean opposition could not develop,
especially given continued material hardship, ideological decline, and state
ineptitude, but it does not exist right now. Even groups of university students, one important source of democratic opposition in South Korea and
elsewhere, have not visibly pressed for political change in North Korea.

These students, who come from privileged families and generally enjoy those same privileges upon graduation, may be hesitant to undermine their own futures just as existing elites are reluctant to press for comprehensive political changes.

Without the pressing demands of a domestic opposition, the state has greater opportunity to gradually modify its roles. With the state facing increased impotence in these core areas, it can alter its mode of operations to recapture its ability to provide basic services to the population and maintain a mantle of legitimacy as defender against imperialist forces champion of a reunified Korea. These developments are important because they demonstrate why North Korea developed the way it did instead of moving in the direction of the postcommunist states of Eastern Europe, post-Maoist China, or elsewhere. By retaining certain elements of the old order and incorporating significant new elements, North Korea looks and acts much different than it did under Kim Il Sung.

Post-totalitarian Politics

The single most important person in North Korean politics is unquestionably Kim Jong Il. This is the most critical holdover from the old system. Kim continues to maintain absolute authority, although not absolute power. He can intervene in any part of the policy decision-making chain and pursue different strategies to ensure effective policy execution. He is an active micromanager and his role should not be underestimated. But he is just one man. Kim Jong Il is not synonymous with North Korean politics. To more fully understand North Korean politics and variant policy outcomes, one must evaluate North Korea's second-order institutions.

This study faces the same two fundamental tasks that faced earlier studies of the post-Stalinist Soviet Union: What are the relevant political institutions below Kim? And how do they affect policy (the criterion for "relevance")? Besides Kim, the party is the clearest example of a holdover from the old regime. It continues to purport an ideologically based policy guide, although it no longer reigns supreme over the government and military. The military continues its same basic function of defending the state but has an additional political role now that it is freed from its subordination to the party. It highlights specific security threats and suggests means to counter them but generally does not articulate a class-based perspective or specifically ideological anti-imperialist orientation. The newest element in the North Korea power equation is the increased role of the cabinet. With its emphasis on tangible results, particularly in the economic arena, it is comprised of technocrats who are pursuing the most rational agenda.

This does not discount the possibility (indeed, probability) of subinstitutional divisions. Nor does it suggest that individuals or groups within an institution may find common ground with others in another institution. On the contrary, I suggest such divisions should exist down to the individual level. However, the most salient division exists at the top. Each bureaucracy is a coherent group with visible differences regarding the most important questions of state. It is at this second echelon—more so than the third or fourth—that variance in important, national policy decisions can be explained and understood.

Policy Formation

These three institutions, the party, military, and government, represent distinct interests. In the course of strategic policy decisions, these interests come in conflict, forcing a new type of institutional interaction. The party in particular must now compete on an increasingly level playing field in policy formation debates. Ideological guidance is not irrelevant, but it has become just one of several arguments for or against a particular agenda. Different institutions with a distinct clustering of personnel, resources and competencies, and with shared backgrounds and (potentially) similar worldviews define various policy options from below rather than having them prescribed solely from on high. Nonetheless, authority remains at the top, and Kim and his inner circle are more than mere mediators of competing options.

North Korea's institutions define the range of policy alternatives. Kim, with or without advice from inner circle advisers, selects from these presented options. Power is more diffuse but authority remains centralized. Institutions are the critical, ignored policy inputs that this study largely focuses on. However, Kim is in no way peripheral to the policy process. He has the final say, but his state increasingly uses rational information inputs as another critical input in a way that the more purely ideologically guided policy choices of his father did not. This new mode of rule necessarily requires more diffuse power.

Experts by their very nature have a more limited professional view. While they may consciously attempt to contextualize their own particular area of expertise by being generally informed about other areas, senior leadership values their opinion for the specific expertise it provides. Experts are expected to develop and sustain a deep understanding of a specific policy area. As a collective body, competent experts should retain a much more detailed understanding of a range of issues than senior leadership. Insofar as this expertise is valued and sustained by senior leaders making decisions, a larger number of nameless people are involved in some way in influencing those policy decisions. Not all knowledge translates into power. It requires a connection of knowledge that authoritative officials value. North Korea's modified institutional structure puts in place the ability of the bureaucracy to provide expert opinion that would aid a rational mode of governance.

I contend that in North Korea, much of the policy innovation comes from below. Experts craft new ideas and form proposals to challenges they confront. They do not merely execute policy. They also seek to inform policy based on rational and ideological arguments. On the most important questions of the direction of the state, the largest group of bureaucrats has some interest in the outcome. Of course, the highest-ranking bureaucrats will articulate these views most commonly. Given that this institutional outlook is shaped and synthesized from below, it is natural for these high-ranking leaders to espouse distinct policy preferences from their colleagues leading other institutions. Since Kim holds final authority, these institutions come in conflict and must articulate specific goals to the Dear Leader and one another as internal and external events give them the opportunity to bolster their position.

The three major institutions present and debate their views of strategic policy choices prior to high-level decisions. Kim continually reminds elite and mass audiences alike through references to his father and to his own paternal wisdom that he is the legitimate heir to the revolution. At the same time, he uses policy experts to improve government performance and reduce discontent, even when such prescriptions contradict revolutionary orthodoxy. Kim is playing a delicate balancing act, trying to avoid undermining his ideological claim to legitimate rule based on his

revolutionary bloodline while improving his regime's basic ability to govern. Kim has not sought out this arrangement any more than he sought
out the Soviet collapse, his father's death, or the famine. It is the product
of a historically dependent process outside his control. Consequently, Kim
and his core set of advisers hear both rational and ideological arguments
from institutions with vested interests in his decision.

The younger Kim's system fosters more rational policy options through
pluralism. Experts apply specific knowledge to policy questions as ideological generalists contribute their own piece to the conversation. Ideology is
no longer the deciding factor in policy decisions, but it certainly has not
vanished from the scene. The central leadership must allow public debate
if it is to occur in the official media, and one can see competing empirical
and normative arguments being advanced through different institutional
organs in the official newspapers. Bringing more expert voices into the
policy arena helps rationalize the North Korean political system in the hope
of improving the state's material condition and security.

High-Level Decision Making

Through the course of these debates, Kim and his core advisers are exposed
to competing expert and ideological opinions on policy direction. Senior
leaders arbitrate between competing proposals but are influenced by the
type of information their institutions produce. How Kim and his inner circle
process these different views is difficult to observe, but certain insights can
be gleamed. Though several of these inner circle advisers wear two hats, as
both an adviser and the head of a major bureaucracy with a separate information stream, the inner circle is reputed to be highly insular. Individuals
may risk their (and their families') lives if they get out of step with the rest of
the group, providing a tremendous disincentive for this group to innovate.

Though inner circle deliberations are not available for scrutiny, the
incentive structure set up by the system discourage inner circle advisers
from articulating new ideas. It is a structure that encourages groupthink.
This does not preclude the possibility of a leader savvy or connected enough
to rise to the top from breaking with the structural incentives. But Kim's
inner circle of advisers does not work as a type of high-level think tank for
policy innovation. Knowledge valued by the central authority and access to

that authority are critical elements of power in any system. Understanding the process of knowledge creation, mediation, and dissemination is critical. The inner circle likely provides independent ideas something like Kim's own ideas. But it may also act as one final filter of introduced ideas.

This is not to suggest that the inner circle is irrelevant. The existence of a unified inner circle has especially important implications for any succession scenario. Since Kim is mortal and unlike his father has not extensively and publicly prepared for his succession, this group may be able to continue Kim's rule in the short term in the event of Kim's sudden incapacitation or death. While it is unclear whether the group could control the state in the longer term, given the Kim family's claim to personal authority and the real possibility of disunity within this group of senior officials, it may be able to draw on the state's repressive apparatus to maintain stability long enough to reassert the anti-imperialist, reunification, and/or economic appeals to legitimate authority to maintain the system in some form over time.

Policy Implementation

While the central leadership holds the final say on policy decisions, even these high-level central decisions face bureaucratic resistance in implementation. Bureaucratic losers do not get on board with national policy and continue to voice opposition publicly to the chosen policy direction. Further, these bureaucracies implement the bulk of policy choices that never reach the inner circle level. Bureaucratic preferences impact policy at this lower decision-making level and in implementing high-level choices. The military, the party, and the cabinet critically define the agenda and the shape of options for even the most fundamental strategic questions. They debate and bargain in the policy formulation stage and present their case to Kim. Preferences do not end because an authority has already decided on a policy question, so my model anticipates that these institutions continue to try to affect policy preferences in the implementation stage whenever the opportunity arises. As such, these institutions influence policy decisions by agenda setting, selectively presenting their case, and making lower-level decisions. Of equal importance, they affect implementation by actively and substantially resisting and modifying even the highest-order decisions promulgated by Kim himself.

This model is a fairly straightforward view of bureaucratic politics with a particularly strong individual on top, but it radically departs from the conventional wisdom on how North Korea functions. Under this model, the three bureaucracies debate policy in the formation and execution stages. Authority remains centralized, but power is more diffuse than the relatively monolithic typologies predict. It shines light on a part of the system that exists in analytical darkness. If my hypothesis is correct, the regime functions in a very different way than previously thought, with different downstream consequences for regime stability and reaction to foreign events.

Rationalization—even when partial—has real costs, including information outflow and loosened control over the bureaucracy, which allows limited political expression within the regime. Likely concerned about internal threats, most notably coups, both Kim regimes implemented a vertical information flow. A party official, for example, can push information and analysis up the party chain of command, but he or she cannot communicate regularly with lateral contacts in the government or military. Institutional stove-piping effectively prevents most cross-institutional communication.

However, the demand for cross-institutional communication to reveal preferences, influence policy, or coordinate effective responses remains. Senior officials can communicate to a wider audience outside of their own institution in the form of speeches, commentaries, and articles. Although they must be cautious not to overstep their bounds, the official media has been increasingly used under Kim Jong Il to reveal policy preferences and foster limited forms of debate. This state that is so concerned about information security allows foreign observers to see some of its internal deliberations but prohibits regular cross-institutional communication. Systematic content analysis of North Korea's elite press is the best way to elicit institutional preferences and interaction.

Research Design

I employ a simple historical analysis to test my theory. This history focuses on evidence of institutional policy positions, institutional debate, and bureaucratic resistance to established policy. My historical analysis has two tasks. First, I identify the strategic policy issue areas to focus my study. If power is diffuse on the most important issues, then the central leadership likely does not try to micromanage issues it deems relatively trivial. This approach has the advantage of not focusing too narrowly on a single issue where its technical nature may predispose it toward technocratic input. But it does not overextend the analysis beyond a digestible set of primary data on important issues.

Once the issue areas are established, I conduct a systematic content analysis of North Korea's elite press and speeches to document stated institutional policy preferences in context. This allows me to demonstrate how institutional leaders respond to each other and their environment. It allows one to see if institutional leaders can reveal preferences and whether differences are institutional or simply vary by the leader of the institution at the time. The remainder of this chapter reviews the specifics of my approach, including coding details, the relevant methodology literature, and data sources.

Establishing Strategic Issue Areas

In the process of synthesizing internal policy debates, any researcher must select documents from a larger body. The most significant test of my theory will be on the most significant issues facing the state. However, reasonable people may disagree on which issues are most important. For the purpose of this study, it is imperative to tease out which issues the central leadership deems most important. As early as 1966 Kim Il Sung laid out the key priorities for the DPRK: anti-imperialism, reunification, and domestic ideological and economic concerns. With minor modification, these core goals remain at the top of the state's agenda today.[26]

The annual New Year's joint editorial (NYJE) also demonstrates these three issues are paramount in Kim Jong Il's DPRK. The NYJE is the North's single most significant policy and propaganda tool. Pyongyang lays out the state's core policy goals and ideological imperatives, and reaffirms the leadership every year in the NYJE. Kim Il Sung delivered a speech on New Year's Day every year until his death. Kim Jong Il has only spoken publicly on one known occasion (and then only to shout a single sentence), so he replaced the New Year's Day speech with the NYJE the first year after his father's death. While important joint editorials between two of the major newspapers are found occasionally during the year, the NYJE is the only document carried by all three major, official media outlets in the DPRK. Domestic and foreign audiences anticipate the NYJE and read it closely. The NYJE is the best, most systematic indicator of the regime's strategic priorities.[27]

I demonstrate that the NYJE focuses on these issues every year by coding each paragraph in the NYJE's policy section by the dominant goal it elucidates. While the NYJE has some intermixing of the leadership, policy, and ideological sections, it does not repeatedly jump between these areas. When more than one goal is mentioned in a paragraph, I decide which goal is dominant. This does not pose a significant challenge, since the North's stark terms make their core point exceedingly clear.[28] I repeat this process for each full year Kim Jong Il has been in power to date: 1995–2009. I use the full-text NYJE translations publicly available from FBIS/OSC.[29]

These three goals made up 95 to 100 percent of this section each year (1995–2005) and are still clearly dominant in the four remaining years. Together, the economy and reunification dictate a median of 92 percent of the issue focus. When incorporating U.S. policies, the three issues make up 100 percent of the issue focus for most years (Figure 2.1). The regime likely considers these issues strategic.

Analyzing Institutional Policy Preferences

My second, longer task is to test whether the state is unified and monolithic as the centralized models describe or is more diffuse as I hypothesize. This section provides the central evidence to support or refute my theoretical expectations. Have the cabinet, military, and party each advocated their own policy agendas within these three issue areas since Kim defined his regime's modus operandi in the 1998 constitution? Do these institutions publicly clash with one another in advocating their own policy agendas? Do policy agendas vary when new leaders assume the top post of a given institution and therefore are better ascribed to the individual than the institution? Do implemented policy choices tend to come from the universe of options publicly presented by North Korea's bureaucracies?

Methodology

I reviewed a set of speeches and articles presented inside the country by the forty-eight most senior members of each bureaucracy and their succes-

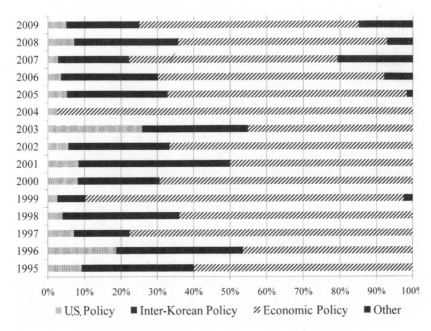

FIGURE 2.1 Policy Issues in New Year's Joint Editorial, 1995–2009

sors as defined in the *North Korea Handbook*.[30] Despite crossover in formal affiliations of many officials, these lists help determine primary affiliation. For example, cabinet premiers have all been party members, but these lists identify their primary affiliation with the cabinet. These officials produced more than 4,460 speeches or articles from Kim Il Sung's death until 2009 on these three issue areas. This is slightly less than half of all publications sourced to Pyongyang. The most senior leaders spoke and published much more often than subordinates, leaving less ambiguity about the institutional affiliation.

North Korea's official, elite media is a critical conduit for the regime to communicate general policy and ideology internally. Two of the three most important newspapers in the country are consistently available to foreigners: the dailies of the party and government. The Korean People's Army daily *Choson Inmingun* is not available outside of North Korea.[31]

I rely primarily on FBIS/OSC translations. This material is translated by professional, full-time Korean linguists with a secondary line of review. This ensures a more accurate translation than a single researcher could likely provide and allows more researchers (e.g., non-Korean linguists) to replicate this study. Even native Korean speakers have made critical translation errors with profound effects on U.S.-DPRK relations, especially given regional variations and the North's occasional use of intentionally vague constructions. Relying on professionally trained linguists with a second reviewer has real advantages over attempting to translate this material myself.

Furthermore, using these translated sources ensures that this study is not missing material. North Korea's relatively small volume of print media articles and commentaries makes a comprehensive review of the material feasible and verifiable. *Nodong Sinmun*, the party's newspaper, is a six-page daily; *Minju Choson*, the government's newspaper, is a four-page daily. Given North Korea's high priority and the relative importance of its official press to OSC's clients, the entire body of relevant articles is available. Skeptics of the translated documents can spot-check the publicly available OSC articles against the original vernacular or compare them to the duplicate, albeit incomplete, BBC Worldwide Monitoring translations. The OSC translations provide a convenient link to the vernacular text. I also include relevant leaked media reports from third-party interlocutors that described specifically bureaucratic positions. I utilize all available databases to include this material.

My research design hinges on the contention that each institution presents its own policy preferences in the elite press. Elites have information needs beyond what the mass media supplies. The elite media serves an important communications function. In a state where regular cross-institutional communication is restricted, the media helps fill this void. To sacrifice this critical conduit of cross-institutional communication for a disinformation campaign would be puzzling. While the central leadership may be able to sow disinformation, this undermines its own ability to rule: elites within the bureaucracies would be less clear about state policy and centralized wishes less effectively translated into action.

Furthermore, the state goes to great pains to continually reinforce the notion that Kim is the nerve center, directing all wise choices. Presenting the state as disunited undermines this critical propaganda purpose that both the regime and comparative politics theory recognize is important for regime survival.[32] If the military or any other institution serves as the excuse for Kim to select a policy, then his power is necessarily constrained. He is not only challenged but also challengeable. This is not a cost-free idea for a dictator. Despite the regime's security consciousness, it is less likely that this disinformation campaign seeks to mislead academic or policy analyses like this one.

Additionally, the deception counterthesis cannot explain why policy divisions are institutional rather than personal. An individual is easier to blame than a whole institution for policy failure. Cadres, for example, know their own unit's performance better than they know the performance of one high-ranking general. Blaming the entire military is a harder sell to this elite audience than blaming a single individual that a smaller group of elites would know personally.

I contextualize these policy positions in a contemporary history. This has several generic methodological advantages for a project like this one. Charles Tilly put the methodological argument most starkly: "In the case of state transformation, there is no way to create comprehensive, plausible, and verifiable explanation without taking history seriously into account."[33] This study at first blush is somewhat limited in time (1998–2009) and space (North Korea), but it is not a particularistic, atheoretical case study. It seeks to explain this case on its own terms and use that knowledge to build and refine comparative politics theory.

This dual purpose lends itself to this approach. This study of state transformation questions our fundamental assumptions about how the state operates. It seeks to define the relevant variables that have not previously been identified and that exist in complicated two-way feedback loops where time intervals are not standard. The project attempts to uncover the processes and mechanisms that produce variable trajectories and outcomes. This is highly context dependent. All social science attempts to simplify reality, but the initially more limited scope of this project requires retaining the specific context as important data. The historical approach allows the incorporation of initial conditions, path dependency, sequences, and interaction effects. In this way, it can expose the political process that evolved and currently exists in history.[34]

More specifically, the historical approach most effectively deals with this research problem. This approach allows me to identify the evolution of North Korea's policy debates over time, given internal and external circumstances. For example, do periods of intensified hostility with the United States favor the military and their agenda? Does South Korean economic aid foster increased international opening and softening of the North's foreign policy choices? More basically, does Kim select policy from the universe of choices debated in the official press? Do institutions hold relatively stable policy advocacy across leaders of the institution or are they a product of new leaders? In short, my detailed historical discussion of this period focuses on whether my theoretical expectations and the downstream consequences of my model hold true.

Integrating the three issue areas into a single chronological history allows one to view the bureaucratic debate within and between these issue areas. Also, the temporal character is important. Are new policy initiatives discussed between agencies prior to implementation? If a new policy idea appears in the elite press as an institutional position before Kim lays claim to it or it is implemented as policy, then that policy likely originated from below. While it is possible that the idea originated within Kim's inner circle, it is unlikely that the top political leadership would allow lower-level bureaucrats to claim credit for their idea. Questioning policy diverges from the more centralized models' expectations. If the bureaucracies have a say in refining policy ideas through interagency debate, then institutions weigh in on policy choices and expert opinion factors into policy decisions.

Furthermore, my hypothesis predicts an element completely alien to the monolithic descriptions of North Korean politics: bureaucratic resistance. I expect the disadvantaged institutions to maintain consistent policy positions on strategic policy *even after* Kim's central decision. These positions may be somewhat muted or presented more cautiously after Kim's decision, but continued opposition to decided policy is strong evidence of a more plural polity. The center does not direct all positions.

Falsifiable Theory

My research hypothesis is falsifiable. It is possible that institutions do not maintain a consistent general outlook on these issues over time. They may simply reflect the wishes of the central leadership, toeing Kim's official national line and not varying on revealed policy preferences. The central leadership may encourage these contrary views to throw off foreign observers and select policy consistently advocated by only one institution. Also, senior leadership may ignore these differences and select policies outside the universe of policy options debated in the elite press. Alternatively, powerful men—and here the gendered term is explicitly warranted—may rotate between the most senior positions of each bureaucracy, bringing with them a new outlook to propound. Finally, men or institutions may be set up as scapegoats, linking certain people or institutions to policies that are bound to fail. In short, the research design can at the outset find supporting systematic evidence for any of the theories documented in the literature review—or it can support my own.

The monolithic ideal types may find support in the following chapters instead of my theory. If the central leadership defines policy and the bureaucracy implements it, then one would not expect to find policies debated in the official press. The central leadership would have no incentive to allow systematic disagreement with their dictated policy. Furthermore, if power is personal and not institutional, then a leader's policy choices should not be tied to the institution he leads. A new cabinet premier, for example, would have no reason to articulate the same policy line as his predecessor. By contrast, consistency across leaders of the institution suggests the expert professional bureaucracy pushes new ideas up to the political leadership to arbitrate, and individual leaders are less important in policy formation than competing models argue. In this case, the institution has expertise and momentum of its own regardless of the top leader.

My theory argues that Kim's power is limited in the sense that he rules through a rational bureaucracy. His policy choices carry the day, but experts within each bureaucracy present him with a partial universe of policy options. While "none of the above" remains one of his multiple choices and preserves a critical role for Kim as policy innovator as well as executor, I test with the analysis in the following chapters whether he usually selects from those options debated in the press. If he does, then this is evidence that power is more diffuse than the monolithic theories present. Defining options for policy selection is a critical power. Bureaucratic resistance is also strong evidence that Kim's power is more limited than the monolithic ideal types indicate.

The falsifiable empirical test will allow me to systematically address this question. My research design does not allow proving the theory beyond a reasonable doubt. Rather it tests which theory holds the preponderance of evidence. If my empirical tests correspond with my expectations, then they are highly suggestive that the monolithic conventional wisdom needs refinement; it demonstrates that my model is more likely to be correct than that of competitors.

In order for this theoretical model to be deemed applicable to North Korea, several empirical regularities must be observed. Bureaucracies must do the following:

1. Be coherent groups
2. Have an ability to aggregate and articulate preferences
3. Conflict with one another on policy questions
4. Have some bearing on actual policy decisions

Bureaucratic resistance to selected policy choices, while more difficult to observe, would provide further evidence that bureaucracies articulate and pursue specific interests in a diffused manner at odds with the totalitarian model.

In chapter 4 I argue that the party, the military, and the cabinet are coherent groups with distinct policy outlooks. They have different histories and composition. Conversely, I argue that the security apparatus is not a coherent group and therefore cannot be considered a fourth interest group. I also show that the other national institutions recognized in the constitution—the rubber-stamp parliament (Supreme People's Assembly) and the judiciary—cannot be characterized as coherent, semiautonomous groups that influence policy decisions.

Chapters 5 through 7 take up specific policy debates within the system. I test whether each of these three institutions has a coherent message over time and whether their policy goals come in conflict with one another. I also test whether one or more of these policy options generally becomes state policy. If each institution does not present a single policy response to arising issues, wavers from institutional interests, does not conflict with other institutions, and/or has its policy options routinely ignored, my theory should not be deemed empirically valid.

Before turning to these critical tests, however, I sketch North Korea's six-decade political history, from the founding of the state in 1948 to the present.

CHAPTER THREE

Historical Context

Kim Il Sung maintained the longest ideologically driven political system of the communist experiment that approached the totalitarian ideal. His system was remarkably resilient and remains popular today even among many North Korean defectors who live in South Korea and blame his son for ruining the country.[1] The elder Kim was credited with fighting the Japanese colonizers, erecting the state, "defeating" the Americans in the Korean War, and providing the perception of a higher standard and respectability of living. Kim Il Sung presented himself as a true revolutionary.

By contrast, Kim Jong Il was born into luxury, lacked his father's revolutionary bona fides and personal charisma, and claimed political legitimacy based on his bloodline rather than his own actions. He avoided public appearances and did not command the same widespread personal loyalty. He also assumed the top leadership position amid economic collapse and incipient famine, further compounding challenges in consolidating his rule. Kim Il Sung spent two decades formally grooming his son for succession, yet the two Kims ruled the state in distinct ways. North Korea's political institutions evolved over the decades and rapidly changed in the 1990s.

I begin with a simple assumption: political evolution is a historically dependent process. Rarely can political institutions be crafted without reference to the political past. In order to understand why and how the contemporary North Korean political system functions, one must start with what the current regime evolved out of. This chapter sketches North Korea's general political history since its founding. The next chapter takes up the related, albeit more specific, task of describing the establishment and evolution of North Korea's political institutions. The central point of these two chapters is to show how Kim Il Sung over time built a totalitarian system with its apex in the early 1970s. Kim Jong Il inherited and precipitated a system in decline. This decline accelerated rapidly in the 1990s and opens the theoretical possibility of discussing the resulting specific variety of post-totalitarian rule.

Foundations of the Founding

Kim Il Sung's North Korea departed significantly from previous Korean political history. It provides a convenient starting point for evaluating the evolution of the state's politics. While Korea's "five thousand years of history" undoubtedly shaped the culture, values, and social relations that make the nation a single people, this history sheds incomplete light on Kim Il Sung's early government institutions, their specific functions, and how they related to society.

Much has been written on the birth of the state and speculation about its impending death. Neither evaluates the entire story. The state changes as it grows older. The formative years critically shape the state's life, but they do not predetermine its destiny. North Korea's relations with its neighbors have affected its political development. Challenges and opportunity alike have fostered its evolution. This chapter looks at that evolution in progress. North Korea is a young state, but it is very ill. The prognosis remains unclear: will North Korea will rebound from the 1990s or suffer chronic illness until its eventual demise. To answer these questions and others, one must look to the evolution of North Korea's politics.

The Choson Dynasty reigned over a united Korea from 1392 to 1910, but its lasting imprint on the structure and character of the North Korean regime is negligible. Korean political culture from the pre–Japanese occupation era would only survive in the North in the most general sense in terms of social values, beliefs, and customs. Japan's occupation and annexation—along with the strong reaction to it—profoundly shaped the creation of new political institutions on the Korean peninsula.

During Japan's thirty-five years of formal annexation of Korea (1910–45), Japan imposed a feudal economic structure with land held by only a few owners, and industrial production and capital investment geared toward extractive and exported goods. The Japanese dealt with the Koreans brutally, suppressing their national identity and language. Resistance groups organized against the Japanese inside Korea and in nearby China before and during the Second World War. Following Japan's defeat in 1945, these guerilla groups vied for power over Korea. The peculiar nature of the right-wing Japanese administration led most resistance groups to take on a leftist persona. The dearth of indigenous, noncommunist groups left the United States, for example, only one serious contender to recognize as the noncommunist Korean government in 1948.

The Japanese occupation made Korea ripe for leftist politics, but leftism was secondary to the primary demand that the new polity be anti-Japanese. Before it had fully consolidated power following the Japanese defeat, the Kim Il Sung faction moved toward a land reform effort that initially privatized the large land holdings the Japanese had consolidated. The socialist goal of collective agriculture was put on hold; the initial effort was to move away from the Japanese administration, prompting the community party to form individual agricultural plots. While the Korean Workers' Party eventually advocated a more socialist line, prioritizing heavy industry and defense over agriculture and light industry, the anti-Japanese element proved more important than socialist doctrine.

The new Korean government was more concerned with its intensely anti-Japanese/anti-imperialist orientation than returning to a premodern Choson political order. Previous land owners and other "collaborators" with the Japanese or Americans lost their social and political standing and were even considered poor marriage partners, radically reshaping social relations in the North. Many of the previous elite were killed outright as collaborators, while others either moved to the South or re-created themselves as part of the new dominant social and political order as the new guerilla government in Pyongyang marginalized and denounced this group.[2]

Despite this intense anti-Japanese sentiment, the party's demand to pursue a more modern state encouraged it to very cautiously utilize the skills of these individuals. The Japanese left thousands of trained administrators on both sides of the DMZ after their abrupt departure in 1945.[3] These administrators brought their skills to the new Korean governments and helped bring traditional Korea into the modern world. Both Koreas developed a modern bureaucracy and increasingly used and developed science and technology as industrializing states. The premodern Choson political institutions had relatively little bearing on the new North Korean polity, in particular. Some Korean nationalists in the North and the South are reluctant to recognize this historical point, but the Japanese colonial period left a tremendous mark on Korea, Koreans, and their political institutions.

Further, Kim Il Sung's faction was geographically and politically distanced from the Choson Dynasty. These guerillas were from Korea's northern provinces and lower classes. This was a double strike against them in the Choson system. The Kim Il Sung faction did not demonstrate any affinity toward or have any significant contact with the Choson government. Kim's guerrillas after the Japanese defeat and even through the Korean War actively vied for power against those who may have had some contact with Choson institutions. Since the Kimilsungists fought the Japanese from abroad, they labeled anyone who remained in Korea, even those who opposed the Japanese, as "collaborators" and tried to purge them. Labeling other anti-Japanese factions of Korean fighters as "collaborators" was a tactical effort by Kim to purge domestic rivals and position himself on top of a new Korean regime. During the occupation, Kim's group was based in China, more distanced from the center of Japanese power on the peninsula, and faced criticism from competing guerilla groups, who claimed they had abandoned Korea during the colonial period. Korean leaders who may have known something of the preceding Korean political order did not participate in building the DPRK's political institutions. The guerilla experience would be the main indigenous Korean influence on the DPRK's founding.[4]

Kim and his comrades did not finish middle school. These uneducated guerillas made up Kim Il Sung's political elite. These men likely did not have much serious exposure to Choson political institutions personally or through reading history. Furthermore, they were focused on ousting the Japanese, not learning how to govern. There were no Lenins among the Kimilsungists; they distrusted intellectuals and actively purged them at various stages after consolidating power. The Kimilsungists lacked the capacity to develop sophisticated political institutions on their own or draw from the past. Instead, they followed the lead of their main international backers and their own collective personal experience leading a small guerilla army.

Finally, the Soviets contributed to North Korean institutions. The DPRK's first constitution was written in Russian and translated into Korean. The 1948 constitution was modeled on the Soviet Union's 1936 "Stalin constitution." In 1948 and 1949 when the North Koreans used the term *suryong* (chieftain), they were referring to Stalin, not Kim. Kim later made sure *suryong* referred only to him.[5] Yet Stalin's aims were limited in Korea. He sought to install a friendly regime rather than get deeply involved in the regime as he did in Central and Eastern Europe. North Korea had greater room to depart from Stalin's political model than the states behind Europe's iron curtain.

Kim was not merely a puppet of the Soviets even in the early years after the Japanese defeat. Kim's political star was already shining among his peers before the Soviet tapped him for the job. He commanded up to three hundred men in a fractionalized guerilla movement only a few thousand fighters strong, mounted at least one offensive inside Korea, topped Japan's "most wanted list" in 1939, and most importantly, unlike many other guerilla groups he avoided total liquidation by the Japanese. After returning to Korea following the Japanese defeat, Kim's political proposals won out among indigenous forces over the Soviet-supported factions in 1946. Following a Soviet fallout with its first choice for a Korean leadership team, Moscow turned to Kim Il Sung.[6] Soviet influence was undoubtedly important, but it was only one element of the founding of the state.

Kim's autonomy grew quickly. The KWP merged the North Korean and South Korean Communist Parties in 1946—a full two years before the establishment of the state. Kim, the party, and the state concentrated on reunification, not foreign policy. With a significant military advantage over the South and a depleted U.S. military presence in Asia following Washington's rapid demobilization after World War II, Kim effectively lobbied Moscow to allow him to reunify the nation by force in 1950, precipitating the Korean War.[7]

The Korean War (1950–53) was a tremendously important event in Korean history, as well as twentieth-century world history. Destruction and deprivation were extreme on both sides of the peninsula. The American general in charge of the Far East Bomber Command reported that there were no more targets in North Korea, because everything had been destroyed. North Korea's population contracted by more than 10 percent; every major industry was devastated; and agricultural production shrank to a fraction of pre–Korean War levels.[8] North Korea was virtually a blank slate in every material way. For ideological purposes, the DPRK media cites the importance of the Korean War experience regularly as the great effort to achieve the state and party's core goal of national reunification.

The Korean War is important, but it was not a revolutionary struggle. For the North, it was an early action of a government that had preceded the war and survived it. A band of anti-Japanese factions with Kim Il Sung the most prominent among them launched the war, and Kim Il Sung emerged from the war still precariously on top. The Japanese occupation and defeat—not the Korean War—revolutionized Korean politics. Before, during, and after the Korean War, Kim Il Sung worked to eliminate internal opponents and strengthen his grip on the DPRK. The Korean War was one more tool, not a cause, for Kim to establish his totalizing regime.

By the end of the 1950s, Kim had eliminated his major domestic opponents and fashioned a totalitarian system. North Korea's institutions did evolve—notably in 1972, 1992, and 1998 with constitutional revisions—but they evolved from this Stalinist-guerilla fusion starting point coupled with a legacy of the imperial Japanese modes of administration. Stalinist Russia, the Kimilsungist guerrillas, and imperial Japan shared totalizing aspects that sought state supremacy over all aspects of society, which profoundly shaped the DPRK's founding institutions and ideology.

Kim Il Sung and Totalitarianism, 1956–1990

Kim Il Sung consolidated his power in the 1950s, purging his remaining opponents and making Soviet support less important for internal control. He removed domestic opposition to allow the Communist Party to monopolize politics under his direction as the totalitarian model predicts.

Consolidating Power, the 1950s

In December 1955 Kim introduced the country to a comprehensive ideology, Juche. Juche is an inherently flexible and radically nationalistic philosophy that promotes Korea's autonomy and guided Kim Il Sung's political institutions until his death. The injection of nationalism is important, because it marked Kim's final departure from Soviet puppet status. Kim had removed enough internal challengers so he could move farther from Soviet influence and assert cherished independence. North Korea never reached its self-reliant ideal. Nonetheless, this ideal serves as a source of pride and ideological conviction to this day. Like the Vietnamese, Koreans of all sorts proudly recognize their independent history and have fought fiercely to defend that status. When other states were absorbed by foreign occupiers, Korea remained independent. This is part of the reason the Japanese occupation was so hated, and why the North Koreans constantly chide the South Koreans as being American puppets. Kim Il Sung tapped into this nationalism and placed himself and the ideologically guided party at the center of the new regime.

At the first opportunity after Khrushchev's "secret speech" that denounced Stalinism, Kim Il Sung's domestic opposition criticized what they saw as Kim's Stalinist tendencies. The Soviet-Korean faction (those residing in the Soviet Union during World War II) and the Yenan-Korean faction (those fighting in Mao's army during the period) departed from Khrushchev's model in one important way—Khrushchev denounced Stalin after the totalitarian dictator's death, and Kim Il Sung was still very much alive.[9] Kim responded to the criticism by finally purging these two other guerilla factions and firmly establishing his personality cult. After Kim liquidated factionalism, North Korea had a party elite of generally like-minded revolutionaries with intense personal devotion to Kim Il Sung, despite concerns about continual purges and evidence of corruption.[10]

Kim Il Sung called the Third Party Congress in April 1956. Rather than following the Soviet lead away from the totalitarian ideal, Kim further centralized his power and the power of the Korean Workers' Party. He instructed the party to implant its representatives within the government and in the military organizations (down to the company level) to ensure proper policy implementation in accordance with the party line. Party representatives would have to approve any operational military action; they also controlled promotions, transfers, leaves, and general indoctrination.[11] Party representatives established youth and women's organizations, agriculture and industry work federations, trade unions. They also closely controlled education.[12] Kim did not develop a strongman dictatorship along the personalist model by maintaining power through simple repression. His new polity proved much more robust, utilizing a massive party apparatus to control society as well as government.

Kim Il Sung utilized a single comprehensive party and all encompassing ideology as the totalitarian ideal type predicts, but he also put himself firmly on top of the party. Kim's oft-cited "personality cult" runs much deeper than most analyses recognize. The Korean War created human suffering that outlasted the war. The large number of orphans encouraged the state to establish the School for the Offspring of Revolutionary Martyrs, later known as Mangyongdae Revolutionary School. The school instilled the idea that the state was the new family, which had a tremendous psychological impact on these boys and young men.[13] It bred intense devotion to Kim Il Sung and the revolution that later generations not personally marred by the Japanese occupation or the Korean War could not appreciate. Though some other totalitarian regimes used similar methods to fill the ranks of the secret police, graduates of the Mangyongdae Revolutionary School came to populate the top leadership positions in the North Korean system as the first-generation revolutionaries aged. Kim Il Sung put in place an ideological system with greater potential to be long lasting among this group of elites than other totalitarian states.

Though the regime used repression extensively, it did not survive by that alone. It was a more stable polity, because it could appeal to intense ideological and nationalistic sentiments and articulate them in Juche thought. The system also gained legitimacy internally in the early years from the economic results it produced. Casual observers of North Korea understandably associate it with economic backwardness. This characterization is generally appropriate after the 1970s, but in the years following the Korean War, the state saw real economic gains. North Korea expanded agricultural production and reduced the number of people required to work the fields. They shifted workers into the greatly expanding industrial sector and developed an educated workforce. The state enjoyed double digit growth annually in the post–Korean War 1950s and roughly 6 percent annual growth in the 1960s, leading one *Le Monde* journalist to note that North Korea was "one of the greatest economic powers in Asia." North Korea was doing better economically than South Korea. The North even accepted defectors from the South. North Koreans did not live in a socialist paradise, but they could reasonably conclude that life was getting better. They attributed this success to the command economy—another area where this regime followed the totalitarian ideal type.

Sino-Soviet Split, the 1960s

The Sino-Soviet split in the 1960s prompted North Korea to play China and the Soviet Union off against each other. It also provided North Korea greater political independence and new economic and security challenges. The Juche ideology's emphasis on independence and more general Korean nationalism produced a reluctance to rely on Chinese or Soviet benefactors. However, what North Korea gained in political independence from this posturing, it lost in critical economic aid. North Korea had to extend its seven-year plan to ten years when it failed to reach economic targets. Greater independence also produced greater insecurity. North Korea could not rely wholly on either the Soviets or the Chinese to provide for its security. It intensified the self-reliant line and started efforts toward its own nuclear capacity.[14] While North Korea's heavy-industry-supporting command economy was based on the Stalinist model, the state followed Mao's lead in the Great Leap Forward to modify the Korean economy in the Chollima march.

With more independence in the 1960s, the state was faced with more responsibilities. Technocrats emerged in the military and economic spheres to augment the revolutionaries with more competent administration. In 1962 Kim Il Sung announced the party must put "equal emphasis" on military and economic goals, signaling his ability to direct all policy spheres.[15] Kim quickly reversed his slight movement away from the ideologically driven command economy. Revolutionary generals argued that the state should provide defense before considering economic goals. Kim Il Sung ultimately heeded his revolutionary compatriots' advice and restricted the role of economic technocrats once again. Consequently, as Soviet aid fell, the initial gains of industrialization reached a point of diminishing returns. As Kim Il Sung's strategy to arm the entire population and build extensive and expensive underground military facilities required a greater share of the country's increasingly scarce resources, the state's economic growth slowed. Kim demonstrated some willingness to listen to and empower institutions other than the party during his reign, but it was limited and always under the watchful eye and formal authority of the party.

The economy slowed starting in the mid-1960s and 1970s, stagnated in the 1980s, collapsed to below subsistence levels in the 1990s, and modestly rebounded in the 2000s. However, a certain segment of society recalled the period of postwar reconstruction and industrialization that produced rapid growth as more than a one-time strategy. With nostalgia, they argued that these socialist strategies could again be put to use, reflecting the party's general position of applying past policies to contemporary situations.[16] This memory had a meaningful impact on policy debates in North Korea in the 1990s and 2000s.

By the Second Party Congress in 1966, Kim had installed his revolutionary brethren in key posts and eliminated the technocrats. By the end of the decade, though, he had purged many of these loyal revolutionary compatriots. Kim alone would be the revolutionary hero; not even this close group of comrades would remain in positions of power. Kim followed the totalitarian model's expectations for a permanent purge. He replaced some of his revolutionary generals with revolutionary civilians and technocrats. One had to demonstrate loyalty to Kim and the party line, but even that did not assure one's (political) survival. Officials naturally develop differing ideas about policy, and they may express them. However, Kim Il Sung's use of purges like other totalitarian dictators prevented these views from advancing or undermining the state's centralized control.[17]

Kim retained the ultimate authority to interpret the Juche ideology and did not wholly delegate this power to the party as Marxist-Leninist doctrine would support. While the party began as an important institution, it came to occupy a decidedly second-place role. The party would sit atop and constrain the bureaucracy but follow the orders of a single man. Party representatives resided inside every major unit of the bureaucracy, military, and workplace. They assured policy implementation did not depart significantly from Kim's orders and ideological correctness. Just as the party maintained tight control over the rest of the system, Kim tightly controlled the party and asserted legitimacy through simple repression, a well-developed personality cult, a general ideology, and even a recognition of economic growth. North Korea approached the totalitarian ideal type in the late 1950s and 1960s with a level of personal power that even Stalin and Mao did not achieve.[18]

Apex of Power, the 1970s

Kim had so solidified his position atop the system that Robert Scalapino and Chong-sik Lee perceptively argued in the 1970s that profound institutional change (through evolution or revolution) was unforeseeable in the near future: "Only when organizations now totally subordinate to the party . . . acquire some sense of separate interest and some degree of autonomy will the present structure of the party, including the methods of ordering authority, undergo significant alteration. The degree of pluralism attained in the total society, in short, will determine the extent to which party monolithism and the cult of personality that tends to accompany it can be reduced." In their view North Korea was the "world's purest monocratic system."[19] Still, this position would not naturally propagate itself and required close and increasingly difficult efforts to maintain.

North Korea's 1972 constitution codified Kim's personal power. On the heels of Kim Il Sung's important and highly celebrated sixtieth birthday, the new constitution created the position of president for Kim Il Sung, instituting an unprecedented concentration of presidential power unseen even in Stalin's Soviet Union or Mao's China.[20] Kim Il Sung drew advisers from his revolutionary brethren and put them in high positions in the party. They were rewarded for general (ideological) knowledge. Specialists and those with technical knowledge were tolerated in the party starting in the 1960s when the Sino-Soviet split provided North Korea greater independence and thus created more responsibilities, but technocrats still had no opportunity for senior leadership in the 1970s.[21]

The 1972 constitution firmly established the supremacy of the party over the state. It formally downgraded the main legislative body, the Supreme People's Assembly (SPA), discarding the previous fiction that the SPA was the supreme organ in the North Korean system. It downgraded the state's main executive body, the cabinet, renaming it the Administrative Council. The new constitution shrank the number of ministries from thirty-seven to twenty-two and granted the party more functional control over the Administrative Council, particularly in economic affairs where economic technocrats had temporarily exerted greater influence in the 1960s. Most of the officially high-ranking revolutionaries held senior positions in the party structure and low- and midlevel officials stopped rotating between the party, military, and government roles. They increasingly developed functional expertise in one institution, compartmentalizing roles and information that Kim Il Sung and his revolutionary comrades could control.

Kim's speeches and writings explicitly and consistently identified the government bureaucracy as an enemy to the good. Like other communist states, party members maintained key posts in the government bureaucracy in order to ensure proper policy implementation. The foreign minister, for example, was a member of the Politburo. The Ministries of Foreign Affairs, Armed Forces, Trade, External Economic Relations, the Committee for Cultural Relations with Foreign Countries, and the Academy of Sciences all had formal roles in foreign policy, but in practice the party was sufficiently staffed and empowered to control these bureaucratic elements under Kim Il Sung's oversight.[22] Foreign policy decision making centered on the party secretariat's Department of International Affairs not the separate Ministry of Foreign Affairs. The party's decisions would be sent to the rubber-stamp parliament and then implemented through the Politburo.

The party was the most important organ: advising policy decisions, making policy decisions, and executing policy. Remaining institutions existed as support staff to the party. This decision-making and implementation process operated under the supervision of the Central Committee of the Party—and the president.[23] Ideology informed macropolitical decision making that was reflected in the state's institutional formation.

Kim continued to rule through the party by implanting political advisers with wide-ranging power in the military and government bureaucracies. These implanted representatives delivered regular reports to the party apparatus. Party control of the government expanded in the Fourth (1961) and Fifth (1970) party congresses, although the extent of this expansion cannot be firmly identified.[24] Particularly in the arena of foreign affairs, the DPRK needed greater capacity in the 1970s. In the early years, North Korea had diplomatic relations with as few as seven countries, allowing the condensed party structure to deal with foreign policy. By the 1970s, Dae-sook Suh notes, the government had to assume greater policy-making roles due to the greater workload reflected in the 1972 constitution.[25]

Suh's analysis was restricted to foreign affairs, but one can surmise that similar pressures faced other areas that increasingly required more specialized knowledge. The government moved from a purely administrative role to having greater policy-making responsibilities as suggested by an infusion of new personnel, more frequent meetings on substantive

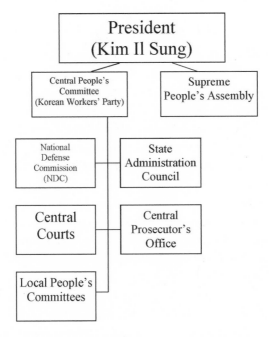

FIGURE 3.1 Macropolitical Organization Under Kim Il Sung

questions, and the cabinet premier introducing the new budget to the SPA. By contrast, the KWP Central Committee had already reduced its plenary meetings to once or twice a year. Government personnel increasingly met in joint meetings with Politburo personnel.

The party was positioned over the military and the government, creating a three-tiered political structure. Kim codified personal power but maintained ideology as a guide and constraint on political action. The important role of the party, ideology, continual purges, and command economy as key conduits for Kim to control the state and society made his state more closely resemble the totalitarian ideal than other models of nondemocratic rule.

After the initial gains of postwar reconstruction and modernization began to wane, Kim Il Sung's ideologically driven process failed to foster prosperity. Kim may have been well informed about what occurred, but his leadership lacked the personal and/or institutional capacity to understand why it mattered. In 1972–74, for example, Kong Chin Tae, the minister of external economic affairs, presided over the purchases of massive Western industrial enterprises, including the world's largest cement factory. North Korea planned to produce exportable products. The enterprise was not economically viable even with cheap North Korean labor. Some industries could not produce a product; others could not market it abroad. The 1973 oil crisis and rise in energy costs made energy-inefficient production even more unsustainable. The short-lived experiment left North Korea with a massive debt and no new productive industry. The North showed no inclination to pay down its debt. It was the first socialist state to default, causing its credit rating to plummet and effectively removing any hope of access to foreign capital other than aid.

Kim was not above blaming and even purging officials for failed policies, but he promoted Kong to vice premier in 1975. In a rare interview with a Western media outlet, Kim told *Le Monde* in 1977 that the investments had failed because the West was not able to purchase the North Korean goods;[26] Kim did not seem to understand the economic folly of the project and its tremendous long-term consequences for the North Korean economy. Kim Il Sung was an ideologue and revolutionary, not a technocrat. He empowered the KWP's State Planning Commission with economic decisions while the government ministries could only carry out policy.[27] Significant events like this suggest that he did not have the institutional or personal competence to rule pragmatically.

The year 1973 marked the introduction of Kim Jong Il to the North Korean political scene. Kim Il Sung demoted his younger brother, Kim Yong Chu, and Kim Jong Il took on a then-unspecified senior party role. The North Korean media started to praise Jong Il as the "party center." That same year the DPRK Academy of Sciences deleted its previous derogatory definition of "hereditary succession" as an exploitative, feudal practice from its *Political Dictionary*.[28] Kim Il Sung effectively maintained political control through the totalitarian arrangement. What was not clear was whether the younger Kim could exert the same power and authority as his father.

By the mid-1970s some observers claimed that the North Korean government was increasing its role vis-à-vis the party, especially in foreign affairs. Dae-sook Suh wrote that the 1972 constitution fostered this change, while Robert Scalapino responded that the dual appointment of party and government officials made such a change of "limited importance." The party and government officials were the same, Scalapino reasoned, and Kim Il Sung could control foreign policy by dividing this authority between several institutions.[29] Others argued that the state had both ideological requirements and national interests to pursue in foreign policy. Shifting between these goals was common to communist systems, including North Korea where economic demands had come to outpace geopolitical ones, but did not represent a division between institutional interests.[30]

Succession Preparation Intensifies, the 1980s

There was some shift afoot by the early 1980s. Kim Jong Il officially became the supreme leader in waiting at the Sixth Party Congress in 1980. To know in what way Kim Jong Il's rule would differ from his father's would have to wait until the 1990s, but North Korea watchers recognized some general social and political changes brewing. At the 1980 party congress, Kim Il Sung warned against a move away from revolutionary principles among a post–Korean War generation. As long as Kim Il Sung was alive, the political objectives of the revolution would outweigh other goals. But the stage was being set for Kim Jong Il. The state saw its first major shift toward employing technocrats and Kim Jong Il loyalists formally in senior positions starting in 1980. Some observers called this not just a transition between top leaders but a generational change in which economic pragmatists might rule over militant ideologues.

Not everyone was enthusiastic about Jong Il's selection for successor. At the 1980 party congress, Minister of Public Security Yi Chin-su warned against opposing the heir apparent—a point reiterated in *Nodong Sinmun* as Kim Jong Il's personality cult intensified. The security apparatus purged those who opposed Kim Jong Il's selection.[31]

Kim Jong Il demonstrated an early willingness to use not only targeted purges but also arbitrary repression to assert his power, even when his specific goals were not clearly formed. Like his father Kim Jong Il rejected empiricism as eroding revolutionary principles and demanded improved empirical performance from state organizations. His bloody crackdown was aimed more at demonstrating his ability and willingness to use arbitrary terror than at advancing a certain goal. Kim Jong Il used "three revolution teams" of young and zealous Koreans to suppress empiricists and support three vague goals of ideological, technical, and cultural advancement. Kim demanded officials be both ideologically committed and expert in their specific area.[32]

In the 1980s Kim Il Sung began moving into the background as his son increasingly took on more responsibility. As early as 1983 one scholar predicted that the state that Kim Il Sung built into a monolith would likely bureaucratize as the tension between competence and ideology expanded, but at that time there was "no clear dichotomy between Red [ideologue] and expert."[33] Tai Sung An and Dae-sook Suh thoughtfully argued that the stage was set for the state to gradually change under Kim Jong Il although it remained unclear what that change would produce. Kim Jong Il modified his father's reunification policy, allowing some family reunions, opening inter-Korean economic discussions, and promoting his own loyalists to senior positions, particularly post–Korean War graduates of the Mangyongdae Revolutionary School. The state might be taking a new path, but where it would lead and what the resulting regime would look like remained unclear.[34]

Even those arguing the state was slowly changing recognized that the party more tightly controlled the state and society than any other political system. The North Korean system still sought to eliminate dissent. North Korea's previous experience with dissent was a factional system in the 1940s and 1950s that the Kims and their senior leadership sought to avoid repeating. Even those early scholars who detailed the prevalence of various groups and generational change within the North Korean system concluded that by the time Kim Il Sung consolidated his rule, he sat atop the party, which in turn dominated the other groups.[35] In every way imaginable, Kim Il Sung's North Korea approached the totalitarian ideal.[36]

On the eve of Kim Il Sung's death, in-depth studies of the North Korean system continued to apply the totalitarian label. Many did not deny change within the system with the ebb and flow of history, but the fundamental character of the regime remained static. The party controlled the military and government, with Kim on top; ideological indoctrination remained important; and the state monopolized the media and planned the economy.[37] In 1994 "the North Korean political structure, in short, [represented] the classic case of the monolithic power" where unity defined all the political institutions of the state.[38] Bruce Cumings argued that "the North Korea of today is still, fundamentally, the one that was formed in the 1940s. But time goes on, things change."[39] Cumings recognized the increased role of the younger Kim, especially by the 1980s, but basically saw the system as the same despite calling the younger Kim "the world's first postmodern dictator" after Kim Il Sung's death in 1994. North Korea approached the totalitarian ideal under Kim Il Sung, but significant events in the 1990s fundamentally reshaped the system. The nature of that system is the primary topic of this study.

The Transition Period, 1991–1998

North Korea's political system grew more rational in the 1990s. The type of information senior leadership demanded required a substantially different bureaucratic structure and a renewed emphasis on expertise. The acceleration of North Korea's political evolution in the 1990s is more than the simple political transition from father to son, although the skills and experience of the top leader played an important role. Three events compounded one another's effect to unleash tremendous economic, social, and political forces that hastened the regime's transformation. The Soviet collapse in 1991, Kim Il Sung's death in 1994, and the onset of the famine in 1995 had a profound combined effect on North Korean politics. This section documents the history of this period, paralleling the theoretical discussion of these changes found in the previous chapter.

Shock One: The Soviet Collapse

North Korea lost its primary economic and security backer in 1991. North Korea depended on Soviet military, energy, and food assistance to keep its economy afloat. Though Soviet secretary general Mikhail Gorbachev reduced Soviet aid to North Korea throughout the 1980s, one-sided "trade" remained at $3.5 billion as late as 1988. In 1991 Moscow completely shut off the aid valve and trade plummeted to hundreds of millions of dollars per year. Furthermore, with the end of the Cold War, North Korea lost its main security guarantor. Moscow eliminated any mention of Russian military assistance to North Korea even in the case of direct attack against the North and formally recognized the government in Seoul in 1991.[40]

North Korea's economy was modeled on the Soviet Union even more than its politics. After the Korean War, Moscow provided technical assistance to build ninety-three heavy industrial factories in North Korea,[41] producing a familiar blend of heavy industrial products mainly useful for the military with little investment in light industry and consumer goods. This economic plan required sustained energy input to keep the production chain moving. With the loss of energy aid, the North's industrial base suffered dramatic declines as the state sought new ways to supply its energy needs.[42]

North Korea's economic woes ran deeper than those of other former Soviet satellite states. The cessation of energy aid put North Korea perilously close to not being able to feed its population. North Korea used potent oil-based fertilizers to sustain some level of food production. The fertilizers did long-term damage to the soil over decades of use, and by the mid-1990s, the soil required these fertilizers to produce food. North Korea also experiences very cold winters. Without oil, North Koreans turned to the forests to provide heating fuel. Burning biomass contributed to deforestation and soil erosion that further hindered agricultural production, especially in the most productive agricultural lands. North Korea is a mountainous country with little arable land; indigenous food production is overwhelmingly concentrated in the "rice bowl" in the south of the country, which is prone to severe flooding. Coupled with the state's policies that contributed to soil erosion, extreme weather could destroy the country's crop.

North Korea's geography produces a natural reliance on food imports to feed its population. Pyongyang's policy choices have magnified this dependence on foreign food supplies, a fact that is particularly inconvenient to an autarkic government. Reduced energy aid shrank fertilizer production and increased the state's reliance on foreign food sources at precisely the same time when friendly aid sources rapidly diminished. North Korea had to purchase a larger portion of its food from abroad at a time when its industrial production—its economic engine—ground to a halt. The state's long-term outlook was bleak, and it was one shock away from a debilitating food crisis.

However, North Korea's new challenges were not simply economic. It still faced off across the world's most heavily fortified border against a newly democratic enemy. South Korea's elected officials had ties to the former military regime and were openly hostile to the North during this period. South Korea clearly outpaced the North economically and potentially militarily—even independent of U.S. backing.[43] Of course, South Korea did enjoy U.S. backing, and the United States maintained troops on the Korean peninsula. While President George H. W. Bush acknowledged publicly that the United States had removed all of its tactical nuclear weapons from South Korea by December 1991, the security-conscious North Koreans still had reason to fear the U.S.–South Korean alliance. With its dilapidated economy and no superpower support, North Korea scrambled to survive.

The following year, the two Koreas made history. In February 1992 North and South Korea signed the Basic Agreement, whereby both committed to peaceful reunification, denuclearization, and cultural and economic projects like family reunions and joint ventures. Pyongyang seemingly recognized the challenges facing the country and sought to negotiate security commitments and obtain the necessary food and energy assistance. Two months later, North Korea revised its constitution. It removed all references to Marxism-Leninism, precipitating calls for "Korean-style socialism." The Cold War was over, and North Korea was searching for a new international strategy that would have long-standing effects on its political structure.

The Soviet Union was not North Korea's only ally. It also cautiously relied upon its northern neighbor, China. The two states have a precarious history. The Kimilsungist guerillas helped the Maoists defeat Chiang Kai-shek's nationalist army in the Chinese civil war. The Chinese reciprocated by sending 3 million troops to fight on North Korea's side in the Korean War. The two states have a relationship forged in blood but a historically uneasy relationship. The Chinese have seen Korea as part of its sphere of influence and sought to explicitly dominate—and at times conquer—the peninsula. North Korea signed formal treaty alliances with both China and the Soviet Union within one week of each other in July 1961 and tried to play the Soviets and Chinese off against one another after the Sino-Soviet split. Eventually, Pyongyang decided to rely more on the Soviet Union, judging loss of sovereignty to China as the greater threat.[44]

China and North Korea grew apart through the later years of the Cold War. In December 1979 Deng Xiaoping announced China's radical economic reforms. The People's Republic of China moved away from its Maoist roots. By the end of the Cold War, the relationship between the two countries had deteriorated. In August 1992, over Pyongyang's strenuous objection, Beijing recognized the Republic of Korea (South Korea). But China's interest in regional stability ultimately led it to protect North Korean interests in international forums, especially the UN Security Council, in the coming years to prevent the real risk of a North Korean collapse. China also provided North Korea with what one former Chinese Foreign Ministry official estimated to be 70 to 90 percent of the North's energy aid and approximately one-third of its food aid.[45] China remains the North's sole remaining military ally, though Beijing's willingness to uphold its treaty commitment militarily even in the face of explicit intervention from foreign powers is highly questionable.[46] China was not North Korea's first choice as an international backer, but the reclusive state cautiously accepted China' support while pursuing the means to provide for its own security and economic needs.

In this context of eroding sovereignty, North Korea took bold action. The state could address its mounting problems by forging a new relationship with a more distant great power, the United States, or seek to address the security part of its new challenges alone with a nuclear deterrent. On March 12, 1993, the North Korean Foreign Ministry precipitated a crisis by announcing the state would withdraw from the Non-Proliferation Treaty (NPT). Three of the top U.S. negotiators in the first nuclear crisis described their understanding of how the regime made this decision:

> According to later accounts, the idea of withdrawing from the NPT was advanced by the Ministry of Foreign Affairs and championed by Kang Sok Ju, the first vice foreign minister. Neither was thought of as a bastion of hard line sentiment within the North Korean system. On the contrary, Kang was believed to belong to a group of Foreign Ministry officials who were relatively more pragmatic. Nevertheless, in a political system where currying favor with the two Kims translated into influence and power (or at least survival), the ministry may have advanced the idea of NPT withdrawal in response to the wishes of Kim Jong Il, who may have been looking for a way out of an increasingly difficult situation. The Foreign Ministry also had its own motives, chiefly to reassert control over dealings with the United States. It had never been happy with Kim Yong Sun's leadership role from his perch as head of the Korean Workers' Party International Department. Since his stewardship had produced few results, by autumn 1992 responsibility had shifted to the Ministry of Foreign Affairs. In December, Kim Yong Sun was promoted, taken off the American account, and put in charge of North-South

dialogue. Later he would claim that he had opposed the North's withdrawal from the NPT. That implied the decision was not simply handed down but perhaps discussed within the small coterie of North Korean decision makers.[47]

North Korea took action that would allow it to reach an agreement in 1994 that traded a nuclear freeze for security guarantees and food and energy assistance. The Kims halted the nation's most potent military program—the plutonium production at Yongbyon—for eight years (1994–2002). The move seemed to address the state's core problems without requiring substantial changes that might more comprehensively affect the regime's rule. The military retained its prestige and prioritized resource allocation; the state's economy remained socialist; and wider society was largely unaffected by the decision with the notable exception of gaining some much needed energy. The 1994 agreement stabilized the situation, but other events outside of the regime's control again intervened.

Shock Two: Kim Il Sung's Death

The second shock came in the midst of negotiating the Agreed Framework. In 1994 Kim Il Sung, the state's founder, president, and national hero, died. Kim Jong Il had fundamentally gained legitimacy from his father's actions half a century earlier. He inherited the reins of power, leaving him with a set of political institutions that he could not immediately change without cost but that were not well suited to his strengths. Though he could not rule with the same revolutionary authority and he faced different challenges, the younger Kim's institutions and system at the outset were essentially those he inherited from his father.

Kim Jong Il came to power during an economic and security crisis. Lacking military qualifications himself and threatened by military coups from the time he was tapped as Kim Il Sung's successor in the 1970s to the latest failed coup only two years prior, he nonetheless concluded the Agreed Framework three months after his father's death.[48] Kim Jong Il did not move immediately to alter his father's institutional structure. He observed a three-year mourning period, traditionally reserved for the death of Korean kings. This show of Confucian filial piety likely appealed to both elite and mass audiences. Traditionally, when a son emerges from the mourning period, he assumes his father's role. In this culturally prescribed way, the younger Kim bolstered his authority as the legitimate heir to his father's rule.

Shock Three: Famine

Within that three-year period of mourning, the third shock hit. Multiyear extreme weather beginning in 1995 compounded the effect of years of failed food and agricultural policies under both Kims, including reducing production incentives and inefficient food rationing and distribution methods.[49] Floods destroyed North Korea's crop, and international assistance was not cost free. It meant recognizing failure. More importantly, international aid came with inspections.

The UN's World Food Program (WFP) requires its staff to certify that the aid is going to vulnerable populations and not being wholly diverted to the military or regime elites. Pyongyang objected to UN inspections. They also objected to other policies, specifically that donated aid bags could recognize the donor's country of origin (including the United States). The WFP grew wary of North Korean demands. While some negotiated aid eventually reached starving North Koreans, the regime's rigid stance caused up to a million people to starve or die from disease and left a generation of North Koreans malnourished.

This third shock, coming on top of the previous two, resulted in social changes in North Korea. The regime had conditioned its citizens to depend on the state for food and other critical resources. When food did not come and regime instructions to work harder or plant patches of grass to eat did not solve the problem, many people died. Still, the regime stubbornly held to its administrative solutions to the famine. Socialist orthodoxy demanded the state lead on these issues and not permit market mechanisms to affect the outcome. Ideologically committed revolutionaries and security-conscious elites alike objected to the idea of increased, individual cross-border traffic. Such moves ran counter to socialist principles and risked dangerous information flows. Party commentaries continually repeated the risk that society might become infected with capitalist ideas in a way that would hasten the collapse of the rest of the former Soviet bloc.

Others defied the regime and survived. Young and able-bodied men and women illegally crossed into China in search of food or consumer goods. A new class of entrepreneurs emerged as farmers sold some production in open-air gray markets and traders brought in new goods from China. Those able to participate in this commerce benefited. China backed high-level reform efforts based on its own experiences, and Pyongyang began to tolerate some of this behavior. While periodically shutting down these markets or cracking down on Sino–North Korean border movement, enough incentive remained for citizens to maintain this trade.[50]

The social and political consequences paved the way for rationalizing North Korea politics and society. Socially, a new class of risk-accepting merchants arose in North Korea. Previously, cadres and party members had topped the status ladder. The state controlled social advancement. However, with the introduction of independent paths to wealth and power, the state inadvertently allowed individuals to gain status based on their own entrepreneurial abilities. Self-made businessmen enjoyed status outside the state. Status is a finite quality, so this move cut into the prestige of cadre and party members, providing both an individual and institutional reason to oppose market mechanisms.

The famine also weakened society's trust in government. While ideology had been eroding for decades, Kim Jong Il's taking power shifted society's focus somewhat from the revolution to effective governance. Under Kim Il Sung's charismatic authority, the psychic needs of elites and the populace could be satisfied by faith in the revolution. Through socialist principle, the state would achieve ultimate victory against the imperialists; promote a moral, nonmaterial way of life; and ultimately transgress the "arduous march." "Good socialists" who entered the party or military earned individual reward in terms of status and wealth as well, providing further incentives for people to pursue this path. During the famine, however, those who made the greatest gains were those who defied the regime and pursued individual interests in markets.

Kim Jong Il announced his regime would pursue "emergency management," permitting implementation of policies that did not subscribe to the socialist orthodoxy for pragmatic reasons. Such a move shifts the elite and popular focus to results. Kim Jong Il repeatedly cited his father, but increasingly he needed to produce effective policy outcomes. The legitimacy of the Kim regime came to rely increasingly on rational calculations.

Such a move was very risky for Kim. Kim Il Sung had been a self-made man. Kim Jong Il was not. He had to walk a fine line between recognizing the role of self-made men and individual expertise without delegitimizing himself. Once Kim started to focus on the effectiveness of his own performance, it raised the possibility that someone else might lead the country more effectively than he was doing. The ruling myth becomes increasingly hollow. Kim's almost supernatural ability to "sagaciously" interpret Juche philosophy and guide the state like a "shining star" becomes less important. Kim did not want to move in this direction, but eventually, after immense human suffering, Kim took some measures to address these new ground realities.

The state accelerated its bureaucratization to rationalize politics. Faceless bureaucrats informed policy based on their individual expertise, not their pedigree or status. While Kim and his core advisers remained on top, the more impersonal hybrid system began to erode charismatic authority.[51] This enhanced the role of technocrats, especially in the economic sphere. They were charged with crafting policy that would help extract the state from this deep crisis. The Administrative Council employed most of these technocrats. All signs indicated that Kim Jong Il would rule differently from his father.

At the same time, Kim needed the military to deter foreign invasion and maintain his ideological mantle of legitimacy. The state still tried to justify its rule in terms of blocking imperialist advances. Kim responded to this dilemma by nominally raising the status of the military. He could hope to garner support from the military. However, he would also need to divide and conquer his bureaucracies by institutionalizing constraints from competing institutions and the security services to prevent the hostile military from threatening Kim himself.

This was not a Kim-directed change, but the exogenous shocks of the mid-1990s put in play important social and political forces that the state, faced with difficult trade-offs, codified in the 1998 constitution. The shocks encouraged the leadership to incorporate novel elements into the political system in face of potential collapse. It did not collapse, but it emerged from these crises changed. North Korea had fewer domestic and international reasons to keep up socialist constraints on policy choices. Ideological correctness would become just one factor in policy choices rather than the guiding policy. It was appropriate, therefore, that South Korea received its highest-ranking North Korean defector in 1997—North Korea's lead Juche theorist Hwang Jang Yop.

Forces outside the state's control prompted changes in North Korean politics. This leads to the conclusion—uncomfortable to many—that Kim Jong Il effectively managed this situation, given his goals. The collapsist school was implicitly correct that the *risk* of state collapse was high. Their error was in overstating their case as deterministic. While one can easily dispute the morality of his choices, Kim achieved his core objective of staving off collapse by overhauling the state's founding institutions and crafting a new ruling order. He codified this new rule in the 1998 constitution. The role of the party, ideologically driven policy, and the command economy all suffered under the new arrangement. North Korea moved away from the totalitarian model not by choice but from necessity.

Post-totalitarian Institutionalism, 1998–Present

By September 1998 North Korea had emerged from its transition period and modified its constitution. The younger Kim modified, or redirected, the state out of an evolving internal and external environment. The state attempted to address challenges in three core areas: inter-Korean relations, U.S. policy, and economics. Each of these issue areas fundamentally related to systemic survival and incorporated competing economic, military, ideational, and political goals.

Toward a New Constitution

In 1998 South Korea elected a political heavyweight, Kim Dae Jung, on a platform that included reconciliation with the North and explicitly discussed reunification as a long-term goal that could be addressed in the future. This gave rise to Seoul's sunshine policy, which involved tension-reduction measures, discussion on reuniting families divided since the Korean War, and economic, food, and energy assistance to prepare for eventual reunification. Pyongyang reacted positively to this development. North Korea sent seventy letters to South Korean politicians through Panmunjom's "truce village," and the secretary of the party's Central Committee commented that the letters signified North Korea's desire to discuss and negotiate with South Korean government officials, political parties, and organizations to "promote coexistence, co-prosperity, common interests, mutual collaboration and unity between fellow countrymen."[52]

The United States focused on North Korea at the beginning of this period through four-party talks. The talks, involving the United States, North Korea, China, and South Korea, never got off the ground. Within seven months, they had ended, with the parties unable to reach basic agreements. However, U.S.-DPRK relations were not yet at a crisis point. Both sides prodded the other to uphold the Agreed Framework commitments; neither had completely abandoned the agreement.

North Korea's economy meanwhile was in shambles. The regime started to emerge from the depths of the famine at the end of the 1990s. Coping mechanisms learned during the famine, as well as Chinese and South Korean aid and investment, were so significant that they began to transform the economy from below. Seoul and Beijing urged Pyongyang to allow greater grass-roots marketization and take more significant political moves to follow China's post-Maoist development model. North Korean generals and party officials objected, arguing that socialism collapsed in Eastern Europe because the system had been opened to foreign and capitalistic influences.[53] But some increased use of markets on a larger scale gradually caught on as economic technocrats cut into the ideological purity and security arguments presented by the party and military.

On the eve of North Korea's constitutional revision, Pyongyang's position on each of these three areas was precarious but not in crisis. The government cautiously but positively responded to its southern neighbor's new overtures of economic aid and investment, accepted eased tensions with the United States, and clung to its socialist economic methods at the commanding heights of the economy. Despite flooding that destroyed much of the country's rice and corn fields and new U.S. allegations of a suspected underground nuclear site, North Korea introduced its new form of government.[54]

The state reintroduced the newly articulated concept of military-first politics in an August 22, 1998, *Nodong Sinmun* editorial and flight-tested the Taepodong-1 rocket over Japan on August 31, prompting substantial international concern.[55] On September 5, the Supreme People's Assembly officially retired the position of president, elected Kim as chairman of the

National Defense Commission (NDC), and codified the new constitution only four days before the anniversary of the founding of the state. Kim uses drama and important anniversaries to highlight important political events. This succession of events suggests he wanted the country—and the world—to take notice.

The "Kim Il Sung constitution" was unveiled with a dedication in the preamble to the country's founder: "The DPRK Social Constitution is the Kim Il Sung Constitution; it legally embodies Comrade Kim Il Sung's Juche state construction ideology and achievements." This preface was necessary because the new constitution departed significantly from the political institutions and modus operandi of Kim Il Sung. The younger Kim sought to bolster his legitimacy through referencing the revered leader in a Confucian show of filial piety, but he did not have the personal charisma to rule like his father. He was not a revered war hero, a gifted orator, or even very self-confident.

The younger Kim codified the mode of rule that had gradually intensified over the last two decades—as Kim Il Sung increasingly passed governing responsibilities to his son. North Korea's political evolution did not start or stop with this constitutional revision. The constitution did not signal an abrupt switch from totalitarianism to post-totalitarianism, but it helps clarify when the regime acknowledged a significantly new mode of governance. Kim laid down a marker for a domestic audience and foreign one indicating clearly that after three years of mourning he was now in charge and would rule in a certain way. He effectively codified a post-totalitarian state structure, not a transitional polity or one in rapid decline. North Korea had found a fairly stable equilibrium outcome as an impoverished authoritarian regime.

The new regime still relied heavily on ideological indoctrination to control the masses and elites alike. This period saw the increased prominence of military-first politics, or military-first ideology, introduced the previous year. Some observers claim the new ideological mantra replaces Juche, while others claim it merely supplements it. The state continually cites both to this day. This debate over the supremacy of the party or the military mirrors questions of whether the party or the military is now the dominant institution in North Korean politics. Of course, this discussion assumes there is a single dominant institution in North Korean politics and Kim does not seek a divide-and-conquer ruling style. Military-first politics reflects the KPA's greater institutional *political* role as well as Kim's need to placate the powerful institution and leaders. In the empirical chapters I support this argument by documenting how the military and party pursue policy preferences through the jostling of bureaucratic politics rather than being able to dictate orders.

The military had long enjoyed prioritized resource allocation, but this military-first ideological move raised the military's political and social status. It marked a move away from the party-dominated totalitarian model. The regime had long credited the KPA with safeguarding and building the socialist revolution. According to the national narrative, without Kim Il Sung's guerilla fighters, there would be no Communist Party in Korea. The new ideology extended the military's ideational and practical roles, however. The military-first policy's goal of building a "powerful and prosperous nation" required focused attention on ideology, politics, the military, and the economy.[56] Under military-first politics, the KPA would have a greater say in national policy in all four of these areas of national policy decision making and implementation, not simply the military arena.[57]

The ideology's flexibility allows central authorities to praise the military and focus on empirical results, while still maintaining Juche and socialist revolutionary demands. This effort to maximize material and ideological gains demanded an institutional structure that could produce these goals more effectively. Central authorities continued to try to balance the concerns of ideologues and pragmatists, and they used competing institutions to promote those goals. Chapter 4 reviews the history and composition of the main institutions in North Korea and shows how they have come to compete for influence and to pursue ideological or pragmatic policy goals.

The new constitution formally removed previous roles of the party and simplified the bureaucratic structure. The military and cabinet no longer reported to party officials. The military did not replace the party as the key organ. The three entities were rebalanced as peer organizations. The Korean Workers' Party, the Korean People's Army, and the cabinet jointly dominated national politics under Kim Jong Il.[58] Despite these important government changes and efforts to highlight the new constitution with a major rocket launch, immediate concern about the rocket launch quickly overshadowed the constitution. Commentators focused on the state's outward actions while voicing bewilderment at the supposedly one-man-rule

state's decision making. With newfound authority, the three constitutionally autonomous institutions discussed the missile launch publicly.

Diverging Policies, 2000–2006

The new constitutional arrangement and systemic change ushered in
a period of disjointed North Korean policy choices. Pyongyang compart-
mentalized its inter-Korean, U.S., and economic policies. The more flexible political system capitalized on Seoul's rapprochement, positioned itself
against toughening American policy, and allowed domestic economic policy to proceed apace with relatively little interference from outside actors.
The combined decade of Kim Dae Jung (1998–2003) and Roh Moo-hyun
(2003–2008) administrations in Seoul saw a general expansion of economic engagement, social interaction, and political trust building. The
gradual reunification policy enjoyed popular support in South Korea following the 1997 financial crisis. Rapid reunification jeopardized the South
Korean economy too much; gradually transforming the North Korean
economy, society, and politics could set the stage for eventual reunification
with fewer costs.

The most dramatic breakthrough on inter-Korean relations occurred in
2000 when Kim Dae Jung and Kim Jong Il met in Pyongyang. The first
ever inter-Korean summit produced a series of cabinet-level civilian and
military meetings and significant South Korean economic engagement
with the North. Progress was anything but smooth and uninterrupted,
but it was discernible. Seoul treated Pyongyang particularly gingerly in an
effort to induce social, economic, and political change to the great conster-
nation of South Korea's conservatives and some foreign allies, including
the conservative administration in the United States.

South Korean public opinion shifted dramatically after North Korea
tested a nuclear weapon in October 2006; South Korea's opposition party's
long-held position that the sunshine policy produced no significant results
developed a newfound resiliency. The charge stuck particularly well against
liberal president Roh Moo-hyun who was now widely identified as an ineffective president. This helped set the stage for South Korea's election a year
later of a conservative president Lee Myung-bak, who promised a competent administration and economic revitalization. Lee also vowed to pursue

a tougher North Korea policy that prioritized near-term denuclearization over long-term reunification preparations. Inter-Korean relations soured significantly in the months after Lee's inauguration in February 2008 as the new administration backed off expanding economic engagement, criticized the North's human rights record more vocally, and pursued a policy Pyongyang generally labeled as "confrontational." The diplomatic fallout from the nuclear test and the reaction to President Lee's approach to the North marked the most significant inflection point in inter-Korean relations in the decade after North Korea's new constitution.

While inter-Korean relations had one dramatic turn in this ten-year period, relations between Washington and Pyongyang, despite many ups and downs, had two quite dramatic inflections in 2000 and 2006. Modest gains were made in U.S.-DPRK relations in the last few months of the Clinton administration in 2000; renewed confrontation occurred in the first six years of the Bush administration; and productive negotiations returned after the nuclear test and U.S. congressional elections in 2006. In late 2000 the United States and North Korea seemed to be reaching some agreement on North Korea's missiles. Secretary of State Madeleine Albright traveled to Pyongyang in October 2000 and met with Kim Jong Il in preparation for a possible summit with President Clinton. Pyongyang sent a high-level emissary to Washington to meet with President Clinton and several cabinet officials. But time was too short: working-level talks broke down, and Clinton left the unresolved issue for the next administration.

Pyongyang voiced skepticism about the new leadership in Washington in early 2001 but refrained from recasting its U.S. policy until Washington completed its policy review. The policy review prompted the new administration to commit to an engagement strategy in summer 2001, though this policy would never be implemented. Bush administration officials noted that "9/11 changed everything," and Washington crafted what Pyongyang labeled a confrontational policy toward it. U.S.-DPRK relations continued in a downward spiral after October 2002 when a U.S. negotiating team traveled to Pyongyang and raised the question of the North's uranium enrichment program. The U.S. delegation reported that the North Koreans admitted to having a uranium program, which prompted Washington to end its Agreed Framework commitments. Pyongyang claimed it had not admitted to a uranium program, but it then refused to confirm or deny whether such a program did exist. It cited Washington's abrogation of the

Agreed Framework to unseal Yongbyon, verifiably frozen for eight years, and begin its withdrawal from the Non-Proliferation Treaty. Negotiations continued on and off with little sustainable progress until the fall of 2006 after North Korea flight-tested its longest range rocket, tested a nuclear weapon, and made nuclear technology available to Syria.

In October 2006 North Korea tested a nuclear weapon. The following month Democrats in the United States won enough legislative seats to reclaim the congressional majority. While the nuclear test prompted South Korea to back off its engagement strategy, it helped jumpstart six-party talks. Key hard-liners in the U.S. administration resigned as engagement advocates enjoyed greater flexibility. Washington reevaluated its squeeze strategy.

As Seoul and Washington traded places in their engagement and confrontational policies, Pyongyang's economic policy saw its own swings. Pyongyang increasingly accepted illegal coping mechanisms during the famine. When the state failed to provide rations sufficient to prevent mass starvation, enterprising North Koreans skirted the law and traded to survive. As the state emerged from the famine, it tried to reassert a measure of control over this activity without prompting another food crisis. On July 1, 2002, it instituted significant wage and price reforms that recognized part of the ground reality. Central authorities also adopted several heavily debated management and enterprise reforms to increase economic efficiency. North Korea took limited steps away from its command economy and the totalitarian ideal.

The state backed off some of these economic decisions in 2005, most notably, reintroducing socialist control over food distribution. Market reforms demonstrated a certain staying power as the regime again slowly backed off its efforts to crack down on market measures in favor of a demonstrated ability to enhance the domestic economy. The debate raged in the official press and has not yet been definitely resolved. On the question of marketization the state continues to move two steps forward and one step back.

The Japanese defeat in 1945 and the rise of Kim Il Sung revolutionized North Korean politics. The system defined itself as anti-Japanese, yet incorporated some modern elements from the Japanese colonial administration. But it also incorporated the guerilla movement's traditions and depended in part on Soviet assistance, especially in the early years. North

Korea increasingly asserted its sovereignty as Kim Il Sung consolidated his power after the Korean War. The Sino-Soviet split in the 1960s allowed Pyongyang to play the Chinese and Soviets off against each other. Kim Il Sung reached the height of personal power in the early 1970s; his totalitarian regime then began a slow decline. Kim Il Sung tapped his son as his successor, and Kim Jong Il's roles in the North Korean system expanded in the 1980s.

The 1990s saw the most dramatic changes as the Soviet collapse, Kim Il Sung's death, and famine modified ground realities. Changes outside of the Kims' direct control produced new challenges that the younger Kim attempted to address. After observing the traditional three-year mourning period following his father's death, Kim Jong Il moved to codify his new mode of operations. The younger Kim demonstrated his intention to divide and conquer the bureaucracies, pitting the cabinet, military, and party against one another. Jong Il's divided political system allowed the state to shape economic policy, inter-Korean efforts, and foreign policy toward the United States on separate tracks. Though these tracks could be linked, the linkages themselves remained a subject of debate between Pyongyang's three main institutions. Kim remained on top and held ultimate authority, but central decisions reflected a greater diversity of state views as central authorities grappled with competing pragmatic and ideological demands.59 I call the new type of politics that emerged in North Korea out of Kim Il Sung's totalitarianism "post-totalitarian institutionalism."

CHAPTER FOUR

North Korea's Political Institutions

North Korea has three main political institutions: the Korean Workers' Party (the party), the Korean People's Army (the military), and the cabinet (the government).[1] This chapter demonstrates that these three institutions are the most important institutional actors in North Korea. The others are either nominal or do not exert a systematic influence on a wide range of national-level policy decisions. These three institutions, along with Kim in a unique role, guide strategic-level policy. They can speak to linkages across issue areas and regularly voice preferences in the North Korean press.

This chapter reviews the history and composition of each constitutional institution and the security apparatus. Since any evaluation of the political history of North Korea under Kim Il Sung must necessarily evaluate the evolving roles of these institutions, much of this discussion is contextualized in the previous chapter. This chapter builds on that discussion, primarily taking up how the three main institutions evolved under Kim Jong Il and evaluating the more marginal constitutional organizations that are not part of the wider national political narrative. In this way, I seek to shed light on how each organization has developed (or failed to develop) a coherent set of policy preferences and how it can turn those preferences into national policy.

The Korean Workers' Party

The party is the most central organization in the totalitarian model. In Kim Il Sung's polity, the Korean Workers' Party was a key organ charged with important ideological work. Applied ideology guided specific policy decisions, and party members were implanted deep within the government and military structures to make sure that government "functionaries" and military cadres carried out the party line. The party was the most important institution under Kim Il Sung, with his closest personal allies in the guerilla struggle and Korean War taking senior posts in this organization. It was charged with strategic policy goals such as pursuing the socialist goals of the revolution, defeating the imperialists—Japanese and American—and forcing national reunification on the North's terms.

In carrying out a comprehensive ideology, the party prescribed right action from the individual to state level. It had formal authority over virtually every aspect of one's life, fusing public and private spheres toward a utopian moral order. In the 1950s and 1960s the party's revolutionary purpose held greater weight as global communism was much stronger than today. Memories of the brutal Japanese occupation and the great losses of the Korean War were also fresh in the minds of the political class and masses.

The North Korean Communist Party in 1945 was fairly diverse. It consisted of roughly equal parts of industrial workers; rural peasants; and a mix of petite bourgeoisie, intellectuals, and businessmen. Kim Il Sung did not control the party completely at this time because the party was insufficiently institutionalized. Lower party units may not have received orders from the top leadership or they simply may not have carried them out at times. Consequently, party consolidation was an earlier priority than even the formation of the state. The North Korean Communist Party merged with the South Korean Workers' Party in 1949 to form the Korean Workers' Party led by Kim Il Sung. The party grew from roughly 4 percent of the population in 1946 to more than 11 percent in 1970 with 1.6 million members.[2] Kim took a diverse set of individuals with competing loyalties and, through purges and indoctrination, forged a unified party under his control. The political history of Kim Il Sung's North Korea is fundamentally a story of the relationship between Kim Il Sung's personal power and his use of the party to run the country (see chapter 3).

However, as communism, having failed to achieve its utopian objectives, died out in most other parts of the world by the end of the twentieth century, the Korean Workers' Party did not reconstitute itself. It remained a revolutionary organization that relied heavily on suppressing information from the outside world that might undermine its stated objectives. The party tried to maintain the totalitarian order, including a monopoly on communication and propaganda. Increased information inflows challenged the party's information monopoly and the narrative that declared the country was proceeding apace toward a socialist utopia. By the time Kim Jong Il came to power, the party was a fish out of water. Aging officials from a previous era continued to trumpet the importance of applying revolutionary principles to specific policies, but the calls rang increasingly hollow.

Furthermore, Kim Jong Il's leadership is quite different from his father's. He does not enjoy Kim Il Sung's claim to revolutionary politics; he also lacks his personal leadership qualities. Kim Il Sung was a very strong leader who mobilized a nation and took it in a tremendously harmful direction. Kim Jong Il lacked his father's abilities; in addition internal and external circumstances prevented him from pursuing the same objectives in the same fashion. The younger Kim modified the way his father ruled and the role of the party declined. The party is no longer preeminent; it operates more on par with the military and cabinet organizations. The three institutions engage one another's arguments rather than the party simply dictating to the formerly subordinate bodies.

Kim has publicly chastised the party, emphasized competing institutions, and gradually rationalized policy against the party's Juche bulwark. In 1992 Kim Jong Il remarked publicly that he read the army's newspaper every morning before reading the party's daily newspaper. The symbolism was not lost on North Korea's populace.[3] At the December 1996 graduation ceremonies at Kimilsung University, Kim Jong Il praised the army while noting the party's dwindling abilities. At this event he publicly blamed the party for policy failures during the famine. The following year, Kim imprisoned or executed several leading party officials but left the military hierarchy untouched.[4]

These events set the stage for shrinking the party's role. While consolidating his power, Kim Jong Il could not afford to alienate large numbers of powerful people, nor could he afford to leave potential opponents in positions of power. Kim had no need to abolish the party or humiliate revolutionaries. He simply demoted the party it by enhancing the authority of competing institutions. Under Kim Il Sung, revolutionaries led key ministries. Kim Jong Il kept his father's loyalists as the head of ministries and other organizations but no longer empowered the positions. Ministers are now largely nominal positions. These positions are still filled by Kim Il Sung's elderly compatriots in many cases, but their deputies have all the power. Just as Kim Jong Il was North Korea's number two leader for twenty years, his number two counterparts in each ministry now rule. This move allowed these men and their families to save face while achieving his goal. Likewise, the 1998 constitution made Kim Il Sung North Korea's "eternal president." Kim Jong Il took a primarily military—not party—title from which to rule the country.

Some important, trusted officials with strong family backgrounds retain their party titles. Yi Chol, North Korea's ambassador to Switzerland, Kang Sang Chun, the head of Kim's personal office, and Won Yong Rok, the head of North Korea's unofficial diplomatic representation in Germany all continue to sign external correspondence with their full party titles. These are long-standing, important figures in North Korea, but they derive their power from their inner-circle status. They do not control large bureaucracies; they gain power by their access to the Dear Leader. Kang's access to Kim is self-apparent as he heads Kim's personal office. Chol and Won head important overseas missions where Kim's family members live or have lived.[5] When Kim's sons were in school in Switzerland, Yi Chol was responsible for them. Yi Chol is also rumored to help manage a significant portion of Kim's personal funds abroad. Kim's second son and possible heir, the twenty-seven-year-old Kim Jong Chul was videotaped at four Eric Clapton concerts in Germany in June 2006; Won was responsible for him.[6] These men are important but do not demonstrate the importance of the party despite their retaining their party titles. This highlights the continued role of a few personal relationships at the apex of power, while the bureaucracies increasingly produce impersonal, expert opinion to inform and influence political decisions.

Kim Il Sung created the Party's Central People's Committee specifically to control the bureaucracy;[7] the younger Kim abolished the guidance organ outright in the 1998 constitution. Kim Jong Il was still concerned about control, but he would not utilize the party as an intermediary between him and the military and the government. The party still proposes policy, but it has lost its critically important function of directing policy across the otherwise stove-piped bureaucracy. The 1998 revision is said to have reduced North Korea's official personnel by 30 percent over five years in order to save scarce resources during the famine.[8] This is one explanation for the bold move; the other requires a closer look at the military.

The Korean People's Army

North Korea's military also claims to predate the state. Although Kim Il Sung's ragtag group of about three hundred anti-Japanese guerillas in the early 1940s looked very different from a Soviet-supplied North Korean military of 1950, the military still argues its origins are rooted in that early guerilla experience. The military holds a sacred place in the state's ideological narrative. The military protects the party and advances the revolution. Under Kim Il Sung, the senior levels of the party and military were highly fused. Many senior party members were four-star generals, and the military valued political correctness at least as much as military effectiveness. Militarism was central to the anti-imperialist and reunification goals of the revolutionary state. Consequently, the history of the North Korean military under Kim Il Sung is closely tied to the general political evolution.

Kim Jong Il separated the political roles of the party and military after his father's death. He granted the military organization direct access to the Dear Leader, without having to subordinate political ideas to party leaders. By 1998 Kim had seemingly raised the National Defense Commission (NDC) to the pinnacle of institutional power. When Kim assigned the position of president to his father, he took the ruling title of chairman of the NDC. The state introduced the military-first concept in 1997 and has reiterated it every year since then. There is little doubt that the military plays an important role in the North Korean system, but questions persist as to whether it is the preeminent institution under Kim Jong Il in the military-first era.

Much has been written on the gradual rise of the military in North Korean politics. In 1991 Kim took the rank and title of vice marshal of the Korean People's Army. In 1995, after his father's death, he had himself promoted to the supreme commander of the military. The seating order at important state events like Kim Jong Il's birthday celebrations and Kim

Il Sung's funeral changed; it listed members of the NDC before Politburo members. These lists historically had provided a pecking order of officials.[9] In 1996 Kim expanded the number of national holidays from five to seven. The two new holidays were both named after the military: Foundation Day of the Korean People's Army and Victory Day of the National Liberation War. Kim had the Supreme People's Assembly elect Jo Myong Rok, the vice marshal and director of the KPA General Political Department (the military's top official after Kim Jong Il), to the second highest office in the land: first vice chairman of the NDC. Jo gave the keynote address at the fifth anniversary of Kim Il Sung's death and visited the White House in 2000 to meet with President Bill Clinton, Secretary of State Madeleine Albright, and Secretary of Defense William Cohen.[10]

Arguments citing the rise of the military generally note Kim's reliance on that organization. One scholar concluded that "it was the military that carried Kim Jong Il through the most difficult times from 1994 to 2000," and Kim emphasized the role of the military over the party because of this dependence.[11] Yet Kim has had an uneasy relationship with the military. He purged six hundred officers after an alleged coup attempt in 1992. He completely dissolved the VI Corps in 1995 and replaced it with personnel from the XI Corps due to massive corruption.[12] Further, both Kims have employed extensive security apparatus. The cabinet, party, and military each has a security service that checks on its own organization as well as the other two. Like most dictators, Kim is suspicious of the military and has sought to keep them close so as not to lose control of their extensive coercive potential.

The core question is whether this shift toward the military is a real shift of power or merely for show. Kim has long had a difficult time with the military, so heralding the military's critical role may be an attempt to keep a lid on its power rather than an increase in its actual authority. It is also possible that evaluating these changes at face value is the correct view. The party is ineffective, and the military's bureaucracy is relatively disciplined. Kim may have decided to rule through the military bureaucracy because it distorts his policy prerogatives less.

It is important to recognize that the National Defense Commission and the Korean People's Army are not the same institution. Arguments citing the rise of the military in North Korean politics inevitably cite the NDC and conflate its functions with the KPA. The NDC is a small senior leadership body, not an institutional representation of military interests. Senior generals take many of these seats, but the NDC is better understood as an extension of Kim's inner circle than a broad, deep, and impersonal policy apparatus. Of course, the "inner circle" concept is sufficiently vague that it is not particularly helpful. It encapsulates very different functional roles to different readers. As a rough parallel, the NDC can be conceptualized as a particularly powerful National Security Council with a large representation of generals and more expansive authorities that extend into domestic areas as well. It is unclear if the NDC coordinates policy formation and implementation with reference to institutional positions or draws on independent perspectives to brief Kim. It is also not clear when the NDC weighs in on policy questions or what influence it has on particular policy choices. What is clear, however, is that the NDC should not be confused with some type of super defense ministry or group of military chiefs with direct and extensive institutional support. The NDC gains power from its direct and personal contact with Kim, not from the depth of new information or policy detail it can provide from an extensive bureaucratic support.

Military-first politics has not catapulted the military into bureaucratic primacy. Rather Kim uses the government, military, and party to check one another and to carry out policy collectively. New benefits granted to the NDC and the military establishment have been largely nominal. Kim has honored the military and raised its prestige. Rhetoric and prestige matter, but as far as honors placate the military establishment, Kim can reduce dissatisfaction enough to pursue interests that are in conflict with the military's actual policy preferences.

With the notable exception of raising the bureaucratic importance of the NDC, these actions are merely honorific. But the actions were not without purpose. Prestige can be a cheap and effective motivating force. Honoring the military allowed Kim to dampen mistrust and provide an excuse for dismantling much of the party's functions. Kim's actions can be better understood not as a shift from Juche-supporting institutions to military-first supporting institutions, but a move that freed his hand in directing the state from many ideological constraints. Kim would pit the military against the cabinet and foster limited debate over some of the core problems facing the country—notably questions of economic reform, reunification, and foreign policy toward the United States. Kim Il Sung's goals of security, prestige, and prosperity remained in an emergency management government where these tangible goals were discussed publicly.

The Cabinet

The People's Committee was the earliest rendition of the North Korean government. Kim Il Sung described it as the linkage between the party and the masses, serving to implement party decisions on land reform and industrialization. It executed orders rather than participating widely in policy decision making.[13] The 1972 constitution not only established Kim Il Sung's position as president but also gave the party a greater role in ensuring that government implemented policy as directed. It renamed the cabinet the Administrative Council to reflect its position as a support body. (The previous chapter describes these changes at some length since the changing roles of the government are integral to the general political history.) The government's position in policy decision making was firmly subordinated to the party under Kim Il Sung. It was a relatively insignificant institution until Kim Jong Il substantially upgraded its roles.

The 1998 constitution changed the State Administration Council into the cabinet and expanded its management authority. The cabinet's primary responsibility is to implement policy promulgated by the rubber-stamp parliament. It is the bureaucracy responsible for executing policy. However, with the abolition of the Central People's Committee and the position of president being vacant, the cabinet has become a formally independent actor, albeit responsible to Kim in practice. The constitution granted the cabinet broad management responsibilities. The cabinet could modify its own structures to implement policy, change rules of administration, modify strategic-level national management practices, and create, inspect, and abolish key administrative organs.

The new constitution also raised the cabinet's status to the second most important bureaucratic element after the National Defense Commission. Nominally, the Supreme People's Assembly remained above all other elements, but the constitution removed the formal authority of this body—which rarely meets in the first place—to check the military and government. Despite the cabinet's heightened authority and real power, the cabinet and its government ministries did not enjoy the praise lavished on the military. On the contrary, the government ministries continued to be blamed publicly for distorting policy directions when policy outcomes did not meet expectations. Furthermore, Kim's new titles do not reference the SPA or the cabinet. He is the general secretary of the Korean Workers' Party, chairman of the National Defense Commission, and supreme commanding general of the People's Armed Forces.[14]

The cabinet is low on prestige but not on power. The cabinet's role expanded in 1998, especially in the area of the economy. The cabinet became the dominant force in economic policy, and each of Kim Jong Il's three premiers gained a reputation as the most influential proponent of economic reform. Economic reform is at the center of many debates on the strategic direction of the state—in and out of North Korea—which cannot be adequately discussed here. Despite widespread disagreement about the nature and extent of economic reform, Pyongyang has certainly decentralized some power in the economic sphere.[15] Technocrats and specialists have a greater role in government guided by policy goals rather than ideology.

The bureaucracy has always housed specialists—even in the political sphere where technical or specialized knowledge seemingly has less utility than in the physical sciences or economics. Kim Il Sung's rule recognized that international politics require expertise. Foreign ministers held posts longer than other ministers and their tenures grew even longer over the course of Kim Il Sung's rule (Table 4.1). While these men were party members, they were granted longer tenures since an effective foreign policy was critical to the state's existence, and an effective foreign policy required specialized knowledge.

This same role for specialized negotiators and advisers existed within the Ministry. Unlike U.S. diplomats, who are trained to become generalists, North Korean diplomats specialize in one area and develop effective tactics to make diplomatic gains disproportionate to the state's power. A string of U.S. negotiators have sat across the table from Kang Sok Ju and Kim Kye Kwan for many years. Whether this is an effective means of training diplomats is not the issue. It shows that the North Korean leadership finds even international politics an appropriate area for specialized knowledge. These specialists report the results of negotiations to Kim. If he did not value this specialized knowledge, he could change the Foreign Ministry's operation or reempower the party's international relations arm.

TABLE 4.1 North Korea's Foreign Ministers, 1948–Present			
NAME	DATES (NO. OF YEARS)		SUBSEQUENT GOVERNMENT POSITION
Pak Hon Yong	1948–1953 (5)		n/a[a]
Nam Il	1953–1959 (6)		n/a[b]
Ho Tam	1959–1969 (10)		Chairman, Committee for the Peaceful Reunification of the Fatherland[c]
Pak Song Chol	1969–1983 (14)		Honorary VP, SPA Presidium
Kim Yong Nam[d]	1983–1998 (15)		President of SPA Presidium
Paek Nam Sun	1998–2007 (9)		n/a[b]
Pak Ui Chun	2007–present		n/a

[a] Executed in 1953 during Kim Il Sung's power consolidation effort.

[b] Died in office of natural causes.

[c] Kim Il Sung's brother-in law; died in 1991.

[d] Served concurrently as deputy prime minister.

The Foreign Ministry has long had an important place in the cabinet. North Korea's first three foreign ministers, spanning the first twenty-two years of the state, all served as vice premier in the cabinet structure, including one of Kim Il Sung's earliest and most important rivals who was executed after the Korean War.[16] It should come as little surprise that a state so extensively concerned about its external security would place great importance on both its military and its foreign ministry. While key personnel in the foreign ministry have direct access to Kim and may even be part of his inner circle, it is possible to include this organization as part of the cabinet. Formally, it resides under the cabinet structure. More importantly, it conducts its business as a specialized organization. Each of the three main institutions have internal divisions, but the generalizations about their composition and advocacy hold even for the cabinet–Foreign Ministry relationship.

The Foreign Ministry and other ministries under the cabinet's authority serve as the main interlocutors with foreign embassies in Pyongyang and in important inter-Korean negotiations and talks with significant regional powers, including the United States. Western ambassadors stationed in Pyongyang consistently report that the party is uninterested in meeting with them beyond an initial courtesy call. The real work of foreign affairs, including economic engagement, flows through the cabinet ministries, which channel this information through the North Korean bureaucracy. Likewise, the cabinet's Foreign Ministry has spearheaded negotiations with the Americans under Kim Jong Il and advocated internally for diplomatic solutions to the North's economic and security challenges.

The Security Apparatus

Especially in a state where the military is recognized as a key institutional actor in politics, one could reasonably expect the security apparatus to serve as a fourth institutional actor. Alternatively, the intelligence and police organizations could support one of the other three political actors, giving it a specific advantage in policy debates. If the security apparatus were a coherent, semiautonomous body, this might be true. Though it is more difficult to cull public and declassified sources on the North Korean intelligence and police services, broad outlines of its structure and functions can be deciphered. The basic conclusion of this section is that under both Kims the security apparatus is not an important political player in its own right.

North Korea's security apparatus developed in the 1950s during a time of great flux for the country. By 1962 the Ministry of Public Security held wide-ranging powers, including stamping out "antirevolutionary" activities, conducting domestic surveillance, running overseas intelligence operations, maintaining prison camps, and providing basic crime control and air defense. The party controlled the ministry at each level of its organization, implanting personnel to keep the organization under its control, as the party did with the government and military as well. The security apparatus under Kim Il Sung had multiple roles, but it was a singular organization firmly controlled by the party.[17] The security apparatus did not have an independent voice in politics.

In contemporary North Korea, the security apparatus is not a political institution. The younger Kim's efforts to divide and conquer the bureaucracy saw a parallel in these coercive bodies. Each of the three major institutional actors has formal control over one of these organizations and the fourth reports directly to Kim. Though informal lines of control further complicate this hazy picture of intelligence control, the general picture still supports the main contention that the security apparatus lacks a discernable influence on a wide range of political decisions. In practice, elites in the party, government, and military, as well as security practitioners themselves, fear different elements of the security apparatus, but they cannot employ it to systematically influence policy. (See Figure 4.1.)

The primary role of the three security apparatuses is to protect the Dear Leader and his state from foreign and domestic threats. Their similarities do not extend much beyond this, and they are better understood as rival organizations than a coherent body. The National Defense Commission controls the State Security Department (SSD). The NDC is a small organization composed of senior leaders, including Kim Jong Il, and the SSD plays a critical role as the regime's most significant intelligence agency. The exact nature of this relationship is not well documented, but it is plausible that Kim Jong Il himself or a trusted colleague such as his brother-in-law Chang Song-taek may spend a considerable portion of their time managing the SSD directly. At this level, Kim or an adviser like Chang could use competing security institutions and military elements to control the otherwise unwieldy SSD.

The SSD has had a long and deadly history of tense relations with the military. In this regard, it is no different from most communist states.[18] After Kim Il Sung designated his son as his successor, the elder Kim purged military officers in 1976–77 who voiced displeasure with this move. Another purge of military officers occurred in 1987–88 for unknown reasons. The SSD likely carried out Kim's orders. When the SSD exposed an alleged military coup attempt in 1992, six hundred officers were purged. Likewise, the SSD uncovered massive corruption in the VI Corps in 1995, prompting the corps' reorganization. The SSD helps the top leadership keep the military in check.

Of course, the military helps keep the SSD in check. Top intelligence officials suffered when they opposed policies favoring the military. In 1998 top intelligence leaders were purged following the introduction of military-first politics. Kim Yong Ryong, the deputy head of the SSD, was executed on trumped-up charges after he voiced his opposition to the military-first doctrine. Kwon Hui Gyong, North Korea's former ambassador to the Soviet Union and the director of the Party's Central Committee on External Information Collection Department was exiled. Other opponents simply disappeared.[19] These types of actions are not publicly debated. They demonstrate one of the repressive tools at the disposal of the North's top leadership. It is highly unlikely that anyone other than the top leader could amass enough power to order mass purges—without himself being purged.

As part of this complicated web of dividing and ruling the security services, Kim Jong Il's personal protection force is separate from the SSD organization. The KPA and Ministry of People's Armed Forces (MPAF) control the Guard Command. The Guard Command is formally part of the KPA, but its personnel have a reputation for arrogance and heavy-handed tactics against their military colleagues. For example, when Kim visits military units, Guard Command personnel keep the rank-and-file soldiers far from Kim. Stories abound about Guard Command personnel forcing soldiers off of military runways, while Kim briefly waves from afar, or hitting the soldiers with rifle butts and generally showing disdain for the average soldier. The truth of individual reports is beyond the point. The Guard Command is another check on potential rogue elements in the KPA and the SSD: its mission of protecting the top leadership.

The KPA and MPAF also technically control the Security Command as a branch of the armed forces, but in reality it is controlled by the SSD. The Security Command has a similar function to the Guard Command. It is responsible for investigating and eliminating individuals or groups disloyal to Kim. However, shortly after the younger Kim came to power, he reportedly gave functional control of the Security Command to the State Security Department. The overlapping functions of the Guard Command (KPA) and Security Command (SSD) foster additional competition and internal checks. The complex web of security relationships demonstrates the top leadership's concern about violent overthrow from within and concerted efforts to spy on the spies.

The party controls a small but elite security services. The central committee secretary in charge of South Korean Affairs (CCSCSKA) has approximately fifteen thousand personnel. The party's CCSCSKA controls the important Operations Department (OD) as well as three other bureaus (Office 35, Unification Front Department, and the Foreign Liaison Department). The OD is credited with carrying out intelligence operations overseas, including high-level assassination attempts and kidnappings in the 1980s, and trying to raise hard currency through illicit activities. The organization is small, but high-level scrutiny is needed to keep it in check.

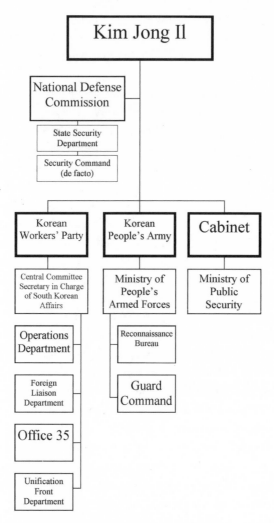

FIGURE 4.1 Security Apparatus Under Kim Jong Il

The cabinet controls the Ministry of People's Security (MPS). The MPS is the lower level security agency that serves as the national police force. It numbers approximately 130,000 people and tries to compete with the SSD. Like the SSD, it was reorganized in the 1990s several times amid concerns about corruption, higher illegal border crossings into China, and an inability to contain low-level disorder after the floods and famine. The MPS lost its responsibility for border control in 1995 and part of its authority to control travel in and out of Pyongyang in 1997; the MPAF took over this role, marking a partial militarization of border control and travel restrictions.[20]

Though the difference between formal and informal lines of control over the various security agencies in North Korea is by no means clear, there does seem to be a real effort to erect a divide-and-rule arrangement to keep a lid on the military, government, party, populace, and the security apparatuses themselves. Though the empirical evidence is much less extensive than that available for national policy institutions, it seems that the three security apparatuses in North Korea check one another. The important point for this analysis is that they do not represent a coherent whole. They do not participate publicly in institutional debates in the North Korean press—even cautiously, as the three main political institutions do. While it is possible that the security establishments' influence on national policy is real and hidden, these divisions suggest that the lack of observed political behavior by the security apparatuses can plausibly be taken at face value. Though one may have only moderate confidence in the specific details of the above lines of control given the anecdotal nature of data points, the broader conclusion for this analysis should elicit less controversy: the security apparatus is not an institutional player on a wide range of policy decisions.

Supreme People's Assembly

The Supreme People's Assembly (SPA) is officially the DPRK's highest constitutional organ and its leader is the nominal head of state. While the prime minister meets with some foreign visitors, the SPA lacks an independent source of power, any real responsibilities, or even a permanent staff. It only meets a few days a year to rubber-stamp policy decisions. Under Kim Il Sung, the SPA held a more important international propaganda purpose as the communist world attempted to present itself as more democratic than the exploitive capitalist West.

The SPA does not reach the "quasi-independent agency" standard. On paper the organization has many of the same powers as most democratic legislatures, but it lacks any real power. The state determines which candidates will be listed on the ballot without any alternative candidates. Citizens can vote yes or no. In many cases citizens must walk to the other side of the voting room to place their ballot in the "no" bin as security officials watch. Kim's regime often claimed a 100 percent return in favor of their candidates. Elections to the organization are meaningless.

The elections themselves are hardly worth protesting since representatives lack any real power. The SPA is not a coherent, permanent institution. At the height of its authority, the SPA would meet twice a year, rarely for more than a week. Even this nominal capacity has shrunk. The SPA now meets once a year and Kim Jong Il himself rarely attends the SPA meetings. The personnel do not appear to have an independent power base or any discernible influence on policy making.[21]

Subnational Governments and the Judiciary

Provincial and local governments and the judiciary round out the remainder of the permanent institutions enshrined in North Korea's constitution. The 1998 constitutional revisions abolished the Party's Central People's Committee that formerly supervised local governments and the judiciary. The judiciary is now subject only to the nominal oversight of the Supreme People's Assembly—a mere figurehead organization. Though subnational governments and the judiciary gained a degree of autonomy in 1998, neither weighs in on national policy questions.

The size of North Korea's subnational governments has shrunk as the state has had increasing difficulty providing basic services to its people.[22] Subnational governments are less powerful in a highly state like North Korea where even a question like food distribution is often delegated to a mobilized national institution—the military. A national police force deals with local crime. Though Pyongyang's increasing inability to function outside of the capital area has given local governments more autonomy but fewer resources, provincial and local governments have not voiced policy positions on strategic questions of national policy.

The judiciary also fails to exert a systematic influence on North Korean national political decisions. The judiciary is divided into prosecutors and courts. The railroads and military have their own parallel legal systems. Both the prosecutors and courts have three layers of administration: national, provincial, and local. Local prosecutors' work is supervised by provincial prosecutors. Provincial prosecutors' work is supervised by national prosecutors. And national prosecutors' works is reviewed by the SPA. National-level judges and prosecutors are appointed by the party and rubber-stamped by the SPA. In this regard, they must have some political connections to reach this level. Once appointed, they need worry only about the informal and potentially arbitrary attention of a small number of high-level officials. There is no serious judicial check on other government institutions. The courts provide a means to try and imprison alleged common criminals and are one stop on the path toward imprisonment for political crimes. They do not protect individual liberties, enforce the rule of law, or otherwise participate in policy decisions and implementation.

Subnational governments and the judiciary complete the permanent bureaucracies that make up the North Korean state. They have some influence on society, but the decentralized nature of these bureaucracies and their parochial outlook prohibit them from contributing systematically to strategic, national-level decisions. Individuals from these constitutional entities do not enter the national debate on questions of redirecting the state. They do not lead on any questions that seek to inform, craft, or implement policy.

North Korea's formal institutions have evolved since the founding of the state, but today's party, military, and cabinet have a systematic impact on national policy creation and implementation. Other constitutional entities—the Supreme People's Assembly, subnational governments, and judiciary, as well as the divided security apparatus—do not systematically influence national policy decisions. The primary argument in this chapter is that three institutions can be understood as coherent groups, not amorphous clusterings of like-minded individuals, that actually coalesce to influence policy outcomes in a consistent direction. These institutions have a corporate identity and act in such a way as to suggest an institutional worldview that colors reactions to specific events and policy advocacy. The next three chapters test these theoretical expectations by evaluating specific policy debates articulated in the North Korean press from the 1998 constitutional revision to the present to ascertain whether these groups do indeed exert systematic influence on the North Korean policy process.

CHAPTER FIVE

Institutional Jostling for Agenda Control, 1998–2001

The next three chapters provide the empirical tests to the theoretical expectations put forward in chapter 2. On specific policy questions, do the cabinet, party, and military provide consistent institutionally derived policy options to the senior leadership? Do they debate policy alternatives in the press? Does the senior leadership select from the policy options presented? Do institutions resist senior policy decisions? In short, have North Korea's second-echelon institutions had a systematic effect on national-level policy since Kim Jong Il's consolidation of power and does the system correspond to the theoretical expectation I put have forward?

This chapter concentrates on the first three years of North Korea's new constitutional arrangement, September 1998 to January 2001. South Korea elected a new president committed to cooperative relations with North. China maintained its policy of backing North Korea, while prodding it to open up economically. Relations with the United States were strained, but North Korea's main nuclear reactor at Yongbyon remained frozen, and the two adversaries made diplomatic progress on the missile issue. China, South Korea, and the United States had many different views about policy toward North Korea but found basic agreement on the need to change Pyongyang's strategic orientation.

In this context, North Korea announced important internal changes in the form of a revised constitution. The party attempted to maintain its position of supremacy over the government and military, while the newly empowered institutions asserted their own policy preferences more forcefully. A systematic reading of the North Korean press reveals divergent policy preferences by institution on questions of both domestic and foreign policy—on the nuclear and missile issues, inter-Korean economic projects, international trade and investment, and resource allocation. The party maintained an ideological approach to economic issues, inter-Korean projects, and relations with the United States. It rejected marketization efforts, international opening, and diplomatic accommodation. The party tried to keep its institutional supremacy despite the constitutional revision that raised the military and the cabinet to peer status.

The military shared many goals with the party but asserted interests distinct from the party and resisted party efforts to claim authority over the military institution. The military rejected economic opening efforts on pragmatic grounds, voicing concern about information security, and it opposed inter-Korean rapprochement and diplomatic agreements with the United States. It expanded its purview beyond traditional state-to-state military concerns. The state's military-first policy encouraged citizens to model their lives on the soldier, not the party member. This highly militarized society now allowed generals—wearing their military hats—to enter the policy fray on questions of economics and foreign policy.

This break from the past was subtle but important. Generals had previously engaged in wider policy debates as party members when these two institutions were more tightly interlinked under Kim Il Sung. Kim Jong Il's divide-and-conquer strategy separated more clearly the party and military institutions. The KPA no longer had to subject its views to party review and could voice institutional positions on a wider range of policy questions. In short, under the military-first policy, the KPA gained autonomy as the party lost its monopoly on controlling a single, comprehensive policy platform. Though military leaders shared many of the same objectives as the party, they articulated a distinct policy outlook based on a different rationale and knowledge base.

The cabinet departed most significantly from the other two organizations under Kim Jong Il's rule. Though the cabinet had been gaining some limited ground for decades, the new constitution gave it more authority to reject party demands to subordinate itself to the institution previously charged with comprehensive policy guidance. Like the military, the cabinet fought back against party efforts to reassert its bureaucratic hegemony. The cabinet advanced an agenda of economic revitalization through greater market mechanisms. Just as the military's main international mission blurred into linked domestic policy areas, the cabinet's domestic authority blurred significantly into inter-Korean policy and foreign relations.[1] The cabinet argued that its formal authority over economic management gave it a voice on key debates centered on inter-Korean economic projects and international trade that fundamentally required improved relations with South Korea and the United States. All three institutions attempted to expand their bureaucratic fiefdoms, creating a natural expectation of conflict.

The specific policy disputes during this period suggest remarkable consistency among institutional platforms. Each institution maintained policy positions that fit squarely within this general framework—including objections to decided policy when it ran counter to this general policy outlook. However, national policy varied tremendously, reflecting the tension between institutional positions and one platform winning out over the other at a given time.

Furthermore, these institutions pursued contradictory policies simultaneously. For example, the military engaged in deadly military clashes with the South Koreans, strongly condemning its southern neighbor, and calling for war at the same time as the cabinet expanded inter-Korean trade to record levels and warmly congratulated the South on its World Cup success. Though one may assert that central authorities could have put some (but certainly not all) of these actions into motion much earlier, it does not support the centralized models' expectations. If central authorities could not shut off a congratulatory message or naval provocation, for example, then institutions have greater power than the centralized model holds. Put differently, focusing solely on the center leaves significant variance in national policy decisions unexplained.

Of course, policy was not always uncoordinated. Central authorities put the brakes on one institution's advocacy and pursued another's. Most policy disputes tended to erupt as reactions to foreign actions, with a few notable exceptions. As a small, security-conscious state, North Korea's policy is greatly affected by external factors. North Korea is tremendously reactive to foreign actions and acts fairly predictably based on its particular internal and external interests. The remainder of this chapter delves into the specific policy disputes during this three-year period to document institutional positions, evaluate institutional interaction, and when possible, evaluate how central authorities ultimately decided policy on each issue.

Taepodong-1 Launch

In September 1998 North Korea revised its constitution. To mark the important occasion, the state launched the Taepodong-1 rocket for the first time. The rocket overflew Japan, evoked substantial international concern, and overshadowed the constitutional revision. All three bureaucratic actors within the North Korean state responded to the launch, demonstrating their conflicting outlooks on the specific incident and related, wider concerns. The party lauded the Taepodong-1 "satellite" launch as a victory for socialism; the KPA praised the Taepodong-1 "missile" launch as a military victory; and the cabinet tried to minimize the launch's impact on its negotiations with the United States, South Korea, and Japan.

The party took credit for the rocket launch, hailing it as evidence of the power of socialist ideology, "The successful launch of our first satellite is the greatest pride of Juche Korea and a brilliant fruition of the prolonged and arduous struggle of our party and people. . . . Today's reality demonstrates the validity of our party's self-reliant economic line. . . . Apart from socialism, we cannot think of S&T [science and technology] development or a worthy life for scientists and engineers."[2] Over the coming weeks, they repeated this idea of the launch demonstrating the value of socialism. This was a noteworthy national achievement to be celebrated, and it never could have been achieved without the party's leadership in pursuing a socialist economic line. The party argued that its policy platform produced long-term achievements and national glory.

The party claimed the rocket was a satellite, not a missile. The party often uses highly inflated and threatening rhetoric, but it refrained from doing so in this case, describing the launch as a peaceful satellite. The launch had dual-use applications: the technology could be used to fire a medium-range ballistic missile, putting Japan in range of North Korean missiles, and have peaceful science and technology satellite applications. The party does not try to avoid heightened international tensions. The party's characterizing the rocket as a satellite was more likely an effort to shift credit from the military to itself, rather than an effort to assuage international concern.

The KPA diverged from the party line, calling the Taepodong-1 a missile launch. As such, it was a military victory, not a party achievement. Kim Yong Chun, chief of the KPA general staff, recognized the role of the party and socialism in a major holiday speech, but he stressed the importance of the launch in building a strong army to "mercilessly annihilate" any invaders.[3] The rocket was not a product of the party's science and technology platform but an outgrowth of investment in defense. Both the party and military hailed the rocket launch in nationalistic terms and claimed credit for the historic event. Beyond the prestige associated internally with the launch, claiming credit may allow either institution to further its own agenda and obtain scarce resources.

The launch demonstrated a recurring theme within the party-military interaction. The two institutions often held very similar objectives but came to their policy positions from different directions. Since many of the most-senior officials in North Korea hold both military and party titles, some observers claim there is no meaningful distinction between the party and military;[4] others prefer to discuss the role of hard-liners within the state.[5] This effort to simplify a description of North Korean politics has real merit but it overlooks an additional benefit of recognizing the diversity within this hard-line camp. There is value in understanding the process of *how* divergent groups come to the same positions that is masked by looking at only the policy outcomes. Those committed to Juche orthodoxy and others committed to military security have different fundamental interests even if they come to similar conclusions in the end. Understanding those interests is important for anyone seeking a fuller understanding of the North Korean system. Military and party hard-liners can and do differ on policy advocacy, but more importantly, they find different arguments persuasive. One advantage of going inside the red box is detailing these differences to craft more effective diplomatic strategies, reduce surprise, and ease "intractable" conflict.

The Foreign Ministry, a key organ of the cabinet, projected a substantially more subdued response to the launch. It did not mention the relationship between ideology or the state's economic system and the launch.

It was the only one of the three institutions to explicitly offer a way forward to negotiate how North Korea would employ the newly demonstrated technological capability.[6] After laying out the rationale for continuing talks with the United States, the Foreign Ministry turned to the rocket launch, "We made it clear that the development, launch, and use of a satellite are internationally recognized rights of a sovereign state for independence. . . . Through the talks, we consider it fortunate that although it is late, the United States has reentered the stage of implementing the framework agreement as promised."[7]

In the wake of the launch, this institution took a decidedly measured tone. It agreed with the party's characterization of the rocket as a satellite but disagreed with the party's policy prescription. The cabinet organization reiterated its commitment to the Agreed Framework—an avenue which its bureaucracy controlled. The institution recognized why the United States did not supply the fuel oil pledged in the framework and encouraged a return to the agreement. A Foreign Ministry spokesperson said, "The United States failed greatly in 1998 to meet the timetable for the construction of the light water reactor project and for supplying heavy oil because of opposition by the U.S. Congress and because it was unable to procure the funds for implementing the framework agreement properly due to the so-called economic crisis of the members of the Korean Peninsula Energy Development Organization. This caused us to doubt the United States' will to carry out the framework agreement, and compelled us to suspend the storage of spent fuel and to prepare for more relevant measures."[8]

In this statement, coming just days after the launch, the Foreign Ministry associated the launch with what it saw as the United States not upholding its part of the nuclear agreement. The cabinet did not revel in the launch the way the party and military did. It used the event to urge a return to the negotiating track. It focused on its own contribution to North Korean history: maintaining the Agreed Framework and fundamentally altering its relationship with the United States and the outside world. The KPA and KWP did not voice support for negotiations, reflecting their consistent preference for a confrontational approach with the United States. The KPA celebrated the technical, military applications of the event; the party highlighted an achievement of socialist science and technology policies, and the cabinet focused on the diplomatic consequences and opportunities it presented.

The rocket crisis that followed the announcement of North Korea's new constitution did not create a situation where a clear decision by the Dear Leader was required. The action put the ball in the court of North Korea's foreign interlocutors. The state presumably sought to prod the United States in particular into supplying the LWRs and heavy fuel oil. Dissatisfied with years of little or no progress on the Agreed Framework's implementation, the small state tried to pressure the larger one. However, revelations outside of the regime's control intervened to change the discussion before the policy process could run its full course on this issue. The Taepodong -1 incident demonstrates how institutional responses vary in accordance with the institution's more general policy outlooks and objectives, and do not necessarily produce a clear, single policy response. Each institution provided different interpretations and policy recommendations to central authorities as the post-totalitarian institutionalism model predicts and creates a new puzzle for the more monolithic models. As such, it does not say much about how policy disputes are resolved. The intervening crisis would help clarify this issue.

The Kumchang-ri Suspected Nuclear Facility

Following the leak of a newly discovered, alleged underground nuclear facility at Kumchang-ri, U.S. demands to inspect the facility started to overshadow the Taepodong-1 launch. The demand provides an excellent early case study of the North Korean bureaucracy in action. The allegation was new, forcing each institution to voice its position, and it required a single, unambiguous decision by a central authority. The state either would allow the inspection or block it; there would be no ambiguity concerning the policy outcome. The inspection demand was related to a more general, important, and ongoing debate within the North Korean bureaucracy over whether Pyongyang should negotiate with Washington at all. Each of the three institutions explicitly linked arguments for or against allowing the U.S. inspection to wider positions of continuing with the Agreed Framework process or abandoning it outright.

Also, the bureaucratic players knew something the Americans did not: the allegation was factually incorrect. This allows one to see the importance various institutions placed on primarily ideological versus pragmatic action. Interestingly, once the inspection demonstrated there were no traces of nuclear material at the underground facility or in its soil and the facility was not suitable for such a purpose, the party and KPA did not gloat.[9] The U.S. allegation had been proved wrong, but the party and KPA had still lost the debate about whether to prevent the inspection in the first place.

The party, military, and cabinet developed three distinct policy responses to the inspection demand. The party rejected the inspections on principle, arguing it undermined the state's sovereignty. Party commentaries likened the inspection to a police officer's humiliating demand to inspect one's house. The party also put the demand in a larger context, arguing this was only the latest example of U.S. tricks to delay implementing the Agreed Framework. They noted their grave suspicion of the agreement and called for negotiations to end.

The military took a different stance in opposing the inspections. The KPA argued the United States should not be allowed to inspect any military sites. Allowing a hostile state to inspect military sites presented a dangerous precedent for the military and likely reflected some concern about inspecting Kumchang-ri itself. Though inspections eventually showed the heavily guarded site had no traces of nuclear residue, it may have contained conventional military technology that the military would have had to move in the months between the allegation and the permission granted to inspect the tunnels. The military took a pragmatic opposition to the inspection, reflecting institutional interests.

The military also connected their position to a wider concern about negotiating with the Americans, arguing the KPA should have access to all necessary weapons to fight and defeat the Americans, including nuclear weapons. The Agreed Framework's commitment to trade North Korea's nuclear program for security commitments and aid did not appeal to this group. Military articles did not focus on abstract ideas like the party's but berated the Agreed Framework on nonideological grounds. Suspicious of paper agreements with the Americans and relinquishing their central role in providing for the state's security, a spokesman reiterated that the KPA as an institution had *always* opposed the Agreed Framework. This reflects a consistent institutional policy position and suggests institutions resist decided policy when possible and actively pursue policy reversals.

The cabinet, again through the Foreign Ministry, first presented the U.S. demand to the rest of the bureaucracy. It initially did not comment on the accusation, but then discussed the possibility of allowing a one-time inspection in exchange for economic aid. The Foreign Ministry took what the rest of the bureaucracy called an offensive demand and turned it into a platform that would advance the cabinet's institutional agenda. The cabinet and Foreign Ministry had long sought economic concessions from the United States. While the United States rejected the cash demand and Pyongyang settled for continued U.S. food aid instead, the cabinet demonstrated both its commitment to achieving substance over symbols and its main vehicle for negotiations—the Agreed Framework. After months of debate, the state implemented the cabinet's advocacy among competing proposals.

The Foreign Ministry led off, announcing the U.S. allegation of the underground nuclear facility. A spokesman for the Foreign Ministry said,

> The U.S. side suspected that we were building an underground facility to promote a nuclear program in secret. During the talks, the talks were also delayed by the assessment that our satellite launch was a ballistic missile test and by the claim that issues that had already been agreed upon [U.S. supplying heavy fuel oil] had to be reconsidered due to the negative atmosphere that was formed. . . . We made our position clear that we will take practical measures to show that we cannot be unilaterally bound under the framework agreement and sacrifice our own nuclear power industry if the United States again takes a backward step in carrying out the framework agreement.[10]

Utilizing brinkmanship tactics, the Foreign Ministry was not shy about making threats to scuttle the Agreed Framework. Four years had passed since the agreement's signing and most of the heavy fuel oil still had not arrived. Yet the institution left an opening at the end of the statement, urging the Americans to take forward steps by supplying the fuel oil. The cabinet was the only institution publicly advocating this line. The inspection demand, coming on the heels of the criticism of the Taepodong-1 launch, accelerated more fundamental debates about whether the state should continue to negotiate with Washington at all at this time.

Negotiations continued despite increased discussions in Pyongyang about abandoning talks. The Foreign Ministry reiterated its statement, implicitly indicating the value it placed on open lines of communication, "at the DPRK-U.S. high-level talks in New York, the DPRK made clear its position to show in practice its will not to sacrifice its nuclear power industry." The party's newspaper spun the Foreign Ministry statement in a different direction, summarizing it with a focus on the ultimatum and missile "slander."[11] The party newspaper concurrently ran a signed editorial—evoking the name of both Kims—describing its view that "enemies within and without were making desperate efforts to disintegrate and stifle Korean socialism with the fictitious 'nuclear problem.' [Kim Jong Il] frustrated their maneuverings with a bomb-like declaration. . . . For dozens of years he together with the president [Kim Il Sung] has crushed every one of the imperialists' moves to isolate and stifle the DPRK."[12] While the Foreign Ministry presented the DPRK's interests in New York, the party advocated crushing U.S. "deception" and refocusing on ideologically driven military means to complete the revolution and reunify the nation.

The party would not stand for the United States trying to "stifle and isolate" Korea, repeating ideological sentiments that questioned Washington's underlying goals. For party ideologues, imperialists schemed to crush socialists, so it was naive to believe one could compromise with them. The party objected on principle to the U.S. inspection demand, indicating such a move undermined socialism, security, and sovereignty. It connected this specific incident with its opposition to negotiations. The cabinet and party highlighted different elements of the same statements and interpreted U.S. moves in different ways.

The KWP's position stemmed from the 1950s thought that through socialism and military might, the state would defeat the imperialists. The party refused to be swayed by imperialist pressure through the Agreed Framework apparatus, including the inspection demand. The party's position arose out of ideological conviction, intense distrust of the "imperialists," and the view that a nuclear weapon strengthened the state's defense and enhanced its international prestige.

Consequently, the party said Pyongyang should block inspections. Through Kim Jong Il's wisdom and "scientific" understanding of world politics, the state would "smash the commotion of the nuclear inspection maneuver of the imperialist allied forces." The party explicitly specified that they based their international strategy on ideological correctness, "Our party was able to consistently adhere to the socialist principle while not even once wavering from the aftermath of the modern revisionism and modern social democracy. . . . This is the secret behind our party and people's display of invincible feats in a time when the imperialists' maneuvers to isolate and crush us has reach[ed] an extreme point."[13] The party expressed its vision for the DPRK's future through a single ideological prism.

The party linked the inspection demand to its more general rejection of the Agreed Framework, "We are not afraid even if the agreement breaks down. We are not willing to be restricted by it while having our sovereignty violated."[14] The party's alternative was clear: the class enemies must be confronted through military might. "No matter how hard they may try to embellish capitalism and launch all sorts of ideological-cultural offensives, they will never be able to avert the hatred of our people for the class enemies. Just as a wolf cannot take the form of a sheep, the aggressive nature of the imperialists will never change. Fighting against the enemies to the end is the thoroughgoing class stance of our people."[15] For the party, U.S. action was a constant. The United States might try to present its position as compatible with mutual gains, but it was simply trying to trick the North. The United States only sought to bring down the socialist system. Opposing the Agreed Framework was a sacred duty of protecting the socialist system.

Suspicion of negotiations extended beyond the specific framework agreement. The party also objected to the pending six-party talks, calling them a platform for "treason," "The so-called multilateral party talks, which profess the security of Northeast Asia, are nothing but a repetition of the six-party talks by divisionists who often used the talks to intensify division and to fabricate the concept of two Koreas. . . . The talks are an anti-reunification idea that is simply unrealistic and cannot be accomplished. . . . Therefore, the multilateral security dialogue is a criminal act that can never be forgiven. . . . On behalf of the nation, we firmly denounce the South Korean puppets' proposal of multilateral security dialogue, which sells national interests and permanently divides the country."[16]

The two Koreas had already joined the UN as separate countries and signed the Basic Agreement, recognizing one another by their formal names as the Democratic People's Republic of Korean (DPRK) and the Republic of Korean (ROK). The party's position again was locked in the past. It used the nostalgic argument for reunification as another talking point against the new negotiating proposal. Bilateral talks were bad enough but multilateral talks that included the South Koreans risked recognizing the government in Seoul as a legitimate, separate state. This "divisionist" move could be presented as an affront to Korean nationalism, but the party's argument failed to carry the day.

More directly, party commentaries denied the underground facility and rocket launch had any military uses but ended with a thinly veiled threat that the satellite could be used as a missile, "whether the launch of our artificial satellite is used for military purposes or not entirely depends on the attitude of the United States and other hostile forces."[17] The party injected more brinkmanship into the situation as it pursued a confrontational agenda. Just as boldly confronting the Japanese in the 1940s allowed them to move from a band of fringe guerilla fighters to the state's elite, confrontation with the Americans might pay off by achieving national goals and glorifying their—or increasingly their families'—lifelong efforts.

The KPA added to the mix, expressing its opposition to negotiations after the inspection demand surfaced. The (North) Korean broadcast station announced, "Our people and People's Army are strongly united around Comrade Kim Jong Il, the respected and beloved supreme commander, and fully prepared for any military adventure by the U.S. imperialist warmongers. If the U.S. imperialists and the South Korean puppets dare to light a fire of aggression against our Republic after all, this will only be a foolish self-destructive act like jumping into the fire carrying gunpowder."[18] This original rhetorical flourish likely demonstrated the military's difficulty in justifying publicly its specific concerns about U.S. inspections of the site. The KPA would not want to admit that the heavily guarded site may have some military applications.

Although less colorful, later publications articulated the KPA's institutional policy more clearly. The KPA expressed its long-held opposition to negotiating with the Americans; negotiations had only gone forward because other, unspecified bureaucratic interests won out. For the military, the United States' inspection demand proved that KPA's opposition to negotiations was correct and its institutional opponents were wrong: "The Korean People's Army expected nothing from the [Agreed Framework] and had no interest in dialogue and negotiation through diplomatic channels. Now, the United States, throwing away the mask of 'appeasement' and 'engagement' which it had once worn for some time, is openly revealing its design to invade the DPRK, threatening to break the Agreed Framework and spreading a plan for the second Korean war. The present developments prove that the KPA's judgment and stand were completely correct."[19]

The KPA opposed the diplomatic track—past, present, and future. The bureaucratic players also blamed the Americans in distinctive ways. The Foreign Ministry sought to inject greater nuance into the debate. Abandoning negotiations outright was not the only way to register displeasure with the inspection demand. Current difficulties in negotiations could be more narrowly sourced and potentially overcome. The Foreign Ministry noted that interbranch conflict in the United States prevented it from upholding its preliminary obligations under the Agreed Framework. By contrast, the party sourced the cause of this outcome to the "insincere attitude of the United States toward implementing the agreement" and dismissed the Foreign Ministry's more nuanced explanation, "The United States has recently been unable to pay a penny to build the light-water reactors, due to this or that pretext." The party expressed a more fundamental suspicion that lent itself to a radical break from negotiations altogether.

When the party commentary recognized the role of congressional opposition at the end of the article, it claimed this showed why the agreement would never be implemented and should be abandoned, "Hard-line conservatives in the United States did not approve in Congress the budget for the heavy oil supply. Therefore, prospects for the heavy oil supply are dim. Nevertheless, the United States is helpless about this. . . . It is self-evident that in this situation, we cannot pin our hopes on the agreement with the United States. . . . We have no intention [of adhering] to the Agreed Framework. Even if the DPRK-U.S. Agreed Framework is broken, we have nothing to fear. Rather, we will be freer."[20] The latest hang-up in the Agreed Framework was more evidence it should be eliminated altogether rather than be addressed at the negotiating table.

Party commentaries drew on historical examples or pure ideological exhortations but overwhelmingly searched for current evidence to bolster their consistent policy advocacy toward confrontation. The party followed up by publishing another ideological article on how the "imperialists' aggressive nature cannot change" and how the United States slyly sought to split the North Korean leadership by falsely presenting a "peace strategy" which is "simply another version of war strategy." The party recognized the possibility (if not current reality) of divisions within the state and concluded by presenting its advocacy as superior to that of its internal opponents: "Only when the revolutionary people of the world, penetrating into the imperialists' aggressive and plunderous nature, further intensify the anti-imperialist and anti-U.S. struggle, can global peace and security be ensured."[21] Accommodation was counterproductive.

An unattributed (North) Korean Central News Agency (KCNA) broadcast presented a more moderate path, "If the U.S. side persists in inspecting our underground structures, we can show them to it. However, if they prove to be civilian structures, the U.S. side must compensate for its aspersions on the DPRK."[22] The policy option did not seem to originate in the party or from central authorities as four days later the party continued to call for preventing the inspection and scrapping the Agreed Framework.[23] The position was out of step with the main current of thinking expressed in the North Korean media. Such a move can be dangerous to the person presenting it and helps explain why the piece was unattributed.

The cabinet later suggested the article probably originated there. The cabinet negotiated specifics of U.S. compensation for inspecting Kumchang-ri and eventually reached a settlement that became state policy. Central authorities selected between the competing options fiercely debated in the North Korean press. The cabinet's proposal to accept food aid for inspections and maintain the Agreed Framework won out, but this was far from a foreordained conclusion. Before the central authorities selected the compensation-for-inspection solution, another crisis intervened to make the decision more difficult. The cabinet's policy of continuing negotiations (albeit in an increasingly difficult environment) was adopted, but its economic construction agenda was denied for the time being. The existence of competing proposals and arguments from below that inform top-level decisions is out of step with the monolithic models in which the nerve center does not select policy without reference to its institutional supports, and those institutional supports present a consistent policy platform in line with the organization's interests.

OPlan 5027

A related crisis soon dominated North Korea's relations with its neighbors and the United States. The newly revised Combined Forces Command's Operation Plan (OPlan) 5027 outlined joint U.S.–South Korean military actions in case of a military contingency on the Korean peninsula. The U.S.–South Korean command wrote the defensive plan in 1973 to prepare for a possible North Korean invasion of the South and revised it several times. The 1998 revision was the first version to detail plans to permanently eliminate the DPRK if it ever attacked the South. Previous plans focused on ending a second Korean War quickly; the revised plan put forward the contingency response goal "to abolish [N]orth Korea as a state."[24]

All of the DPRK's institutions united in opposition to this development, but they still maintained divergent responses. The party linked the OPlan development to the inspection demand, highlighting a general U.S. "hostile policy" toward the DPRK. They capitalized on the negative atmosphere the OPlan revelation created to advance its opposition to inspections and the Agreed Framework. The new facts fed into its existing platform. The KPA reacted in stronger terms, calling the move tantamount to a declaration of war. Though the military and party use the "declaration of war" characterization loosely, it does register a high level of dissatisfaction and a call to stiffen defense measures. The cabinet explicitly recused itself from this public discussion, noting that bilateral relations had deteriorated so much that the cabinet could not present an alternative to the confrontational approach in the current political climate.

The party jumped on the OPlan news, connecting the document to the inspections issue, "Worse still, the U.S. Defense Department in a recent 'Report on U.S. Security Strategy for East Asia' said that they would 'exercise military power' to prevent the DPRK from resuming 'nuclear development.' As seen above, developments are turning for the worse and the U.S. is putting tougher pressure upon the DPRK for its refusing to accept the 'inspection.' However, any 'pressure' and 'threat' will not break our determined position of principle. We declare once again that our underground facility is not related with nuclear activity and that, accordingly, we will not in the least allow any 'inspection' of the facility."[25]

Although not explicitly sourced to the party, the party newspaper subsequently published another ideological article elucidating many of the same points, stressing that the party's ideological pureness could transcend any challenge.[26] The OPlan was a long-term document that surfaced during this crisis. It did not have a clear linkage to the inspection issue, but the party was willing to connect the issues to advance their agenda. The party sought to link these actions so it could advance its principal argument that Pyongyang should harden its U.S. policy.

The KPA opposed the inspection in stronger and more direct terms than the party as one might expect from the institution most directly responsible for military plans. The spokesman for the KPA's general staff also linked the OPlan with the inspections demand. The state had to respond to the OPlan news, the military argued, by adopting the military's position on inspections and emphasizing the military's interests as one would during wartime:

> Our revolutionary Armed Forces will respond toward the challenge of U.S. forces of aggression with annihilating strikes without forgiving it at all. . . . The puppet South Korean traitor, who had maintained his existence with flunkeyism and submission, curried favor with his master in response to this bragging [of regime change in OPlan 5027], and preposterously raved that the North must accept the inspection of the underground facility. The Japanese reactionaries, who viciously raved that our satellite launch was a ballistic-missile launch, are again making vicious attempts. At such a time, U.S. conservative hard-liners made the violent remarks that they would abrogate the DPRK-U.S. Agreed Framework and make a resolute response if no inspection of our underground facilities was conducted. This is, in essence, like a declaration of war.[27]

Referring to U.S. actions as a "declaration of war" is common enough that it does not merit particular attention, but a long series of articles and broadcasts delineated the statement as important. For the next week, soldiers, sailors, veterans, workers, students, intellectuals, and foreigners all allegedly supported the KPA general staff's view.[28] North Korea's elites likely did not read these propaganda articles as genuine expressions of interest by these groups, but the repetition indicated that the KPA wanted to highlight this statement in a way that is rarely seen. The position had apparently taken some hold in senior KPA circles.

The KPA general staff statement rejected negotiations in general and built on the negative atmosphere to advance its institutional agenda against economic reform and opening. The institution never wavered in its core precepts. The KPA linked the launch response, inspection demand, and OPlan to its long-held argument that the state should reject U.S. "appeasement efforts" (negotiations) and economic opening. North Korea should be a closed society and emphasize military security:

> Lately, the U.S. imperialists are hyperbolic about aggravating a situation which resulted from the matter of our nonexistent underground nuclear facility and satellite launch because they aim to come up with an excuse to light the fuse of war in accordance with Operation Plan 5027. It is obvious why the United States has launched into implementing Operation Plan 5027, relieving itself of appeasement and engagement, with which they briefly disguised themselves. As it has failed to destroy our socialist system even with its strategy of isolation and suffocation and the strategy of appeasement intended to lead us to reform and openness, it finally has lost its sense and launched into a reckless adventure. Originally, our revolutionary forces never had any expectations toward the appeasement policy proposed by the United States, which is inherently trying to demolish our socialist system. . . . The general situation formed today clearly reveals that the sharp caution and the revolutionary position of our revolutionary forces were extremely just. . . . Although we do not want a war, we also will not avoid a war.[29]

The KPA statement pays some lip service to socialism, but it is not a class-focused statement. However, it fit well into the party's ideological conviction that capitalism and socialism cannot coexist. A party commentary draws out the class distinction at much greater length and shows how the party took a different path, and yet also concluded that reform and opening must be abandoned:

> Today, when the U.S. imperialists and their dirty hirelings have openly taken off their cunning masks of dialogue and negotiation and have taken out their swords of aggression, what do we realize most keenly, and what awakens us once again? They are the firm anti-imperialist revolutionary idea of our party, which is firmly holding revolutionary arms in its hands, and its firm anti-U.S., class spirit with which we have always fought relentlessly. . . . We are keenly realizing now how just and wise it is for us to have consolidated our resolve, a thousand times, to firmly hold our bayonets and cherished a class-oriented belief in our hearts. . . . Based on their class-oriented stand, they also

must have clear-cut views, a firm faith, and a firm resolve. . . . [We are engaged in] a life-and-death class struggle in which for us to live, they must die, and in which for them to live, we must die.[30]

The party's position is necessarily zero-sum, removing any possibility of effective compromise or value in give-and-take negotiations.[31] The central problematic is the class struggle not a more narrow military confrontation.

U.S.-DPRK relations had soured. Pyongyang had to object to the OPlan; it could not accept as legitimate a document that threatened to eliminate the state—regardless of the circumstances or caveats outlined in the military plan. However, the OPlan leak did not likely change any planning or strategic thinking in Pyongyang. The state operated under the oft-repeated assumption that the United States wanted to wipe the country off the map—even absent North Korean aggression. It probably came as little surprise that in the event of a second Korean War the United States and South Korea would attempt to eliminate the DPRK. Both Koreas had attempted to force reunification in the Korean War and committed themselves to this principle in their respective constitutions throughout the Cold War.

In this case, unobservable, private discussions may have significantly diverged from the public rejection of the OPlan. In particular, the Foreign Ministry's public role may show only part of its advocacy. A Foreign Ministry statement said, "DPRK diplomats have little to do because the DPRK-U.S. relations are rapidly turning toward military confrontation."[32] The Foreign Ministry removed itself from the public discussion, but it likely did not remove itself from behind-the-scenes politicking. Such a move would be anomalous and puzzling given its general policy advocacy, access to Kim's inner circle, and important institutional equities. Though no one continued to press the compensation-for-inspections idea in the official press, the party continued to publicly oppose it.[33] These commentaries would be puzzling if no one was pushing this agenda privately.

The Foreign Ministry was the only institution not on record opposing the phantom proposal. Vice Foreign Minister Kang Sok Ju negotiated the Agreed Framework and is reputed to be one of Kim's two dozen or so inner circle advisers. Given his institution's advocacy and personal ties to the Agreed Framework, it is possible that he attempted to leverage his position privately to present the inspections-for-compensation idea to central authorities. Indeed, the proposal eventually became state policy over party and military objections. Although impossible to verify at this point, the pieces of the puzzle seem to point to a role of the Foreign Ministry in pushing this agenda.

Outcry over North Korea's rocket launch, inspection demands, OPlan 5027, and continued failure to provide Agreed Framework commitments effectively muted cabinet moderates who publicly advocated negotiations. Party and military hard-liners seemed to gain the upper hand. Though the regime eventually exchanged inspections for aid, hard-liners won out in internal deliberations for a change in linked issue areas. Their calls for a more planned economic structure—for ideological and security concerns associated with increased openness—carried the day. Though this trade-off process remains hidden from view, it is plausible that Kim, not completely comfortable with ceding to the U.S. demand during this heightened state of tensions but taking actions to preserve the Agreed Framework, sought to placate party and military demands in other areas. Such moves could also reduce Pyongyang's dependence on its neighbors and the United States at a time when such reliance seemed even less prudent than normal. Indeed, each institution had previously advocated publicly that the state should link issue areas. The state announced the change in economic policy in the important New Year's joint editorial.

The Second Chollima March

The 1999 New Year's joint editorial announced the state would pursue a "second grand Chollima march" as advocated by the party and the military. Chollima is a winged mythical horse reputed to be especially fast. The first Chollima march was an administrative push to accelerate economic construction and provide for the country's food needs by collectivizing agricultural land. Started in the late 1950s, Kim Il Sung's plan mirrored Mao's Great Leap Forward in actions and initial failures. The first Chollima march finally started to produce gains once Kim Il Sung introduced private incentives for overquota production a few years into the program.

The Chollima march has a positive connotation in North Korea. The economy grew following the post–Korean War reconstruction until the

1970s. There are several large statues of the Chollima horse in Pyongyang to commemorate the administrative push credited with pulling the state out of poverty. For much of the isolated and indoctrinated population, the improved economic situation was because of—not in spite of—forced collectivization. Kim's announcement of the second Grand Chollima march was a nostalgic move to renew centralized economic control over agriculture.[34] It marked a tremendous policy win for the party and military and a defeat for the cabinet. It committed to recentralizing economic plans and cracking down on market activities. For the party, this was an ideological win; it was a move toward socialist orthodoxy. For the military, it was a move to restrict information outflow and reassert state control over the economy. For the cabinet, it meant removing production incentives and more inefficient food distribution methods that had contributed to prior food shortages.

The renewed administrative push for economic construction filtered into all three strategic issue areas: the economy, reunification, and anti-U.S. policy. The party in particular attempted to reassert its larger "rice bowl," or bureaucratic domain, following this first post-1998 constitution NYJE. The move to annex more bureaucratic fiefdoms triggered a reaction, especially from the cabinet. National policy became more disjointed than during any other period under consideration, with different institutions simultaneously pursuing different agendas. The result is puzzling for the monolithic ideal types but easily explained by post-totalitarian institutionalism's theoretical expectations. The monolithic ideal types expect top-down control of a unified policy. Policy should not be significantly self-contradictory, nor should institutions openly fight over controlling the agenda, yet the rise and fall of one institution's influence relative to another's continued.

The party began to reestablish its bureaucratic clout over the economy. In a front-page editorial in the government newspaper only four days after the NYJE, the KWP interpreted Kim Jong Il's new guidance as requiring a "redoubled" socialist push to build a powerful country. North Korea's ideological mantra refers to a "powerful and prosperous nation." The party editorial makes clear its preference for powerful over prosperous and calls on the cabinet to implement the party's policy preferences:

No goal of nation building is more sacred and greater than the building of a powerful nation. . . . The most important in this is for all the [cabinet] functionaries to grasp the wishes reflected in the New Year's joint editorial and have their minds made up to implement them to the end. The basic idea of the joint editorial is that we glorify this year as the year of a great turning-point for building a powerful nation by accelerating another great Chollima march under the leadership of the respected and beloved general just like we have built the social-ist fatherland of independence, self-reliance, and self-defense from scratch under the guidance of the great leader through the [first] Chollima march. Building a powerful socialist nation is a long-range blueprint that the great Comrade Kim Jong Il has long elaborated as well as a shining milestone for nation building.[35]

The party's position was not a stretch; it cited Kim's decision to give it greater power in economic management and tried to preemptively whip the competing bureaucracies to get in line.

The party continually reminded the government that Kim Jong Il ruled on this economic question and insisted they get on board. The cabinet did not reply in the press initially, but the party was well aware of their opposi-tion. In case the cabinet "functionaries" did not get the message the first time in the front-page article in their own newspaper, the party continued, cabinet functionaries "must see that the rules and order are thoroughly observed in the economic work and remain vigilant against and reject any tendency that runs against the principles of the socialist economic man-agement, no matter how trifling it may be."[36] The party published further articles on functionaries' duties under the new NYJE guidance, clearly rel-ishing their newfound authority.[37] For the party, their role to direct policy ran deep. It must apply to all sectors at every level. They even published articles on the proper Juche method of the "cannon's roar signaling the potato farming revolution," noting its "grandeur" and contribution to a powerful state.[38] The party pushed its authority quickly and forcefully while it had the bureaucratic upper hand.

The party addressed the possibility, and their expectation, of bureau-cratic resistance. This expectation suggests bureaucratic resistance is not uncommon but rather part of the system. The party would not be surprised if the cabinet tried to subtly subvert the NYJE. In fact, it prepared for this real possibility. And the cabinet did exactly as anticipated. It recognized the NYJE's clear policy guidance that awarded leadership on economic policy to its institutional rival with a very different economic agenda, but it also immediately began undermining the party's goal. The possibility of bureaucratic resistance is completely alien to the monolithic ideal types but an expectation of the post-totalitarian institutionalism model. It is an important component of the model that shows these institutions do not simply set the agenda for senior decision-makers—a key function in its own right—but can actively press their own agenda. Though this certainly does not rise to the level of resistance found in democratic states with well-established opposition parties and organizations, it does indicate a level of bureaucratic autonomy not recognized in monolithic descriptions of the North Korean system.

The cabinet replied in a front-page article in the party newspaper that they would adhere to socialist principle but made clear the need to focus on rational results. In short, they waved a white flag while holding their guns steady. They resisted decided policy, capitalized on the inherent vagueness of high-level proclamations, and attempted to push their agenda against the tide of decided policy: "What is important in the cabinet's work as the nation's economic headquarters is to precisely establish combat operations to thoroughly implement the party's economic policy *in conformity with actual conditions* and to carry out works in a revolutionary *and effective* way. . . . The goal of combat, which was legislated through the cabinet's decision, is to revive the economy, which has suffered temporary difficulties, within the next few years, and raise the level of production already attained by all sectors of the national economy" (emphasis added).[39] The NYJE was a win for the ideological purists but the general guidance could still be cloaked in a pragmatic need for results. The party cited its delegated claim to authority over economic management but had a difficult time implementing this agenda.

The party attempted to expand upon this policy win by interpreting Kim Jong Il's Chollima march declaration as a clarification of the new constitutional arrangement. The party presented the government as its subordinate. The party contended that the government must relegate its preferences to the party's ideologically guided demands and follow its planning, citing authority granted from Kim Il Sung rather than Kim Jong Il. The party wanted to claim victory in the bureaucratic war, while the cabinet refused to recognize complete defeat even in this individual economic battle:

In the course of leading the socialist economic construction, the great leader [Kim Il Sung] consistently adhered to the principle of giving priority to the ideological work. The great leader's firm creed was that as long as their ideas are set in motion, the masses can fulfill any kind of difficult and vast tasks. . . . Armed with the spirit of self-reliance, the whole population is vigorously speeding up the second grand march of Chollima aimed at opening a new great turnaround in the economic construction. The centralized, planned guidance over the economy is further strengthened and the work of establishing discipline and order in the economic construction is being deepened in accordance with the demand of the new state organizational system.[40]

For the party, the "new state organizational system" looked very similar to the old one; it meant the party on top, pursuing a centralized, planned economy with ideologically directed decision making.

The party asserted that the NYJE did not simply grant it more discretion in economic affairs; it insisted that its guiding roles were comprehensive. The Chollima march reference implied that the party was back on top and the constitutional revision three months earlier could be "reinterpreted" into nonexistence. Kim Jong Il had completed the three-year mourning period for his father a year earlier. The party tried to present the constitutional revision not as the final word on the younger Kim's modus operandi but as a decision that could be undone. The party wanted its institutional supremacy back, but neither the military nor the cabinet was prepared to satisfy the party's desire.

Kim Ki-nam, secretary of the KWP's Central Committee, laid out the party's view that the economic guidance extended into reunification and anti-U.S. policy issue areas too. In a speech marking the sixth anniversary of Kim Jong Il's election as the NDC chairman, Kim Ki-nam emphasized economic self-reliance and the need to enhance the role of the defense industry to promote economic growth, "Our national defense industry has also become a precious asset in building a country with a powerful economy . . . . It is our party's consistent principle and firm position to advance the construction of the economy and national defense and to invariably adhere to and develop our independent economic structure. We should consider the foundation of the self-reliant economy, which we established by tightening our belts and exerting every effort, and the national defense industry, which is based on its foundation as a valuable asset to the revolution, and further enhance and develop them."[41] Since the party's economic agenda meant investing in defense to promote growth, it naturally addressed policy toward those states that the military expenditures sought to counter. Lower-level party officials drew out this point more forcefully and more starkly.

The party's economic policy gave it a pretext to address reunification and U.S. policy. The North's administrative push in economic policy and greater self-reliance meant reducing its dependence on South Korean investments in inter-Korean economic projects. Party officials returned to traditional arguments that the South must join the North in communism to reunify the nation, "The country-selling traitors in South Korea, given to toadyism and reliance on outside forces under the veil of 'the government of the people,' have raised increasingly high barriers on the path to reunification. This reality demands even more pressingly the nation's adherence to the principle of national independence. Today the only way out for South Korea from its present crisis lies in the attainment of reunification through coalition with communism and with the North."[42]

Likewise, the party took aim at the South Korean Ministry of Unification. The Ministry is charged with inter-Korean dialogue and economic projects. Their main interlocutors in the North are in the cabinet. The party labels the ministry antireunification, citing again the party's preference for reunification through force: "The South Korean people should step up more courageously their struggle to get all anti-reunification institutional devices—including 'the National Security Law,' 'the ministry of Unification,' and 'the National Security Planning Agency'—scrapped or dismantled. . . . And, by doing so, they will hasten the day for the 70 million to reunite as one."[43] Having achieved the goal of reapplying Kim Il Sung's economic policies, the party now attempted to implement the long-term Kimilsungist peninsular policy of removing U.S. troops and pressing the South into submission.

Not surprisingly, the KPA agreed with the party that the state should prioritize military resources and take a militaristic stand in the areas of reunification and anti-imperialism. Citing again only half of the "powerful and prosperous nation" mantra, Kim Yong-chun, the chief of the general staff, said, "We have to achieve independent reunification of the fatherland

and consummate the Juche revolutionary cause amid the fierce struggle against the enemies. The people's army should . . . guarantee with military force our people's struggles for the reunification of the country and for building a powerful state. . . . All the situations more clearly show how the imperialists' aggressive and brutal nature will never change and that the victory of the socialist cause can only be guaranteed through the bayonets of the revolution. . . . This is our army and our people's unchanging firm standpoint and firm will."[44]

These two institutions openly and consistently advocate a reunification policy line that some observers claim is so unrealistic that no institution or individual could genuinely hold such a view. North Korea's reunification rhetoric must be mere propaganda. By 1999 South Korea could likely have defeated North Korea on the battlefield even without U.S. support.[45] North Korea's military hardware has become increasingly antique, and an emphasis on missile and nuclear technology suggests a deterrent rather than an offensive orientation of the portion of its military that gains the most resources. Reunification propaganda serves to keep the masses in check by reinforcing an empty ideology, but serious policy advocates must have abandoned this view.

However, dismissing these positions as rhetoric without substance misses the DPRK's peculiar reality and the difference between short- and long-term objectives. Kim Il Sung reportedly could not sleep at night in the late 1940s, because he was so consumed with thoughts of his nation's division.[46] Today's Kimilsungists likewise seek to strengthen the North's means to force unification despite its requiring tremendous sacrifice and even greater risk. They take the long view and emphasize that their resolve is greater than the Americans'. They emphasize guerilla tactics and special operations forces and encourage the severely weakened radical left in South Korea. Though conditions are far from ripe for invasion or fomenting revolution in the South, these revolutionaries and military men argue that history is not predetermined, and the conviction of the North Korean soldier would mean victory for the North.

Those permitted to read this study may find these people's logic unrealistic and flawed, but that does not suggest it is not their genuine advocacy. With the personal risks an accommodation-driven reunification poses to elites and their families, it is perhaps not surprising that some elites prefer the status quo as opposed to the faint possibility of a unified Korea working in their favor. Indeed, imposing this same metric of rejecting "unrealistic expectations" as impossible and mere rhetoric makes the North's nuclearization and attending extreme sacrifice equally implausible, yet it is their reality. These institutions have taken observable steps to advance these general agendas. In short, North Korea is not well positioned to reunify the nation by force but that does not preclude ideologues and cadres from trying to position the state now for the long-term possibility of completing the revolution.

The party and military sought to expand their authority after the NYJE to each of the major policy areas by rearticulating their comprehensive platform. Both institutions continued to link the reunification question with anti-U.S. policy. The United States must be driven off the peninsula if Pyongyang is to reunify the country. Reunification means absorbing the South's economic and agricultural production potential and makes the state sustainable. As such, both the party and the military took the opportunity to reiterate their long-standing, institutional opposition to the Agreed Framework—the cornerstone of addressing U.S. policy through accommodation rather than confrontation.

Laying out its complete U.S. policy anew, the party explained only eight days after the NYJE why it objected to negotiations with the United States:

The U.S. implemented none of the Geneva agreement although four years have passed since its adoption. Moreover, the ground for the light-water reactors has not been broken today when nearly half of the set time elapsed. The U.S. has not faithfully discharged its obligation to supply heavy oil, with the result that its shipment is in arrears. The U.S. sanctions against the DPRK have not yet been lifted, and the nuclear threat is increasing. In fact, the DPRK-U.S. Agreed Framework has been reduced further to an empty paper. In the final analysis, we have gained nothing but economic losses in 'reward' for earnestly implementing the Geneva agreement. The U.S. is clamoring about "missile threat" and the "suspected underground nuclear facility" in the DPRK, politicizing humanitarian food assistance together with its followers. What it seeks in this is to disarm the DPRK. This is a declaration of abandonment of the DPRK-U.S. Agreed Framework, a declaration of war and provocation against the DPRK. If the U.S. wants, let us kill the Agreed Framework and take our own way. This is our position.[47]

The party's position was stretching the authority that the Chollima march reference provided it. It attempted to run as far as it could with the new authority. Seeing an opportunity, the military jumped on board too. Within days of the NYJE, the KPA announced its renewed institutional opposition to the Agreed Framework, which, the statement claimed, stemmed from the very inception of negotiations:

> The United States' insincere attitude and stand toward the Agreed Framework prove once again that the position of the Korean People's Army is right. From the outset, our People's Army did not have expectations for the Agreed Framework, nor was it interested in dialogue and negotiations through diplomatic channels. When the nuclear crisis was concocted on the Korean peninsula in 1993 and hostile forces violated our sovereignty by raising the ridiculous issue of inspecting the objects, our Army strongly called for responding to this with resolute self-defensive steps. There has been no change in such position and attitude by our Army thereafter. Rather, its position and attitude have become more solid. . . . The KPA's position is that diplomatic negotiation is not the only way for solving matters.[48]

The military once again argued that it had never supported accommodation with the United States. It went so far as to explicitly note its institutional opposition to high-level decided policy. It wanted to continue the nuclear crisis created in 1993 when the North announced its intention to withdraw from the Non-Proliferation Treaty and reprocess plutonium. For the military, this was not an empty threat or a diplomatic tactic. It was part of a long-standing military plan to enhance its war-making potential. A nuclear North Korea may be able to raise the stakes high enough to dissuade the United States from joining a peninsular war and eventually allow the North to move forward on its historical mission to reunify the peninsula on its own terms.

All bureaucratic actors were not on the same page. The NYJE did not indicate a permanent policy win for the party. They no longer sat atop the bureaucracy and directed all policy choices as editorials earlier in the year hopefully claimed. The cabinet reasserted its role in economic affairs. It published an article citing the "cabinet's plan of operation" in regards to agricultural policy without reference to party guidance.[49] The cabinet decided to ignore demands that it get on board with the party's agenda. The cabinet continued to rely on pragmatic policy metrics in making economic policy and opposed efforts to end the Agreed Framework. The North's main avenue to nuclear weapon status—the Yongbyon nuclear reactor—remained frozen. Relations with the United States were strained and diplomatic progress slow, but Pyongyang did not radically depart from the diplomatic structure. Inter-Korean projects experienced the most national-level policy variance in the coming months. Policy coordination declined as the three institutions pursued policies in conflict with one another—a development unexplained by and puzzling for the monolithic theories but accounted for by institutional politics under Kim Jong Il's authority.

Uncoordinated Institutions

Despite the decisive statement on socialist economic construction in the New Year's joint editorial, the cabinet actively undermined the policy. While the party attempted to extend its domain, the cabinet largely disregarded party guidance—or at best provided lip service to it. As a result, each institution pursued contradictory, strategic objectives simultaneously. Though the regime had already demonstrated its willingness to shift strategies over time, this period would be particularly puzzling for those subscribing to the monolithic ideal. The military, party, and cabinet each maintained a consistent strategy, but the nation did not. During this period, national-level policy was notably fragmented and disjointed.

One scholar describing inter-Korean relations during this time frame perceptively noted how the North's uncoordinated bureaucratic actors pursued their own policy lines. "Rarely have they [inter-Korean relations] seemed more bifurcated or more puzzling than in June [1999], when a naval battle erupted on the West Sea while simultaneously on the other side of the Peninsula cruise ships of the Hyundai group—Korea's largest *chaebol*—continued to ferry South Korean tourists to the scenic Mt. Kumgang on the northern side of the demilitarized zone as if nothing was happening."[50]

The KPA was the sole participant and spokesperson for naval clashes, while the cabinet controlled the economic projects. The bifurcated policy that worked at cross-purposes is puzzling if one expects the state to act as a monolith or at least as a coordinated entity. These actions square well, however, with each institution's consistently expressed preferences. Institutions started to move on their agendas as lines of institutional dispute resolution appeared not to be fully developed. Indeed, events beyond inter-Korean relations further demonstrate that distinct bureaucracies tried to cautiously test the extent of their authority during this period.

North Korea continued to negotiate in Geneva with the United States on its demand to inspect the suspected underground nuclear facility despite party and military opposition.[51] Washington rejected Pyongyang's demand for $300 million but offered to continue food aid. Bilateral talks reached an impasse. After months of stalemate, Kim Jong Il traveled to China—his first trip abroad since his father's death. The move marked a long trend of private North Korean consultations with the Beijing leadership, followed by Pyongyang announcing its willingness to talk. Two weeks after Kim's trip to China, North Korea consented to U.S. demands to inspect Kumchang-ri in return for continued U.S. food aid and U.S. training on potato farming.[52] Despite losing on the administrative economic push, the cabinet won on the compensation-for-inspections proposal.

Unfortunately, no data are available on the final stage of decision making. Such information would undoubtedly improve our understanding of the policy process, but its absence does not prohibit a theoretical understanding of the state's policy formulation and execution. What is most important for validating post-totalitarian institutionalism's theoretical expectations over the monolithic ideal types is the consistent policy expectations of each institution, conflicting policy goals and approaches between institutions, and the separation of wins and losses on an issue basis. Institutional divisions exist on core political questions and central authorities tend to select from these options in crafting and implementing policy.

The cabinet won its advocacy on the inspections issue but lost on the economic agenda. No single institution could claim permanent, comprehensive supremacy over another as the party enjoyed under Kim Il Sung. Institutions continued to resist one another's wins according to their preconceived policy platforms even after central authorities decided policy. Institutional leaders attempted to get the rest of the regime on board for policy implementation after decisions were made. Such acquiescence was not automatic. Kim's central authority is critical, but it often does not end debate. The North Korean system is locked in an equilibrium outcome of institutional interaction defining the range of policy options, institutional competition informing and influencing policy decisions, and similar competitive dynamics playing itself out in implementing decided policy.

The United States inspected Kumchang-ri in May 1999. The inspection turned up empty tunnels without nuclear traces. The news opened the door for further diplomatic overtures. At the end of the month, former U.S. defense secretary William Perry traveled to North Korea to offer a deal: if Pyongyang halted missile flight tests, then Washington would remove substantial sanctions and improve diplomatic ties.[53] Perry met with the figurehead SPA Presidium chairman and held meetings with key players in the Foreign Ministry, Kang Sok Ju and Kim Kye Kwan. The Foreign Ministry issued a simple statement: "The talks took place in a sincere and frank atmosphere full of mutual respect."[54] The cabinet's win put it in an advantageous position to expand its comprehensive policy agenda.

Two weeks after the long-debated inspection and Perry's visit, the North Korean media first mentioned the inspection. Instead of continually repeating in ideological essays that the North Koreans were correct that the tunnels indeed lacked any traces of nuclear activity, the Foreign Ministry issued a statement calling for a return to the Agreed Framework: "The visit proved objectively that the underground facility in Kumchang-ri is an empty tunnel, not related to nuclear development at all. As a result, it was clearly proved once again that we have been sincerely implementing the Geneva Agreed Framework."[55] There were no party commentaries or KPA statements on the inspection. Their enthusiasm for pursuing a confrontational policy toward the Americans was on hold. They had to find other ways to undermine the state's decided policy of accommodation with the United States.

Instead of commenting on the inspection issue, the KPA responded with actions. It sent patrol boats across the northern limit line (NLL)—the disputed sea border between North and South Korea.[56] The UN Command had drawn the line in 1953, although the North Koreans refused to recognize it in the armistice. The NLL proceeds from the military demarcation line at the center of the DMZ and hooks northward, hugging the North Korean coast. The NLL recognizes portions of the West Sea north of the thirty-eighth parallel as South Korean waters. Pyongyang prefers the maritime military demarcation line, which continues as a straight line from the middle of the DMZ. The land border between the two Koreas slopes southward as it reaches the west coast of Korea, providing the North with segments of the West Sea south of the thirty-eighth parallel. The border dispute has triggered multiple naval clashes for years.

The KPA regularly sends patrol boats across the NLL. However, this time they engaged a South Korean warship. The South Korean navy attempted to chase the North Korean warship back across the Northern Limit Line. When the North Korean warship refused to retreat, the two navies exchanged gunfire, and the South Korean navy sank the North Korean vessel, killing all twenty North Korean sailors onboard.[57] An unnamed source familiar with the overhead imagery leaked: "There was plenty of time for North Korea's military leadership to tell them to back off, but clearly they wanted to send a message that they were not about to back down."[58]

Interestingly, the KPA statement blamed the Americans for their role in establishing the northern limit line decades earlier and called Seoul a "puppet military, under the command of the U.S. Forces."[59] Nevertheless, the KPA's actions stalled the cabinet's inter-Korean negotiations. The next day, the North suspended talks with South Korea "for the time being."[60] However, the cabinet quickly resumed them, concluding an eleven-day inter-Korean negotiating session within three weeks of the incident. The talks broke down over the unrelated question of family reunions.[61]

Without recognizing the competing bureaucratic interests within North Korea, U.S. officials called the clash a "stupid" mistake; others said the regime was not serious about negotiations. This incident provides more evidence of the importance of correctly understanding North Korea's internal politics if one seeks to interact with or influence them. Donald Gregg, a knowledgeable former U.S. ambassador to South Korea, noted "like everything the North Koreans do, no one is entirely sure why they did it" while another unnamed senior official simply labeled the action as the North Koreans again doing "something stupid." Some congressional opponents to the Agreed Framework cited the clash as evidence of the talk's futility; viewing the state as a singular entity, they said North Korea was not serious about negotiations.[62]

In fairness, these comments may have been aimed more at influencing the U.S. foreign policy agenda than analyzing the situation. Nevertheless, they demonstrate the analytical paucity of the monolithic model of North Korean politics. These analysts did not recognize—at least publicly—the possibility that the clash was uncoordinated bureaucratic freelancing that reflected different agendas within the DPRK. It would be entirely consistent to expect that the KPA wanted to derail inter-Korean and U.S.-DPRK talks, while the cabinet seriously pursued diplomatic rapprochement.

The naval incident delayed negotiations briefly. The next month, the Foreign Ministry issued a statement calling on the United States to return to the Agreed Framework. Competing institutions interpreted the statement differently. Facing different interpretations of its statement within the DPRK, the North Korean Foreign Ministry had to publicly clarify its own statement:

> It has only been [a few] days since the press statement of the spokesman for the DPRK Foreign Ministry was issued, but this is already drawing great attention at home and abroad and bringing about a positive response. In the press statement, we once again put forth the principled position that we do not consider the United States the sworn enemy, and that if the United States recognizes our sovereignty and freedom of choice and treats us with good faith, we will develop relations with the United States based on the principles of equality and reciprocity. This is our Republic's fundamental position and consistent attitude regarding the United States.[63]

On behalf of the entire system, the Foreign Ministry was ready to deal. However, the whole republic did not support the Ministry's position. As the Foreign Ministry called for developing relations, the party indicated its desire to escalate military confrontation. Three days after the Foreign Ministry clarified the state's "consistent attitude," an unnamed detractor using the party's boilerplate language cited the Foreign Ministry's statement and concluded quite differently: "The touch-and-go situation prevailing on the Korean peninsula reminds one of a time bomb that may go off at any moment. The present situation compels us to maintain a higher vigilance and stronger revolutionary stand than ever before. Our armed forces and single-hearted unity, which have become invincible thanks to our party's military-first politics and military-first revolutionary leadership, regard it as their inborn quality and intrinsic mode of counteraction to return fire for fire and artillery fire for pistol fire. The further the United States escalates pressure upon us, the stronger our reaction will become, bringing unpredictable consequences."[64] The Foreign Ministry had authority to entertain negotiations, but the party actively sought to derail those negotiations and advocated military escalation. Its efforts for the time being would not bear fruit as the Foreign Ministry could pursue its own agenda. The KPA's effort in the West Sea and the party's more general opposition did not prompt the regime to reverse course on its U.S. policy.

Missile Negotiations and the Inter-Korean Summit

At the same time, a U.S. intelligence leak revealed that North Korea was preparing its Taepodong-2 rocket for launch later in the summer. If the launch was successful, the rocket would put the United States within North Korean missile range.[65] Party and army organs denounced the allegation and the United States more generally until the Foreign Ministry announced that the United States had agreed in Berlin to remove some sanctions against the DPRK.[66] The Foreign Ministry called that move "a reflection of the U.S. political will to stop pursuing its policy hostile to the DPRK and to improve relations . . . [which] create[s] an atmosphere favorable for a negotiated solution to outstanding issues between the two countries."[67] The announcement again only temporarily took the wind out of the sails of institutional opponents. The state stepped down its threat to test-fire another long-range missile and planned to return to the negotiating table.

The party and military again lost. The KPA dug up the NLL issue again, rejecting the maritime border's validity and reiterating earlier claims that the border extended thirty-five to forty miles south of the NLL.[68] It was a effort to antagonize the other side. The old trick garnered little attention, as much bigger agreements were in the works. U.S. and North Korean negotiators agreed in Berlin that the United States would "ease some sanctions" in exchange for North Korea suspending any long-range missile launches.[69] The Clinton administration upheld its pledge five days later, marking the first easing of U.S. sanctions against North Korea since 1953. The Foreign Ministry could point to concrete progress as a result of the negotiating track, which shored up its position internally vis-à-vis the party and military.

A Foreign Ministry statement paralleled the divisions within the U.S. political establishment on North Korea policy with divisions within North Korea on U.S. policy. The institution stated explicitly that some elements within the North Korean leadership preferred the confrontational path to the cabinet's negotiating path:

At the Berlin talks held in September and November both sides agreed to hold high-level talks to discuss pending issues in near future, depending on a climate to be created for them. However, Republican congressmen are threatening to prevent the administration from carrying out its policy towards the DPRK. . . . It is hard to guess which is the true U.S. policy out of the conflicting policy options of the two parties. . . . In fact, we hear assertions made by different domains in the DPRK that the present U.S. administration's policy toward the DPRK is intended to disarm and destroy it step by step in the end. They prefer the Republicans' assertion to be adopted as a U.S. policy to compel them to confront the U.S. militarily. In other words, we are fully prepared for both events: improvement of relations with the U.S. And showdown with it.[70]

The Foreign Ministry's discussion of "different domains in the DPRK" and use of the third person to refer to North Korean institutions that prefer a confrontational approach further suggests that the Foreign Ministry is the institution committed to a negotiated solution to outstanding issues between the United States and North Korea and that it battles internally against those that fundamentally disagree with this approach.

Despite historic movement on sanctions, the KPA continued to press its concern about South Korean warships in the West Sea. The KPA reaffirmed its resolute stand against South Korean ships in "North Korean waters," arguing that the United States had prodded the South Korean "puppets" to sink the North Korean warship. The statement is particularly interesting since it came in December, a full six months from the height of the crab season that makes the waters lucrative and around which the inter-Korean naval clashes usually develop. The KPA usually denounces any clashes shortly after the event, and they could not cite any new evidence that the United States had "prodded" the South Koreans to defend their territorial waters. The KPA was grasping at straws to find any recent evidence to object to negotiations with the United States: "The U.S. imperialists have worked hard to disarm the DPRK under the name of 'improvement of relations,' while escalating its military pressure upon the DPRK. However, the Korean people have taken firm and resolute measures against their moves, neither yielding to their military pressure nor being taken in by any appeasement and deception." The KPA, the communication concluded, stood ready to win another Korean War.[71] Lacking more recent evidence of U.S.-DPRK or North-South confrontational policies, the KPA's argument against diplomatic progress was weakened. Central authorities did not register any sympathy with the KPA's argument.

The cabinet had enjoyed a string of recent policy wins, but they were not permanent. Engagement continued in a stop-and-go fashion. Working-level U.S.-DPRK talks in mid-November 1999 failed to produce results, while Japan and North Korea announced the following month that they would resume normalization talks that had been stalled since 1992.[72] At the end of January 2000, North Korea agreed to send a delegation to Washington to discuss the missile issue. However, by the end of March, the state had reversed itself: "We cannot visit the United States with the cap of a terrorist," according to the North Korean ambassador to China, Chu Chang Jun, referring to North Korea being on the terrorist list. Such a move would force North Korea to negotiate from a position of weakness, he reasoned.[73] Meanwhile, the state established new diplomatic relations with Western states, including Italy, Australia, and Britain.[74]

Pyongyang seemed to be moving generally in the direction of accommodation, although it would not abandon its brinkmanship tactics. Deciphering between tactics and strategic reversal is difficult but essential. When the cabinet raises a new demand, such as being removed from the terrorist list, just as an agreement is about to be concluded, it suggests a brinkmanship tactic to secure more concessions rather than a more strategic effort to abandon negotiations altogether. The party and the military's negotiating demands are more far-reaching, preventing any real possibility of acceptance by the other side: such as a complete and immediate withdrawal of U.S. troops from the Korean peninsula or South Korea joining the North in communism. Neither the military nor the party advanced the terrorist list removal demand this time, indicating the Foreign Ministry was just trying to get more out of the deal than was originally negotiated. Still, the tactic delayed the missile meeting until the following fall. In the interim, the two Koreas made historic progress toward easing tensions.

The June 13–15, 2000, summit in Pyongyang between South Korean president Kim Dae Jung and North Korean leader Kim Jong Il was the first summit between the two Koreas. Ending only ten days before the fiftieth anniversary of the start of the Korean War, Seoul and Pyongyang pledged to pursue wide-ranging cooperative endeavors aimed at reducing inter-Korean tensions and paving the way for eventual reunification. Kim Dae Jung argued that rapid absorption of North Korea, even if it could occur peacefully, would severely damage the South Korean economy.[75] Seoul sought international cooperation to develop and open North Korea's economy to pave the way for gradual reunification and to exert some leverage over Pyongyang in the process. Meanwhile, North Korea gained economically from this cooperation but some within the regime voiced concern that significant opening risked unraveling the state. They cited the former communist states of Europe as evidence that economic change precipitated political regime change. These distinct views between the DPRK bureaucracies came into sharp focus around the historic summit.

The cabinet argued that the political consequences of economic changes were manageable. Economic projects could be contained to avoid political consequences while providing a means to rehabilitate the North's dismal economy. Immediately following the April 8 announcement of the June summit, the cabinet quickly and publicly supported the inter-Korean dialogue. It is possible to infer that the cabinet even had a role in pushing the summit behind the scenes, considering that all other major actors were in opposition before and after the Summit announcement and had opposed earlier cabinet efforts to promote inter-Korean economic projects. Only two days after announcing the first inter-Korean summit, Premier Hong went on record in support of the talks: "Our people . . . fully support and concur with the North-South agreement reached on 8th April on holding highest-level talks between the two sides. They are also filled with the burning determination to expeditiously realize the fatherly leader's behest for the fatherland's reunification."[76]

During the summit, Kim Jong Il openly admitted to Kim Dae Jung that the party objected to the inter-Korean negotiations. Party Secretary Kim Yong-sun told South Korean president Kim Dae Jung that the U.S. military must remove all its troops from the peninsula. Kim Jong Il interrupted, "What problem would there be if the U.S. military remained?" Kim Yong-sun began presenting the party line, and Kim Jong Il again interrupted: "Secretary Yong-sun, stop that. Even though I try to do something, people under me oppose it like this."[77]

This incident could have been staged. However, North Korea's highest-level defector has described Kim as one who often publicly castigates senior officials on a whim.[78] Political psychologists note he is prone to impulsive remarks and stances.[79] In short, it is possible that this display actually reflected different bureaucratic positions within the state. Indeed, public debate in the North Korean media after the summit and a joint announcement of a dramatically new inter-Korean policy further suggest Kim's statement reflects the political reality in Pyongyang rather than an effort to deceive international observers.

Diplomatic progress between the two Koreas spilled over into U.S.-DPRK relations. Clinton administration officials announced on the final day of the inter-Korean summit that the United States would drop an array of sanctions against North Korea and leave open the possibility of removing the DPRK from the terrorist list.[80] Two days later Secretary of State Madeleine Albright announced a newly scheduled trip to South Korea and China and noted her intention to build on recent momentum to reach an agreement with North Korea to halt its missile launches.[81] North Korea responded quickly, announcing its suspension of missile launches during Albright's trip to the region. The United States pledged to reopen missile talks with North Korea on the development and proliferation of long-range missiles.[82]

The fiftieth anniversary of the start of the Korean War occurred on June 25. North Korea canceled its annual celebration of the anniversary. In South Korea, Kim Dae Jung scaled back the remembrance and used the holiday to highlight the importance of promoting inter-Korean peace.[83] By the end of the summer, the two states had reached tentative agreements on family reunions, opening liaison offices, establishing military-to-military communications (e.g., hotlines), economic cooperation, and rail and road connections across the DMZ.[84] North Korea joined the ASEAN Regional Forum (ARF) in July and sent its foreign minister to the ARF meeting. In August, Pyongyang held a ten-day meeting for the leaders of South Korea's major print and broadcast news outlets. South Korea repatriated sixty-three North Korean spies serving prison sentences in the South, and Kim Jong Il's aide, Kim Yong-sun, visited Seoul to reaffirm inter-Korean economic projects. The cabinet's agenda was on a roll, and the party and military were marginalized for the time being.

U.S.–North Korean negotiations proceeded apace on the missile issue. Russian president Vladimir Putin announced that Kim Jong Il had voiced support for a deal that would allow foreign governments to launch satellites on North Korea's behalf. Such a deal would permit North Korea to maintain and advance its rudimentary satellite presence and the accompanying economic benefits without worrying the region and the United States about its missile capability. The North Koreans asserted that this offer had been made in jest, raising questions about whether the offer had been miscommunicated or had been rescinded due to reconsideration of the idea.[85]

During this period, missiles and nuclear developments dominated the U.S. agenda for negotiating with the North. Based on interviews with senior North Korean officials and direct experience with the U.S. deliberators, Bob Carlin and John Lewis concluded that bureaucratic politics helped explain Pyongyang's reaction to U.S. negotiation efforts:

In some cases, the United States faced perplexing DPRK demands or delays, which were often connected to turf battles within the DPRK. For issues on which the DPRK Foreign Ministry had the lead—and that meant virtually anything directly connected with the Agreed Framework—the Americans could usually arrange meetings with minimal difficulty. Issues outside the clear purview of the Agreed Framework, by contrast, raised problems because they engaged competing bureaucracies within the DPRK hierarchy. As noted above, the missile talks were difficult for many years because the Foreign Ministry could not make a convincing case that this subject was a significant foreign policy issue for the ministry rather than purely (or mostly) a subject that fell to those elements in the Workers' Party and the military involved with the production and sale of missiles. In this instance, moreover, the Foreign Ministry had an even more difficult case to make, not least because the United States did not act if it were seriously concerned about the issue, and which it did not begin to do until 1999. Before that, the talks never had a chance to develop a momentum of their own or move beyond mere repetition of the U.S. position. Repetition of talking points, not surprisingly, was never sufficient to put the message through to the right places in the DPRK leadership on a priority basis.[86]

In October 2000 President Clinton's time in office was short. His administration rushed to make progress on the missile issue. With less than three months left in the second term, President Bill Clinton, Secretary of State Madeleine Albright, and Secretary of Defense William Cohen met in Washington with North Korea's second-highest-ranking official, Vice Marshal Cho Myong-rok. The North sent a uniformed official but one representing the state; Cho carried a letter from Kim Jong Il. Both sides signed an agreement to "improve fundamentally their bilateral relations. . . . The two sides agreed to work together to develop mutually beneficial economic cooperation and exchanges to explore the possibilities for trade and commerce. . . . To further the efforts to build new relations, the DPRK informed the U.S. that it will not launch long-range missiles of any kind while talks on the missile issue continue. . . . It was agreed that Secretary of State Madeleine Albright will visit the D.P.R.K. in the near future . . . and to prepare for a possible visit by the President of the United States."[87]

Later that month Secretary of State Albright visited Pyongyang. Both governments labeled the trip productive, but high-level commitment to improved relations soured as technical discussions the following month yielded no results.[88] Citing the ongoing Supreme Court battle in late 2000 over who won the U.S. presidency, President Clinton decided to forego a U.S.-DPRK summit and left the missile issue to his successor.

In 2001 North Korea's movement on the missile issue and inter-Korean reconciliation again became disjointed. Pyongyang adjusted its policy toward the United States considerably as the incoming Bush administration defined a new approach. Pyongyang reacted in predictable ways as the cabinet's continued advocacy for a negotiated solution became more difficult to sustain. Party and military positions on U.S. policy began winning out internally. They effectively argued that the United States sought to "suffocate" North Korea and foster rapid regime change. Nevertheless, the state showed its ability to pursue distinct policy lines on U.S. policy, reunification, and economic management. The cabinet focused on maintaining its momentum in inter-Korean relations and market-based economic construction.

The first twenty-seven months after North Korea's September 1998 constitutional revision saw tremendous institutional jostling for bureaucratic supremacy and agenda control. The party tried to treat the military and cabinet as its subordinates, directing policy through an ideologically guided lens. The military and cabinet resisted this power grab. The constitutional revision formally made them peer institutions, thus diluting the party's ability to dictate to the others. The military's and cabinet's fighting back against the party's assertion of continued dominance reflected interinstitutional jostling over specific policy questions. Institutions advocated and even implemented policy preferences that contradicted each other.

Although central arbitration between institutional policy positions remains hidden from view, policy was markedly uncoordinated in the early months after the announcement of the new constitution. The three institutions simultaneously implemented contradictory policies, leading some observers to note that these contradictions posed a theoretical puzzle for the monolithic interpretations of the North Korean state. If policy was defined at the top, how did one explain the fundamental contradictions pursued simultaneously in North Korean policy? The post-totalitarian institutionalism model helps explain this puzzle.

The party, military, and cabinet held distinct policy outlooks on a broad array of strategic policy questions. They debated policy in the controlled media and advanced institutionally consistent policy platforms. National policy varied as central authorities selected between one of the policy options presented from below. Policy innovation did not originate from the "nerve center." In every major case, policy was first proposed by one of the state's institutional organs. The range of policy alternatives is more restrained and predictable than previous analyses have allowed. Kim may be impulsive, but a close reader of the North Korean press can delineate the type and scope of North Korea's policy responses to external events.

This chapter demonstrates not only distinct institutional views and advocacy, but the critical role of these institutions in defining the agenda. Though Kim and his central leadership are not bound by these options, they have generally selected from a range of ideas presented and debated between these institutions. The North Korean system is more inclusive of a wider group of elite opinion and more pluralistic than previous characterizations have suggested. Institutional debates are prevalent and observable, and they provide the contemporary analyst charged with predicting North Korean actions an opportunity to critically narrow the body of possible actions by looking at those being seriously discussed within the regime. Recognizing the drivers of North Korean strategic decision making further reduces the uncertainty laden in any effort to predict a state's meaningful actions.

Chapter 6 evaluates a distinct time period after North Koreans generally agreed in the press that the external environment had changed. It provides another opportunity to confirm or deny the empirical validity of this new model's theoretical expectations. It also shows how institutional positions remained constant but central authorities responded to the new U.S. policy with a confrontational policy. The state also compartmented its U.S. policy from inter-Korean and economic marketization efforts. In short, North Korea continued its pattern as a post-totalitarian institutional state beyond the time frame analyzed in this chapter.

CHAPTER SIX

Segmenting Policy and Issue Linkages, 2001–2006

From 2001 to 2006 North Korea continued to react to its external environment. The three major bureaucracies maintained their general policy frameworks, and the state pursued a moderately varying policy. This period demonstrates how Pyongyang can segment different aspects of its policy. Each institution advocated a comprehensive platform, but each could only pursue part of its agenda at a given time. During this time, institutions tried to extend policy wins in one area by arguing that other issues were closely related and therefore should be linked to the original policy question. The most significant instance of this linkage strategy was found in U.S. policy. With the downturn in U.S.-DPRK relations, the party and the military enjoyed greater freedom in this area and repeatedly attempted to link the United States with South Korea and with marketization efforts in hopes of stemming the cabinet's agenda in those areas as well. The linkage strategy failed as Washington and Seoul diverged significantly on North Korea policy, and Pyongyang's central leadership pursued distinct policies toward the two allies. Though the party and the military cited contemporary examples of what they termed the United States' "hostile policy" to put U.S.-DPRK diplomatic progress on hold, central leadership still accepted the cabinet's advocacy of inter-Korean projects and marketization efforts at the same time, demonstrating how Pyongyang can separate issue areas.

The Bush administration reviewed Washington's North Korea policy in the first few months of 2001. During this period, the North Korean bureaucracy debated its future direction toward the United States, but the state deferred major changes until the end of Washington's policy review. The policy review concluded in the summer of 2001 that engagement was the only option but before it could be implemented, terrorists struck the United States on September 11, 2001. Washington's focus changed to fighting terrorists and state sponsors of terrorism. Citing statements by high-level officials, including the 2002 "axis of evil" State of the Union Address, party and military officials argued that North Korea too might be targeted for regime change operations. In late 2002 U.S.-DPRK relations hit a low point as Pyongyang concluded that the United States "abrogated" the Agreed Framework. Party and military calls to scrap the Agreed Framework won out as the state reversed course, ending its eight-year nuclear freeze of the Yongbyon nuclear complex and moving to withdraw from the Non-Proliferation Treaty.

The U.S.-DPRK relationship was only one of the three major issues at play during this period. Inter-Korean relations and marketization efforts proceeded on a different track. Inter-Korean relations generally improved as the liberal South Korean presidents Kim Dae Jung (1998–2003) and Roh Moon-hyun (2003–8) prioritized inter-Korean engagement where the previous conservative governments in Seoul had pursued tougher lines. The North Korean cabinet likewise pushed an agenda of inter-Korean rapprochement. Party and military actors tried to undermine inter-Korean projects by linking Seoul to Washington, now seen in Pyongyang as especially hostile. The tactic had some limited success but central authorities seemed to recognize the stark differences between Seoul's and Washington's policies.

North Korea's marketization also progressed during this period. The cabinet actively pushed economic changes, and on July 1, 2002 the state introduced significant wage and price reforms. The party objected to these "capitalist" impulses on ideological grounds, and military officials openly worried about foreign ideas seeping across the border as trade intensified. Defectors and spies could penetrate the state more easily, they argued in the press. Though the state has implemented several market reforms, it has not yet shown a deep, irreversible commitment toward reforming its economy, mirroring the contradictory positions of institutional opponents.[1]

Internal debate continued in the press on all three issue areas, and central authorities selected from the universe of policy options presented from below. These discussions took place prior to policy decisions. Though the internal social and economic situation, along with South Korean and Chinese aid decisions, seemed to drive central authorities' decisions on marketization, Pyongyang again demonstrated a reactive orientation in its U.S. policy and inter-Korean efforts. North Korea's institutions presented distinct policy lines, but the external environment pushed central authorities toward one institution's policy advocacy over another's.

Toward Economic Reform

Pyongyang debated and made preparatory moves toward marketization during the U.S. policy review, but it refrained from announcing any major changes. As President Bush was sworn in to office in 2001, Kim Jong Il made a trip to Southern China. The trip was noteworthy as it provides rare insight into how Kim arbitrates between competing interests below him. Kim took an unusually large and diverse delegation on this lengthy trip to China's financial centers and special economic zones. In Kim's rare trips abroad, he usually takes only a few senior Foreign Ministry and party officials. This time, however, he took multiple senior members of the party, military, and cabinet organizations. He brought all the major players needed to establish a coherent, long-range economic policy for the state. The state moved significantly toward marketization plans, but it did not implement these changes while relations with the United States remained in limbo. Full realization of economic opening required improved relations with the United States to provide security amid opening.

The delegation visited cities that had developed rapidly since 1985 under China's relatively open economic arrangement for these areas. The most important stop was in China's main financial center, Shanghai. Kim Jong Il had last visited Shanghai in 1983, when its level of development was roughly akin to Pyongyang's. Kim was reportedly shocked at the differences between Pyongyang and Shanghai when he returned in 2001 despite being briefed prior to the trip.[2] North Korea's press coolly noted that "Comrade

Kim Jong Il expressed his opinions on visiting Shanghai, which has changed beyond the imagination of the world's people in a short period of time." Privately, he reportedly exploded in anger, harshly scolding the party secretary in charge of reunification, Kim Yong-sun, upon seeing how far Shanghai had eclipsed Pyongyang. Those close to Kim report that he is subject to fits of rage and his uncontrollable screaming can "shake the windows."[3] His screaming was so loud that foreigners could hear his words through a door. The Dear Leader blamed the KWP secretary for Pyongyang's insufficient development—when every major institutional actor had representatives in the room. He seemed to blame the party's economic model for the state's lack of development; the state soon thereafter departed in some substantial ways from this economic model.

The North Korean media reported that the premier of the Chinese State Council Zhu Rongji allegedly congratulated the Korean Workers' Party on its "correct leadership" that had "reaped big achievements in all sectors." Kim Jong Il replied publicly, however, that Shanghai "carried the sublime ideal . . . demonstrating pride on the land of China." He lauded China's "cataclysmic change," approving of Shanghai's specific development path that incorporated substantial marketization and special economic zones.[4] China and North Korea have long had a tenuous relationship. North Korea has attempted to assert its sovereign place as an equal while being concerned that China treats it as a younger brother. It would not be an easy decision for a North Korean leader—especially if he was primarily committed to a nationalist ideology—to follow China's lead, but within a few months, Kim had empowered the cabinet to take a different approach to economic development that borrowed some steps from China's early reform path.

The party minimized Kim's statements, which touched off a debate after Kim's decision. It did not simply accept the supreme leader's pronouncement, and the cabinet still had to engage the party to pursue its economic agenda that Kim authorized. Again, this resistance shows the relative autonomy of North Korean institutions in advancing the organization's interests. The fact that the party would cautiously dispute the wisdom of Kim's pronouncement is more significant than the substance of their argument.

The party argued that socialism improved the state's material condition in face of distinct crises that China never faced. China's experience simply was not particularly relevant. The party tapped into the anti-Chinese, Korean nationalist sentiment by presenting the party's goals as a moral imperative that should be judged by historical, not short-term, standards. The party's achievements were more comprehensive than a narrow reading of the economy. Viewing all three issue areas together, the party argued, it had created a dignified, Korean system in line with revolutionary principles:

> [Chinese] general secretary Comrade Jiang Zemin expressed satisfaction with the fact that the DPRK people have overcome manifold difficulties and achieved significant developments and new achievements in many sectors, including economic construction, North-South reunification, and foreign relations under the leadership of the DPRK's Workers' Party . . . our people regard living and carrying out the revolution under a superior socialist system by upholding the great leader and under the party's strong leadership, as the utmost dignity and pride. They are also overflowing with the firm determination to advance toward the independent road, the socialist road, which they selected to the end.[5]

The party noted its involvement in all three strategic issue areas, pushing North Korea's specific, "superior" variety of socialism. Their position, they claimed, exemplifies what it means to be Korean, for which Koreans have struggled for centuries. Koreans are not Chinese, and the party defends the Korean way.

The cabinet's economic journal shot back with its own spin on socialist ideology, nationalism, and the party's proper role. The cabinet criticized the party's position as focused only on the short-term morality of individual actions without recognizing the downstream consequences of building a socialist utopia. Through promoting "actual profits," the DPRK could return to the socialist paradise and civilized life in line with its revolutionary principles: "We are accelerating the construction of a powerful state while highly displaying superiority of socialism in all fields of revolution and construction. However, this is not merely intended to overcome impending economic difficulties but to turn our nation into a paradise of people where people would enjoy a better wealthy life. For us to resolve the problems on life including the food problem and to make a breakthrough in building

an economic power, we should thoroughly discard shortsighted work attitude and work style in overall economic works. It is particularly important
to ensure actual profits."[6] These two institutions offer competing ideas of
moral action and pride in Korea's specific path. The party focuses on the
road—the individual action—to determine its morality; the cabinet injects
the consequences of actions into the decision-making calculus.

The cabinet publication instructs workers on how to produce agricultural products "in the Juche method" albeit according to foreign prices and
"investment effectiveness." The cabinet tried to stretch the flexible Juche
ideology to justify its policies, but the argument was tenuous. Economic
data tended to favor the cabinet's position; marketization proved more economically beneficial in contemporary North Korea than the party's socialist
push. However, the party's advocacy enjoyed an ideological advantage; it
represented the socialist principles more simply and more clearly. Neither
side conceded either the empirical or the ideational debate completely,
which reinforced the ideology versus pragmatism back-and-forth.

As part of its refusal to cede the anti-Chinese, nationalist position to the
party, the cabinet portrayed marketization efforts—even if it had parallels
in China—as "Korean-style socialism." It did not cite the Chinese experience as justification for its policies, rather this was used to discredit the
moves internally. Nevertheless, the cabinet remained on the defensive on
these questions, as their party and military critics drew parallels to China
and Eastern Europe. The Eastern European example was used more often
by marketization's internal critics: the cabinet's position risked unraveling
the socialist system and collapsing the state. For North Korean elites, this
was something to be avoided.

Kim's authorizing the cabinet's economic position based at least in part
on his observations in Southern China indicates a degree of pragmatism
in his decision making. He essentially worked as an unwitting comparativ-
ist, viewing the outcomes of China's distinct policy path with some envy.
Ideological and nationalist arguments about the morality of the decision
itself or the "Korean-ness" of the policy failed to dissuade a policy change.
Likewise, party contentions that the cabinet effectively cited a spurious cor-
relation between marketization and development failed to persuade central
authorities. The tremendous differences that had grown between Shanghai
and Pyongyang seemed to push the state to develop significant economic

changes similar to some early moves by Deng's China that Pyongyang would implement the following year.

The cabinet won this policy battle, but it did not stop the party from resisting the cabinet's authority. Within a month, an article in the government's newspaper appeared, demanding that the cabinet follow the "party's policy-level guidance . . . in this year's socialist economic construction."[7] The cabinet ignored the demand and pursued its economic agenda as the state's decided policy line. Indeed, it increasingly seemed that real power of the economy lay with the cabinet. Foreign business and government officials treated the cabinet as the key economic policy bureaucracy. Premier Hong met with the Russian railways minister Nikolay Aksenenko to discuss a highly lucrative project to connect South Korean and Japanese markets to Europe via North Korea and the Trans-Siberian railway. He did not meet with party or military representatives.[8] Likewise, several European ambassadors to the DPRK have noted that their official business, most notably including economic cooperation efforts, flow almost exclusively through the cabinet bureaucracy. The party is not interested in meeting with them to discuss projects that require some degree of opening.[9] The cabinet had an increased role in economic affairs, but it would still take several months for Pyongyang to decide on its specific course of action. At the end of 2001 central authorities reportedly decided to inject more market mechanisms into the North Korean economy; they began implementing these changes on July 1, 2002.

Issue Linkages: Inter-Korean and U.S. Policy

Pyongyang's inter-Korean policy remained ill defined during this period as the state considered whether to segment warming inter-Korean relations from cooling DPRK-U.S. relations. Party officials considered negotiating with South Korea as an affront to the state's dignity. The party could only support inter-Korean talks if the South met all of the North's core demands before negotiations began.[10] The party again showed that it did not measure success or failure based on pragmatic metrics but on the morality of the act itself; the party tried to monopolize the moral discourse, citing its role as the authoritative interpreters of Juche. Predictably, the cabinet refuted the party by citing the need for continued inter-Korean projects for economic advancement.

South Korean president Kim Dae Jung prioritized inter-Korean cooperation and planned a trip to Washington to convince the new administration to follow his lead. The dynamic Kim was reportedly convinced he could get Washington on board, allowing inter-Korean policy to transform North Korean society, economics, and eventually, politics. By most accounts, the March 2001 summit was a disaster.[11] The South Korean media speculated widely that if Washington moved away from the Agreed Framework, it might kill Kim Dae Jung's sunshine policy. The South Korean president would have a difficult time convincing his divided political landscape to continue to follow the sunshine path.[12] As it would turn out, Pyongyang's reaction to the summit was a greater concern than South Korean internal politics. Party commentaries claimed the summit demonstrated that Washington only had aggressive intent, so the KPA stood ready to fight another war.[13] The state followed the party's advocacy and postponed inter-Korean ministerial meetings two weeks later.

However, two weeks passed between the U.S.-ROK summit and Pyongyang's postponement announcement. In the interim, North Korea made several conciliatory gestures toward the South. Pyongyang allowed separated families to exchange six hundred letters—an important South Korean demand—only two days after the summit. Furthermore, North Korea sent an unprecedented delegation to Seoul to express the state's condolences at the funeral of Chung Ju-yung, the founder of South Korea's largest *chaebol*, Hyundai. Only after two weeks of internal debate did North Korea take action by postponing—not canceling—scheduled inter-Korean ministerial meetings. The weak response demonstrated that Pyongyang sought to register its displeasure but had not yet given up on engagement with Seoul or Washington. Central authorities could select a middle path between different institutional positions. Importantly, North Korea's post-totalitarian institutionalism moderated state policy in both a general sense and in specific instances—a point taken up again in the concluding chapter. The following month, the North Korean cabinet reached out to Washington.

Cabinet Premier Hong addressed the Supreme People's Assembly to present his economic vision and extend a foreign policy olive branch. This is the most high-profile speech the cabinet premier regularly delivers each year. After giving the necessary accolades to the party and socialism, the cabinet premier described his dual commitment to market incentives and promoting "friendly" relations with the United States. "In keeping with the changed environment and conditions, the cabinet will uniquely pioneer the method of the management and operation of the socialist economy in our own way. All the sectors and units of the people's economy should thoroughly embody the demand of the Taean work system, properly combine the state centralized uniform guidance with the creative ingenuity of lower units in economic management, and strictly apply the socialist principle of distribution so that everyone can work to his best ability and get paid according to the work done."

The premier advocated modifying the very essence of the 1960s-era communist (Taean) work system with monetary incentives for individual workers; Taean specifically sought to root out this type of individualism. He placed his institution's advocacy within a specifically Korean context, protecting his argument against critics charging it betrayed the nation. Future commentaries modified the "socialist economy in our own way" language to "our-style socialism" or "Korean-style socialism," indicating again the continued importance of nationalist sentiment and how all institutional actors tried to tap that nationalism.

Hong also discussed the cabinet's Juche foreign policy. The cabinet interpreted this ideological phrase as promoting friendly relations with all countries and without mentioning confronting the United States militarily, "In the future, we will continue to implement our Juche-oriented foreign policy in a consistent manner, and develop friendly and cooperative relations with other nations so that the sovereignty of our country and the dignity of our nation shines even more. We will expand and develop great unity in a full-fledged manner with *all countries* of the world who are *friendly to our country*" (emphasis added).[14] If Washington decided to pursue cooperative relations with the DPRK, the cabinet could push for reciprocal action. The premier's major speech is noteworthy not because the regime claimed to be peace loving, but because it came amid constant party commentaries calling for confronting the imperialists and developing the state's military capabilities instead of negotiating.

In May 2001 Kim Jong Il authoritatively announced that the jury was still out on the North's strategic direction in relation to the United States. Institutions debated policy options for months, but Kim had not yet made a decision. He pledged to a high-level EU delegation in Pyongyang led by

Swedish prime minister Goran Persson in his position as president of the EU that North Korea would "wait and see" about the Bush administration's policy review. The state was at a fork in the road; institutions defined the paths ahead in different directions, but the final direction would be decided by Kim on his and his institutional advisers' interpretations of Washington's new policy. In the meantime, North Korea pledged a unilateral moratorium on launching long-range missiles until 2003 despite objections from the military. Kim Dae Jung welcomed the announcement and said he hoped Washington would resume missile talks with Pyongyang.[15] The U.S. deputy secretary of state Richard Armitage announced Washington would resume negotiations with Pyongyang within a few weeks as the policy review was reaching its conclusion.[16]

Selig Harrison, an American scholar, traveled to Pyongyang the following month. He warned that the perception of a tougher line in Washington's policy had emboldened hard-liners within the DPRK: "What I sensed in this visit is that the hard-liners in North Korea have gotten a new lease on life as a result of the Bush administration. They have put North-South progress on hold and I am afraid they will continue to gain strength unless the tone of the administration changes and the Bush administration reiterates its commitment to pursue normalization."[17] Some may dismiss Harrison's "sense" that hard-liners were gaining as nonfalsifiable interpretation of meetings of one engagement advocate. But the wider point is that Harrison's interviews document differences of opinion among elites and their willingness to express differences to a foreigner.

Indeed, in advance of a decision from Kim, North Korea pursued divergent policies simultaneously. North Korea's bureaucracies acted in accordance with standard operating procedures and contradicted one another but did not take any truly bold decisions. The KPA indicated its willingness to launch more short-range missiles—a regular occurrence—and sent its naval vessels south of the NLL again, prompting another clash with the South Korean navy on the anniversary of the Korean War's outbreak.[18] As the two Korean navies engaged each other in the West Sea again, the cabinet hosted a unification forum at Mount Kumgang on North Korea's east coast, celebrating the one-year anniversary of the June 15 declaration on North-South cooperation. Official representatives from the two Koreas attended the forum, South Korean visitors continued to vacation at Mount Kumgang, and inter-Korean trade set another new record high.[19] However,

Yongbyon remained verifiably frozen and the state refrained from test-firing any long-range missile systems. Central authorities waited for a critical variable to decide which road to take and which bureaucracies to empower. Kim seemed to be still committed to "waiting and seeing" as he pledged to the EU delegation. He would not have to wait much longer.

Pyongyang Reacts to New U.S. Policy

The completed U.S. policy review concluded in late July that the United States should engage North Korea. Secretary of State Colin Powell announced the administration's "strong support" for Kim Dae Jung's sunshine policy and the United States' willingness to meet the North Koreans anytime, anyplace without precondition.[20] The announcement was good news for the cabinet, but the North Korean media did not sound off in response. It only repeated standard calls for the United States to remove all troops from the Korean peninsula and reiterated the party's "principled stand" against the United States.[21] After waiting for months for the result of this policy review and debating courses of action, one would have expected a robust response in short order, but Pyongyang's bureaucracies did not reply for weeks.

When Powell announced the result of the policy review, Kim was en route to Moscow via the Trans-Siberian railroad.[22] It is unclear if no one left in Pyongyang had the authority to respond to the U.S. proposal in the North Korean media or whether doing so would have little utility with the main decision maker away for the next month. Only upon Kim's return did the bureaucracies begin presenting their contradictory views on the policy review in the official press. This seemed to suggest at the very least that Kim's train contained the core audience of the institutional debate. However, before Pyongyang reached a conclusion on the U.S. policy review, new instructions coming out of Kim's trip to Russia intervened to change the emphasis of debate.

Upon Kim's return from his summit meetings with the Russian president, all North Korean media outlets ran editorials lambasting the United States' pursuit of missile defense and the U.S. "exaggeration" of North Korea's missile threat. This was certainly not the first time Pyongyang objected to U.S. missile defense plans, but it was a notable increase. Putin sought North Korean assistance on missile defense for over a year. North Korean missile launches strengthened Washington's arguments in favor of deploying the high-tech defense despite Russian and others' objections. The North Korean Broadcast Station even read a translated Russian newspaper article on the air that rejected U.S. pressure on North Korea as an excuse to create a missile threat to justify missile defense. North Korea also focused its speech at the UN General Assembly that month on denouncing missile defense and the U.S. decision to withdraw from the Anti-Ballistic Missile Treaty as creating a new nuclear arms race.[23]

Kim's Moscow trip helped the cabinet's position. Presumably, this highly unusual spike in missile defense discussions stemmed from Kim's personal instructions after his summit meetings with Putin. This incident demonstrates how Kim can get information from sources other than his own regime and act on it. Such sources of information are notable and significant but not regular. For the purposes of this study, the military's resistance to Kim's position is the most significant point. Flight tests provide the military with technical information to develop their missile systems, but they also undermine ongoing diplomatic efforts. In this case, the Russians likely opposed North Korean flight tests and convinced Kim to maintain his flight test moratorium. The cabinet did not need to convince Kim Jong Il and did not publish articles in support of the position at this time, but it tracks with their general policy preferences. Still, the party voiced opposition to Kim's policy.

The party called for a principled, independent foreign policy. The party regularly discussed issues with clear foreign policy implications, but it discusses them in an anti-imperialist context. It is rare to see the phrase "foreign relations" in a party article. The party's call for an independent foreign policy in this case, therefore, likely did not communicate a need to create policy independent of the United States (the imperialists), rather independent of some other country. The party likely was calling for Pyongyang to resist Russian influence to end missile launches to support Russia's antimissile defense agenda. The party called on the government to join it in asserting a principled, independent foreign policy.[24] The media response suggests that institutional actors can and do cautiously oppose Kim's policy guidance. Still, neither the party nor the military took observable action against Kim's policy line other than voicing dissent cautiously.

Before clearly deciding on a policy course in response to the U.S. policy review, Kim Jong Il decided to go to China. Kim traveled much more than normal during this period. He went to China the month after his Russia trip, suggesting the leader was considering significant policy choices and personally consulting with the major states around him. One day before Kim left for China in early September 2001, North Korea agreed to resume inter-Korean talks. China had long advocated North Korea's gradual economic opening, and Kim may have made the move in anticipation of Beijing's demand.

However, Pyongyang waited too long to reply to the U.S. policy review. International events interceded to block diplomatic progress. On September 11, 2001, terrorists attacked the United States. North Korea joined the international chorus in condemning international terrorism. Already a signatory to all the other major international conventions on terrorism, the Foreign Ministry announced in November that the state would sign the International Convention for the Suppression of Financing of Terrorism and the International Convention Against Taking Hostages. Washington's focus changed substantially and results of the policy review seemed to be erased as the White House recrafted its foreign policy, including policy that affected North Korea. Kim again stalled his response to U.S. policy, looking for Washington to focus on Northeast Asia.

Inter-Korean talks continued in the immediate aftermath of the terrorist attacks. In September and early October, the two Koreas held two successful meetings. However, after the United States invaded Afghanistan on October 7, the United States and South Korea placed their militaries on the Korean peninsula and elsewhere on alert. The security-conscious leadership in Pyongyang consistently voiced concern about military exercises and alerts. To register its objection, North Korea insisted that all family reunions take place only at Mount Kumgang, North Korea, citing security concerns from the raised alert status.[25] The October setback would seem minor. In November, inter-Korean relations hit a real snag. The Sixth Ministerial ended without agreement, marking the first time such a meeting had failed to make demonstrable progress since the June 2000 summit.[26] The sunshine policy's honeymoon period was over.

The party expanded their objections to inter-Korean economic projections. They modified their normal exhortation of capitalism to include a condemnation of marketization. Previously, the party had objected to "capitalism" but refrained from criticizing "market socialism" and cabinet calls for "actual profits."[27] Now, the party argued that markets destabilize the political system, and the state must return to planning the economy,

> Fully promoting the superiority of the socialist planned economy is one of the principled issues that emerge in the process of executing the party's ideas for constructing a powerful socialist state. . . . The superiority of a socialist planned economy over a capitalist market economy lies in its ability to guarantee the maximum economic gains. . . . In a market economy whose production is dominated by spontaneous and anarchical aspects due to a private ownership of the production means, it is unthinkable to rationally distribute the resources across the entire society. Pursuit of profits is a physiology of the capitalist market economy, and exclusive competition is the capital's fundamental method of survival.

In this period of heightened insecurity for North Korea, the party sought to reassert state control over society more firmly. Nevertheless, the prospects of inter-Korean meetings improved as South Korea removed its troops from alert status.[28]

Regime Change Short List Concern Closes Ranks

U.S.-DPRK relations deteriorated after 9/11, and Pyongyang responded to the new environment. In a December 1 speech in Asia, President Bush warned Iraq and North Korea that they would be "held accountable" if they developed weapons of mass destruction, and the January 29, 2002, State of the Union Address grouped Iran, Iraq, and North Korea together as an "axis of evil." The Foreign Ministry rejected Bush's "slanderous remarks," and an unattributed North Korean radio address focused on the U.S. military alert on the peninsula and repeated comments previously made by KPA officials, "We simply cannot casually overlook the violent remarks coming out of Bush's mouth." Pyongyang appeared to be united in opposition to the U.S. stand. Subsequent articles worried that U.S. regime change efforts would first concentrate on Iraq and move next to North Korea or Iran.

Two weeks after the State of the Union address, President Bush traveled to Seoul to meet with Kim Dae Jung. Bush told reporters that he remained open to negotiations with North Korea, but Kim Jong Il had failed to call him. Bush followed up by noting, "Yet I will remind the world that America will not allow North Korea and other dangerous regimes to threaten freedom with weapons of mass destruction."[29] He reiterated in Seoul that the United States had no intention of attacking North Korea and voiced support for the South's sunshine policy. He also questioned the character of his North Korean counterpart and voiced concern about human rights, North Korea's forward deployed conventional forces on the DMZ, and nuclear and missile issues. While the Clinton administration's goals had narrowed, Bush's goals vis-à-vis Pyongyang at the outset of his administration were more comprehensive. For a political establishment in Pyongyang concerned about U.S. intentions to force regime change, Bush's more comprehensive efforts to affect all of these issues simultaneously seemed to require a change at the source of each of these problems: the North Korean regime itself.

North Korean elites of all stripes took little stock in U.S. assurances that it had no intention of invading. KCNA cited Bush's "slander[ing] its political system" to sharply reject the U.S. offer to negotiate under these circumstances.[30] Party commentaries increasingly commented on individual foreign policy issues as the Foreign Ministry remained silent. Party commentaries cited U.S. officials' remarks in the following weeks—including issues as diverse as NPT commitments, nuclear weapons developments, human rights and religious freedom stances, and continued missile defense cooperation with Japan—as further evidence that the United States planned to "suffocate" and then invade the North.[31] The party spoke out against the Pentagon's unveiling a new nuclear policy document that recommended developing a nuclear weapon to target North Korea, Iran, Iraq, Libya, and Syria.

Despite the party's objection, the Foreign Ministry kept its meetings two days later in New York with U.S. negotiators. The New York talks did not immediately yield a commitment for higher level negotiations, but Pyongyang agreed to continue monthly technical meetings related to building the Light Water Reactor promised under the Agreed Framework.[32] However, four days later President Bush delivered another address during his five-day trip to Asia. The Foreign Ministry seized on his idea that the North

Korean political system must "change" as reiterating a U.S. regime change policy and noting that the state was "single heartedly united" against this policy. Faced with a perceived threat to the regime's very existence, the cabinet had little room to maneuver on U.S. policy and refocused its energies on inter-Korean and economic policy.[33]

The North Korean bureaucracies coalesced in opposition to engaging Washington for the time being. A party commentary indicated that "the DPRK can never pardon Bush for unhesitatingly slinging mud at the supreme headquarters of the DPRK and even calling for a 'change' in its people-centered political system, most dignified and independent, where the leader, the party and the masses form a harmonious whole. His outbursts once again betrayed his true colors. . . . The DPRK will not sit any longer with the Bush group keen on inventing pretexts for invasion in a bid to change the political system in the DPRK."[34]

Faced with a perceived threat to their existence, elites closed ranks. More significantly, the cabinet released a rare paper severely criticizing the United States and calling the United States, Japan, and Israel its own "axis of evil." The cabinet paper concluded that "the strained situation this month" required a rebuke, but the time element also left open the possibility of near term reversal.[35] Reversing the U.S. regime change policy—namely, recognizing the DPRK's right to exist—became a new prerequisite to resumed dialogue. The government emphasized that the DPRK was not boycotting talks. It blamed the United States for stifling genuine dialogue: "Dialogue is intended to discuss problems candidly and frankly between the two parties with equal qualifications through a meeting and to seek ways for a solution to the problem. However, in a situation that one side hurts the feelings of the other without hesitation and furthermore, one side does not recognize the other, how can dialogue be held? . . . We cannot concede our ideology and system being pressed by the United States nor can we renounce the revolutionary principle."[36]

The cabinet paper concluded in a call to reject the regime change policy and return to negotiations on their terms, "Dreaming a silly dream is worse than not dreaming anything, and the faster one comes out of a dream, the better."[37] The cabinet took a tougher line with Washington than previously but did not make particularly unrealistic demands like the military and the party did.

The United States responded. Vice President Dick Cheney repeated the axis of evil reference, drawing predictable criticism from party organs. The United States announced it had developed new tactical nuclear weapons for targeting seven countries, including North Korea and its underground military facilities. The cabinet's efforts to reengage Washington failed. The Foreign Ministry responded by announcing its own "comprehensive review" of the Agreed Framework. The institution said the review was warranted, since the new U.S. policy threatened the existence of the state. Pyongyang should study options before responding.[38] This effectively silenced moderates in the regime seeking a negotiated solution to outstanding differences. Kim did not need to mediate between competing interests. By 2002 the state was united in opposition to engaging the United States for the time being. Institutions focused their debates instead on economics and inter-Korean policy.

Linking and Delinking Issue Areas

With its foreign policy agenda stifled, the cabinet put its energies into its economic agenda. The government's quarterly economic journal argued for the need to "achieve informatization in all sectors of the people's economy" most notably in planning itself. The article called for increased use of Information Technology and rational information to guide decisions. The journal emphasized the need for data that was "characteristically different" from the previous mode of purely ideological policy inputs.[39] The role of economic technocrats was on the rise as the role of party ideologues eroded.

Government and party organs debated whether markets were compatible with a socialist system. The government held that markets are not antisocialist. It outlined a history of the term "markets" and argued that they were essential to a socialist economy. The government document distinguished between socialist markets and capitalist markets, desperately trying to avoid the pejorative label "capitalist." The government journal argued:

Properly resolving the issue of markets—a realm where products are circulated through the commodity-money relation—is an essential demand for more properly satisfying the residents' demands and for stepping up the socialist economic construction. . . . What has been elucidated anew in the Juche-oriented theory regarding the socialist domestic market for the circulation of production means is, above all, that the essential difference between the socialist domestic market and the capitalist market has been disclosed from a completely new perspective by fully clarifying the socialist market characteristics as an organized market with a unique theory concerning the character-istic of the commodity-money relation in the socialist society.[40]

Through Korean uniqueness, the power of Juche allowed the state to incor-porate markets into socialism.

The party responded by repeating its claim that markets are capitalist—period. They should be opposed by all good socialists. The party's piece repeated the phrase "capitalist market economy" twenty-seven times and concluded that "progressive people . . . should entertain absolutely no kind of fantasy about the capitalist market economy," referring to their govern-ment counterparts advocating increased marketization.[41] Party commentar-ies also warned against the abuse of information technology (IT). Markets, combined with IT, produce "casino capitalism" and dangerous financial speculation. Further, trade brings increased international communica-tions and increased risks of drug trafficking, mafias, globalization, and the "criminal gang [that] discuss actions to be taken via e-mail or 'online con-ferences.'" Increased information flow meant a "world without borders and guards," in this case, a situation infused with a negative connotation.[42] While the cabinet noted the benefits of marketization and increased inter-national trade, the party focused on possible drawbacks.

The debate extended into the education sector. After Kim Jong Il decreed that economic training at universities should reflect "developing realities" instead of ideology, the party resisted, publishing a commentary that inter-preted this guidance to "foster students to be revolutionaries and patriots before being intellectuals under the guidance of party organizations . . . [while] at the same time . . . strengthened the training on practical tech-niques and skills."[43] The party downplayed the disparity between teaching ideologically correct economics and empirically grounded economic theo-ries. The party continued to assert that functionaries should be subordinate to the party's ideological guidance and opposed efforts that enhanced the training of the next generation with a less ideological bent.

By mid-April 2002, ten weeks before the July 1 reform measure, there were no observable signs that the economic debate was going anywhere. However, with the North Korean uproar over the latest U.S.–South Korean military exercises quelled, North-South contacts resumed. The party stressed that the resumption of North-South dialogue was in spite of, rather than because of, U.S. pressure.[44] Red Cross representatives from the two Koreas agreed to restart family reunions and announced that the two sides agreed to "fully restore inter-Korean relations."[45] The party newspaper ran a commentary noting Kim Jong Il supported inter-Korean reconciliation through dialogue. However, the same article criticized the main conduit of South Korea's efforts to negotiate, the Ministry of Unification, and concluded by refocusing reunification efforts through militaristic terms.[46] The party recognized Kim Jong Il's decision but resisted its implementation.

The KPA again managed to disrupt inter-Korean contacts by provoking another naval clash. Inter-Korean naval clashes are fairly regular events. In June the KPA Navy crossed the disputed maritime border between the two Koreas ten times, mirroring a similar number the previous year. However, this time the two Koreas exchanged fire, and the North sank a South Korean patrol boat, killing five South Korean sailors.[47] A spokesman of the KPA's naval command stated the South Korean Navy perpetrated a "grave act of military provocation." The KPA navy placed the blame squarely on South Korea.[48] Three days later, the North Korean media shifted blame for the incident from the South Korean military to the United States. The unattributed television broadcast surmised that U.S. military surveillance must have detected the pending clash and aggravated the situation to undermine North-South reconciliation efforts. The KPA issued another statement, along with a party commentary, blaming both the United States and South Korea for the clash.[49] The military and the party were again seeking to link the United States to South Korea in internal debates.

Seoul placed its military on high alert and called North Korea's actions a violation of the armistice; the North claimed South Korean patrol boats operated in North Korean waters and the South Koreans fired first. The incident roiled the South Korean political establishment, but the public largely ignored the incident as the country was in the middle of hosting the World Cup. Meanwhile, within days of the deadly clash, Pyongyang warmly congratulated the South on its World Cup victories, leading some to call the confluence of events perplexing while others suggested that different North Korean actors might have simultaneously pursued different policy lines.[50]

South Korea hardened its rules of naval engagement and increased military surveillance with the United States. The United States cited the naval clash as the reason to cancel the following week's bilateral talks. Three weeks later, Pyongyang sent Seoul a letter expressing rare regret for the naval incident. South Korea accepted the North Korean apology. The KPA continued to reject the validity of the NLL and threatened more clashes in the West Sea. The party newspaper wrote: "The North-South dialogue has been suspended and North-South relations are also headed for a dangerous situation of confrontation and war." The day before the United States and North Korean military representatives met, the party ran another article calling the NLL an "illegal, unjust bogus line," and that "we cannot prevent the danger of military clash in the West Sea."[51]

With these seemingly conflicting signals and no definitive interinstitutional resolution, Washington attempted to engage North Korea. Secretary of State Colin Powell said he was "not ruling out" the possibility of meeting with North Korea's foreign minister Paek Nam Sun at the ASEAN Regional Forum after Pyongyang's "very positive statements," referring to the apology but not the provocative comments that followed. The informal fifteen-minute meeting between Powell and Paek set the stage for Jim Kelly, the assistant secretary of state for East Asian and Pacific affairs, to lead a small delegation to Pyongyang in October.[52]

Amid this activity, North Korea pursued significant economic policy change. On July 1, 2002, with hardly a mention in the North Korean press, the state implemented far-reaching economic reforms. The changes rationalized the exchange rate, dramatically increased prices on basic goods and salaries, and granted more autonomy to industrial and business managers. It helped turn money into a rational instrument of exchange, wiped out the value of retirees' and black marketers' savings (those who kept at least some wealth in cash), and narrowed the gap between black market and official exchange rates. The moves had a decentralizing effect intended to bolster economic growth. The premier was at the forefront of advocating the economic changes, and the government's advocacy demonstrated a willingness to risk certain political costs associated with lessened central control in exchange for greater economic efficiency.[53]

While the move was not immediately announced in the North Korean press, the party continued its warnings against capitalism. Capitalism in Eastern Europe brought regime downfall and pursuing profit contradicted socialist morals.[54] Markets, in the party's view, were roughly synonymous with capitalism. Characteristically, the cabinet was silent after its policy victory. It did not revel in its win but orchestrated a series of follow-on actions that extended the reforms.

Seoul seized the momentum, proposing more inter-Korean talks and bilateral talks between the United States and North Korea. Inter-Korean talks could not fully address the West Sea naval clashes. The U.S. has a dog in this fight. One month after the armistice failed to resolve the issue, the United Nations Command, led by a U.S. general, unilaterally declared the NLL the maritime boundary. Consequently, U.S. and North Korean generals needed to discuss means for resolving this dispute. Pyongyang reversed its position and agreed to the South Korean proposal to meet with a U.S. military representative. Meanwhile, inter-Korean talks on rail and road connections stalled despite South Korea's unilateral pledge to increase food aid to the North. In a prepared statement the North said: "Both sides agreed to make a proposal to their military." South Korean negotiators indicated the North Korean negotiators in the cabinet did not have the authority to agree to road and rail connections without the KPA's approval.[55] Pyongyang shifted course on economic policy, took modest steps to improve inter-Korean relations, and awaited a visit by U.S. negotiators to Pyongyang to refine its U.S. policy.

End of the Agreed Framework and the Second Nuclear Crisis

At the end of August 2002, the United States agreed to send a U.S. envoy to Pyongyang even as Washington announced new sanctions against North Korea.[56] The North Korean Foreign Ministry responded in a low-key manner—by privately asking Japanese negotiators in Pyongyang for normalization talks to help convince Washington to return to the table. Meanwhile, the party publicly denounced the new sanctions as further evidence of hostile U.S. policy.

John Bolton, a key U.S. proponent of applying more robust pressure strategy against North Korea, delivered a speech in Seoul reemphasizing

President Bush's axis of evil designation and highlighting North Korea's missile proliferation connections with states in the Middle East.[57] Pyongyang's bureaucracies again reacted according to the post-totalitarian institutionalism model. The party newspaper warned against a U.S. "preemptive strike" on North Korea, citing OPlan 5027, whereas the Foreign Ministry downplayed Bolton's remarks as "bereft of reason [and] therefore, his recent outbursts do not deserve even a passing note."[58] Pyongyang acknowledged divisions within Washington's foreign policy establishment on North Korea policy, and waited to see if the U.S. envoy would proceed along Bolton pressure path or the Powell engagement path.

North Korea delayed any decisions on U.S. policy until after Washington's envoy traveled to Pyongyang in October. But September was especially active for inter-Korean and DPRK-Japan relations. Inter-Korean family reunions continued, and Pyongyang announced its willingness to consider allowing such gatherings to take place in South Korea once a railroad connected the two Koreas across the DMZ. The defense ministers from the two Koreas agreed to clear enough landmines in the DMZ to connect the railroad. Cabinet Premier Hong attended the groundbreaking ceremony for the railroad, but despite the military's critical involvement in the negotiations, KPA and party representatives did not attend the ceremony.[59] Athletes from the two Koreas competed under a single flag in the Asian Games—doubly significant as the games were hosted in Pusan, South Korea. Also in September, North Korea pledged to open a special economic zone near the Chinese border to attract foreign investment.

The same month, Japanese prime minister Junichiro Koizumi visited Pyongyang for the first ever Japan-DPRK summit. In the resulting Pyongyang Declaration, Kim Jong Il admitted his country had abducted thirteen Japanese citizens, apologized, and pledged to extend the missile moratorium beyond 2003 in exchange for Prime Minister Koizumi's pledge to normalize relations.[60] Pyongyang's previous long-range missile launch in 1998 rattled Japan in particular, as the missile overflew the country. In each of these areas, the cabinet enjoyed significant policy wins. The summit with Japan was highly significant, but Pyongyang still put Washington at the center of their quest for security. The main event was the following month. In October the U.S. envoy reached Pyongyang.

Foreign Ministry representatives hosted their U.S. counterparts in Pyongyang. The party apparently did not approve. In a "special article" citing Kim Jong Il's guidance, the party newspaper uncharacteristically described the army as one that is "struggling for peace" in a defensive role. But the article concluded with an admonition to reject any "slavish peace" that accommodation with the imperialists may demand.[61] This passage again reflected a pattern in bureaucratic resistance. Articles must start with Kim Jong Il's position if a decision has already been made, but it can spin an interpretation of that decision to mean something very different. Each institution's statements and commentaries are generally consistent with the individual organization's outlook in the final conclusions if not the originating argument. The party emphasized defense and nuclearization at the very time that U.S. negotiators were in Pyongyang to get the state to move in exactly the opposite direction.

The Foreign Ministry's talks with their U.S. counterparts did not go well. The U.S. delegation left Pyongyang a day early without substantial comment. The Foreign Ministry publicly called the talks unproductive. The U.S. delegation confronted North Korea on its alleged uranium enrichment program. Two weeks later, Washington announced that the North Korean negotiators had admitted to having a uranium enrichment program—an admission one member of the six-person delegation called perplexing. The "admission" became the centerpiece of U.S. policy, noting that North Korea had admitted to cheating on the Agreed Framework, which justified rolling back U.S. commitments made during the Clinton administration[62]

The Foreign Ministry announced that talks broke down as "it has become clear, through the special envoy's explanation that the U.S. Bush administration is continuing to pursue—instead of dialogue—a hardline hostile policy."[63] The Foreign Ministry's statement cited Leon Sigal—a rare reference to an American in the North Korean press—whose work has recognized the division between hard-liners and negotiators within the North Korean system. The Foreign Ministry statement said that "the United States should treat the other party based on a clear understanding of it," suggesting the United States should recognize that North Korea had its own bureaucratic divisions, and the decision to pressure the North would "embolden hard-liners" as Sigal warned.

The Foreign Ministry continued, "Currently, the DPRK-U.S. Agreed Framework is facing the serious turning point of being nullified or not. . . . We say this once more: the lesson the United States should learn is that it will have nothing to gain from the hostile DPRK policy. Should the United

States faithfully implement the pledge it made *with us* and head in the direction of improving DPRK-U.S. relations, it will be commensurate with the U.S. people's interests" (emphasis added). [64] The term "with us" can be interpreted either as an agreement with the North Korean state or with the Foreign Ministry personnel advocating engagement. The statement suggests that the Foreign Ministry was on the verge of losing its bureaucratic battle. As the actual negotiators, the Foreign Ministry got the first word; the party and the military had stated their opposition to negotiations much more directly and forcefully.[65] Following the fallout, South Korea, Japan, Russia, and China all called on the United States to resume negotiations.[66]

Despite the most notable setback in U.S.-DPRK relations in almost a decade, it did not disrupt inter-Korean projects. The cabinet labeled inter-Korean cooperation "astonishing" and argued progress should be "expedited."[67] In November the two Koreas announced a substantial industrial zone just north of the DMZ in the historic city of Kaesong. The Kaesong Industrial Project broke ground the following year and become the centerpiece of South Korea's engagement strategy with North Korea. Meanwhile, South Korea and Japan actively advocated continued Korean Peninsula Energy Development Organization (KEDO) oil shipments to North Korea as outlined in the Agreed Framework as the United States pushed to stop the oil tanker in transit to the DPRK given the recent alleged uranium enrichment admission.[68] The United States diverged from its Asian allies on North Korea policy, and Pyongyang reacted to each state in turn.

The North Korean Foreign Ministry announced its view of the international situation, the recent developments in the inter-Korean and economic issue areas, and how stalled U.S.-DPRK relations could get back on track. It also asserted that the United States interpreter had not correctly translated Pyongyang's uranium enrichment message, claiming that negotiators said North Korea was "entitled to have nuclear weapons" rather than saying they "had nuclear weapons"—a one-syllable difference in the original Korean complicated by regional dialects. The Foreign Ministry statement stated its position for the following fifteen months as U.S.-DPRK negotiations faltered. It is worth quoting at length:

> Entering the new century, new, epoch-making changes are taking
> place in the Korean peninsula situation and the rest of the Northeast
> Asian region. . . . Bold actions have been taken to eradicate the old

leftovers of the past, including linking the North-South railways that were severed over half a century ago and liquidating the past with Japan. In line with the currently changed situation and our concrete situation, we have devised a series of new measures in economic management and back-to-back actions to boost the economy, including establishing a special economic region. All of these developments in the situation are practical contributions to peace in Asia and the rest of the world. Therefore, almost all the countries of the world, except for the United States, have supported and welcomed the developments, which greatly encouraged us. Under such circumstances, we recently received a U.S. presidential special envoy with the hope we might be able to fundamentally forsake hostile relations with the United States and solve pending issues on an equal footing. To our regret, however, we confirmed through the special envoy's visit that the Bush administration's hostile attempt to crush us by force and reverse the positive development of the situation on the Korean peninsula and in the rest of the Northeast Asian region has climaxed. Providing no concrete evidence, the U.S. special envoy asserted we were violating the DPRK-U.S. Agreed Framework by engaging in a program to enrich uranium with a view to manufacturing nuclear weapons. He said there would be no dialogue between the DPRK and the United States, and in particular, the DPRK-Japanese or North-South relations will be jeopardized unless we suspend the program. We could not help being stunned by the United States' much too unilateral and arrogant attitude. . . . We clearly told the U.S. presidential special envoy that we are entitled to have nuclear weapons and more powerful weapons than those to safeguard our sovereignty and right to survive. . . . We, with greatest magnanimity, clarified that we were ready to seek a negotiated settlement of this issue on the following three conditions: first, if the United States recognizes our sovereignty; second, if it assures us of nonaggression; and third, if the United States does not hinder our economic development. Nowadays, the United States and its followers assert that negotiations should be held after we put down our arms. This is a very abnormal logic. Then, how can we counter any attack with empty hands? Their assertion is virtually a demand that we yield. Yielding means death.

Concluding with another ambiguous "we," the Foreign Ministry said: "There may be negotiations or the use of deterrent force to be consistent with this basis, but we want the former, as far as possible."[69]

Party commentaries were less concerned with possible gains from negotiations. They railed against international aid, markets, and international accommodation.[70] Likewise, the KPA, citing Kim Il Sung and the Korean War experience, announced that the U.S. position amounted to a

> direct challenge to the great military-first politics, which is our life and dignity, and the cause of national sovereignty and reunification. . . . The United States blocks us, imposes sanctions on us, and gravely impinges on our right to exist, even forcing us to dismantle our armament. Historical experiences confirm that military-first politics is the wisest choice, based on the history of national tragedy in which the nation's sovereignty had been relentlessly abused by foreign powers. . . . In the name of the entire nation, they must strike a decisive blow on the United States' arrogant and rude maneuvers, which gravely threaten our nation's sovereignty, and more courageously wage a struggle against the U.S. imperialist forces of aggression.[71]

The state faced a choice, and the party strongly advocated one option over the other. At the same time Japan-DPRK normalization talks waned on unrelated grounds, and Japan continued to raise the nuclear issue to Pyongyang's dismay.[72] North Korea's Foreign Ministry responded that the "relevant organs" within the DPRK were pushing for an end to the missile moratorium, forcing the state to "reconsider" the moratorium. Foreign Ministry statements tend to be much less redundant than party commentaries, only rarely reiterating points to emphasize them, but this statement concluded by reiterating and expanding upon the political process sentiment: "Our related organizations and people are strongly calling on the DPRK Government to discreetly consider various issues concerning security guarantees, including the nuclear and missile issues, under the condition where Japan's words and actions regarding the DPRK-Japan Pyongyang Declaration's implementation do not match. In particular, our related sectors are even voicing the view that, should DPRK-Japan normalization talks become prolonged without making progress, like they did this time, the measure of extending the missile launch moratorium should be reconsidered."[73] The Foreign Ministry again explicitly cited proponents voicing distinct views that affect policy outcomes.

By the end of November, the KPA and "other organs" used the same construction, pushing for the reevaluation of the missile moratorium, "now that Japan is zealously joining in the U.S. policy to isolate and stifle the DPRK, there is no need for the DPRK to show such magnanimity as maintaining moratorium on missile test fire any longer. . . . The right-wing bellicose forces of Japan should not act rashly, clearly mindful that the Korean people's army and organs concerned of the DPRK are increasingly assertive for the reconsideration of the moratorium."[74] The KPA and cabinet came down on different sides of this issue, but they agreed that organs within the North Korean system advocated different policy responses regarding Japan.

Faced with failed negotiations with both the United States and Japan, the North Korean Foreign Ministry took concrete steps to salvage U.S.-DPRK relations. Instead of calling the Agreed Framework dead, Vice Foreign Minister Kang Sok Ju said the agreement was "hanging by a thread" and provided a means to get it back on track. In ten hours of talks, Kang, a political heavyweight in Kim's inner circle, told the former U.S. ambassador to South Korea Donald Gregg that the United States had misinterpreted the Korean statement when the U.S. envoy had visited Pyongyang the previous month. Kang said North Korea's chief nuclear negotiator Kim Kye Kwan responded to his U.S. counterpart's claim that North Korea was secretly enriching uranium by noting that North Korea was "entitled to" possess nuclear weapons and even stronger weapons, a common euphemism in North Korea for ideological strength. South Korea and China agreed with North Korea's account of the translation. But despite North Korea's attempt to clarify its position and linguists pointing out the possibility of translation error, the United States did not back off its position that North Korea had admitted to enriching uranium in violation of the Agreed Framework.[75] The Foreign Ministry's last-ditch effort to get negotiations back on track had failed.

Following North Korea's October 2002 "admission," Washington said North Korea must completely and verifiably dismantle its uranium enrichment program before U.S.-DPRK dialogue could resume.[76] Washington required that Pyongyang move first. North Korea's response was mixed. An unattributed broadcast reflecting the previous Foreign Ministry statement announced the DPRK wanted the two adversaries to "live peacefully with one another" and Pyongyang would consider giving up its nuclear program once the two sides concluded a nonaggression pact. The broadcast reasoned that absent a security guarantee from the United States, North Korea needed its nuclear deterrent.[77] However, the same day, the party newspaper said: "The U.S. escalated policy to stifle the DPRK by force of arms would only prompt the DPRK to step up its arms buildup to cope with the policy and further increase its army's combat capacity than ever before," and once again openly discussed the possibility of war.[78] Different opinions remained in Pyongyang's official circles. The Foreign Ministry could entertain giving up the North's nuclear weapons; but the party and the military opposed such a measure.

The United States maintained that it had no aggressive intentions toward North Korea as it encouraged KEDO to terminate fuel shipments, marking the end of the Agreed Framework. The Foreign Ministry argued that the United States violated the only provision of the Agreed Framework that it had begun to implement—oil deliveries—and urged Washington to uphold the agreement. The KPA did not support the resumption of the Agreed Framework. Rather, following the model's expectations, the KPA navy issued a statement that a skirmish between the two Koreas' navies must be a part of the U.S. pressure strategy and warned South Korea of the perils of associating with the United States.[79] The KPA was still trying to link the United States with South Korea. The cabinet's mild advocacy failed and the Agreed Framework was scrapped. The Foreign Ministry announced two weeks later that the state would resume construction on the plutonium reactor at Yongbyon that had been verifiably frozen for the previous eight years. Yongbyon would supply all of the nuclear material for North Korea's nuclear weapons test in 2006.[80]

The United States moved toward a strategy of further isolating North Korea economically, running into an obvious contradiction with South Korea's sunshine policy.[81] Barred constitutionally from reelecting Kim Dae Jung, South Korea elected a new liberal president, Roh Moo Hyun, who pledged to continue Kim Dae Jung's Nordpolitik.[82] China too continued to support economic engagement with North Korea, prodding the state to roughly follow its economic reform model. Wedged between these two states, the U.S. economic squeeze strategy faced serious difficulties.

With little meeting of the minds between Washington on one hand and Beijing and Seoul on the other, Secretary of Defense Donald Rumsfeld noted that the United States alone could defeat North Korea militarily even while engaged in a war with Iraq. At the same time, the United States continued to say it had no intention of invading North Korea. North Korea dismantled the monitoring equipment of the International Atomic Energy Agency (IAEA) and ordered its officials to leave the country. The government then began repairs on Yongbyon and cancelled inter-Korean meetings.

Following Pyongyang's actions at Yongbyon, Washington supported the IAEA's effort to refer Pyongyang to the UN Security Council, urging a chapter 7 UN resolution that recognized North Korea's actions as a threat to international peace and security. Chapter 7 resolutions allow military actions to respond to such threats. Unnamed senior officials announced the new U.S. strategy toward the North included seizing shipments under a new Proliferation Security Initiative and sanctioning the state.[83] At the end of 2002 internal debate in Pyongyang again went silent. At least publicly, the North Korean political establishment was unified in its confrontational response to the United States.

In early 2003 the United States indicated its willingness to talk to the North Koreans while resolutely rejecting any quid pro quo, arguing that North Korea must uphold its existing obligations under the defunct Agreed Framework. The Foreign Ministry did not bite, as the state labeled the U.S. offer to talk without negotiating "insincere." Pyongyang withdrew from the Non-Proliferation Treaty and threatened to resume long-range missile tests. Washington sweetened the offer by expressing a willingness to consider economic aid and security commitments. The North Korean Foreign Ministry said it was ready to talk bilaterally if the United States provided a security guarantee and lifted economic sanctions. This response would soon be overtaken by events.[84] President Bush again criticized North Korea in his 2003 State of the Union Address, pledging that the United States would not be blackmailed. The Foreign Ministry denounced the address and called for a nonaggression pact, while the party noted, "It is necessary to reinforce our own defense capabilities in every way possible."[85] The KPA announced it was ready to take preemptive military action in the next two to three days as the United States moved warships into the Sea of Japan and awaited the IAEA's scheduled referral of North Korea to the UN Security Council.[86]

The bureaucracies reacted consistently and according to the model's expectations, but this period did not require internally contentious decision making. By the time central authorities took bold actions on their U.S. policy, internal debate had been temporarily resolved. High tensions did not provide political space for alternatives to confrontational policies. The Foreign Ministry response to U.S. offers to negotiate were pro forma and lacked traction at home. Central authorities moved the state incrementally down the U.S. policy path advocated by the KPA and the party.

The United States and North Korea ratcheted up the pressure in the next three months. The KPA threatened to withdraw from the 1953 armistice agreement, fired short-range missiles during the South Korean president's inauguration, intercepted a U.S. spy plane with MiG fighter jets, and fired an antiship missile. The United States pressed China and its regional allies to exert political and economic pressure on the North, resumed food aid to the North at reduced levels, and imposed new sanctions. President Bush indicated that "all options were on the table." After sending two dozen bombers to Guam, which was within range of North Korea and as the United States prepared for war in Iraq, President Bush argued that if efforts to deal with the North "don't work diplomatically, they'll have to work militarily."[87]

With U.S.-DPRK relations in a steady downward spiral and engagement advocates silenced, China sent Vice Premier Qian Qichen to Pyongyang to meet with Kim Jong Il to encourage him to restart negotiations with the Americans. The contact was reportedly contentious and did not immediately result in North Korea returning to the negotiating table.[88] Pyongyang was dug in. If central authorities did not want to hear from Beijing that they should resume negotiations, they certainly did not want to hear it from their own subordinates. China temporarily suspended North Korea's oil shipments, officially citing a technical problem. North Korea depends heavily on Chinese energy assistance to keep its energy-inefficient industrial base moving—at a fraction of its Cold War level. It is North Korea's economic lifeline. Following the pipeline incident, North Korea's Foreign Ministry announced it would accept the U.S. offer to meet in Beijing. The announcement came shortly after the United States invaded Iraq and two days after North Korea's NPT withdrawal date elapsed. There was no indication that the state was interested in seriously negotiating with the Americans.

North Korea's lead Foreign Ministry negotiator told his U.S. counterpart in Beijing that North Korea reprocessed its spent fuel rods and was ready to "physically demonstrate" or export them. That seemed to indicate the

North's willingness to test a nuclear weapon and/or export nuclear material. For its part, the United States demanded North Korea completely, verifiably, and irreversibly dismantle its nuclear program before other issues could be discussed. Both sides reiterated positions that had been established for months. The talks ended a day early without progress, but both sides did agree to meet again. The party and KPA continued to promote "physical deterrence," referring to a nuclear test.[89] Pyongyang's threat was clear: if it doubted that the United States was sincerely negotiating security guarantees, North Korea would test a nuclear weapon.

The United States unsuccessfully encouraged China and its regional allies to pressure North Korea into submission. South Korean foreign policy officials said "coercive measures are not on the table"; China actively encouraged bilateral negotiations between Washington and Pyongyang; and Japan voiced concern over the prospect of sanctions although it responded to the U.S. request for action by reaffirming existing laws that barred military-related exports to North Korea and continued missile defense cooperation with the United States.[90] As the North Korean Foreign Ministry prepared for scheduled talks, KCNA indicated for the first time that the 1992 North-South Basic Agreement, which ensured peninsular denuclearization, was "nullified," citing U.S. hostility, although only the two Koreas were party to the agreement.

While in Seoul to discuss the relocation of U.S. bases in South Korea, Deputy Secretary of Defense Paul Wolfowitz announced that North Korea was "teetering on the edge of economic collapse. That, I believe, is a major point of leverage."[91] The comment emboldened those in Pyongyang who argued that the United States only wanted to bring down the regime and could not be engaged. With a united political establishment in Pyongyang on U.S. policy, the state pursued a consistent confrontational policy toward the United States.

Inter-Korean Relations: A Separate Track?

Seoul and North Korean cabinet officials tried to keep inter-Korean engagement on a separate path from U.S.-DPRK relations. Cabinet officials presided over the historic opening of rail connections across the DMZ and the groundbreaking ceremony for the Kaesong Industrial Complex. Party and military officials did not attend.⁹² The KPA warned that the previous year's naval clashes risked further South Korean aggression on land. The military institution did not document how such a clash could result, since the DMZ was a firmly recognized, unambiguous border unlike the disputed sea border.⁹³ A month later, the two Koreas exchanged gun fire across the DMZ. No one was injured.⁹⁴

After inter-Korean talks started, the KPA again demonstrated their commitment to a consistent policy line, arguing the talks should be abandoned, even though central authorities had already authorized them. The KPA, noting that South Korea was conducting military exercises and portraying them as provocative, questioned the usefulness of inter-Korean dialogue. The KPA noted that the military exercises "cannot but be seen as an act of impure challenge that deeply provokes the dialogue partner, casts a dark shadow over the results of the talks, and, moreover, throws cold water on brethren's vigorous footsteps toward national reconciliation, unity, peace, and reunification."⁹⁵

Likewise, the party again tried to link the South Koreans to the Americans, arguing that the United States was responsible for the divided peninsula and that the South Korean military was subject to U.S. control.⁹⁶ During the inter-Korean ministerial session, the party newspaper ran an article describing what the cabinet's goals should be at the talks. The talks "must yield good agreements," defined as ones that improve the state's physical security without mention of the cabinet's primary focus in inter-Korean projects: economic goals. By framing the goal of the talks as one to enhance the state's security, the party could erect a straw man and criticize the talks for failing to move toward this end.⁹⁷ Each bureaucracy demonstrated an ability to frame the debate to favor preconceived policy options.

Cabinet senior councilor Kim Yong Song replied by citing Kim Jong Il. Kim granted the cabinet the authority to go forward with the ministerial talks and the cabinet represented Kim's reunification policy. The cabinet moved forward as long as they had the lead. As the main negotiators in inter-Korean talks, cabinet officials outlined the economic benefits such negotiations provided, implicitly refuting their institutional critics and refocusing the expressed goals of the talks. Later in the summer, in one of his last statements as cabinet premier, Hong encouraged continued dialogue at the opening ceremonies of the National Rally for Peace and Reunification saying, "all anti-reunification forces must be opposed and dialogues, exchanges and cooperation encouraged."[98] The cabinet's policy line remained static, and they advanced it whenever possible. The policy was more than just one premier's policy; it was an institutional position. Hong started his tenure as premier with similar comments, and his successor advanced the same agenda.

U.S.-DPRK confrontation continued, but it did not fundamentally threaten inter-Korean rapprochement. The United States organized the first meeting of ten countries that agreed to join the Proliferation Security Initiative (PSI) to interdict ships suspected of carrying illicit and missile cargoes on the high seas. Despite repeated requests, Seoul refused to join the PSI. Referring to the PSI effort, party officials threatened war if the United States imposed a "blockade" against North Korea. The United States circulated a new draft resolution on North Korea at the UN Security Council, and the Bush administration sought congressional approval for a nuclear bunker buster to target North Korea's underground forward deployed forces.[99] After John Bolton visited Seoul to pitch the PSI and UN Security Council referral again, the North Korean Foreign Ministry issued a statement saying it would return to the six-party talks, while ideologues in the North returned to inflammatory personal attacks against Bolton. The pattern continued.

Six-party talks resumed in August with much the same result: North Korea again threatened to test a nuclear weapon, citing U.S. demands that North Korea first shut down its nuclear facilities before other issues could be discussed. The North Korean Foreign Ministry called the talks "not beneficial," and party commentaries unrelentingly criticized the United States. The National Defense Commission's highest ranking official called for reinforcing the state's "nuclear deterrent" by testing a nuclear weapon.[100] The North Koreans attended the six-party talks, possibly to appease their Chinese backers and six-party hosts, but did not soften their position.

As the six-party talks flailed, the two Koreas participated as a single team in the international summer Universiade collegiate athletic competition. The North Korea rubber-stamp parliament elected Pak Pong Ju as the new cabinet premier. As Hong's successor, Pak Pong Ju took up the same institutional position and developed a reputation as a key economic reformer. Immediately after Pak was named premier, KCBS summarized his comments to the Supreme People's Assembly (SPA): "The new premier said . . . North Korea's production power would be increased by improving economic management, and vowed to work towards the reunification of the two Koreas under the banner of the 15 June Joint Declaration."[101] Pak prioritized the same two issues as his predecessor, using the same construction to denote greater marketization in economic policy and more robust inter-Korean negotiations.

The following month, U.S. Forces Korea announced an $11 billion military buildup on the peninsula as U.S. spy satellites reportedly detected that Yongbyon was shut down. North Korea announced it was uninterested in resuming talks until the United States offered a security guarantee. The Foreign Ministry announced the following day that North Korea had shut down Yongbyon to remove eight thousand fuel rods from the reactor—a move required for building a nuclear bomb.[102] Inter-Korean ministerial talks continued as President Bush said the United States would offer a written security guarantee below the treaty level. The party newspaper immediately rejected the offer as "laughable" and emphasized the state should pursue its "nuclear deterrent," although the Foreign Ministry indicated ·"we are ready to consider Bush's remarks on the written assurances."[103] North Korea's provocative move forced Washington to react and reopened Pyongyang's bureaucratic debate on U.S. policy.

The Chinese again stepped in. China's third highest ranking politician, Wu Bangguo, traveled to Pyongyang to meet with Kim Jong Il and Cabinet Premier Pak Pong Ju. Wu delivered Chinese grants and a message that the state wanted to see six-party talks resume. Before Wu left Pyongyang, North Korea announced its willingness to restart talks.[104] Talks resumed with some prospect of movement given the Foreign Ministry's apparent willingness to consider the written assurances pledge, but the talks ultimately broke down. The Foreign Ministry may have had too little too late to overcome the party's and military's inertia.

Three months later, in mid-January 2004, an unofficial delegation of former senior U.S. government officials and academics returned from North Korea and said the North Koreans had showed them the eight thousand fuel rods were no longer in storage; the North Koreans claimed they had been reprocessed.[105] Meanwhile, the United States initiated its planned move of troops away from the DMZ to a base farther south and moved six B-52 bombers to Guam, within striking range of North Korea.[106] The Foreign Ministry did not advocate for renewed talks in the that political climate.

North Korea and the United States talked again in February to little avail as the United States continued to demand North Korea dismantle its nuclear program as a prerequisite to further talks, and North Korea continued to insist the reactors were for peaceful energy purposes.[107] The talks ended with agreement to form lower-level working groups, although Pyongyang took its time forming them. The Foreign Ministry called the talks "disappointing," characterizing them as a way for the United States to stall for time as it tried to "suffocate" North Korea.[108] North Korea remained outwardly united in opposition to further negotiations with the United States.

Chinese foreign minister Li Zhaoxing's subsequent trip to Pyongyang in March 2004 and meetings with Kim Jong Il did not change the dynamics. When Kim Jong Il traveled to Beijing to meet with Chinese president Hu Jintao in April, Kim reportedly sought more Chinese aid to return to negotiations. No specific quid pro quo was ever revealed, although North Korea did agree to participate in the working group meetings after the trip. The North Korean media remained overwhelmingly negative about the prospect for those meetings. The Foreign Ministry issued a single statement, defining the meeting's agenda as one to advance a proposal of "reward for freeze" and empathetically ruling out any "talking about 'irreversible' or something like that." In essence, the Foreign Ministry required a complete capitulation on the American side to continue to "sit at the table."[109] Both financial rewards and a temporary or partial nuclear freeze were anathema to the Bush administration, which regarded them as Clintonesque ideas.[110] Pyongyang—and certainly the Foreign Ministry—knew this. The move was likely tactical. No one in the North Korean system was observably pushing for negotiations in this environment, but showing up at the talks gained Chinese support.

Cabinet officials meanwhile concentrated their energies on inter-Korean projects and economic changes. On Kim's return to Pyongyang from China, a massive explosion rocked the Ryongchon train station. Kim's train had traveled through the station only hours earlier, leading to speculation that the explosion may have been a failed assassination attempt.[111] The explosion created a tense international environment as the North cracked down on Sino–North Korean trade and communications. The KPA and party cited the explosion as a risk of increased opening. The state must reassert control. It is noteworthy that, despite the tense environment, the cabinet premier hosted a South Korean trade delegation only two weeks later. The South Koreans reported a cordial atmosphere.[112]

The cabinet defended its role in economic affairs and its advocacy of greater opening against other bureaucratic interests. Cabinet Premier Pak addressed his detractors, contrasting the ideological approach with a realistic approach, and integrated a vague promise to pursue science and technology into the cabinet's platform.[113] The same month, Kim Jong Il purged his brother-in-law and possible successor, Chang Song Taek, and his supporters amid concerns that he might be developing his own power base and taking on too much of an economic role.[114] The rest of the bureaucracy went silent on this politically sensitive subject, possibly out of fear of being purged themselves. On April 9 the DPRK trade minister Ri Kwang Keun was replaced with a younger economic technocrat, Rim Kyong Man, and the socialist Public Distribution System was suspended in exchange for an increased emphasis on markets. U.S. policy did not seem to directly affect the state's economic policy decisions. Pyongyang could accept some of the risks of lessened control that accompanied economic opening and inter-Korean economic projects even after a major explosion that some within the regime may have portrayed as an assassination attempt.

In May 2004 Japanese prime minister Koizumi returned to Pyongyang for a second summit with Kim Jong Il.[115] Within two weeks, the two Koreas agreed to open road links and end loudspeaker broadcasts across the DMZ. They established a hotline in case of future naval clashes, and South Korea promised rice aid to the North.[116] The cabinet spearheaded only some of these inter-Korean efforts, and even KPA representatives noted some improvement in North-South military relations.[117] Meanwhile, the United States announced it would cut one third of the thirty-seven thousand U.S. forces stationed in Korea. The party called this a victory and a U.S. "retreat."[118]

Washington offered Pyongyang a new incentive, one that Libya had recently accepted—immediate aid and eventual removal of sanctions as soon as Pyongyang pledged to verifiably dismantle its plutonium and uranium programs. North Korea's Foreign Ministry called the idea "constructive" and said it would be studied in Pyongyang.[119] During that study period military officials opposed the proposal. Speaking on the tenth anniversary of Kim Il Sung's death, Minister of the People's Armed Forces Kim Il Chol voiced deep skepticism about the six-party talks and emphasized military preparations instead of dialogue. The argument seemed to take hold among central authorities, presumably up to Kim himself. The Foreign Ministry reversed its initial characterization of the idea, announcing the U.S. offer was a "sham" and renewing calls for U.S. compensation. With President Bush's reelection in question and his Democratic opponent offering direct talks with the North Koreans, the rest of the year saw little advancement in nuclear deliberations.[120]

Nuclear Declarations

South Korea announced in September that it had enriched uranium and extracted plutonium under both the military dictatorship and democratic regimes. IAEA inspectors indicated Seoul had tried to hide the event for six years as it claimed the two small experiments were only on an academic research scale and did not constitute a weapons program.[121] As the IAEA investigated, North Korea's media highlighted what it saw as international hypocrisy and double standards applied to the two Koreas. The Foreign Ministry downplayed the revelation as a U.S. fabrication and urged continued inter-Korean contacts.[122]

KCNA called the news an "open secret" and noted that South Korea could not make a nuclear weapon without U.S. help. The article blamed the United States and the IAEA for creating a "double standard" for the two Koreas but largely refrained from criticizing Seoul. The North's only criticism of Seoul came from the *Tongil Sinbo* website—one of the least authoritative means for the regime to communicate messages. The website, officially independent of the regime, is run out of Shenyang, China, and claims to be the voice of an overseas Korean expatriate group committed to reunification on the North's terms. It argued that the South Korean nuclear experiments provided further reason to be cautious of the United States and to boycott the six-party talks.[123]

The KPA and the party had a good talking point. Uncharacteristically, they did not capitalize on it. For months, they had attempted to link North-South relations with declining U.S.-DPRK relations. Here was an excellent opportunity to not only bash the South but also link Seoul and Washington together by alleging nuclear cooperation between the two countries. The North Koreans are not beyond stretching the truth considerably, but the official reaction was quite muted. The party and the military did not downplay the event actively like the Foreign Ministry, but it did refrain from speaking out. Inter-Korean relations were improving, and a higher authority may have squelched their dissent.

Pyongyang moved toward its own more developed and well-publicized nuclear declaration. In January 2005, prior to President Bush's second inauguration, KCNA announced that North Korea was prepared to try talks again and "treat it [the United States] as a friend," and expressed the that the second Bush administration might change its policy toward the North. The North often uses anonymous offers to test politically sensitive messages. In this case, they used an official DPRK publication, more authoritative than an affiliated expatriate organization, but not a formal diplomatic offer. They soon backed off this idea.

Pyongyang probably increasingly viewed Bush's second term as following a similar North Korea policy as the first term. During Condoleezza Rice's confirmation hearings in January 2005, she called North Korea one of the "outposts of tyranny." Two weeks later, President Bush delivered the State of the Union Address. In the paragraph following the only discussion of the Proliferation Security Initiative and naming North Korea as the only state outside of the broader Middle East as a country of concern, the president said, "And we've declared our own intention: America will stand with the allies of freedom to support democratic movements in the Middle East and beyond, with the ultimate goal of ending tyranny in our world."

The North Koreans put these two statements together in official press reports. Washington considered Pyongyang a tyrannical regime, and it was committed to ending those regimes completely. Two days after the State of the Union, a Foreign Ministry statement, citing Rice's "outpost of tyranny" and Bush's "ending tyranny" remarks, argued that North Korea was still high on the U.S. list for regime change. It announced that North Korea had "manufactured nuclear weapons" to deter military intervention, suspended indefinitely North Korea's participation in the six-party talks, and reaffirmed its military-first politics.

Debate continued in Pyongyang but the North Korean readings of events changed the conversation to not *if*, but *how*, the state should announce its nuclearization intent. An American scholar met with several North Korean officials in Pyongyang and reported that the incongruity in the North Korean approach reflected bureaucratic divisions within the regime:

In the February [2005] showdown, I was told by several of those involved, the dealers argued in favor of preserving ambiguity concerning the extent of North Korean nuclear capabilities as part of a continued effort to get economic quid pro quos in return for step-by-step denuclearization. The hard-liners countered that it would be naive to continue hoping for a beneficial deal with the Bush administration, which in their view is seeking regime change and wants to use the six-party talks in Beijing to drive Pyongyang into a corner. It is demeaning for North Korea to let the United States keep it on the defensive in the six-party talks, they contended, even though Washington has 7,400 operational nuclear weapons of its own. The only self-respecting course for North Korea, they said, would be to rule out any discussion of dismantlement for now and to declare unambiguously that North Korea is already a "nuclear weapons state" in order to make Washington think twice about any military adventure.[124]

This account is a helpful window into regime dynamics but still tends to conflate the military and the party representatives together as a single hard-liner entity. Though the more general grouping has a certain utility, this idea can be refined to the two separate sets of arguments the scholar notes were used to advance the nuclear declaration. Hard-liners objected to six-party talks on militarily pragmatic grounds (they fail to provide for the state's security and limit more tangible defensive actions) and on ideological grounds (talking with the imperialists is an affront to the state's dignity). Despite these distinct arguments, these two hard-line groups had the same goal. Their argument seemed to win out as engagement skeptics in North Korea increasingly defined the state's policy toward the United States.

Diplomatic Impasse, Mutual Pressure

Pyongyang returned to its earlier demand of bilateral negotiations. Washington refused, noting its long-standing view that the issue was multilateral in nature, not simply a responsibility of the United States. China called on North Korea to return to the multilateral talks as U.S. plans to intensify its illicit activities initiative to reduce Pyongyang's access to the international financial system leaked to the press.[125] After the head of China's Central Committee's International Department met with Kim Jong Il in Pyongyang, North Korea announced it would participate in the six-party format in principle but did not change its substantive demands. The pattern continued. Secretary of State Condoleezza Rice called her Chinese counterpart in March to urge China to pressure the North Koreans. China refused and offered North Korea "substantial" new "loans" when Cabinet Premier Pak Pong Ju and Vice Foreign Minister Kang Sok Ju visited Beijing in April. North Korea does not repay the Chinese and South Korean "loans" that are better understood as aid. Beijing reportedly may have increased North Korea's aid by up to 40 percent, reflecting Beijing's stated primary interest in peninsular stability.

The following month, some media outlets in Pyongyang suggested the state might test a nuclear weapon—traditionally seen as a Chinese red line—while others called such allegations U.S. propaganda. The state indicated its willingness to return to the six-party talks while others rejected negotiations. *New York Times* columnist David Sanger reported that the U.S. intelligence community was divided in its interpretation of North Korea's actions, relying on satellite imagery of possible preparations for a nuclear test while seeing diplomatic overtures toward resuming talks.[126] Based on these empirical observations, North Korea seemed to be moving in two different directions simultaneously—a position puzzling for those analysts who viewed North Korea as monolithic. Personalizing this disparity led some to call the state a two-faced, though monolithic, entity that fundamentally could not be trusted enough to be engaged.

Similar skepticism about negotiations came from the chief of the KPA general staff who said in a major anniversary address that negotiations were fruitless and only delayed meaningful progress toward the North's "nuclear deterrent." His advocacy seemed to find a receptive ear among central authorities. In May the Foreign Ministry announced that the state had completed reprocessing the eight thousand fuel rods from the Yongbyon reactor. Meanwhile, the United States and North Korea met "secretly" two days later in New York. The Foreign Ministry announced its desire to keep the back channel open while rejecting U.S. "punitive measures." The divergent institutional stands again cannot be explained by monolithic theories of the North Korean state. If policy was solely defined at the top, one should not be able to point to such divergences.

South Korea offered to sweeten the negotiated settlement pot for North Korea to denuclearize with its "important proposal." Pyongyang agreed to an inter-Korean ministerial meeting where South Korea added two hundred thousand tons of fertilizer to the North's aid package, but the North still refused to return to six-party talks. In mid-June 2005, 40 South Korean officials and 295 other citizens celebrated in Pyongyang the fifth anniversary of the inter-Korean summit. A hundred thousand North Koreans attended the opening ceremony at Kimilsung Stadium, and the cabinet premier welcomed "the South Korean delegation with my brotherly love." Meanwhile, the Pentagon suspended searches with the KPA for remains of soldiers killed in the Korean War and ordered Nighthawk stealth fighter planes to South Korea as the U.S. publicly considered pushing for a UN Security Council action against North Korea.[127] Seoul's and Washington's approaches were not in step.

The party again focused on poor relations with the United States instead of advances in inter-Korean relations. The party central committee secretary Choe Thae-bok said in a speech commemorating the anniversary of Kim Jong Il's work at the Party's Central Committee that North Korea "is responding to the imperialists' hard-line policies with an ultra-hard line. . . . Our army and people are sharply watching the United States and its servile followers' foolish acts of recklessness and hostile attempts, and are fully ready to smash any crushing offensive and military attack by the enemies in a single stroke. . . . We will mercilessly annihilate and sweep away the aggressors by fully putting in motion our political and military might."[128]

By the end of the month, the party had more bureaucratic ammunition to cite. President Bush issued Executive Order 13382 as part of WMD Commission recommendations. The order barred U.S. persons from doing business with foreign entities in North Korea, Iran, and Syria suspected of transferring WMD- or ballistic missile–related technology. The party called the move a new sanction.

"The Atmosphere Has Improved"—for a Day

In mid-June 2005 China sent a delegation representing President Hu to Pyongyang to try again to convince Pyongyang to return to six-party talks.

This time Kim Jong Il said peninsular denuclearization was his revered father's "dying wish." It was difficult for party or military leaders to resist this authoritative claim. Within a week, North Korea's Foreign Ministry said replacing the armistice with a "peace mechanism" would end the U.S. hostile policy toward the DPRK and eliminate North Korea's need for a nuclear deterrent. South Korea revealed the details of its "important proposal," and Washington named an accomplished diplomat, Chris Hill, as its new lead negotiator.[129] Absent a new stumbling block, it seemed that all parties were getting on the same page and were willing to move forward. This turn of events reexposed bureaucratic differences in Pyongyang.

The new U.S. negotiator reportedly enjoyed more leeway than his predecessor as he announced the United States would pursue a "words for words and actions for actions" strategy toward disarmament. Pyongyang previously called for "simultaneous" actions to bridge the lack of trust between parties. In his opening statements at the July six-party talks session, Hill reportedly recognized North Korea's sovereignty and repeated the U.S. line that it had no intention of attacking the North. Hill also presented evidence that North Korea had enriched uranium, reportedly drawing on A.Q. Khan's confession. Despite North Korea's reluctance to accept the U.S. information, the six parties worked on drafting a set of principles to guide the talks.[130] The Chinese Foreign Ministry announced that "the atmosphere has improved."

Talks stalled over North Korean's light water reactor (LWR) demand.[131] The 1994 Agreed Framework pledged to build a LWR, and the international consortium charged with the project had broken ground by the time the framework agreement fell apart in 2002. Pyongyang claimed the state needed the reactor to harness the scientific and medical benefits of nuclear power, support its focus on science and technology to transform its economy, and produce badly needed energy. The move also would help Pyongyang save face and would placate internal opponents to negotiations. For Washington, the LWR was politically unpalatable as a centerpiece of the Clinton-era agreement.[132]

China proposed a compromise where the six parties agreed in principle to North Korea's right to develop nuclear energy while delaying the question on building a LWR until an "appropriate time." In exchange, North

Korea agreed to return to the NPT. All sides eventually agreed to this September 19 joint statement.[133] Within three months of the new U.S. negotiating team's having been granted more flexibility, Pyongyang reacted. The North Korean Foreign Ministry had news they could bring back to Pyongyang. Six-party talks gave them something to cite as a benefit of the diplomatic track when presenting their case internally. This state of affairs would not last long. The first significant agreement in years was quickly undermined in both Washington and Pyongyang.

LWR Demands and Banco Delta Asia

As the six parties met in Beijing, the U.S. Treasury Department designated a Macao bank, Banco Delta Asia (BDA), as an entity of "primary money laundering concern" under Section 311 of the Patriot Act because of its ties with North Korean entities allegedly involved in illicit activities and missile sales. The move, published in the *Federal Register* the day after the conclusion of the September 19 agreement, had the effect of cutting North Korea off from the international financial system over an allegation of $27 million worth of illicit funds.[134]

Also on September 20, Pyongyang announced that the critical sticking point of the LWR had to be resolved *before* the state began to denuclearize. Pyongyang interpreted that the "appropriate time" for providing an LWR was now. North Korea's powerful vice foreign minister repeated the LWR demand in his speech at the UN General Assembly five days later. The Foreign Ministry objected to U.S. claims of illicit activities, but it was the party newspaper that first labeled the 311 action a "sanction" incompatible with continued negotiations.

Chinese president Hu again visited Pyongyang, and Pyongyang returned to talks in November. Hu toured the Chinese-funded glass factory and reportedly pledged more aid. Six-party talks resumed without making any progress as the North Korean negotiators took up the party's position. North Korea's chief negotiator told reporters that progress could not be made until the U.S. removed the new sanctions; the LWR demand fell from prominence for the time being. Pyongyang boycotted the six-party talks over the BDA issue for the next fourteen months.

Cross-Border Cooperation: The Only Game in Town

As the United States and North Korea reached an impasse over the BDA issue, South Korea pledged $2.6 billion to the North, more than doubling its aid pledge. The amount pledged was worth approximately 100 times more than the one-time amount in dispute with the United States. South Korea would open its first liaison office in Pyongyang, agreed to finance a multiyear $10 billion joint textile project, and planned to double the size of the Kaesong Industrial Complex. The two Koreas also agreed to field a joint Korean team for the 2008 Olympics in Beijing.

With South Korean and Chinese aid and good weather, Pyongyang enjoyed a bumper harvest. Inter-Korean relations reached a new height, and North Korea's food situation improved markedly. But the improved food situation allowed central authorities to heed party demands to crack down on market mechanisms to distribute food. The state reinstituted the socialist public distribution system (PDS) and expelled UN World Food Program (WFP) staff, who were involved in humanitarian assistance. WFP food aid requires inspections to guarantee food reaches its intended recipients; South Korean and Chinese aid to North Korea largely lacked these oversight provisions. Pyongyang preferred its neighbors' less intrusive food aid to the UN aid. The expulsion reflects long-standing arguments by the military that intrusive food inspections undermined the state's information security. International aid workers channeled information to hostile governments, exposed North Korea's citizens to more outside influences, and somewhat hampered central authorities' ability to distribute food as they saw fit, including feeding the military first, as opposed to reaching vulnerable populations as aid agencies insisted on.

Reintroducing the PDS also addressed growing inequities and corruption that accompanied the markets. Markets provided farmers an incentive to produce more than their quota amounts, because they could sell their surplus. However, unintended side effects from the partially marketized food distribution system emerged, creating arbitrage opportunities and depriving certain at-risk populations from accessing food, including the unemployed, disabled, and elderly. Market incentives created an unsavory side effect of rewarding those who violated the law and put vulnerable populations at greater risk of starvation. Notably, it also smelled of capitalism to party officials who had long opposed this type of incentive. With food secured (for that year), the state rolled back market reforms and reintroduced the PDS. The state seized food and tried to distribute it through state channels. The move shows competing demands on North Korean decision making. Central authorities do not seem to embrace market mechanisms and have not undertaken a top-down economic reform project, but cabinet officials argue they should tolerate some market mechanisms to address critical problems that the state cannot efficiently resolve.[135]

Despite three premiers' documented role in advocating marketization, Premier Pak had to announce the significant change in national economic policy. With Kim Jong Il in rare attendance at the Supreme People's Assembly, Premier Pak spoke on the reintroduction of the PDS. He proposed an administrative solution to food distribution and labeled it the party's position, "By all means, we must reach this year's grain production targets by thoroughly implementing the party's policy of agricultural revolution by fully concentrating and mobilizing the entire country's efforts into the agricultural front."[136]

The speech was significant in that the cabinet premier held out other roles for continued marketization. Following the party's usual strategy of first presenting the required position and then undermining it by the end of the speech or article, Pak said, "We will present the renovation of plants and enterprises with modern communication facilities within the next few years as one of the significant economic strategies." This may have meant legalizing cell phones, already pouring in over the Chinese border, and authorizing more widespread use of international phone lines. Both were necessary to grease the wheels of international business but were opposed by the security camp fearful of information outflows.

Pak continued, "While actively conducting external economic activities in line with the changed environment, we should raise the level of the secondary and tertiary goods that are great in demand to the world level so as to actively develop the overseas market, and effectively carry out economic cooperation with other countries in a way that helps to introduce advanced science and technology." He interjected the role of supplying foreign markets with exportable goods while supporting the party's position on advancing science and technology. Pak presented the benefits of his institution's advocated policy and included minimal party demands, such as state-led science and technology development, that did not fundamentally contradict his own platform.

The most interesting compromise in the speech came when Pak tried to balance ideological requirements with market principles: "All economic guidance functionaries . . . should organize and conduct the activities of production and management by strictly adhering to the principle of socialism and the principle of guaranteeing actual profits." This cloaked the cabinet's profit policy in socialist garb. North Korea would roll back its market efforts in the politically sensitive and economically significant agricultural sector, but the move would not seep into other sectors as the regime continued to use market incentives in business-to-business transactions, decentralize administrative responsibilities to the regions, and deemphasize the plan in industrial policy. It also continued to expand the special economic zones and cross-border trade with South Korea and China. Nevertheless, economic reformers suffered a policy defeat that would remain for the foreseeable future.[137]

Bureaucratic Cracks on "Sanctions" and Missile Tests

In early January 2006 Kim Jong Il made a secret ten-day trip to China as the chief U.S. negotiator visited Beijing to meet with his North Korean counterpart. Negotiations were at a stalemate because North Korea insisted the United States remove new "financial sanctions" before they would negotiate further. The United States maintained the "defensive measures" were a law enforcement issue unrelated to negotiations.[138] Party commentaries opposed negotiations in characteristic rhetorical flourishes, lambasting the U.S. imperialists. The Foreign Ministry took a more pragmatic approach. They agreed with the party and KPA that U.S. "financial sanctions" aimed to pressure North Korea, but the Foreign Ministry claimed the move was intended to denuclearize the Korean peninsula, not change the regime. Pyongyang too sought a fully denuclearized Korean peninsula where all parties could enjoy security. Therefore, both sides should resume negotiations toward this common goal in the most productive manner—through the six-party talks.[139]

The Foreign Ministry's nuanced pitch failed to produce results, and Pyongyang continued to refuse to talk because the financial measures hampered its economic activity and injured its pride. Beijing dispatched its vice foreign minister Wu Dawei to Pyongyang for a five-day visit in mid-February 2006. Again, the Chinese sought to break the impasse as all three bureaucratic organs opposed the U.S. "sanctions."[140] In March the United States and North Korea held bilateral meetings in New York. The United States termed the meeting a "briefing" and sent Treasury Department technical experts; the North Korean delegation called it a "negotiation" and sent Foreign Ministry personnel. Failure was predictable as the U.S. technical experts came prepared only to describe U.S. actions, while North Korea officials sought to roll them back.

With the New York failure, North Korea's bureaucracies again united on U.S. policy. The KPA spokesman denounced the financial sanctions, noting they must be related to U.S.–South Korean military exercises as a pretext to invasion. The Foreign Ministry announced the United States did not have a "monopoly" on preemptive military strikes. Negotiators from the six parties attended a conference in April in "unofficial" capacities. South Korea and China tried unsuccessfully to convince the U.S. delegation to meet informally with the North Koreans. During the conference, North Korea's Ministry of the People's Armed Forces proclaimed that the United States' unwillingness to negotiate further demonstrated its resolve to invade. Pyongyang continued to boycott six-party talks.

The United States issued new foreign asset control regulations targeting DPRK-flagged vessels in May and urged KEDO to finally scrap the LWR project. The U.S. State Department issued new, controversial allegations in its trafficking in persons report, criticizing the low wages paid to North Korean workers at the Kaesong Industrial Complex.[141]In June the North Korean Foreign Ministry issued a statement inviting Chris Hill to Pyongyang for bilateral negotiations. The White House rejected the offer, citing U.S. policy to only negotiate with the North Koreans in the six-party format.[142]

As North Korea's Foreign Ministry proffered this invitation, the KPA readied a long-range missile launch. Neither the invitation to Hill nor the long-range missile launch likely could have gone forward without central authorization, showing how Kim can utilize his distinct institutions to create a range of opportunities. Long a back channel for negotiations, North Korea's second highest ranking official at its office at UN headquarters, Han Song Ryol, offered to discuss the pending flight test with the Americans but the White House refused. Meanwhile, the KPA air force warned the United States to stop flying reconnaissance flights over its territory or risk getting shot down. High-level Bush administration officials rejected a proposal from former Clinton administration officials to strike the missile on the launch pad as too provocative; instead, they moved sea-based missile defense assets into the region, potentially to take a shot at the rocket in flight if given the opportunity.

The United States' rejection of the Foreign Ministry's invitation made it easier for Kim to authorize the KPA's launch. North Korea prepared its longest range rocket for its first flight test—the three-stage Taepodong-2, suspected of being able to reach the continental United States. North Korea ended its self-imposed six-year moratorium on missile launches on the fourth of July (U.S. time). The missile only flew for a few seconds before it failed, according to declassified sea logs of the U.S. Aegis cruisers tracking the launch. The United States pushed for a new round of six-party negotiations as the UN Security Council again condemned North Korea. Washington and Tokyo began deploying sensors for missile defense. South Korea cut off food aid although they would resume it the next month when floods in the North threatened mass starvation. South Korea's president also demanded wartime operational control from Washington as South Korea's generals worried openly about the military utility of the political move. With divergent strategic interests and threat perceptions, the U.S.–South Korean military alliance loosened.[143]

The Foreign Ministry issued a statement rejecting the latest UN Security Council resolution, and the minister of the People's Armed Forces, Kim Il Chol, went one step further, saying that North Korea must provide for its own self-defense "in every way . . . without being hindered by anything." The launch did not prompt a resumption of bilateral talks nor did the United States lift its "financial sanctions." A senior U.S. Treasury official called the line between North Korea licit and illicit finance "nearly invisible" and openly urged countries to cut off all business contacts with any North Korean citizen or entity, in contradiction to the administration's previous argument that the BDA action was a targeted legal action rather than a general political "sanction." The North Korean Foreign Ministry rebuffed the "expanding financial sanctions" and vaguely pledged to "seek all the necessary countermeasures." The state, moderately divided before the launch, united as the Foreign Ministry did not see any opening to make advances with the Americans. Pyongyang would quickly move to another, even more serious, provocation.

Hitting Rock Bottom: The Nuclear Test

Marshal and Defense Minister Kim Il Chol used the anniversary of the Korean War "victory" to lay out the KPA's strategic vision toward the United States. The position was not new. The KPA is openly skeptical of negotiating with an enemy it considers untrustworthy and considers tension reduction measures as impediments to reunification. Putting the nuclear program on hold for phantom gains only delays the North's nuclear deterrent. And reducing the military's actual budget share for economic projects—especially those without military uses outside the heavy industry sector—reduces the KPA's role in domestic and foreign policy:

> Under the aggressive ambition of overturning our socialist system and dominating all of Korea, the United States is blatantly translating into practice its evil scheme for a second Korean War. . . . The United States is increasing its large scale state-of-the-art military equipment and modern homicidal weapons in South Korea and in its surrounding areas and is waging one war exercise commotion after another, such as the "RIMPAC" [rim of Pacific] joint military exercise. . . . The United States picked a fight over the missile launch our military carried out and . . . had the UN Security Council adopt a so-called "resolution," which took serious note of the exercise of our self-defensive right.[144]

The position was not merely one for public consumption. Another high-level KPA official made the same argument in private conversations with his Russian counterparts. Chief of the KPA general staff Kim Yong-joon noted the importance of investing in a "powerful deterrence force" against the United States, according to a Russian media leak.[145] The missile launch was an abysmal military failure that the state misrepresented to its population as successful. However, officials knew their foreign counterparts were keenly aware of the failure. In this context, Pyongyang decided to push forward with another major provocation.

Only three months after the failed Taepodong-2 launch, the Foreign Ministry announced the state would test a nuclear weapon since it considered previous agreements abrogated.[146] North Korea pursued the test despite strong international objections, including Beijing's temporarily suspending critical oil supplies to North Korea. On October 9, 2006, North Korea tested its first nuclear bomb. The bomb's plutonium came from the Yongbyon nuclear reactor that had been unfrozen after the 2002 scrapping of the Agreed Framework. The test "marks an historic event as it greatly encouraged and pleased the KPA and people that have wished to have powerful self-reliant defense capability."[147] The party newspaper ran an epic poem in jubilation over the successful test.[148]

International outcry condemned the test, but few real punishments were forthcoming. Pentagon officials privately told reporters that the United States could not sustain a war effort in Korea due to commitments in Afghanistan and Iraq and questioned the effectiveness of a naval blockade. U.S. efforts in the UN Security Council moved further as China proved less reluctant to sanction Pyongyang in wake of crossing this Chinese red line. The UN resolution cited article VII explicitly, noting that North Korea's actions threatened international peace and security. The UN article allows for militarized responses to such threats; a similar resolution allowed the creation of the UN Command in 1950 and internationalized the Korean War. Still, South Korea and China refused to abandon their engagement strategies. South Korea indicated it would not stop its investment in Kaesong, and China said it would not stop trading with North Korea. They remained firmly opposed to any military action against North Korea.[149]

Two days after the test, North Korea's Foreign Ministry called on the United States to return to negotiations.[150] President Bush responded two days later that signing the North Korea Non-Proliferation Act of 2006 had allowed the United States to sanction entities that transfer missile- or WMD-related components to North Korea, and the next day the UN Security Council authorized sanctions against North Korea. The Foreign Ministry called the Security Council action a "declaration of war," and North Korea's highest constitutional official, Kim Yong Nam, warned of a second nuclear test. He also boasted that North Korea's economy had improved despite previous UN sanctions, highlighting the important role of South Korean and Chinese aid and investments. The cabinet officials intimated that Washington could try, but it lacked the power to pressure Pyongyang into submission.

The series of events demonstrated again the conclusion of the Perry policy review completed years earlier. The United States had few sticks to employ against North Korea, especially given diverging South Korean and Chinese interests, short of direct military action. A second Korean War would be very costly in treasure and blood. The policy review estimated such a scenario would kill hundreds of thousands and create over a million refugees—not including the possibility of nuclear escalation or Chinese involvement. North Korea had an aged, but effective, military deterrent. It would likely lose a peninsular war if fought to a military conclusion without Chinese aid, but the costs would be high enough to dissuade Washington or Seoul from pursuing this policy. Once North Korea went nuclear, the United States modified its strategy toward the North.

This period shows the reactive nature of North Korea's U.S. policy and its ability to segment the three policy issue areas under consideration. Pyongyang viewed Washington's policy as fundamentally hostile and committed to regime change. As these ideas became increasingly accepted in Pyongyang, internal debate on U.S. policy faded away. External events effectively silenced cabinet advocacy on U.S. policy. Short-term gains in diplomacy had little prospect for success and did not have long-lasting impact during this time. Though not responsible for North Korea's sovereign choices, Washington has tremendous power over North Korea. It can shape Pyongyang's internal debates about missile and nuclear policy that critically shape its response and it has the ability to eradicate the regime if it is willing to accept the high costs that would attend such a decision.

Pyongyang responds to both symbols and substance. When U.S. officials criticize Kim, for example, it provides ideologues in Pyongyang another talking point to demonstrate in internal debates that the regime must hold onto its missile and nuclear forces. Those not carefully evaluating the North Korean system may scoff at such a claim that a brutal regime would seriously react to international name-calling, but verbal attacks threaten the prestige and pride of the regime's top leader and institutional leaders have to come to his defense. Advancing negotiations in such an atmosphere is difficult. Understanding the North's internal mechanisms can help inform the cost-benefit calculation of such a decision.

Likewise, efforts to enact sanctions, regardless of their economic impact, prompt much the same reaction from North Korea. Ironically, many proponents of sanctions against North Korea have cited Pyongyang's loud reaction against them as evidence of their effectiveness, miscategorizing Pyongyang's complaints about a poisoned atmosphere for bilateral negotiations with genuine economic pressured being applied. Most prominently during this period, some argued that freezing roughly $25 million of North Korean accounts that resulted in cutting the country's entities off from the international financial system prompted it to make certain strategic decisions out of economic pressure. North Korea lost 80 to 90 percent of its industrial capacity in the 1990s and its severe economic contraction prevented it from feeding its own population, yet it still maintained the core elements of its system as this study has continually noted. Additional economic sanctions have only marginal impact economically, and understanding the regime's internal functions helps explain how these moves simply antagonize the regime rather than making any strategic advance.

This understanding of the North's internal dynamics leads to the conclusion that moderate carrot and stick approaches to the North are difficult to sustain. One institution will inevitably present the stick, no matter how small or ineffective, as an affront to the leader and a threat to the regime's dignity, requiring an even larger inducement than otherwise would be required to shape regime responses. More focused and sustained strategies that try to embolden the cabinet's agenda internally or eradicate the regime outright are likely to be the only means to address concerns about North Korea's long-term actions, the latter strategy having particularly high opportunity costs.

Despite repeated efforts by party and military officials to link inter-Korean relations and marketization efforts to souring U.S.-DPRK relations, cabinet officials successfully managed to keep this policy on a separate track. This development disputes the idea that the regime is strategically committed to creating a wedge between Seoul and Washington; instead, institutions use linkage strategies tactically to bolster their predetermined advocacy. It was the cabinet—not the party or the military—during this period that tried to distance Washington and Seoul to prevent the soured U.S.-DPRK relations from undermining its efforts on inter-Korean economic projects. This did not prevent the military and the party from objecting to established inter-Korean policy. The military demonstrated bureaucratic resistance and its semiautonomous capabilities by provoking a naval skirmish in the West Sea. Both the party and the military used the event to argue for a policy change on inter-Korean projects.

Economic policy was also subject to interinstitutional debate. The regime tolerated additional forms of market mechanisms to address its inability to provide for its citizens' basic needs. But when economic conditions improved enough so that such coping mechanisms were not deemed absolutely necessary, the regime reintroduced administrative control over the economy. Pyongyang seemed to fashion its economic policy in response to the economic situation rather than linking these decisions to the external environment. Seoul's hope that engagement would drive North Korean economic policy decisions was not directly met as other variables proved more important. Perhaps counterintuitively, one could argue that improvements in North Korean food security as a result of Seoul's efforts actually contributed to Pyongyang's 2005 decision to crack down on markets and reimpose greater regime control over the economy.

U.S. policy, inter-Korean relations, and economic policy are inherently linked at some level in North Korea's decision making. Institutions use conditions in one of these issue areas as a debating point for policy agenda in other issue areas. Nonetheless, the state has demonstrated an ability to segment policy areas when it deems it appropriate. This segmentation allows more nuanced policy decisions but also contributes to impressions that North Korea is simply "muddling through"—that the state lacks an overarching agenda to bring it out of the current depressed situation. Top leadership has not shown a consistent commitment to economic reform and international opening that could transform the state into a more sustainable polity, nor has it consistently retrenched in policies of the late 1950s and 1960s where a planned economy supported socialist ideals and a strong defense sector hoped to prepare for the right time to launch a reunification drive by force. A reunified Korea on the North's terms provides a logically consistent alternative to transforming North Korea as reformers advocate. The state is not of one mind on these fundamental questions. Different ideas about the future of the state come through in the bureaucratic jostling on specific agenda items.

After the nuclear test, these issues remained unresolved, and Pyongyang's response to Seoul and Washington flipped. Seoul started to back off the unconditional engagement policy and turned toward a harder line with the election of a conservative president in December 2007. As Seoul moved toward a tougher line, Washington began increasingly to accommodate the North. Divergence between Washington's and Seoul's policies remained—but on a reversed footing. Pyongyang's institutional debates again reflected these changes.

CHAPTER SEVEN

Policy Reversals, 2006–2008

Fall of 2006 proved to be another watershed in North Korea's U.S. policy and inter-Korean policy, though economic policy remained on a different track. The external environment changed in fall 2006, prompting the regime's bureaucracies to cite different data in their institutional debates. The changes raised the cabinet's role on U.S. policy at the expense of the party and military while having the reverse effect on inter-Korean projects. Economic policy remained static. North Korea tested a nuclear weapon in October 2006 and Democrats in the United States Congress won substantial gains in the November elections. Washington increasingly changed its policy toward North Korea, and Pyongyang's institutions reacted.

In South Korea, Seoul's embattled president became an increasingly lame duck, largely on grounds unrelated to North Korea policy. However, the nuclear test affected South Korean public opinion of the government's North Korean policy. Increasingly, conservative demands for greater short-term reciprocity in inter-Korean relations took hold over liberal arguments that unconditional engagement could gradually change the North Korean economy, society, and politics. A year later, South Korea elected a new president who was committed to a tougher North Korea policy. Pyongyang eventually responded to the new inter-Korean policy with greater hostility, favoring party and military positions.

Return to Six-Party Talks

A month after the nuclear test, congressional Democrats took over both houses of the U.S. Congress and demanded changes in policy toward North Korea. Key members of the administration pushing the pressure strategy resigned,[1] and the new Congress pushed the administration to appoint a single coordinator of North Korea policy. The White House tapped lead negotiator Chris Hill. The United States offered aid in response for North Korea's nuclear dismantlement and offered to discuss North Korea's outstanding concern about the frozen assets at Banco Delta Asia.[2] Washington cautiously pursued a more flexible approach, and the United States and North Korea met bilaterally in Berlin in late January 2007.

The North Korean Foreign Ministry announced that the two countries had reached an agreement.[3] In a terse statement, the Foreign Ministry noted: "The talks took place from Jan. 16 to 18 in a positive and sincere atmosphere and a certain agreement was reached there."[4] There was no elaboration on the statement. The Foreign Ministry had been pushing for bilateral talks with the United States for years, and they were finally bearing fruit. Nevertheless, the party newspaper ran a commentary the same day suggesting that "the United States is viciously pursuing the policy hostile to Korea." No recent evidence was given to support that claim. The commentary in the party newspaper the next day focused on the four-month-old news that the United States had moved a squadron of stealth fighters to South Korea and was "hastening preparations for a war of northward aggression behind the curtains of six-party talks."[5] The party was grasping at straws to oppose renewed momentum in the U.S.-DPRK diplomatic track. Central authorities would rule against them.

The following day, North Korean state policy became clear. A senior party representative reversed course and uncharacteristically supported the cabinet's foreign policy advocacy: "Kim Ki-nam, secretary of the Central Committee of the Workers' Party of Korea, in a statement on January 20 fully supported and approved the joint statement released by the political parties, government and organizations of the DPRK, recognizing that the statement is the most just and patriotic appeal indicating the path of a sacred struggle to achieve earlier the national reunification, the supreme task facing the nation at present."[6] The party tends to employ rhetorical flourishes; this statement was more subdued and more straightforward than many party announcements. The party supported the long-held position of the government, representing a bureaucratic defeat. The subdued statement suggests Kim Ki-nam was unenthusiastic about the move but was directed to issue it. The party had to publicly back off its opposition to negotiations. Kim Jong Il likely personally weighed in on this watershed change in the North's policy. Stated institutional positions from each of the bureaucracies supporting negotiations with the Americans signaled that the state was ready to deal.

Six-party talks resumed on February 8. In the two weeks between Kim Ki-nam's statement and the resumption of talks, the party managed to express restrained doubt about the outcome of the negotiating session. A party commentary noted: "Whenever the opportunity presents itself, the United States says that it will resolve the Korean peninsula issue through 'dialogue.' As reality shows, however, the United States is acting diametrically contrary to its words."[7] The party's criticism was more reserved than previous statements had been and did not affect diplomatic progress.

After five days of negotiations, the six-party talks adjourned. North Korea pledged in the joint document to seal and dismantle the Yongbyon nuclear facility and provide a list of its nuclear facilities. Japan and North Korea also promised to reopen normalization talks and "the Parties agreed to cooperate in economic, energy and humanitarian assistance to the DPRK" starting with heavy fuel oil shipments.[8] The DPRK media did not carry the joint document's text. Instead, the Foreign Ministry announced the deliverables it had secured, prompting external observers to conclude there must have been some internal debate in Pyongyang on the joint document itself.[9]

By the following month, U.S.-DPRK talks were under way, and Cabinet Premier Pak Pong Ju emerged from a five-month public hiatus around the nuclear test to host South Korea's unification minister Lee Jae-joung for four days in Pyongyang. In these first post-test inter-Korean talks, Pak requested the resumption of rice and fertilizer aid, economic projects, and a peace treaty to end the Korean War saying, "Now is the time for the two Koreas to step on a springboard planted on firmer ground."[10] North Korea's cabinet sought to maintain Seoul's conciliatory northern policy. KCNA paraphrased Chief Councilor of the Cabinet Kwon Ho Ung's keynote address, "Recalling that the North-South relations witnessed repeated suspension and resumption, he held that this abnormal situation should not be allowed to repeat itself any longer. To this end, it is necessary to refrain from sacrificing the interests of the nation for the sake of the relations with the outsiders under any circumstances."[11] The South Korean administration agreed that inter-Korean engagement should be permanent and sustainable as this sentiment became the first thought expressed almost verbatim in the joint press statement at the meeting's conclusion.[12] Government-to-government inter-Korean relations continued to improve even as the South Korean public grew more wary of dealing with the North after the nuclear test.

Meanwhile, for the first time since 1992, the IAEA sent a delegation to North Korea to discuss implementing the February[13] six-party agreement. Lower-level working groups of the six parties met in Beijing to discuss energy and economic assistance. Washington also dispatched a Treasury Department official to Macao to finalize the removal of the U.S. financial measures against North Korea. Before the month was over, the six-party talks had resumed again. The political stage was set for more progress, but citing a technical problem in transferring funds, the United States claimed the North Korean money could not be unfrozen. The talks ended four days later without progress as the North Korean delegation refused to negotiate until the BDA funds were actually unfrozen.13

With the delay in six-party negotiations, KPA officials took the opportunity to repeat the KPA's opposition to accommodation and that it stood ready to defeat the Americans. The KPA's endgame is clear: defeating the Americans by getting them to leave Korea would pave the way for reunifying the nation. "Should the U.S. imperialists infringe even a bit upon the sovereignty of the DPRK and its right to existence, the KPA will wipe them out at a single stroke and accomplish the historic cause of national reunification, the cherished desire of the nation, without fail."[14] The call seemed particularly hollow in a general atmosphere of negotiating progress, much like previous cabinet and Foreign Ministry statements holding out the prospect for continued negotiations as other bureaucratic actors' policy preferences won out.

Cabinet Economic Reformer Replaced with Economic Reformer

Cabinet Premier Pak Pong Ju had a difficult balancing act, having to continuously advocate for economic reforms always couched in socialist language. In light of military and party opposition to the cabinet's accommodating foreign policy with the Americans and its economic opening
platform, Kim Jong Il removed Pak from power. But instead of being
executed as other economic reformers had been, Pak was moved into a
managerial position in a chemical factory.[15] Furthermore the regime did
not distance itself far from Pak's advocacy. His replacement was a former
subordinate the transportation minister Kim Yong Il.

A week after Kim Yong Il replaced Pak, the new premier held a meeting
on the state budget. His first public comments in his new position articulated the same institutional goals as Pak's: "The meeting noted the need
for all of the economic guidance functionaries to strictly guarantee actual
profits in industrial management and to attain their units' state budget-
ary payment plans without fail every month and every quarter . . . [while]
resolutely maintain[ing] the principle of socialism."[16] Kim Yong Il was the
third consecutive cabinet premier since the 1998 constitutional revision
who had upgraded the institution's formal powers, and all three premiers
articulated the same vision, which was contrary to that espoused by their
party and military colleagues.

Premier Kim's first major speech took place a few months later, on the
anniversary of the state's founding. It largely reinforced state ideology,
but on the economy, the premier carefully balanced demands for heavy
industry with consumer goods, light industry, and agriculture: "We will
firmly adhere to the socialist economic construction line of the military-
first era and while developing the national defense industry first, we will
vigorously ignite the flames of the agricultural revolution and the light
industry revolution, thus the food problem and the issue of the people's
consumer goods should be smoothly resolved."[17] The new premier was not
as outspoken and effective as his predecessor, but he still presented the
same institutional policy line.

Party leaders also continued to argue that the state should favor heavy
industrialization and communal agricultural production and distribution.
They cited the need for administrative, not market, solutions to economic
problems. By working harder and applying science and technology, the

state could remedy underproduction.[18] It is unclear whether Pak's dismissal actual placated military and party hard-liners who had suffered major policy losses on both domestic and foreign policy. The replacement, after all, was simply another individual advocating the same positions, albeit with less personal clout and less effectiveness.

Chris Hill in Pyongyang

In late June 2007 Chris Hill traveled to Pyongyang for bilateral meetings with his North Korean counterparts—marking the highest-ranking official to visit Pyongyang since Hill's predecessor had led a delegation in 2002 when North Korea supposedly admitted to having a uranium enrichment program.[19] The Foreign Ministry labeled the discussions "comprehensive and productive" and said "both sides shared the view that they would start implementing the agreement on the premise that the issue of the remittance of the funds is finally settled and had an in-depth exchange of views on the actions to be taken by each side in the next phase."[20]

On June 25, the anniversary of the start of the Korean War, the North Korean Foreign Ministry confirmed that the $27 million of Banco Delta Asia accounts had been returned and the state would begin dismantling its nuclear complex at Yongbyon.[21] The following day, IAEA deputy director Olli Heinonen led a delegation to North Korea's nuclear facilities. The Foreign Ministry announced it would start shutting down Yongbyon as soon as the first delivery, or 10 percent of the pledged heavy fuel oil shipments, arrived rather than waiting for the entirety of the pledged oil.[22] Within a week, South Korea had made the first delivery. Pyongyang began to follow through on its pledge by shutting down and sealing Yongbyon; party and military personnel could not offer new evidence for delaying the dismantlement.

Lacking new evidence, the military attempted to cite historical reasons to scuttle this agreement. In a long article detailing a selected history of U.S.-DPRK confrontations from the 1950s to the present, and noting the fundamental untrustworthiness of the Americans on nuclear policy, the KPA attacked the agreement. "The KPA cannot but clarify its stance on the persistent maneuver of the anti-Republic fanatics of the United States. . . . Nobody can dare to deny that confrontation between the DPRK and the United States becomes a life and death confrontation of who beats whom.

As the other side to the engagement, we have the undeniable and legitimate right to prepare all the self-defensive means necessary to defend
one's right to existence from the threat and blackmail of the United States."
The KPA statement declared that if the regular U.S.–South Korean military
exercises continued, "the implementation of the 13 February agreement or
the six-party talks will evaporate"; it called on the United States to negotiate
a permanent peace regime to end the U.S. presence in Korea.[23]

The army's desperate effort did not produce the desired results, mirroring earlier unsuccessful cabinet efforts to forestall a confrontational policy.
U.S.-DPRK relations had improved, and the cabinet had the policy lead.
The Foreign Ministry announced the suspension of activities at Yongbyon,
and the IAEA inspectors confirmed the reactor was shut down.[24] Again, the
details of senior leadership's decision making remains obscured from view,
but two days later, six-party talks resumed. The North Korean negotiating
team called for an LWR in exchange for dismantling Yongbyon and providing a full declaration of its nuclear inventory to the IAEA. The Foreign
Ministry called for more talks as the round yielded no new agreement.[25]
Meanwhile, the two Koreas held another summit. Kim Jong Il and the
unpopular South Korean president Roh Moon Hyun met in Pyongyang.
With only three months left in office, Roh promised Pyongyang that Seoul
would expand multiyear, multibillion dollar economic projects.[26] Whether
any future South Korean administration would honor this late term presidential pledge was questionable.

U.S.-DPRK bilateral talks proved more effective. In early September the
United States and North Korea reached agreement—in Geneva, the site of
the signing of the 1994 Agreed Framework. North Korea pledged to declare
and disable all of its nuclear facilities by the end of the year in exchange
for the United States removing North Korea from the terrorism list and
ending Trading With the Enemy Act (TWEA) sanctions.[27] In North Korea's
mass media, the Foreign Ministry said it was "grateful" for "sincere" international aid, naming the United States as one of the donors of food in
response to recent flooding.[28] Party commentaries warned about U.S. and
IAEA inspections of Iraq prior to the U.S. invasion and pointed to regular
military exercises as further evidence of Washington's untrustworthiness,
but the party's efforts were futile as the United States and North Korea
were firmly on the engagement path.[29] In October a U.S. technical team
traveled to North Korea to verify the disabling of the nuclear facility and

announced that North Korea had made a "good start." Chris Hill visited North Korea in December and said dismantlement was "going well."

Presidential Turnover in South Korea

In December 2007 South Korea elected its first conservative president in a decade, Lee Myung-bak. The Korean Workers' Party had long published articles severely criticizing the South's conservative Grand National Party (GNP), but Cabinet Premier Pak's institutional successor, Kim Yong Il, carried on inter-Korean dialogue despite the election of a president from the GNP. Pyongyang preferred the liberal candidate, but the cabinet prior to the election pledged to work with the conservative administration if it was elected. The North Korean premier met with his South Korean counterpart, Prime Minister Han Duck-soo, in November 2007 and argued that the North's ideology supported negotiations with the South: "The experience and lesson over the past seven years following 15 June show that North-South relations can successfully develop when we are faithful to the idea of By Our Nation. Though our fellow countrymen are divided into the North and South, we have the power to safeguard the national dignity and interests and infinite potential that can achieve the nation's shared prosperity and development."[30]

The report documented concrete efforts to expand inter-Korean cooperation, stating that the cabinet premier "emphasized the importance of sincerely implementing the economic and cooperative issues pointed out in the declaration and said that the North-South cooperation projects are not simple economic dealings but are lofty projects that contribute to the nation's reconciliation, reunification, and prosperity."[31] The talks sought to head off conflicts in the West Sea that the KPA had routinely used to aggravate inter-Korean relations and accommodation with the Americans. The two premiers discussed turning the disputed area in the West Sea around the northern limit line into a "peace and cooperation zone." They also made concrete progress toward expanding rail and road links across the DMZ and expanding joint economic projects worth an additional $11–$15 billion.[32] At the end of the year, the two Koreas opened regular freight train service across the DMZ.[33] The cabinet continued to work for continued progress in inter-Korean relations.

President Lee took office in February 2008 and upheld his pledge to substantially modify his two predecessors' engagement policy. Candidate Lee had presented a harder line than his two predecessors; President Lee moved even farther to the right than his campaign pledges. He attempted to abolish South Korea's Unification Ministry, the institutional lead on Seoul's previous Nordpolitik, but settled for marginalizing it politically. Lee insisted his policy advocated engaging North Korea but increasingly tied economic aid to North Korea's denuclearization. The new administration declared its policy "pragmatic" by rejecting previous administrations' more unconditional engagement as ideologically driven and focused on short-term results.

Pyongyang's reaction for the first several months was notably restrained. When the North Koreans sought to register displeasure with a U.S.–South Korean alliance move, they put the blame squarely on Washington. Though Pyongyang still had a strong interest in maintaining momentum with the Americans, there still seemed to be a fairly uniform requirement for the North Korean bureaucracies not to speak out too harshly against the new government in the South. In the Security Consultative Meetings where Washington and Seoul discussed alliance wartime operational control, the party newspaper blamed the Americans for providing military support to South Korea but Seoul was not blamed for accepting it.[34] Normally, the party would label the South "puppets" of the Americans and culpable for this decision. After a U.S.-Japan-South Korea summit that the party newspaper called "triangular pressure cooperation," the article blamed Japan and the "United States, the master of Japan," but not South Korea.[35]

Pyongyang grew impatient with discussions in Washington on the future of its diplomatic engagement. The party used a U.S.–South Korean military exercise to argue that negotiations should end: "It has already been publicly recognized that the war exercise the U.S. warmongers are about to conduct is a war exercise of northward aggression. Conducting a war exercise against a party to dialogue now, when the DPRK and the United States are in the process of dialogue, proves that the position of [the United States] is that it does not want to settle the issue through dialogue."[36] The party abandoned its previous restraint against the United States and noted that these joint U.S.–South Korean exercises were the "full responsibility" of the United States.[37] The next day, however, another unattributed radio broadcast placed joint blame on the United States and South Korea without any indication that one was innocent or even a junior partner.[38]

The party showed an early willingness to criticize the new Lee government. First unattributed sources, then the party, and finally all bureaucracies criticized South Korea. The official press started cautiously blaming the new South Korean administration in late February, growing substantially more pointed by April. The North's Secretariat of the Committee for the Peaceful Reunification of the Fatherland blamed "the hard-line U.S. conservative forces and their followers—the belligerent South Korean forces . . . [for] expanding the current South Korea–U.S. Combined Marine Forces Command." Though it does not mention the South Korean president and lays the blame on a segment of the South Korean military, clearly Pyongyang was willing to make low-level jabs at the South.[39]

In mid-March, Pyongyang demonstrated an even greater willingness to criticize the new government in Seoul. A party commentary led the way after unattributed talks. "The pro-U.S. conservative forces in South Korea are now clinging more impatiently to a racket of confrontation against their fellow country with the backing of outside forces."[40] The party followed up with another direct criticism of Seoul, criticizing it for missile defense cooperation and making only a passing reference to the United States.[41] Previously, Pyongyang had focused on Washington's role in this type of military cooperation.

Though early party commentaries had blamed only the United States for military exercises, by late March, a cabinet article placed blame squarely on the shoulders of both Washington and Seoul: "The culprits that increase the threat of a new war, a nuclear war, by damaging peace and stability on the Korean peninsula today, are the United States and the following pro-U.S. conservative forces of South Korea."[42] This shift, coming from the cabinet, suggests a real downturn in inter-Korean relations. Each of the bureaucratic players started to voice opposition to Seoul. Lacking opposition to increased confrontation with the South, the model expects that the state will take a more aggressive stand toward its southern neighbor. This would not be a tactical move but a strategic turn that would require a significant change to reverse.

Relations deteriorated quickly. The technically independent *Tongil Sinbo* webpage took issue with the South Korean unification minister's comments that Seoul would tie Kaesong development assistance to nuclear progress. The article concluded: "The conservative ruling forces in South Korea—who seek nothing but confrontation in homage to outside forces bent on harming their fellow countrymen and pay no attention to the reconciliation, unity, and reunification of the nation—will be made to pay for their sins without fail."[43] The same day, the head of North Korea's general-level military talks with the South criticized the "violent remarks on a preemptive strike against us made by the chairman of the Joint Chiefs of Staff of the South Korean forces." The military representative noted, "Our army will counter even a slight move for a preemptive strike attempted by the South side with a more rapid and more powerful advanced preemptive strike." He demanded an apology, threatened to suspend all North-South dialogue, and prevented all South Korean officials from traveling to the North.[44]

On April 1 the North launched its most scathing attack on the South, severely criticizing the new South Korean president by name in a party commentary. The article was run repeatedly on North Korean television and radio; it ushered in a period of unrestrained criticism of their southern neighbor.[45] Within days, party commentaries had linked the Lee government with the Japanese imperialist period; an unofficial North Korean webpage satirized Lee in poetry and openly criticized him in prose.[46] And each institution harshly denounced the South Korean government.[47] Several months after Lee's inauguration, Pyongyang's prodding to convince Seoul to maintain the position of Lee's two predecessors took a decidedly different turn. The North Korean bureaucracy was united in its opposition to the new government in Seoul.

South Korea received most of the blame for U.S.–South Korean cooperation, whereas before Washington had taken the heat. The cabinet joined the party and the military in criticizing South Korea for a variety of offenses, from accepting U.S. beef imports to education changes to military exercises to Seoul's summits with Washington and Tokyo.[48]

Though the Lee government reiterated that it was pursuing an engagement policy and even offered the North economic aid, compared to the previous two governments, Seoul offered Pyongyang very little. In the coming months, Seoul offered corn aid, instead of the preferred rice. And whereas Lee's predecessor had discussed economic projects worth upward of $11 billion, now South Korea discussed providing $7 million worth of humanitarian assistance. Pyongyang refused all of South Korean offers, putting more

pressure on the South Korean government to revert to the liberal engagement policies of Lee's two predecessors. In effect, Pyongyang gambled $7
million in the hopes of hitting the $11 billion jackpot. This may not be a bad
strategy by casino standards, the regime was gambling with food when its
citizens still suffered from chronic food shortfalls.

North Korea demonstrated an ability to adapt to a changed environment
in inter-Korean relations. It could change suddenly as it had done with previous scenarios or gradually as with this one. First unattributed and then
party commentaries increasingly called on Seoul to shape an engagement
policy on the North's terms. Each bureaucracy joined in the anti-Seoul
chorus after the April 1 denunciation. Inter-Korean relations continued to
deteriorate throughout 2008. In an apparent accident, a North Korean soldier shot and killed a South Korean tourist who had entered a restricted
area in July. The incident reenergized South Korean public opposition to
unconditional engagement with the North when Pyongyang refused to
allow an investigation. Though making some minor concessions to the
North, Seoul maintained its firm position, and Pyongyang continued to
stonewall, calling on the conservative government to return to the liberal
engagement policy.[49] After Kim Jong Il reportedly started to recover from a
mid-August stroke, the North gradually ratcheted up pressure on the South
by first threatening and then taking action to sever all official inter-Korean
contact. Even the sunshine policy's flagship project, the Kaesong Industrial
Complex, came under attack from Pyongyang.

Just as the cabinet had previously concentrated its energies on inter-
Korean issues when tensions with the United States were at a high point,
the organization shifted to the exact opposite. The cabinet now defended
its progress with the Americans despite periodic setbacks from the rest of
the year. Resolving inter-Korean tensions seemed to be a bridge too far,
presumably due to a high level decision and few signals of a substantial
change in Lee's principled stand.

Refocusing on the United States

Everything was not coming up roses in U.S.-DPRK relations in 2008, but
fragile progress moved forward. In January the Foreign Ministry noted that
North Korea had initiated disablement in November and urged the United

States to uphold its part of the most recent agreement, including removing North Korea from the State Sponsors of Terrorism list and completing fuel deliveries. "Now that other participating nations delay the fulfillment of their commitments, the DPRK is compelled to adjust the tempo of the disablement of some nuclear facilities on the principle of 'action for action.' The DPRK still hopes that the October 3 agreement can be smoothly implemented should all the participating nations make concerted sincere efforts on the principle of simultaneous action."[50] The cabinet newspaper rejected calls for the North to give up its nuclear weapons before the United States took action.[51]

The party took a more aggressive stand in accordance with its wider policy agenda. Citing a White House announcement that the United States planned to reduce its nuclear arsenal to one-fourth of Cold War levels, party commentary noted: "The United States' announcement of its plan to reduce nuclear weapons-related facilities is nothing but a petty trick to deceive the world's public opinion."[52] The party spun news to portray the United States in the worst possible light. Another party commentary lashed out at the news that a U.S. division would soon serve on a rotational assignment to South Korea. For the party, this "clearly laid bare the aggressive and criminal plan of the United States that is trying to indefinitely occupy South Korea as a bridgehead for nuclear war and thereby realize the wild ambition for northward aggression and the strategy for the domination of the world at any cost."[53] It spoke out against F-16s stationed in South Korea and U.S. efforts to engage South Korea in the Proliferation Security Initiative, which the party labeled a blockade.[54]

The Foreign Ministry, stressing repeatedly the United States' "sincerity," said the United States should uphold its commitments in the six-party talks.[55] It hosted a U.S. Track II delegation of senior current and former government officials in February; military officials turned down the delegation's requests for a meeting.[56] Senior congressional staffer Keith Luse commented in a trip report: "Is the North Korean military resisting MFA efforts to substantively engage with the United States and the other five countries? Chairman Kim's best efforts to orchestrate a balance among competing interests within the North, may be a 'stretch too far' for North Korean military hardliners. Declaring and discarding the jewel of their arsenal will be difficult for those viewing it as the ultimate deterrent."[57] Former director of the Los Alamos National Laboratory Siegfried Hecker came to a similar conclusion. He reported that cooperation between the North Korean nuclear specialists and Americans monitoring the disablement was "excellent." But the Foreign Ministry hosts had explained, in Hecker's words, that the "DPRK military and industrial officials were extremely unhappy with the access the Americans were granted and with the fact that they were given samples of the aluminum tubes in question," which provided evidence of enriched uranium in North Korea.[58] The Foreign Ministry again demonstrated a willingness to deal with the Americans in official and nonofficial realms while the military and party resisted such efforts.

Indeed, the party publicly contradicted the Foreign Ministry's statement that the Americans should uphold their commitments sincerely, concluding that the United States could not sincerely engage Pyongyang. Washington would always find some pretext to scuttle paper agreements,

> The national sovereignty is a prerequisite for peace and prosperity, and the nation's dignity and happiness depend on sovereignty. That is why our party eloquently made an appeal again in the joint editorial to firmly maintain the position of the national independence. . . . The United States is continuously raising the level of pressure against our Republic, persistently finding fault with us by fabricating the 'nuclear issue' and 'human rights issue,' and so on. . . . Peace, which is a prerequisite for development and prosperity, should be seized by struggles. Self-defensive national defense capabilities are the guarantee of defending peace. . . . Our party's position on peace and prosperity is firm.[59]

The party questioned U.S. sincerity based on ideological convictions of the aggressive nature of the imperialists, but it did not call for a scrapping of six-party talks outright. The party registered its objection and pledged to struggle on.

Talks stalled in April when the Bush administration briefed Congress on its evidence of North Korean nuclear assistance to Syria. The briefing came eight months after Israeli air strikes destroyed the facility, raising ire that the administration was trying to sidetrack the legislative branch to maintain diplomatic momentum. Some members of Congress argued against continued negotiations with the North Koreans.[60] In this situation, the Foreign Ministry remained fairly quiet. It made a single pro forma objection to a U.S. democracy report, and an unattributed radio broadcast mildly rebuked President Bush for supporting missile defense in Europe.[61] Party commentaries noted that "hard-line elements" in Washington sought to undermine diplomatic progress and disguise their true hostile intent with "cunning" diplomatic overtures.[62]

However, largely conservative opposition in Congress to a conservative White House's foreign policy did not derail the administration's new focus. In mid-June the Foreign Ministry announced that U.S.-DPRK negotiations in Pyongyang had "proved successful," as Pyongyang moved to supply a nuclear declaration and Washington started efforts to remove North Korea from the terrorism list.[63] The military and the party made some effort to turn the tide in U.S.-DPRK negotiations. Party commentaries rejected the U.S. defense secretary's comments that nuclear weapons could help deter states like Russia and Iran. Though the speech did not mention Korea, the party pointed out increased American nuclearization even as North Korea took steps away from this.[64] They continued to note the United States was the "root cause of war" on the peninsula.[65] Still, they refrained from the most outlandish calls to reject the diplomatic track altogether and rely on military means as they had done at other times. The military condemned American and South Korean criticisms of North Korea's human rights record; the KPA linked the United States with South Korea and argued that the allies wanted to see the collapse of North Korea and its integration into South Korean society. But the focus was mainly on Seoul's criticism of North Korea's human rights violations, not Washington's criticism.[66]

In mid-July the U.S.-DPRK diplomatic option was on track. North Korea had destroyed the Yongbyon reactor's cooling tower, a largely symbolic move that signaled the state's decision to dismantle the nuclear site. The United States began the process of delisting and also delivered its first shipment of the five hundred thousand tons of pledged food aid. The World Food Program's Asia director commented that his organization, which was delivering most of the American food aid, enjoyed "the best monitoring conditions the WFP has ever had in North Korea."[67]

However, when Washington did not remove North Korea from the terrorism list as quickly as Pyongyang expected, U.S.-DPRK relations soured. Washington noted that the nuclear declaration required verification, citing its lack of several key nuclear installations, before removing North Korea from the terrorism list. The Foreign Ministry called on the United States to uphold the letter of the published agreement that did not provide for the document's verification prior to delisting. The party took a different view, running articles saying Washington's actions demonstrated the true intent of the imperialists.[68] With great fanfare, Pyongyang had already demolished Yongbyon's cooling tower. Though it could be rebuilt with relative ease, the highly publicized demolition would embarrass the country if Washington did not follow through on delisting the North.

Party and military criticisms of the United States spiked. The party objected to the U.S. Forces Korea commander having compared North Korea and Iraq, was again critical of new U.S. nuclear weapons, objected to U.S. naval assets moving into Korea for military exercises, and stressed the strength of socialist ideology to defeat imperialists—all within two days.[69] They linked U.S. policy to economic policy, arguing that opening was dangerous and impractical while terrorism list sanctions remaining in place.[70]

As the model predicts, the cabinet continued to take a more moderate view. It openly urged American delisting, condemning the delay as tactical and not a strategic move. The cabinet held that the United States was trying to extract more concessions at the negotiating table, not threaten the state's basic existence. Nevertheless, the cabinet warned that the delisting delay jeopardized recent diplomatic gains:

> The question is why the United States is continuously committing such acts of military provocation that irritate us—its dialogue partner—at a crucial time when diplomatic efforts are under way to resolve the pending issues between the DPRK and the United States and thereby to put an end to hostile relations which have persisted between our Republic and the United States for many decades. . . . Since the situation has entered an important crossroads where the DPRK-U.S. relations of deep-rooted hostility should be brought to an end, and peace and stability on the Korean peninsula should be achieved through the denuclearization of the Korean peninsula, now is the time for the United States and other relevant countries to act with discretion.[71]

The cabinet did not explicitly issue an ultimatum, but it warned that failure to delist would have significant, long-term, strategic consequences.

With the delisting delay ongoing, even the government's newspaper began running more critical pieces of the United States.[72] The party newspaper criticized "U.S. imperialism" and American nuclear policy, and the Foreign Ministry took issue with renewed U.S.–South Korean military exercises.[73] In September, the Foreign Ministry announced that the state would begin efforts to restart Yongbyon "as a countermeasure against the action taken by the United States to indefinitely put on hold the effectuation of the measure on removing our country from the state sponsors of terrorism list. This was a natural, logical result in accordance with the principle of action for action." As "a natural, logical result" no bureaucracy voiced support or condemnation of the decision.[74] Pyongyang was playing hard ball to secure delisting but also indicated its willingness to verifiably dismantle Yongbyon in exchange.

North Korea's vice foreign minister Pak Kil-yon expressed the same sentiment the following week in the country's address to the UN General Assembly and other Foreign Ministry statements bolstered the point.[75] Meanwhile, party commentaries called for a strategic shift: provide security through nuclear weapons, not negotiations, and secure the state's sovereignty and dignity.[76] The internal controversy over the terrorism list was resolved in mid-October when the United States removed North Korea from the list.

With a new president slated for the White House, the United States and North Korea continued their tenuous engagement in the six-party venue. Though Pyongyang said it would treat Japan as if it was not present at six-party talks due to a bilateral dispute, the negotiating structure remained in place through the end of the year. Washington remained highly skeptical of the North's supposedly complete nuclear declaration, raising real concerns that the agreement had narrowed to one where North Korea was only giving up the aging Yongbyon reactor, not its full nuclear program. Concerns about the North's uranium enrichment program had long sat in the background in nuclear negotiations due to differences over whether Pyongyang had admitted having such a program in 2002 and the more substantial question of verifying dismantlement of this more easily hidden program. U.S.-DPRK relations were anything but friendly, but Pyongyang seemed to be angling for more concessions from the incoming Obama administration by backing off its verbal commitments to verification.[77] By the end of the Bush administration, U.S.-DPRK relations had made a dramatic comeback. Whether those improved relations would allow a negotiated solution to the long list of outstanding issues between the countries, however, remained to be seen.

Continuity Amid Change: The North Korean Economy

North Korea's third strategic issue area, the economy, saw a great deal of changes over the decade under analysis. But during the last two years when North Korea's relations with the United States and South Korea flipped, Pyongyang maintained the status quo in the economic realm. The party's advocacy for retreat from the 2002 economic reforms continued to carry the day, and after the nuclear test, souring relations with South Korea and China—the main backers of the North's economic changes—did not aid the cabinet's argument. The party had the lead on economic matters and tried to reinforce this institutional reality through regular pronouncements to that effect.

The party argued that the rest of the government should follow it in this ideological position, rejecting alternative institutional views. "If a country wants to develop and be strong, it should be politically stable and its society should be united. . . . Unity is a root of socialism, and the power of ideology eventually comes out of the power of unity that firmly solidifies all the people as one under the column of the Party and the leader."[78] Party unity means squelching unwanted dissent within the state. More directly, the party demanded that cabinet functionaries follow party guidance in all cases, "All functionaries should display all the more higher the revolutionary trait of unconditionally implementing the party policy to the end. . . . The party line and policy are filled with fighting tasks and methods and strategy and tactics for embodying the Juche idea and the military-first idea in all areas of revolution and construction."[79] The party's guidance was comprehensive. The rest of the system should get on board not only for U.S. policy but also for economic construction and all other areas.

The party enjoyed authority granted in the 2008 New Year's joint editorial and cited it time and again throughout the year. The important planning document reiterated that the cabinet must adhere to party economic

guidance: "Leading functionaries of economic establishments at all levels, including the cabinet, should strictly adhere to the socialist principle and the collectivist principle in conducting economic management,
regarding the party's economic ideas, theories, and policies as unbreak-
able guidelines for the construction of an economically powerful state."[80]
The emphasis on unity over divergent policy options indicated the cabinet
should not attempt to chip away at the party's economic position, prioritizing defense and "guaranteeing the planned and balanced development of
the national economy."[81]

The party repeated this emphasis on planning over markets several
times throughout the year. The party's commitment to socialist economics was in line with the Juche ideology and must be adhered to.[82] Cabinet
functionaries should implement the party's economic planning guidance:
"The socialist economy is a planned economy, which can be rapidly developed only when its superiority is adhered to and unreservedly displayed.
For this reason, this year's joint editorial importantly stressed the issue of
strengthening the planned discipline in all sectors and all units of people's
economy. In order to brilliantly realize the grand goal of building an economically powerful state presented by the party, all functionaries and working people must cherish the superiority of socialist planned economy as
their firm faith and put great strength into displaying it highly."[83]

Furthermore, communal ownership and abandoning markets allows the
state "to fully secure the true freedom and rights for the people masses and
provide them with prosperous and happy lives," while "economic reform
maneuvers of the Lee Myung-bak gang for 'opening up the North' are an
attempt to degenerate our system and to 'absorb' our Republic into their
'liberal democratic system' and thus will unfailingly bring nothing but
North-South confrontation and war."[84] The party comprehensively rejected
all cabinet efforts to reform the North's economy, claiming that they were
contrary to Kim's NYJE guidance, socialist orthodoxy, party direction, and
even the country's basic national interests.

The post-totalitarian institutionalism model suggests that the cabinet
would likely try to resist. And the cabinet did continue to cautiously present
the benefits of marketization, even expounding upon conceptions such as
a price index on the same day that inter-Korean relations took a substantial
and sustained downturn.[85] The cabinet also noted that "the DPRK government is consistently pursuing the policy of encouraging joint venture with

various countries over the world." This meant expanding the number of foreign companies willing to invest in the state, "transcending differences in ideology, ideal[s] and social system."[86] The cabinet held that North Korea should expand international economic cooperation at least with the friendliest states that may establish joint ventures with the regime and develop the tools for rational macroeconomic policy, including basic economic data.

The party refuted these cabinet arguments with a special article in *Nodong Sinmun* noting the party's role in guiding a "collectivist" economic policy and imploring cabinet functionaries once again to simply carry out the party's orders. In short, the party told the cabinet to stop debating; they had already lost. Efforts to "convert the socialist planned economy to a market economy . . . [were] imperialist maneuvers" that should be avoided at all cost.[87] The party also noted its institutional role in upholding the planned economy in the government newspaper. The party often uses this vehicle when it seeks to speak directly to a government audience, "It is the proud fruit of the planned socialist economy that our economy—which has broken through harsh trials under the wise leadership of the party—is achieving active orbit, vigorously displaying its might."[88] Though marketization was far from dead, it suffered continued setbacks as the time frame under analysis closed. The cabinet continued to mildly assert the benefits of markets and greater openness, but poor relations with Seoul and Beijing created an unfavorable external environment for this stance. The cabinet had little contemporary evidence to cite and the economic situation, while still dire, was not as bad as previous years, allowing the party's economic advocacy to remain on top.

Since its October 2006 nuclear test, North Korea demonstrated an ability to gradually reverse course on its policy positions. Though each of its three main political institutions kept their same basic platforms, the state moved significantly. Ten years of active inter-Korean relations collapsed in a matter of months, and six years of highly hostile dealings with the Americans moderated significantly. Pyongyang's economic policy remained constant amid these changes as economic issues largely receded from the headlines. North Korea's three bureaucracies reacted in predictable form, but external events largely drove their policy. As a small, reactionary state, Pyongyang again showed how external actors can largely shape its internal debates, which ultimately affect national political outcomes.

With new congressional leadership in Washington and a growing sense that the 2001–2006 policy had not prevented Pyongyang's nuclear test, Washington's shift to engage the North started to bear fruit. Though it remains unclear if negotiators will convince North Korea to give up all of its nuclear programs and weapons, diplomatic efforts by the end of the Bush administration had achieved the initial dismantling of Yongbyon. The nuclear reactor that provided all of the plutonium for Pyongyang's nuclear test and an unknown number of nuclear weapons was verifiably shut down and was being taken apart—at least for a time.[89] This was a dramatic shift from the North's decision in 2002 to restart that same reactor, which had been shut down for eight years at that time.

Pyongyang's ability to change its strategic position in inter-Korean cooperation is likewise notable. While ten years of engagement by the Kim Dae Jung and Roh Moo-hyun administrations yielded the establishment and expansion of the Kaesong Industrial Complex, Mt Kumgang Tourist Site, family reunions, and other economic projects and government-to-government efforts, Pyongyang managed to freeze or significantly limit activity in each of these areas of cooperation. And at the time of writing the risk of inter-Korean conflict was higher than anytime since the Kim Young Sam administration in the 1990s. The state's bureaucracies came together in opposition to the new Lee Myung-bak administration, mirroring an earlier period when these institutions united to oppose American policies.

Amid these changes, economic policy remained somewhat separated from international politics. Each bureaucracy kept its position on the economy, but the party and military won out over the cabinet. Pyongyang did not announce any new efforts to reintroduce significant marketization as the government sector in areas like food distribution grew at the expense of markets. Though the regime did not reverse all changes that had come with the markets over the years, including bottom-up changes that produced a slowly revising social structure, it did show how the North's economic policy can be explained by the post-totalitarian institutionalism model.

CHAPTER EIGHT

Conclusion

North Korea more closely resembles the post-totalitarian institutionalism model than previously presented theories of nondemocratic rule. Kim is unquestionably the single most important person in North Korean politics. His role should not be minimized, but Kim is not the state. To more fully understand North Korean politics and explain variant policy outcomes, one must evaluate the second-order institutions that Kim seeks to command. Authority remains centralized, but power is more diffuse than the relatively monolithic typologies of totalitarian, corporatist, and personalist rule ascribe.

North Korea's Post-totalitarian Institutionalism

North Korea's bureaucracies have sufficient autonomy, corporate identity, and conflicting objectives that their advocacy and actions help explain variant North Korean policy outcomes. The cabinet, party, and military interact by applying three distinct, individually coherent institutional policy platforms to specific policy debates. These general policy outlooks are stable across leaders of each institution, further indicating that these groups do not fundamentally change with the personal position of the institution's leader. Though the institutions are formally stovepiped, they express conflicting ideas and spin facts and events in the official press. Institutional actors resist decided policy and take actions in contradiction to the regime's overall policy to shape the agenda according to these preconceived platforms. They operate under the ultimate authority of the supreme decision maker, but their operations have a meaningful and systematic impact on national policy.

Policy choices are not simply a function of institutional interaction without reference to Kim and his top advisers, but institutions do have power in North Korea. They impact policy decision making by framing the agenda and defining most of the policy alternatives. Policy innovation does not merely come from Kim's mind; it often comes from below. Central authorities generally select between these presented options. Institutions frame decisions by contextualizing specific contemporary events in a particular historical or ideological context or present recent empirical data to bolster their advocacy. Though leaders make decisions and can reject advice, this advice in the aggregate is important. In a post-totalitarian institutional state like North Korea, inner circle advisers have an incentive to avoid getting out of line with mainstream thinking lest they jeopardize their personal and professional survival. Impersonal institutions have more room to innovate—a characteristic not generally associated with bureaucracies in a democratic context. Put differently, inner circle groupthink and innovation-discouraging incentives limit this authoritative body's power over policy direction and variance by institution helps explain more divergent national policy decisions than hidden inner circle deliberations.

Institutions also influence implementation, modifying central decisions when they can. Central authorities make every effort to control bureaucratic action, but a single individual's ability to do so is limited. This is not to suggest the Kim family's rule is fragile. It is to suggest that its power is not as thorough as the totalitarian and personalistic ideal types suggest. Kim and other leaders of states that fit the post-totalitarian model must contend with institutional opposition and freelancing. Kim relies on peer institutions and a divided security apparatus.

Kim must manage these bureaucracies through the divide-and-conquer arrangement that he molded. North Korea no longer has a single, monolithic party that guides strategic decision making under the power of a single man nor is the command economy or ideological correctness sacrosanct today as under Kim Il Sung. North Korea has moved away from but not totally abandoned these core elements of totalitarianism. Institutional interaction has replaced party monolithism; markets have etched cracks in the command economy; and ideological arguments compete with rational ones in policy debates. The party competes with the military and cabinet in advocating national policy. The party's efforts to reassert its dominant, comprehensive institutional position after the 1998 constitutional revision have failed. Post-totalitarian institutionalism is not simply an interim state but a regime type more robust and sustainable than many other typologies of nondemocratic rule with relatively short lives.

An Evolved Polity

Totalitarianism comes closer to explaining an earlier period in North Korean politics under Kim Il Sung. The younger Kim's government is still highly centralized, but not as much so as its predecessor. Due to the exogenous shocks to the system in the 1990s, North Korea's political system changed. Kim Jong Il did not have the personal gravitas to hold together a united polity. The younger Kim accepted the inefficiencies of a divided government to aid his effort to maintain control over the state. Pitting one institution against another allowed Kim to restrain one large modern bureaucracy with another. Placing greater emphasis on rational results even when in competition with ideological imperatives allowed the state to stave off collapse amid serious challenges to regime survival. Kim did not choose to move away from his father's totalitarian state and likely would have preferred the stronger, totalitarian state, but the natural progression of totalitarian states and particular accelerating dynamics in the 1990s forced his hand.

It is important to recognize that post-totalitarianism institutionalism is an outgrowth of a totalitarian state. In this sense, it is a subset of the generic post-totalitarian umbrella type. Kim maintained much of the old system, changing only what he thought he must in order to address the changing internal and external situation and avert collapse. Kim implemented changes to the political and economic structure over time based on particular needs that in the aggregate created a political system different than his father's.

Consequently, the post-totalitarian institutional state retains some key elements of totalitarianism. In North Korea's case, the state still uses arbitrary terror and regular purges to instill fear and anxiety in elites and the masses alike. Despite extensive elite privilege, the system holds long-range goals beyond simply enriching the leadership, including broad national goals like reunification, macroeconomic improvements, and anti-imperialism. Pyongyang monopolizes the media and does not allow civil society or popular dissent to develop. North Korea's state institutions carefully provide distinct views in the controlled press, but that press should not be misunderstood as being even remotely free.

North Korea also lacks a comprehensive opposition within the country. The population does not have an alternative to the status quo and has no semiorganized means to pursue it due to continual purges and extensive repression. There are not significant non-governmental groups that can resist state power as the Solidarity movement and Catholic Church did in communist Poland. Forces of moderation and reform are firmly within the authority of, and indeed sanctioned and employed by, the state. This does not mean opposition could not develop, especially given continued material hardship, ideological decline, and regime ineptitude. But the current reality is that no organized opposition to the state exists within the country. By thwarting domestic opposition, the regime has more opportunity to gradually modify its positions. Facing increased impotence in these core areas, Pyongyang could alter its mode of operations to recapture its ability to provide basic services to the population and maintain a mantle of legitimacy as a protector against imperialist forces and champion of a reunified Korea.

North Korea's specific post-totalitarianism also involved addressing ideological change. Ideology and tradition are still critical inputs into policy decisions in all issue areas under consideration. Juche, military-first politics, and the Kims' personality cults are important parts of regime stability. Kim does not want to be measured only on the rational outputs of his governance, because this raises the specter that another individual could do the job more effectively. Kim references his bloodline to bolster his legitimacy and the regime continues to expend great energy to uphold the integrated ideological justifications of its rule. At the same time, ideological erosion is common to totalitarian regimes. As the promised utopia is not realized, regime calls for extreme sacrifice for a better future ring hollow. Propaganda pays diminishing returns.

The state increasingly must focus on tangible results to augment this decline in ideological furor while not discounting the importance of ideology. At a basic level, the regime must provide for the fundamental needs of its citizens. The declining material condition of the state where it cannot prevent chronic food and heating shortages makes ever delayed promises of a better future more difficult to accept. The state uses repression as a check on ideological decline to keep its grip on power, but it has not shifted to a simple, personalistic rule where repression is the cornerstone of regime maintenance. Such a shift away from ideology would represent an important change in North Korea's post-totalitarian institutionalism, greatly weakening its tools for maintaining social control and political stability. North Korea's broad and deep institutional arrangements also continue to distinguish it from the less stable personalistic state.

North Korea has developed meaningful groups that influence policy decision making and implementation. Though these groups operate within the state, this group identity and shared purpose breaks down the individual atomization that the totalitarian regime type encourages. Elites can engage in group politics in this restricted way. More directly, the state is not as monolithic as totalitarianism suggests. These groups advocate distinct policy purposes, conflict with and undermine one another at times, and even resist central decisions. This disunity and structural conflict is the most significant difference between the post-totalitarian institutional model and totalitarianism and corporatism that predict relative intragovernmental harmony.

Decision Making

Over the eleven-year period under consideration, there were periods of time when one institution's preferences prevailed over another's. With very rare exceptions, no single institution could claim victory on all three issue areas at once, nor did any institution sustain its victories indefinitely. North Korea's evolution is not simply the rise of one institution as the expense of the other two. There is no easily identifiable linear progression that accompanies the relative rationalization of the system. Table 8.1 documents the institutions that wrestled agenda control on all three issue areas. Though not all debates have a clear winner and loser, nor are they of equal importance

TABLE 8.1 Institutional Lead by Issue Area, 1998–2009			
DATE	ISSUE AREA	POLICY ISSUE	LEAD INSTITUTION
September 1998	U.S./Inter-Korean policy	Taepodong-1 launch credit	n/a[a]
October 1998–May 1999	U.S. policy	Kumchang-ri suspected nuclear facility	Cabinet
November 1998	U.S. policy	OPlan 5027	n/a[a]
January 1999	Economic policy	Second Chollima march	Party
January 1999	U.S./Inter-Korean/economic policy	Institutional supremacy claimed by party	Military/cabinet
June 1999	Inter-Korean	Northern limit line naval clash	Military
July 1999	Inter-Korean	Ministerial negotiations	Cabinet
July 1999	U.S. policy	Renewed contacts	Cabinet
September 1999	U.S./Inter-Korean policy	Taepodong-2 launch preparations	Cabinet
June 2000	Inter-Korean policy	First North-South summit	Cabinet
June 2000	U.S. policy	Missile moratorium	Cabinet
October 2000	U.S. policy	High-level visits to Pyongyang and Washington	Cabinet
January 2001	Economic policy	Kim's tour of Southern China	Cabinet
March 2001	Inter-Korean policy	Letter exchanges; North Korean delegation to Seoul	Cabinet
May 2001	U.S./Inter-Korean policy	Missile moratorium	Cabinet
May 2001	U.S. policy	Kim's "wait and see" comment	Neutral
June 2001	Inter-Korean policy	Naval clash	Military

TABLE 8.1 Institutional Lead by Issue Area, 1998–2009 (*continued*)			
DATE	ISSUE AREA	POLICY ISSUE	LEAD INSTITUTION
July 2001	U.S. policy	Policy review conclusions/ negotiation offers	n/a[b]
August 2001	U.S. policy	Missile launches	Cabinet
November 2001	Inter-Korean policy	Ministerial meetings at standstill	Military
December 2001– February 2002	U.S. policy	High-level U.S. comments urging comprehensive change in North Korea	Party/military
June 2002	U.S./Inter-Korean policy	Naval clash	Military
June 2002	Inter-Korean policy	World Cup congratulations	Cabinet
July 2002	Economic policy	Wage and price reforms	Cabinet
Aug 2002	U.S. policy	Quiet engagement on new sanctions	Cabinet
Sept 2002	Inter-Korean policy	Road/rail links; family reunions; unified sports team	Cabinet
October 2002	U.S. policy	U.S. visit to Pyongyang	Party/military
November 2002	Economic policy	Economics education	Cabinet
November 2002	Inter-Korean policy	Kaesong groundbreaking	Cabinet
March 2003	Inter-Korean policy	Continuation of economic projects amid challenges over rail explosion	Cabinet

(*continued*)

TABLE 8.1 Institutional Lead by Issue Area, 1998–2009 (*continued*)

DATE	ISSUE AREA	POLICY ISSUE	LEAD INSTITUTION
May 2005	U.S. policy	Announcement regarding reprocessed fuel rods	Party/military
June 2005	Inter-Korean policy	Anniversary of inter-Korean summit celebration	Cabinet
June 2005	U.S. policy	Dying wish comment	Cabinet
September 2005	U.S. policy	Agreement on guiding principles	Cabinet
September 2005	U.S. policy	LWR demand and reaction to BDA	Party/military
November 2005	Economic policy	Reintroduction of the PDS	Party/military
July 2006	U.S. policy	TD-2 flight test	Military/party
October 2006	U.S. policy	Nuclear test	Military/party
January 2007	U.S. policy	Berlin agreement	Cabinet
February 2007	U.S. policy	Six-party agreement on denuclearization	Cabinet
February 2007	Inter-Korean policy	Renewal of contacts	Cabinet
April 2007	Economic policy	Less influential technocrat as Cabinet Premier Pak's replacement	Party/military
June 2007	U.S. policy	U.S. official in Pyongyang; BDA resolved	Cabinet
September 2007	U.S. policy	Lifting some sanctions for disablement deal	Cabinet
November 2007	Inter-Korean policy	Commitment to economic projects with South	Cabinet

TABLE 8.1 Institutional Lead by Issue Area, 1998–2009 *(continued)*			
DATE	ISSUE AREA	POLICY ISSUE	LEAD INSTITUTION
February 2008	Inter-Korean policy	Beginning of North's negative reaction to new ROK president	Military/party
July 2008	U.S. policy	NK destruction of cooling tower; start of U.S. food aid deliveries	Cabinet
July 2008	U.S. policy	Delay in terrorist list removal	Party/military
October 2008	U.S. policy	Terrorist list removal	Cabinet
January 2009	U.S. policy	NK's attempts to recast terms of ongoing talks with new U.S. administration	Party/military

[a] No resolution

[b] No immediate response

or have the same lasting effect, the table demonstrates that no single institution has won out over the others in a sustained fashion.

North Korea's polity has grown relatively more rational than in the past, but this does not suggest that the cabinet is the new preeminent institution in North Korean politics or that one should expect it to take on this role in the future. Quite the contrary, the most recent evidence points to a reversal of many of the cabinet's early gains in economic and inter-Korean policy. North Korea's current system is stable because institutions check one another and blend rational policy justifications with ideological ones. Policy decisions oscillate between favoring the party's, the military's, and the cabinet's agendas. Each institution has won and lost bureaucratic battles, but the war has no clear end in sight. Institutional conflict, not cooperation, contributes to the regime's stability.

The table also shows that simplifying these three institutions to hardliners and "pragmatists" by collapsing the party and military into one hard-liner category has only limited usefulness and overlooks the decades of bitter divides between the party and military. The "party/military" label, for example, should not be read as a joint policy win. These institutions argued separately—with distinct justifications—for a similar outcome. The military institution, for example, is actually quite pragmatic but also hard-line. It does not reject accommodation strategies with enemies because they are imperialists but because in their estimation doing so undermines state security. Furthermore, defining elites as "pragmatists" and "hard-liners" without reference to institution creates artificial, amorphous groups that are not coherent political actors within the state. These "groups" are not discernible clusters of regime elites influencing decisions or modifying policy implementation in any organized fashion. The nature of the table's effort to summarize outcomes hides the more complex picture of interbureaucratic struggle. However, it is important to note that there are no permanent coalitions between institutions and no observed evidence of explicit and sustained collusion. Table 8.1 does not clearly show a systematic pattern in North Korean politics. No single institution is on top of the others.

If this table does not show a discernable pattern influencing North Korean decision making, the natural question remains: what does? Figures 8.1–8.3 help bring out some of the core conclusions of this study not found in the table. The picture is much clearer if one breaks down agenda control by issue area. These figures show the most general sketches of agenda control over the decade under consideration in this study. I smooth out the trend lines to bring to the fore strategic and long-lasting shifts in North Korean institutional agenda control. The empirical reality is much messier than this trend, of course, and is documented in detail in Chapters 5 through 7, but the big picture should not be lost in the weeds and is fairly straightforward, especially on inter-Korean and economic policy.

Kim Dae Jung's sunshine policy ushered in a new period in inter-Korean relations that lasted throughout his and his successor's administrations. Delays and difficulties abounded in inter-Korean relations, but the cabinet's agenda won out internally in North Korea as the primary strategic orientation toward the South. However, with a new administration in Seoul in early 2008 and its tougher line toward the North, the cabinet lost its control over inter-Korean relations as the party and military's advocacy gained increased resonance in Pyongyang.

Cabinet Lead

Party/Military Lead

1998 1999 2000 2001 2002 2003 2004 2005 2006 2007 2008 2009

FIGURE 8.1 Institutional Lead on Economic Policy, 1998–2009

Control over economic policy likewise had two major inflection points during this time. Kim empowered the cabinet to take over economic policy after his tour of Southern China's financial centers and special economic zones in 2001. For four years, the cabinet implemented various economic reforms, emphasizing greater reliance on markets and localized management to distribute goods and provide workers incentives to produce. However, the party observed that this created social irregularities, including creating a new wealthy class of businessmen that might be harder to control and leaving vulnerable populations so destitute that the stark contrast further eroded the regime's claim to protect socialism, Pyongyang eventually shifted. Once food security could be reasonably assured for the year, Kim gave power over strategic economic questions back to the party, which then reversed several of the cabinet's liberalizing endeavors.

The regime's approach to U.S. policy has been more complicated. Figure 8.2 shows considerably more variance than the two-inflection point figures on inter-Korean and economic policy. However, the trend here can be somewhat simplified as well. Cabinet organizations, particularly the Foreign Ministry, led on U.S. policy until shortly after terrorists struck the United States on September 11, 2001. The Foreign Ministry engaged both the Clinton and Bush administrations primarily on the North's long-range missile programs. When repeated comments by senior U.S. administration officials in late 2001 and early 2002 convinced Pyongyang that, as the party and the military maintained, Washington could not be trusted and sought to eradicate the North Korean regime, the cabinet lost its lead over U.S. policy. Party and military outlets emphasized armaments over paper agreements as U.S.-DPRK confrontation intensified. The cabinet

FIGURE 8.2 Institutional Lead on Inter-Korean Policy, 1998–2009

ultimately failed to wrestle back agenda control over U.S. policy until after the North's first nuclear test in 2006.

The cabinet briefly regained agenda control in late summer 2005 when Washington appointed a new lead negotiator with seemingly greater authority to deal, but this quickly fell apart after the six parties agreed to the guiding principles of future negotiations. The party and military pointed to Washington's new financial sanctions on Banco Delta Asia that cut the North off from the international financial system and were labeled internally as part of Washington's "suffocation" strategy that revealed the "imperialists'" efforts to promote regime change through other means. The argument carried the day in Pyongyang as the cabinet lost its newly acquired leeway.

Strategic change in the North's policy toward the United States occurred after North Korea's October 2006 nuclear test. With a tested nuclear deterrent in hand, the cabinet reengaged the Americans from what the regime considered a position of strength. The party and the military temporarily took back agenda control in late summer 2008 over what Pyongyang saw as the U.S. backtracking on its commitment to remove North Korea from the terrorism list. But the cabinet again took center stage once Washington completed this action in October 2008. As Kim Jong Il's succession took on greater urgency in early 2009, the leadership would place the regime on a more escalatory path with the United States to accompany its tough position toward the South and administrative control over the economy. The regime would essentially hunker down and possibly modify this existing political structure to suit his son's budding effort to control the regime and society.

Cabinet Lead

Party/Military Lead

1998   1999   2000   2001   2002   2003   2004   2005   2006   2007   2008   2009

FIGURE 8.3 Institutional Lead on U.S. Policy, 1998–2009

Importance of the Internal Mechanism

One may argue that understanding this internal mechanism is not necessary to understand North Korean policy responses. An observer could
theorize that treating North Korea as a reactive black box explains its
responding to a perceived hard-line policy from Washington or Seoul with
its own hard-line. Conversely, Pyongyang could simply scapegoat Washington's or Seoul's latest policy position to justify its predetermined policy
choices to other foreign audiences. Economic policy is more difficult to
explain without reference to the internal situation, but one may dismiss
it as relatively unimportant as unrelated to questions of high politics.
Though there is some value to this basic shorthand for explaining North
Korean actions, this section argues that the explanation and prediction of
North Korean actions is not nearly as specific or productive without a full
understanding of the internal mechanism of policy formulation, execution, and sustainability.

The primary difficulty with the contention that North Korean policy
choices can be explained without reference to the internal mechanism
is that it makes mediating between competing theories of North Korean
actions more difficult. For example, is North Korea proactively pursuing
security through nuclear, missile, and other asymmetric military capabilities without reference to foreign actions? Or is it willing to halt or even
reverse this nuclear drive in exchange for progress toward other core
regime goals that foreign powers can confer? Fundamentally, this asks

whether a negotiated settlement of the nuclear issue is at all possible with North Korea.

There is a logical claim to both answers based on theoretical expectations with tremendous impact on foreign policy choices of several states in East Asia and the United States. If Pyongyang is pursuing nuclearization without reference to foreign actions, then denuclearization negotiations are a waste of time and resources and unnecessarily limit more coercive options against the state. Likewise, if foreign powers can convince North Korea to give up its nuclear drive without force, then the relevant actors can potentially avoid a high-cost military conflict to achieve these goals.

One purpose of this study is to argue that the empirical evidence should mediate between these theories rather than preconception. As is often the case, empirical reality is much more complex than neat theories allow, but policy-relevant conclusions are not beyond the pale. Seizing on data selectively rather than systematically can bolster either theory but is not a fair evaluation of either argument. A contextualized, systematic analysis is required to make meaningful judgments.

This study shows that Pyongyang, beyond tactical posturing, has demonstrated a strategic commitment at times to abandon negotiations with the Americans outright and develop its nuclear and missile capabilities. But the regime also has shown an ability to slow or halt this drive at other times. The more useful question, therefore, is what explains these variant North Korean strategies? Put differently, under what conditions does the regime consider halting or reversing its nuclear drive? If these conditions can be identified, policy makers can proceed to the normative question as to whether those conditions are worth meeting.

The evidence presented here indicates North Korea is a highly reactive state, specifically in its U.S. policy. The cabinet, party, and military consistently advocate their agenda on U.S. policy and define the specifics of what each of those agendas consist of. The party and military have consistently objected to any measures that would trade away its missile and nuclear capabilities, while the cabinet has argued at times that there is value for Pyongyang in certain negotiated solutions. Internal bureaucratic politics affect policy outcomes more on questions of low politics where it is more difficult for central leadership to micromanage the process, but Kim still listens to his institutions on the nuclear issue as well. He has the greatest incentive for independent movement on these matters of high politics, but the model does provide some useful lessons.

North Korea's threat perception is not merely a hollow, tactical move to extract additional concessions in negotiations. When internal voices note recent and substantive evidence (in Pyongyang's view) that foreign actors, usually the United States, are not seriously committed to satisfying its demands at the negotiating table or threatens the regime's existence, party and military arguments to recoil tend to win out as cabinet advocacy goes silent. Negotiations also tend to stall or fail when foreign actors hit an ideological tripwire. Insulting the Kim family—inadvertent or not—poses an ideological threat to the regime that has no real parallel in American politics but can still shut down a process. Those attempting to negotiate with the North Koreans may find such concerns mere excuses to sidetrack talks, setting up a scenario where the North Koreans can "give" on these invented concerns and "take" on the real substance of talks. North Koreans diplomats angle for tactical advantage, but they often have to abandon a process they defend as fruitful to the national interest in the official press when military and party elements argue the ideological or security downsides preclude an agreement.

This is not to suggest that a concessionary policy from Washington or Seoul can promote meaningful diplomatic progress. When the cabinet argues that foreign adversaries are ripe for providing a good deal, it often takes center stage internally and diplomacy becomes active. Naturally, the regime attempts to minimize its own concessions and maximize its adversaries'. Kim Dae Jung's sunshine policy demonstrates how the cabinet could continually pocket South Korean concessions and respond by asking for more rather than offering something in return.[1] Hardening one's diplomatic position is necessary to ensure something in return from the North. The cabinet is not a reservoir of dissidents or soft-liners but a hardened arm of the regime used to maximize its advantage.

Furthermore, the appearance of a concessionary policy risks the cabinet overplaying its hand internally by overpromising the adversary's concessions and creating expectations that Seoul or Washington are not actually ready to meet. This seemed to be the case at the end of the Bush administration as the cabinet argued the incoming Obama administration would be a group of relatively soft negotiators who were willing to give more simply for the sake of a deal. When the new administration in Washington showed signs that it did not intend to meet these expectations and Kim reemerged after his stroke and began succession preparations, the benefits of engagement probably looked relatively unimpressive compared to the expectations the cabinet created, especially given more pressing, competing regime goals. Though the new administration had not yet assembled its Asia team, let alone clearly defined a North Korea policy, Pyongyang seemingly decided approaching Washington with an "unclenched fist" took a backseat to other priorities.

Diplomats therefore have the difficult task of demonstrating that their country will not threaten the regime's security (or pride) to empower the cabinet's agenda but not give the impression that their country is willing to give more than it actually is so as to keep North Korean expectations in check. One must recognize that no one in Pyongyang is interested in merely a good or fair deal. North Korea's negotiators want the best deal achievable under any circumstances, including breaking off past agreements explicitly or in practice, while their detractors want to actively undermine any diplomatic agreements completely. The task of moderately empowering the unscrupulous first group is the unpalatable path to diplomatic progress.

North Korea is not strategically proactive in its U.S. policy. It will take the lead to get Washington's attention, try to define the agenda, or simply advance its long-range missile and nuclear programs when diplomatic conditions are not in its favor, but it usually does not pass on an opportunity to enhance its security and economic situation when it deems the time is ripe. This is not to suggest that the United States is responsible for North Korea's actions but simply to note that it has more power over the state in terms of inducements than it usually recognizes and less power of coercion than it often assumes. Moderate inducements can empower the cabinet to begin and sustain a process. Coercion is often employed to avoid giving the impression to the North that they can act with impunity, socialize their actions and those of observer states, and satisfy domestic political demands. However, these actions usually empower military or party advocates to abandon the diplomatic track altogether.[2] The pressure of limiting inducements or taking them away often serves a more useful function, keeping the issue internally in the cabinet's purview to negotiate.

Pressure must be much more robust and sustained to effect change. At the most extreme end, a regime change strategy that seeks to topple the North Korean leadership to force near-term reunification or otherwise install a new leadership could change the regime's behavior (depending on the successor regime) but with very high opportunity costs and prospects for success far from assured. Advocates of increased pressure on North Korea often have a much more nuanced approach than this. They may present the case for economic pressure on the regime, including traditional bilateral or multilateral sanctions, innovative financial measures, and encouraging North Korea's neighbors to limit certain types of trade and aid.

The United States and its allies can also attempt to surveil and interdict North Korean shipments of internationally prohibited cargoes or advance more limited military means such as intercepting or otherwise preventing pending ballistic missile launches, providing greater political support to our South Korean ally for robust responses to the North's naval provocations against its navy, or even surgical strikes on key nuclear, missile, or other military facilities. Each of these efforts brings with them varying degrees of escalatory risk that has led to a general preference for economic sticks over military ones, but this model helps explain why coercive efforts are usually insufficient to prompt North Korea to change its policy.

Bureaucratically, such efforts provide fodder for military and party elite to argue that the diplomatic track should be abandoned. Pyongyang generally prefers to sit out discussions than engage under such circumstances. After coercive tools have been employed, the cabinet consistently goes silent; they do not argue that North Korea must reengage to get such pressure lifted. The party and the military are empowered to deal with these coercive strategies, and North Korea tends to have a greater risk tolerance for escalation than its democratic counterparts.

More limited pressure by its very definition does not fundamentally challenge the state's near-term existence. Consequently, the leadership can withstand the blows and escalate until the other side calls off the pressure. In the recent case of financial measures against Banco Delta Asia, Pyongyang abandoned the negotiating track and escalated continuously, culminating in its first nuclear test. Pyongyang demonstrated a willingness to escalate and wait out the measures Washington labeled as law enforcement but Pyongyang characterized as politically attuned. Indeed, some pressure advocates in Washington, Seoul, and elsewhere noted these financial measures were effective, showed an ability to pinch the regime, and should have been reinforced, not rescinded. More broadly, the argument claims that states should not tolerate North Korean escalation as it teaches them the value of escalation as a means to head off pressure strategies.

In order for pressure strategies to be effective, they must bypass the bureaucracy and reach the top of the system. The military and party will not sue for peace. Kim must recognize that this pressure is causing real damage to an interest he values and engagement vice counterpressure is the best way to resolve his problem. The first condition is relatively easy for foreign states to affect in some way, but the latter is very difficult. Countering such pressure with escalation has simply been an effective way for Kim to stop such campaigns. Long-standing coercive policies have been integrated into part of the North Korean existence and serve a continuing role in the regime's basic internal justification of its existence.

Other sanction advocates claim that economic or financial tools can directly target North Korea's internal politics and exert pressure from the inside out. They claim that financial measures against the regime elite can undermine elite loyalty to Kim by restricting access to luxury items or foreign bank accounts. If Kim cannot provide certain luxury items and privileges to senior leaders, this line of logic argues, then such measures may undermine political stability. The argument is premised on an understanding of the regime's internal politics fundamentally at odds with the one documented here. It presumes that such gifts are the glue, or at least a significant component of, elite loyalty. Removing this glue may lead elites to organize against the Kimist system that they are so integrally a part of.

Elites and their families going back at least two generations owe their social standing, livelihood, and physical safety to the system; if it collapses, they are collectively well aware that those repressed by them, their fathers, and their grandfathers are unlikely to treat them well. Foreigners are likewise unlikely to be particularly receptive to protecting the interests of the elite. Given the regime dynamics discussed in this book, it is hard to imagine a scenario under which an organized group of elites could change regime behavior in a way conducive to U.S. or other outside interests, because their access to certain luxuries was temporarily suspended or even outright eliminated.

But not all efforts to pressure the regime are bound to fail. Efforts that undermine the regime's claim to legitimacy without reinforcing its role as protector against the imperialists are potentially powerful tools for a long-term strategy. This includes encouraging information transparency by means of radio broadcasts, international phone access, and people-to-people exchanges. Pyongyang certainly considers radio broadcasts such as Voice of America and Radio Free Asia, illicit cell phones that can call internationally, and even student exchanges to all but a small handful of countries as subversive efforts that undermine the regime.[3] In a sense, these efforts are subversive and do undermine the regime's long-term viability and therein lies part of their value. These efforts expose the importance of information in a regime like North Korea's and force us to reconceptualize what constitutes pressure. Effective pressure tactics are policies that push North Korea in a positive direction that it is not willing to go on its own. Informational pressure tactics like radio broadcasts, foreign media, and cell phone towers can accelerate the erosion of ideological appeal that undergirds the party's platform and regime legitimacy claims more broadly.

These are pressure strategies that rarely get much discussion or even included as part of the traditional arsenal of coercive tools. Viewed not as pressure moves but more neutral diplomatic tools, these mechanisms are often left only partially implemented out of concern that they could undermine ongoing negotiations.[4] In effect, they are often undervalued for their coercive potential in favor of more immediate coercive economic tools or high-profile UN Security Council resolutions. While I do not contend there are not diplomatic tradeoffs and inherent risks to North Koreans caught with illicit radios, cell phones, and even South Korean dramas, this study demonstrates that this type of "stick" is more likely to impact one important basis of the regime's claim to legitimacy than economic or financial sanctions with small marginal returns.[5]

This study shows that the conception that "no one" in North Korea still believes the regime propaganda or subscribes to its ideology overstates the case. North Korean defectors regularly voice surprise at some element of the outside world and often have a difficult time fully integrating even into South Korean society with substantial material support. Information penetration can help instill a wider acceptance of notions that there may be a better future available for the masses and perhaps influence some elites over time to support a more moderate domestic and foreign policy.[6]

This study also exposes how the North Korean regime responds to both symbols and substance. Symbols have greater role for North Korea's ideologues, in particular—a point lost if one treats the country as a black box. Ideology is eroding in North Korea but has a residual role. This model helps one explain concretely the effect of ideology on policy decisions and the regime's functions. Ideology remains an important component of regime legitimacy and one set of arguments for or against certain policy options. It helps explain North Korean actions that seem to defy logic at first glance without serving as a simple excuse for failure to understand the North's decision. Put differently, the ideology variable is not akin to arguing that Westerners cannot understand the Confucian or Korean mind—a contention I find neither accurate nor helpful. Ideology is not a "spigot variable" to be turned on and off when the model fails—either by overpredicting or underpredicting a certain behavior—but concretely points toward pressure on policy choices in a specific direction.

More broadly, another important question addressed by this study is what are the regime's core goals? It is a relatively simple enterprise to identify managing its relationship with the United States and South Korea and revitalizing its economy are core goals, but there are very different paths that Pyongyang can take to address each of these three issues with tremendous impact on the future of the country and region. The regime has demonstrated its ability to try a diversity of approaches that are inexplicable and puzzling without reference to the internal mechanism. Given the country's dismal economic situation, the cabinet articulates economic revitalization as critical to the regime's existence; it places the economic question on par with other existential security threats, which military opponents criticize. The regime must balance between competing goals—ideological and rational.

Consequently, analyses that begin with a clear presumption about the regime's goals and conclude that it will never attempt a certain course of action without qualification of circumstances overstate their case and miss the nuance of competing agendas. Most critically, the fashionable argument that Pyongyang will never give up its nuclear weapons now that it has demonstrated that capability through nuclear tests is overly pessimistic. North Korean denuclearization is undoubtedly more difficult today than it was just three years earlier and certainly more difficult than when the regime faced new and pressing security challenges in the early 1990s, but there still is room for maneuvering. The regime still faces structurally competing goals, represented institutionally, that provide opening, albeit small in the near term, for shifting emphasis away from expanding (or even retaining) its nuclear arsenal.

Understanding how these three strategic issue areas interact helps explain why the regime does not react consistently to foreign policy options from Washington or Seoul without reference to the other issue areas. Importantly, Kim's divide-and-rule governance would make empowering a single institution on all three issue areas itself puzzling. Though providing consistency in advancing one of the policy platforms, this move would weaken Kim's institutional check on the empowered institution. Kim would be skirting the system of rule he has molded if he granted the military, for example, its comprehensive agenda and would have eroded the most significant barriers from the military ruling the system—de facto or otherwise. Indeed, as Table 8.1 shows, no single institution has been able to sustain its agenda on all three issue areas for any significant period of time in the decade since the 1998 constitutional revision.

During this period of post-totalitarian institutionalism, Pyongyang has demonstrated an ability to manage this interaction by linking and delinking issue areas. All three institutions utilized contemporary information at their disposal to present arguments to advance their internally consistent, comprehensive agendas. And while each institution's comprehensive agenda had a certain logic, the leadership empowering one institution on one issue and another institution on another issue simultaneously blocked each of these comprehensive platforms from being advanced. In other words, I suggest that it is incorrect to say that North Korea does not have a strategy for the way forward or an explicit cause for being. It has three, and the regime as a whole has simply only empowered certain aspects of each strategy at any given time, giving some foreign observers the impression that it lacks a central purpose or is not doing anything more than "muddling through."

This point has important implications for those crafting foreign policy toward North Korea. Part of Kim Dae Jung's sunshine policy, for example, theorized that unconditional engagement toward the North that included significant economic aid and development assistance would provide incentives for Pyongyang to reform its economy and open up to the outside world. Faced with serious economic problems, the regime would come to realize the necessity of diplomatic rapprochement with Seoul and Washington if sanctions were to be removed and North Korea integrated into the international order. The policy also planned to gradually shift the social structure by encouraging a new class of businessmen in North Korea who developed their wealth from nonstate employment and may press for greater business freedoms and engagement with the outside world.

The policy was a sophisticated and proactive approach toward the North that slowly made inroads into changing the North's social structure, but it ultimately proved inconclusive in governing the North's economic choices. The North's strategic economic choices have not correlated with its inter-Korean policy. For a time, Pyongyang empowered the cabinet to pursue economic reform policies but South Korean aid largely did not correlate with the state advancing or retreating from these strategic choices. This study demonstrates that the North Korean leadership empowered one institution over another on economic policy based on two considerations: internal politics and realization of ground realities within North Korean society.

Gradual social change in North Korea, aided by South Korea's sunshine policy, has improved the standing of business elites over party and military ones. While these individuals are certainly not democrats, they take a more pragmatic view than security-conscious officers and ideologically inclined party officials. Businessmen largely already enjoy a privileged place in society that requires collusion with the regime but is not solely dependent upon it. Though these people do not seem inclined at present to press their business interests in the political realm nor is there real evidence that they can even yet be considered a coherent "group," there is potential for foreign states to craft policies to encourage a North Korean business identity with greater distance from the state. Businessmen react to demand for their services; given the small size of North Korea's trading economy, minor amounts of more profitable trade can increase these people's wealth and political clout.

Businessmen are usually not political revolutionaries, but they do tend to exert political power and can be effective lobbyists for their interests. Primary among these interests is greater access to foreign markets. The great prize for any coherent business lobby in North Korea, if it could develop, would be to convince their own government to take a more moderate foreign policy to encourage the international community to allow greater flows of trade in and out of North Korea. Under these circumstances, those poised to engage in international commerce could profit handsomely. The United States has appropriately held out this prospect of integration into the international community for decades in exchange for North Korean denuclearization. Efforts to further cut off North Korea from the international financial system have the unintended consequence of squeezing the very group that could potentially press this long-offered initiative within the North Korean regime as part of a denuclearization process.

Likewise, foreign non-governmental organizations and academic groups that attempt to build universities in North Korea that teach science, technology, business, and economics or sponsor academic exchanges to a budding group of elites assist the long-term effort to change North Korea. Governments do not need to actively support such efforts, but they do need to avoid blocking them to have an impact on the wider North Korean society.[7]

Foreign travel also can impact North Korean elites. One North Korean's foreign travel and exposure to foreign development had a profound impact on Pyongyang's economic policy. Kim Jong Il dramatically empowered the cabinet on economic policy after he saw for himself the tremendous differences in level of development in Southern China and North Korea. His scathing attacks on the party's policy produced the most sweeping economic changes in North Korea to date. He backed off these policies with much less fanfare but only after opponents noted that these economic changes were actually pinching the regime's modus operandi. Party arguments that the economic changes produced a rising class of rich businessmen that could skirt regime control (via corruption), general modification of the social structure, and claims that unequal food distribution undermined regime ideological commitments to socialism prompted the central leadership to switch course.[8] Exposure to foreign ideas, business practices, and development, as well as encouraging business interests, can have a positive, long-term impact on further undermining the regime's ideological character and pressing for greater openness.

This analysis also points to the importance of Washington and Seoul finding common ground in its approach toward the North. Though it is popular to note that Pyongyang tries to create a "wedge" between these two allies in their approach toward the North, it has not required much help in this regard over the period in this study. Electoral politics in the United States and South Korea have stimulated significantly different approaches to North Korea. For example, by the time the Bush administration completed its policy review of North Korea policy and shortly thereafter shifted to a harder line toward North Korea after 9/11, a liberal president occupied the Blue House in Seoul intensely committed to inter-Korean engagement. The critically important U.S.–South Korean alliance failed to produce a unified view of policy toward North Korea. President Bush reversed course after the October 2006 nuclear test and the November 2006 elections that gave Democrats control of both houses of Congress. As the United States reached out to North Korea diplomatically, South Korean public opinion turned against engagement, and its lame duck president could do little to stem the tide. By the end of 2007, South Korea had elected a conservative president committed to a tougher line as the United States continued to engage.

Pyongyang exploited these differences tactically, but this study shows how certain bureaucratic actors tried to do precisely the opposite. Party opponents to inter-Korean engagement tried to *link* Washington and Seoul's policies to make its case against a separate, generally conciliatory policy toward the South. Pyongyang's strategic interests do not always call for separating Washington and Seoul. Instead its strategic objectives are more straightforward. If one ally is offering it concessions and pursuing a conciliatory policy, then it tries to get the other to do the same. Arguments that the North needs an enemy and oscillates between identifying the Americans and South Koreans for this purpose are interesting and theoretically persuasive as distinct possibilities, but the empirical evidence does not support them.

North Korea, Comparative Politics, and Downstream Consequences

Like all states, North Korea is unique at a certain level of specificity. However, asserting that it is noncomparable is unproductive and unpersuasive. Understanding the state requires reference points, and building comparative theory has wider applications beyond this one state. North Korea presumed oddity does not discount the ability to derive more general lessons about a group of post-totalitarian states. There is a variety of post-totalitarian states that makes subclassifying these states fruitful. Post-Maoist China looks very different from contemporary Romania, for example. Refining the *varieties* of post-totalitarianism helps us understand the state's functions and, consequently, contextualize and predict its policy responses. In short, North Korea and states like it should be brought into the comparative politics tradition more thoroughly.

Classifying a state as a part of a particular typology should have some utility. This is not simply a labeling exercise. In North Korea's case, post-totalitarian institutionalism's variant of the post-totalitarian set has specific, nonobvious downstream consequences. These are important factors for answering the question why this characterization matters. They are not necessarily intuitive without the model, making the effort to classify and characterize post-totalitarian states more helpful to both academics and foreign policy practitioners.

Post-totalitarian institutional states like North Korea are more moderate than their totalitarian predecessors. Observers rarely label North Korean actions as measured or moderate, but the appropriate comparison must be made. Pyongyang's actions are certainly more out of step with international norms than other post-totalitarian states like Russia, China, or even Cuba. One may argue that North Korea is one of, if not *the*, most extreme state in the world. It is a small, impoverished state, surrounded by three of the largest economies in the world. It officially clings to socialist mantras when the world movement has long since faded. It maintains the highest conscription rate in the world and holds to self-sufficiency despite failing— chronically—to feed its own population. However, recognizing the differences between North Korea today and North Korea two decades ago requires comparing these two states in time. Comparing North Korea today to other contemporary states has other uses, but understanding the moderation thesis requires a comparison to itself. Simply put, one must look at how the state has evolved to see if it has moderated or grown more extreme.

North Korea's post-totalitarian institutionalism under Kim Jong Il is more moderate than the totalitarian North Korea under Kim Il Sung. Post-totalitarian institutional states bring the expert and compartmented knowledge of its modern bureaucracy into national-level decisions. The modern bureaucracy is more than a transmission belt, implementing ideologically defined policy; bureaucrats contribute specified knowledge to national decisions. A greater diversity of policy inputs affects policy decisions and implementation than under the previous regime where a single party applied a general ideology to make decisions. Under post-totalitarian institutionalism, technocrats and ideologues moderate one another in the sense that more components of the perceived national interest are integrated into policy making. Policy making becomes more representative of the state's composition, and the state's composition reflects a broader set of interests. This does not make the state in any way democratic or democratizing but it does make it more liberal than its predecessor.

Moderation does not necessarily mean aligning policy decisions with internationally proscribed norms. However, it does institutionalize a counterweight to a singular policy metric, and, in practice, the post-totalitarian institutional state also moderates according to international norms. Communist orthodoxy is out of step with contemporary global norms, and pragmatic national interests are closer to international norms, ceteris paribus. This does not mean that a sovereign state may not decide to develop nuclear weapons or maintain a large military to provide for its security, restrict foreign influences or capital, or take actions with international repercussions to satisfy domestic political needs. Indeed, one may argue that some democracies do many of these things to a certain degree. This does mean, however, that the post-totalitarian institutional state is more rational. It places less emphasis on a radical ideology to guide policy. It makes economic decisions, for example, more in accordance with contemporary international norms than under Kim Il Sung. Though North Korea could not join the International Monetary Fund tomorrow, it has at least voiced a tenuous interest and with some effort could conceivably meet its requirements for admittance. Its policy toward its southern neighbor is not exclusively dominated by a leadership committed to reunifying the state by force at the earliest opportunity. Reaching strategic accommodation with the hegemon is a distinct possibility. In effect, post-totalitarian institutional states are more moderate than their predecessors, because the current international norm favors pragmatic self-interest over ideologically guided policy.

The model also suggests that this category of states is stable. North Korea is not muddling through or seeking a new, more democratic modus operandi. Post-totalitarian institutionalism is sustainable. Though no one within the state chose this type of systemic function, it is still a stable political outcome. Party efforts in North Korea to reassert the old system have repeatedly failed. Nor has the cabinet or the military been able to dominate. These peer institutions advocate at cross-purposes under the authority of central leadership, and one does not have to eventually win in a permanent way. Indeed, an extensive set of checks prevent one institution from trying to usurp power over the others, and a security-conscious central leadership has a strong interest in maintaining a balance that it can control. Changing this order is certainly possible but would require concerted and sustained effort by the leadership, and the new system would be a revision of the current system rather than a completely new creation. Regime leadership has not forsaken terror or the permanent purge to maintain control. Though the state is engaged in a precarious balancing act where tipping too far to one side in these interinstitutional debates could unravel the system, maintaining a long-term balance is indeed possible.

Kim Jong Il did not modify his father's more unified totalitarian regime toward this divide-and-conquer post-totalitarian institutional arrangement, because he found it more stable or effective. He did so as an outgrowth of a particular historical reality. He was not as powerful as his father, lacking his charisma and revolutionary bona fides. The younger Kim also faced a more difficult internal and external situation than his father did in the last few decades of his rule amid economic collapse, legitimacy crisis with his father's death, and the collapse of the Soviet Union. Post-totalitarianism is borne out of weakness, not strength. Efforts to reassert a more unified polity require greater domestic political power than Kim Jong Il maintains. Kim's sons face even greater internal political difficulties in terms of legitimacy, grooming, and expertise than he did. Sustained efforts to unify a post–Kim Jong Il regime under a weaker leader would suggest political miscalculation and a greater risk of political instability in North Korea.

More specifically, this concept of interinstitutional balance and a balance of competing interests means the model provides analysts specific areas to watch that may portend a strategic shift in policy. This study has consistently demonstrated that a close reading of these debates can effectively show where the state is likely to move. When one institution goes silent for a prolonged period of time in face of strong advocacy from another rival institution or when an institution mildly supports its rival institution's position, then the state shortly thereafter generally takes action in accord with the strongly presented advocacy. When the three rival institutions agree on policy in media debates, the central authorities usually follow by implementing that unanimous bureaucratic position. On both the policy level and more significant regime structure questions, there are some indications of change.

North Korea's Future

The search for balance among the three institutions also gives analysts special ability to forecast longer term changes as well. If the balance is permanently broken, then the system is undergoing significant change. If one institution is able to thwart another not on specific policy disputes or corruption allegations in a deep and sustained assault on the other that affects its ability to function, then one should expect noteworthy alterations. Likewise, if the supreme leader imposes a different bureaucratic structure, then one can expect modifications to the ruling structure over time. Put differently, post-totalitarian institutionalism requires a plural set of institutions. Breaking this institutional balance breaks the system. The specific circumstances would help determine whether such a change meant moving away from post-totalitarian institutionalism toward a more liberal polity or retrenchment. Regime intentions are less important than the consequences of those decisions.

The most predictable shock is the death or permanent incapacitation of Kim Jong Il or his planning for such a contingency. Kim's health came into sharp relief in early fall 2008 when he suffered a stroke. It raised to the forefront a basic point: Kim is mortal, and he is not the system. The system will eventually have to address leadership change at the top, and there are some indications this has already begun. The top decision maker is important, but a new leadership will not immediately and necessarily revolutionize the system. In the short term, decisions defined by these institutions may shift within the margins as a new and possibly young leader attempts to establish his position as supreme leader. The regime is unlikely to fall apart quickly or suddenly shift course in an unprecedented way with another person or group of people at the top if the interinstitutional balance can be sustained. The succession issue is critically important, but there is an overabundance of attention on this variable compared to the minimal attention paid to the larger systemic question for which the Kims are but one important part.

Nevertheless, the Kims are an important component in the system and recent changes merit consideration. In late 2008 and the first half of 2009, there were some indications that political evolution from this divide-and-conquer ruling style had begun. North Korea's three institutions started to speak with unprecedented unison on all strategic issue areas. Inter-Korean relations had long since soured, and all three organizations lambasted the South. Economic policy too had moved into the party's orbit, but socialist economic policies advanced more quickly and the cabinet started to strongly endorse the policies it had previously rejected for years. Likewise, Pyongyang's institutions spoke and wrote from a single set of talking points on U.S. policy, taking an increasingly belligerent stance for months without serious reference to empirical reality. Analysts continue to ponder what has motivated this round of escalation with some credible indications that Kim may have been preparing his political institutions and the country for North Korea's second hereditary succession process, albeit in a less pronounced and forceful way than his father did three decades earlier.[9]

At the last six-party talks session in December 2008, the North Korean Foreign Ministry attempted to exclude Japan from the talks, citing Tokyo's not paying its portion of economic compensation to North Korea and Japanese demands that North Korea address the abduction issue. However, it did not boycott the round when Japan was included, blamed South Korea and Japan but not the United States for shortcomings in negotiations, and ultimately called the round "successful . . . on the basis of 'action-for-action' principle," explicitly rejecting widespread disappointment in the final discussions of 2008.[10]

Nevertheless, Pyongyang apparently wanted to wait for the Obama administration to take office in a few weeks, concluding that it might offer a better deal. In December the North did not seem poised to begin an escalatory spiral, but this quickly changed. North Korea started diverging from the familiar ruling pattern highlighted throughout this book. The cabinet and party started to speak with one voice, and as early as mid-December the cabinet published an article noting the importance of the sovereign right to peaceful space exploration, suggesting a budding plan for the April 5, 2009, rocket launch.[11] Repeated commentaries also argued that the United States had effectively recognized Pyongyang's place as a nuclear weapons state, citing unclassified U.S. Defense Department and National Intelligence Council documents and related congressional testimony indicating North Korea possessed nuclear weapons.[12]

In January 2009 the Foreign Ministry broke its verification pledges, which had been given to get off the terrorism list just a few months earlier, by announcing that normalization of relations must come before any agreement on verification.[13] The KPA general staff reiterated the same position.[14] Meanwhile, the military issued a political statement condemning South Korea's inter-Korean policy and threatening preemptive military strikes against South Korean ships in the disputed West Sea waters. Raising the West Sea issue was not new, but it was odd for the North Koreans to raise it in January since these disputes generally arise during the lucrative crabbing season in late spring and summer. The KPA announced an "all-out confrontation posture" as continued newscasts supported the KPA statement.[15] The cabinet again uncharacteristically got on board, adding a criticism of South Korea's president Lee's selection to lead the Unification Ministry.[16] North Korea said it nullified "all agreements adopted between the North and South in the past." The party publicly supported this comprehensive nullification of inter-Korean agreements.[17] The pattern of institutional back-and-forth seemed to be gone on all issues.

About the same time, Kim Jong Il started reappearing in public, and succession talk accelerated. Visibly weakened by his stroke, Kim may have been attempting to eliminate interinstitutional debate in advance of introducing his young and inexperienced son as his heir designate. Indeed, many of the same characteristics that accompanied Kim Jong Il's formal accession to power as North Korea's top leader came at the end of a three year mourning period in September 1998 as the regime unveiled a new constitution, reformulated political institutions, and launched a Taepodong rocket to make the world take notice. In April 2009 North Korea followed many of the same steps. North Korea's rubber-stamp parliament convened and greatly expanded the National Defense Commission (NDC) to include civilian members with deep links to the party and North Korea's most powerful intelligence organizations.[18] It also produced a new constitution that was not released until almost six months later, launched another Taepodong rocket, and tested a second nuclear weapon.

By presenting his third son as his heir apparent and submerging interinstitutional debates, Kim may have been attempting to eliminate differences to avoid factionalism in the coming succession and pursue a more aggressive foreign policy to appeal to those regime elites with the coercive means as their disposal to stage a coup or otherwise threaten the succession process. Cabinet members were not included in this expanded NDC, suggesting they or their positions were at least temporarily out of favor.

Much of the first half of 2009 saw a set of policy priorities consistent with previous military and party platforms but a marked departure from policies of late 2008. On April 5 North Korea launched a Taepodong-2 rocket that it claimed was a peaceful satellite launch but advanced its long-range ballistic missile program. When the UN Security Council imposed sanctions, North Korea's institutions again reacted, universally condemning the UN action.[19] At the end of the month, the Foreign Ministry announced the regime would reprocess spent fuel rods. The Foreign Ministry and party both blamed the Obama administration for pursuing sanctions and continuing joint military exercises with the South Koreans; they also rejected comments that Secretary Clinton delivered months earlier.[20] When Stephen Bosworth, special representative for North Korea policy, visited Seoul later that month, the party and government dailies again spoke as one, objecting to the trip generally and the perceived lack of change in the Obama administration's foreign policy.[21]

On May 25 North Korea continued its back-to-back provocations without pause and conducted its second nuclear test. Each of North Korea's institutions hailed the event but did not compete for credit for this "nationalistic achievement"; rather even the cabinet daily lead by noting "Another round of nuclear test was carried out at a majestic time when the entire party, the whole army, and all the people are vigorously accelerating the general onward march for the construction of a powerful socialist state."[22]

The UN Security Council again sanctioned North Korea, which the Foreign Ministry predictably denounced. Again, the North escalated, threatening to weaponize all extracted plutonium, begin uranium enrichment work "in accordance with the decision to build a light-water reactor on its own," and respond militarily to any efforts to impose a blockade.[23] The military strongly supported this line. Pak Chae-kyo'ng, vice minister of People's Armed Forces, said at a mass rally in Pyongyang that "as solemnly proclaimed by our people's army, the nuclear weapons in the grip of our hands are means of defense. . . . A barking dog does not stop a march's advance, and no amount of desperate struggles by the U.S. imperialists and their peons will be enough to make us abandon the sovereign right to space development and stop righteous efforts to further strengthen the nuclear deterrent, not even for a moment."[24]

The military's argument was consistent, and now the cabinet had started actively articulating the same message. The Foreign Ministry did not offer ultimatums, demands, or a diplomatic way forward. North Korea seemed committed to escalation until it satisfied its internal concern. Considerations of foreign policy or the consequences of additional sanctions no matter how robust did not deter Pyongyang. Track II discussions or back channels tend to be more productive venues when relations hit such an impasse. The U.S. national security adviser James Jones recognized publicly that "we do have channels to talk to the North Koreans" that reach

Kim Jong Il personally, which prepared Bill Clinton's trip to Pyongyang to secure the release of two captive American journalists.[25] A few weeks earlier, a Foreign Ministry's spokesman presented a subdued argument that broke with months of unconstructive barbs. The Foreign Ministry argued that North Korea would not accept the six-party talks format but concluded with this opaque line in reference to the nuclear issue: "There is a separate method of dialogue that can resolve the current situation."[26] It is unclear if they were referring to the same channel or merely noting a preference for bilateral talks in an unusually vague manner. In any case the North signaled an opening in its policy.

Some unobservable internal shift seemed to take place in June or July that again made diplomatic progress possible. The Clinton visit that Pyongyang had sought since 2000 helped sustain that opening for diplomatic progress in other areas. In a short news release, North Korea called the Clinton trip "sincere" and "courteous" four times—important indicators of its willingness to engage—concluding that the visit "will contribute to deepening the understand between the DPRK and the U.S. and building the bilateral confidence."[27]

North Korea watchers disagreed on the rationale for Pyongyang's second reversal in 2009. One thoughtful observer noted that while the exact causal force cannot be precisely determined, the most recent round of UN sanctions were the most likely stimulus for Pyongyang's recent "smile diplomacy" over "nuclear and ballistic missile diplomacy."[28] Another credited the Clinton visit as providing Kim internal justification to reengage Washington.[29] I come to a different conclusion. Though sanctions preceded Pyongyang's move, this study shows how Pyongyang tends to react negatively in the short run to pressure tactics, recoiling from the diplomatic environment. Washington continued to support the UN sanctions on North Korea, suggesting Pyongyang took the more conciliatory line despite, not because of, the sanctions. Likewise, the Clinton visit and presumably the announced preparatory meetings made diplomatic progress more likely but seem to have come after the North Korean switch. Receiving former president Clinton with very positive pronouncements and releasing the two American captives was the *result* of a political decision, not the catalyst. More conciliatory gestures and statements preceded the early August visit.

The seeming policy shift on U.S. policy and a more modest thaw in inter-Korean ties accompanied more appearances of a healthy-looking

Kim Jong Il in public and reports of halting the dizzying propaganda campaign for Kim Jong Un on July 9.[30] The proximate cause of the heightened nuclear and ballistic missile activity—the succession preparation—seemed to be removed for the time being. The immediate prospect for more provocations waned, as Pyongyang completed only two of its three publicly threatened provocations: a satellite launch and a nuclear test. It did not launch an ICBM as it separately warned from its satellite launch.[31] The midstream reversal is precarious but suggests significant changes in North Korea's ruling structure and a retrenchment in provocative policies is not inevitable or even necessarily on the table.

After releasing the two American journalists, Pyongyang also freed a South Korean citizen previously working at the Kaesong Industrial Complex. At the end of August, it released four South Korean fisherman captured in the West Sea's disputed waters, indicated a willingness to reinstate family reunions, and sent an official delegation to former South Korean president Kim Dae Jung's funeral. A North Korean report on the funeral delegation recognized President Lee by title, a break from a year and a half of name-calling. While it is certainly possible that these developments are separate from the turnaround in U.S. policy and reflect Seoul's own new offerings to the North, concurrent advances in long-strained inter-Korean ties further suggest a more fundamental cause of the policy change linked to North Korea's succession preparations.[32] Kim Jong Il's postponing succession preparations freed his hand to halt several aggressive stands against all of Pyongyang's sworn enemies: the United States, South Korea, and after its change of government, even Japan.[33]

This shift may suggest an end to the short-lived party/military dominance in all three issues areas and a return to a more divided political establishment that has governed the regime since 1998. Indeed, the new constitution announced in April 2009 amid Pyongyang's escalatory spree appeared with no great fanfare almost six months later. After completing a 150-day work campaign that could have culminated in an important announcement, Pyongyang unveiled the text of its new constitution on a foreign hosted webpage without any explicit indication it was the new constitution. This is not the type of action Pyongyang takes when it tries to highlight an important new change to its own population and the world. The new constitution does not break with the past but does codify the military-first ideology on a par with Juche and highlights the NDC's constitutional responsibilities in both military and political affairs. It does not formally downgrade any competing institution or clarify the relationship between the institutions. Indeed, if 1998 is any guide, one would expect the three institutions to jockey for interpretation of the marginally changed document in future debates over specific policy issues.[34] At present, it does not look like an even moderately revolutionary document.

The Foreign Ministry articulated an alternative to simple escalation and North Korea demonstrated a willingness to finally free the two American reporters. It is too early to tell if this will have any lasting effect, but a return to a Foreign Ministry articulating alternatives to the party and military preferences suggest the recent governance changes are a temporary and tactical shift to shore up the succession process at the appropriate time rather than a permanent and fundamental shift away from the current modus operandi.

It bears repeating that Kim can effectively squelch differences of institutional opinion on core policy questions for a period of months, but it is unlikely that his son would be able to do so as a long-term governance strategy. Kim Jong Il's divide-and-rule governance method is a demonstration of relative weakness, and Kim Jong Un faces an internally weaker position than his father. Kim Jong Un is more distanced still from the ideological base of the revolution and ideological erosion is even more advanced. Kim Jong Il benefited from a prolonged grooming period during which his powerful father could purge dissenters and encourage revolutionary brethren to support his choice. Kim Jong Un will not have this advantage. Kim Jong Il does not command the loyalty his father. Jong Un is also young and inexperienced, making it potentially more difficult for regime elites to respect him and perhaps offering a chance to unseat the heir after the father has left the scene.

Given these structural difficulties, assuming that this third-generation Kim can meaningfully control a group of ambitious, experienced, and cunning senior leaders with no personal loyalty to this young man and with every expectation that he might install his own advisers at their expense, makes such a permanent arrangement of unchecked institutional power inherently unstable. Such a leader would not necessarily have difficulties reestablishing a more concentrated polity for a short time period but would face increasing difficulties sustaining it. With greater access to outside information, expectation of rational results with the erosion of ideology, total elimination of powerful individual with firsthand experience in the revolution, fewer second-generation ideologues orphaned by the Korean War and powerfully indoctrinated to think of the state as family, Kim Jong Un faces systemic barriers to sustaining a closed North Korea. Barring unforeseen personal abilities, Kim Jong Un's attempting to rule in such a fashion presages political instability.

Consequently, while Kim Jong Il may again escalate tensions in foreign policy to clear the way for his son's succession, I would expect him to attempt to reinstitute the divide-and-conquer ruling method to assist his son's governance once he achieves an enhanced level of familiarity with these institutions and secures the personal loyalty of his own entourage. Under the veneer of institutional unity, differences almost certainly remain. Kim's move to unify positions can change official statements and even unify policies while he is in command, but it cannot force the change in preferences. The outcome of transitions are difficult to predict, but Kim Jong Il's death before Kim Jong Un is able to establish these basic requirements of rule raises the risk of political instability in a transition scenario.

Despite the many unknowns, one can say with a high degree of confidence that North Korea's current institutions will be a relevant feature in any transition scenario. Even in the most radical political change in North Korea that occurred after the Japanese defeat in World War II, Kim Il Sung's revolutionary polity had to deal with existing trained administrators and institutional structure to modify it. Focusing on the known rather than the unknown helps narrow the range of more likely outcomes. If these internal checks explained in the model can be maintained, then it suggests that the military would have a difficult time taking control by force. The long and lethal history between the Korean People's Army and the State Security Department suggests that one will attempt to prevent the other from usurping control. These organizations could conceivably fight one another for control in a sort of civil war, but they could also simply deter one another as well.

One can also note with confidence that individual ambition and fear of what may come if a rival takes power will likely trump the collective interest in stability if top leadership constraints prove inept at controlling the regime. Though most North Korea analysts predict a peaceful transition, there is certainly a possibility that individual groups, especially if faced with a rival coming to power, could risk everything to secure their own position on top. A transition could be bloody and destabilizing in the short term, but Kim's senior inner circle, with tentacles in every major institution, may be able to keep a lid on this type of leadership crisis. In short, one should not rule out the possibility of a bloody transition. But it is important to understand the histories and interests of the players who might be involved in such a scenario, which is contingent on the breakdown of senior-level leadership that does not seem forthcoming at this time.

Nevertheless, the top still matters tremendously. Kim is not a passive broker of his bureaucracy, and leadership change matters. Despite clear indications that Kim Jong Un will be his father's heir, there are several other plausible options for leadership at the top after Kim's death. Kim's brother-in-law Chang Song Taek, one of Kim's other three sons, or someone else could replace Kim as the top leader. Alternatively, a collective leadership composed of representatives from each of these three powerful institutions could emerge. Though Kim is seemingly grooming Kim Jong Un, it remains an open question whether even a formal and unambiguous designation would have much weight after Kim Jong Il's incapacitation or death. The twenty-seven-year-old Kim Jong Un could rule the state with substantial governing assistance from his uncle Chang Song Taek and an expanded National Defense Commission with broad and deep links to each of the three institutions.

Kim's eldest son, Kim Chong Nam, resides in China and is reportedly out of favor with his father.[35] He does not hold onto any of the reins of power that would make him likely to emerge as the sole leader without help from someone within the state. Chang Song Taek could possibly align with this nephew Kim Chong Nam, but why he would choose this course is unclear. Chang may simply become the new supreme leader himself. However, this guessing game of who will be the next supreme leader is truly irrelevant if one cannot say anything about how those successors may rule differently from Kim Jong Il or each other. It is unclear if swapping Kim Jong Un with Kim Jong Nam would make much difference as they seem to espouse many of the same positions as the current supreme leader and would face ruling the same institutional system currently in place.

The individual best positioned to be a real power broker is Chang Song Taek, who has extensive experience and the contacts necessary to control some of North Korea's most formidable institutions. Indeed, Kim Jong Il purged Chang for gaining too much of a personal following in the mid-2000s but brought him back into his inner circle after a few years of "reeducation." Chang has significant responsibilities over the party and government but, until recently, lacked control over the military. The most significant change in early 2009 involved Chang Song Taek and his new-found role in the military apparatus. When Kim raised the profile of the National Defense Commission and expanded its membership to twelve individuals, he included Chang in the NDC for the first time.[36]

Chang does not have a blood relationship to Kim Il Sung. If he replaced Kim Jong Il, he would need to find a way to establish his legitimacy in North Korea's long history of myth making. Both Kims significantly embellished and rewrote their résumés before and after coming to power, so this may not be as difficult of a task as some commentators have suggested. Kim Il Sung's legitimacy stems from his claims of revolutionary heroism, so Chang would need to link his family to the revolution more than Kim Il Sung to tap into this source of internal legitimacy. Alternatively, he could establish his legitimacy over time by actually improving the rational functions of the North Korean system. If Chang decided to turn the state in another direction from his predecessor, he would need to do so through the North's current institutions. He could modify the institutional structure over time, but Chang or any one of the Kims would initially manage Kim Jong Il's bureaucracy, as Kim Jong Il initially sought to manage his father's system.

It seems more likely at this point that Chang would cooperate with Kim Jong Un in ruling the regime. The greater powers of the NDC and Chang's ability to significantly advise and carry out Kim Jong Un's resulting orders through the three institutions points to a concentration of power at the top. The party may be more marginalized as an institution and the cabinet silenced and instructed to carry out orders when the succession process goes forward. It would require substantial effort for the young Kim to fundamentally revise the divide-and-conquer operations Kim Jong Il institutionalized.

North Korea's political future is still a great unknown, inevitably shaped by future events. But it will change from a knowable present, likely within certain structural parameters. Understanding how the state functions currently helps guide policy decisions from neighboring states that could influence not only short-term policy choices but long-term ones as well. Kim Jong Il's system has reacted with a certain level of predictability. Washington has more power over the country than it may realize, albeit of a different nature than often assumed. Sanctions and military moves can have some effect with opportunity costs, but the lessons of this study are that Washington and Seoul have an important role to play in influencing North Korea's internal debate. Empowering the cabinet's agenda is a more effective way to achieve American and South Korean policy goals than is trying to strong-arm a country that is deeply entrenched against military moves and has an isolated economy relatively immune to sanctions.

North Korea is a reactive system that is knowable and moldable. It is not an unknowable enigma that should be addressed without reference to comparative theory or historical interactions. It is an extreme polity that produces a great deal of suffering for its own people and insecurity for an important region, but it can be known and tamed. Understanding the bureaucratic positions of the main political institutions helps us peer inside North Korea's red box, explain why this state responds to events the way it does, and proactively craft policies in Seoul and Washington that influence its decision making and, eventually, strategic orientation.

Notes

1. Introduction

1. "Kim Jong-il Interrupts Own Official to Say U.S. Forces May Stay After Reunification," *Choson Ilbo*, August 9, 2000, BBC Summary of World Broadcasts, August 11, 2000. "Kim Jong Il Could Accept U.S. Military Presence," *Daily Yomiuri*, August 10, 2000. Don Kirk, "A North Korean Shift on Opposing U.S. Troops?" *International Herald Tribune*, August 10, 2000.
2. Hwang, *Nanun Yoksaui Chillirul Poatta*.
3. Post, "Kim Jong Il of North Korea."
4. Sigal, *Disarming Strangers*. Wit, Poneman, and Gallucci, *Going Critical*. Pritchard, *Failed Diplomacy*. Chinoy, *Meltdown*.
5. "Army's Anger Over U.S. Nuclear Moves Has 'Reached Its Limit,'" KCNA, December 12, 1998, BBC Summary of World Broadcasts, December 14, 1998.
6. Jae-jung Suh, *Power, Interests, and Identity*.
7. This self-interest applies to cabinet officials as well, albeit in a different way. Cabinet officials are regime elites and do not want to see an end to North Korea as a political entity. Unlike military and party officials, however, cabinet officials contend that the deterioration in economic and other arenas poses a different kind of threat to the existence of the regime. These officials tend to be younger, with a longer time horizon and a more expansive view of national security. They do not observably reject the argument that party and military officials present that there are risks involved in opening but hold that the alternative poses greater threats to long-term regime maintenance.

8. Koh, "Ideology and Political Control in North Korea," 655–74.
9. Sigal, *Disarming Strangers*.
10. Ahn. "The Man Who Would Be Kim," 94–108. Bueno de Mesquita and Mo, *North Korean Economic Reform*. Eberstadt, *The End of North Korea*.
11. Chen and Lee, "Making Sense of North Korea," 459–75. Lankov, "North Korea," 4–14. Cumings, *Korea's Place in the Sun*. Scobell, "Making Sense of North Korea," 245–66. Cho, "The Characteristics of the North Korean Political System," 44–54.
12. Kwon. "State Building in North Korea." 286–96. Hassig, "The Well-Informed Cadre." Scalapino, "In Search of Peace and Stability," 367–78.
13. Gwak, "Guiding Role," 43–53.
14. Bermudez, "Information and the DPRK's Military and Power-Holding Elite." Yi Yang Su, "Analysis of DPRK Power Group," parts 1–3, *Chungang Ilbo*, January 4–6, 2007. Chong, "Changes in North Korea's Hierarchy," 16–21.
15. Carlin and Wit, *North Korean Reform*.
16. Gause, "North Korean Leadership."
17. Choi, "Changing Relations." Mansourov, "Disaster Management and Institutional Change," 1–19.
18. CIA World Factbook, https://www.cia.gov/library/publications/the-world-factbook/index.html.

2. Post-totalitarian Institutionalism

1. Oh and Hassig, *North Korea Through the Looking Glass*, 4.
2. Samuel Kim, "Introduction," 12, 22.
3. Lankov, "The Natural Death of North Korean Stalinism," 95–121.
4. Scobell, *Kim Jong Il and North Korea*, vi.
5. Hak-chun Kim, *North and South Korea*, 150.
6. Choi, "Changing Relations," 1999. Carlin and Wit, *North Korean Reform*. Paik, "North Korea's Choices for Survival and Prosperity," 249–92.
7 S. Neumann, *Permanent Revolution*. Arendt, *The Origins of Totalitarianism*. F. Neumann, *The Democratic and the Authoritarian State*.
8. Linz, *Totalitarian and Authoritarian Regimes*.
9. Oh and Hassig, *North Korea Through the Looking Glass*, 39–40.
10. Weber, *Economy and Society*, 1121–56.
11. Eckert, Lee, Lew, Robinson, and Wagner, *Korea Old and New*, 132–54.
12. Skilling and Griffiths, *Interest Groups*. Gleason, *Totalitarianism*.
13. Hough, *The Soviet Union and Social Science Theory*.
14. Linz and Stepan, *Problems of Democratic Transition*. Goldfarb, "Post-Totalitarian Politics," 533–54. Thompson, "To Shoot or Not to Shoot," 63–83.
5. Ceausescu's Romania is a notable exception. See Greg Scarlatoiu, "The Role of the Military in the Fall of the Ceausescu Regime and the Possible

Relevance for a Post-Kim Jong-il Transition in North Korea," KEI Exchange, February 2009, Korea Economic Institute, www.keia.org/Publications/Exchange/02Exchange09.pdf.

16. Chehabi and Linz, *Sultanistic Regimes*. Geddes, *Paradigms and Sand Castles*.

17. Molina and Rhodes, "Corporatism," 305–31.

18. Cumings, "Corporatism in North Korea," 269–94. Cumings, *Korea's Place in the Sun*.

19. Bruce Cumings, interview by author, March 11, 2008.

20. Skilling, "Interest Groups," 3.

21. Ibid., 4, 9. Truman, *The Governmental Process*, 23–33.

22. Skilling, "Interest Groups," 17.

23. Ibid., 23.

24. Groth, "USSR: Pluralist Monolith?" 445–64. Odom, "A Dissenting View," 567.

25. Scalapino and Lee, *Communism in Korea*, 604.

26. Domestic policy goals such as maintaining social control are broadly wrapped into the debate on economic opening with few other domestic issues demanding cross-institutional conversations at this level. The only other countries of sustained foreign policy importance to Pyongyang that could merit a prolonged conversation for systematic analysis are relations with Japan and China. With rare exceptions noted in the empirical chapters, relations with Japan are often debated in the "imperialist" context of relations with the United States. Sino-DPRK relations are not discussed in any depth in the media.

27. Inference is not the only tool to highlight the importance of the NYJE. The North Korean regime explicitly says it is the core policy document for the year. North Korea's semiofficial webpage, the People's Korea, describes the NYJE: "As the DPRK's key policy statement for the year replacing late president Kim Il Sung's New Year's Address, the Joint Editorial [has been] published annually on New Year's Day since 1995 by the country's three major newspapers—*Nodong Sinmun* (organ of Workers' Party of Korea), *Joson Inmingun* (organ of the Korean People's Army), and *Chongnyon Jonwi* (organ of the Kim Il Sung Socialist Youth League). Following the line of the late president Kim Il Sung's annual New Year's address, the joint editorial sets forth the new task of the year [and looks] back upon the previous year." "QandA on DPRK's Joint Editorial," 2000, *People's Korea*, www1.korea-np.co.jp/pk/127th_issue/2000011901.htm.

28. My judgments on the subject of the paragraphs are available for replication. Since this is a single-investigator project, my coding has not yet been subject to intercoder reliability efforts.

29. The Foreign Broadcast Information Service (FBIS), renamed the Open Source Center (OSC) in 2005, translates foreign media into English. Articles date back to 1953 and are publicly available in research libraries.

30. Yonhap News Agency, *North Korea Handbook*. Updated list of successors compiled from multiple sources.

31. The Open Source Center estimates *Nodong Sinmun*'s circulation is 1 million and *Minju Choson*'s is 600,000 out of the country's approximately 23 million people.

32. Linz and Stepan, *Problems of Democratic Transition and Consolidation.*
33. Tilly, "Why and How History Matters," 421.
34. Ibid.

3. Historical Context

1. Martin, *Under the Loving Care of the Fatherly Leader.*
2. Cumings, *North Korea*, 132–33. Ilpyong Kim, *Communist Politics in North Korea*, 10–11.
3. Mansourov, "Kim Jong Il's Military-First Politics," 40–41.
4. Armstrong, *The North Korean Revolution.*
5. Armstrong, "Nature, Origins, and Development of the North Korean State," 50.
6. Armstrong, *The North Korean Revolution.*
7. Halberstam, *The Coldest Winter.*
8. Foster-Carter, "North Korea," 115–20.
9. An, *North Korea: A Political Handbook*, 34–47. Yang, *North and South Korean Political Systems*, 374–79.
10. Scalapino and Lee, *Communism in Korea*, 775.
11. An, *North Korea: A Political Handbook*, 99–100.
12. Scalapino and Lee, *Communism in Korea*, 701–11.
13. Cumings, *North Korea*, 106–7.
14. Hoare and Pares, *North Korea*, 117–19.
15. Scalapino and Lee, *Communism in Korea*, 594–602.
16. Foster-Carter, "North Korea," 120–28. Hoare and Pares, *North Korea*, 37–45.
17. Dae-sook Suh, *Kim Il Sung*, 159–268. Ilpyong Kim, *Communist Politics in North Korea*, 117–31.
18. Armstrong, "Nature, Origins, and Development of the North Korean State," 43–53.
19. Scalapino and Lee, *Communism in Korea*, 756, 788.
20. An, *North Korea: A Political Handbook*, 133–45.
21. Hak-chun Kim, *North and South Korea*, 68.
22. Buzo, *The Guerilla Dynasty*, 16–52. Koh, "North Korea's Foreign Policymaking Process," 49–55.
23. Yoo, "Change and Continuity."
24. Dae-sook Suh, "Organization and Administration of North Korean Foreign Policy," 3–6.
25. Ibid., 9–11. Park, "Power Structure in North Korea," 111–42.
26. Buzo *The Guerilla Dynasty*, 89–100.
27. An, *North Korea: A Political Handbook*, 114.
28. Ibid., 150.
29. Dae-sook Suh, "Organization and Administration of North Korean Foreign Policy," 1–19. Scalapino, introduction, x.

30. Ahn, "North Korean Foreign Policy," 15–38.

31. An, *North Korea: A Political Handbook*, 150–68. Park, introduction, 3–14.

32. Lee, "The 1972 Constitution and Top Communist Leaders," 192–222. Lee, *Korean Workers' Party*, 114–34. Dae-sook Suh, *Korean Communism*, 444–48. Kim Jong Il, "Let Us Step Up the Three-Revolution Red Flag Movement," November 23, 1986, www.korea-dpr.com/lib/Kim%20Jong%20Il%20-%204/ LET%20US%20STEP%20UP%20THE%20THREE.pdf. Scalapino and Lee, *Communism in Korea*, 559–684.

33. An, *North Korea: A Political Handbook*, 176.

34. Dae-sook Suh, *Kim Il Sung*, 287–97.

35. Dae-sook Suh, "Communist Party Leadership," 159–91.

36. Foster-Carter, "North Korea," 130–33. An, *North Korea in Transition*, 7–34.

37. Yang, *North and South Korean Political Systems*, 223–57, 584–93.

38. Ibid., 265.

39. Cumings, *North Korea*, 134.

40. James Moltz, "Russian Policy on the North Korean Nuclear Crisis," May 5, 2003, North Korea Special Collection, Center for Nonproliferation Studies, http://cns.miis.edu/north_korea/ruspol.htm.

41. Vorontsov, "Current Russia–North Korea Relations," 5.

42. Peter Hayes, "North Korea's Uranium Exports: Much Ado About Something," May 25, 2004, Northeast Asia Peace and Security Network, Special Report, www.nautilus.org/archives/pub/ftp/napsnet/special_reports/Hayes-DPR Kuranium.txt. Duk-Hwan Hwang, "Energy and Mineral Resources of Russia (East Siberia and Far East) and North Korea," Summary of Research Paper, August 2003, Energy Cooperation in Northeast Asia, www.neasiaenergy.net/ nea/e_publications.nsf/ 1b408c7e1ee7e412492570d0004c5f07/a8070cb4997 2e0a249256ecb000dec11/$FILE/DHHwang.pdf.

43. Jae-jung Suh, *Power, Interests, and Identity*, 29–62.

44. "Some New Aspects of Korean-Chinese Relations in the First Half of 1965," Excerpts from the Report of the Soviet Embassy in Pyongyang, June 4, 1965, Cold War International History Project, Virtual Archive, www.wilsoncenter.org/ index.cfm?topic_id=1409&fuseaction=va2.document&identifier=5035023B -96B6-175C-93B025BE065B82E8&sort=Subject&item=Korea,%20DPRK,%20 Korean%20Worker%E2%80%99s%20Party,%20KWP. "Record of Conversation Between Soviet Politburo Member Nikolai Podgorny and Kim Chung-wong," January 20, 1967, Cold War International History Project, Virtual Archive, www.wilsoncenter.org/index.cfm?topic_id=1409&fuseaction=va2 .document&identifier=5035025A-96B6-175C-939A231E7DF03C10&sort =Subject&item=Korea,%20DPRK,%20in%20Sino%20Soviet%20Split. For complete text of North Korea's July 1961 treaties with the Soviet Union and China, see Basic Documents of Postwar International Politics, "The World and Japan" Database Project, Database of Japanese Politics and International Relations, Institute of Oriental Culture, University

of Tokyo, www.ioc.u-tokyo.ac.jp/~worldjpn/documents/indices/docs/index
-ENG.html.

45. Wu, "What China Whispers to North Korea," 42.

46. The nature of China's political commitment to North Korea is hotly debated today, though few argue that Beijing would prop up the current regime in Pyongyang militarily if called to do so. For a collection of contemporary articles on the China–North Korea political relationship and their foreign policy impact, see Jayshree Bajoria, "Backgrounder: The China–North Korea Relationship," July 21, 2009, Council on Foreign Relations, www.cfr.org/publication/11097/.

47. Wit, Poneman, and Gallucci, *Going Critical*, 36.

48. For more on attempted military coups in North Korea, see Oh and Hassig, *North Korea Through the Looking Glass*, 119–20. Alexandre Y. Mansourov, "Korean Monarch Kim Jong Il: Technocrat Ruler of the Hermit Kingdom Facing the Challenge of Modernity," CanKor, Nautilus Institution, DPRK Briefing Book, www.nautilus.org/DPRKBriefingBook/negotiating/issue.html. "Leadership Succession," GlobalSecurity.org, Military, www.globalsecurity.org/military/world/dprk/leadership-succession.htm.

49. Haggard and Noland, *Famine in North Korea*.

50. There has been some debate as to the whether labeling this market activity as "illegal" or "black market" is appropriate. Though North Korean law clearly prohibits this activity, some argue that the rule of law is not established and the regime's commitment to tolerating this market activity makes it more appropriate to label it "gray market" activity. However, the state has shown only intermittent tolerance, occasionally enforcing the law in the form of crackdowns. The activity, though increasingly widespread, remains technically illegal and therefore somewhat risky. Readers can draw their own conclusions of the appropriate terminology based on this type of arrangement.

51. Weber, *Economy and Society*, 1148–49.

52. "North Korea Urges South to Try to Reconcile," *New York Times*, February 20, 1998. "Yonhap Views Thawing of ROK-DPRK Relations," Yonhap News Agency, February 20, 1998.

53. "North Korea, Army Chief Addresses War Anniversary Meeting in Pyongyang," KCBS, July 27, 1998, BBC Monitoring Asia-Pacific, Political, July 29, 1998. Though Chinese diplomacy toward North Korea was a quiet affair, they presumably could point to China's own stable communist political system as evidence that economic opening did not necessarily produce political revolution.

54. "North Korea May Run Out of Grain in April: U.N.," *Asia Pulse*, March 13, 1998. John Gittings, "North Korea Admits Food Crisis," *Guardian*, March 1998. "ROK to Contribute 50,000 Tons of Food Aid to DPRK," *Choson Ilbo*, March 9, 1998. "ROK 'Ready' to Provide Additional Shipments of Fertilizer," *Korea Herald*, March 13, 1998. David E. Sanger, "North Korea Site an A-Bomb Plant,

U.S. Agencies Say," *New York Times*, August 17, 1998. "ROK Trying Hard to Confirm NYT Report on DPRK Facilities," Yonhap News Agency, August 17, 1998. Pak Tu-sik, "'Material Evidence' Is Found for North Korea's Resumption of Nuclear Activities," *Choson Ilbo*, August 18, 1998. "Torrential Rains Take Heavy Toll in North Korea," Associated Press, August 26, 1998. "DPRK Plagued by Flood," Xinhua News Agency, August 22, 1998.

55. The Taepodong-1 rocket can be configured as a medium-range ballistic missile or as a space launch vehicle to put satellites into orbit. The third stage of the rocket was configured for a satellite launch during the 1998 launch, but the tested technology had dual-use missile implications.

56. Byung Chol Koh, "'Military-First Politics' and Building a 'Powerful and Prosperous Nation' in North Korea," Nautilus Policy Forum Online 05-32A, April 14, 2005. www.nautilus.org/fora/security/0532AKoh.html.

57. Some have argued that the military-first politics marked a new role for the military as the supreme institution in North Korean politic, replacing the party. Indeed, one sophisticated take on this new dynamic noted that military-first resembles imperial Japan's "enriching the state and strengthening the army" rallying call or South Korea's developmental dictatorship under Park Chung Hee's Fourth Republic. In some respects, military-first politics more closely resembles fascism than socialism. See Kihl, "Emergence of the Second Republic," 14.

58. Choi, "Changing Relations."

59. For another view on competing regime goals and policy linkages during this time period, see Paik, "North Korea's Pursuit of Security and Economic Interests," 95–126.

4. North Korea's Political Institutions

1. One may reasonably argue that Kim Jong Il himself is an institution. I do not dispute this, but for the sake of clarity, I refrain from referring to him as such.

2. Ilpyong Kim, *Communist Politics in North Korea*, 3–8.

3. Sung Chull Kim, *North Korea Under Kim Jong Il*, 95–98.

4. Hak-chun Kim, *North and South Korea*, 108–9.

5. Yonhap News Agency, *North Korea Handbook*, 98–104.

6. Bertil Lintner. "The North Korea Enigma: Sons and Heirs," *Asia Times Online*, August 18, 2006, www.atimes.com/atimes/Korea/HH18Dg01.html.

7. An, *North Korea: A Political Handbook*, 52.

8. Mansourov, "Kim Jong Il's Military-First Politics," 45.

9. Moon and Kim. "The Future of the North Korean System," 236. Yonhap News Agency, *North Korea Handbook*, 189.

10. Hak-chun Kim, *North and South Korea*, 90–112. Samuel Kim, *North Korean System*, 16.

11. Jae-jung Suh, *Power, Interests, and Identity* 79–81.
12. Oh and Hassig, *North Korea Through the Looking Glass*, 119–20.
13. Ilpyong Kim, *Communist Politics in North Korea* 8–9.
14. Yonhap News Agency, *North Korea Handbook*, 93.
15. For debates surrounding North Korea's economic reform, see Ahn, Eberstadt, and Young-sun, *A New International Engagement Framework for North Korea?* Frank, "Economic Reforms in North Korea," 278–311. Y. Kim and Choi, *Understanding North Korea's Economic Reforms*.
16. Dae-sook Suh, "Organization and Administration of North Korean Foreign Policy," 6.
17. Scalapino and Lee, *Communism in Korea*, 818–24.
18. Barghoorn, "The Security Police," 78–90.
19. Mansourov, "Kim Jong Il's Military-First Politics," 46–47.
20. Bermudez, *The Armed Forces of North Korea*.
21. Scalapino and Lee, *Communism in Korea*, 792–800.
22. North Korea is first divided into provinces and special (larger) cities. Below this level of organization reside the counties. Finally, at the bottom one finds municipalities (*si*), towns, wards, villages, and workers' settlements. Each has a legislative, executive, and judicial organ responsible to the higher level of organization. See, An, *North Korea: A Political Handbook*, 56.

5. Institutional Jostling for Agenda Control, 1998–2001

1. Both Koreas recognize in their constitutions authority over the entire Korean peninsula. Consequently, neither officially considers inter-Korean relations "foreign policy."
2. "A Historic Event Having Demonstrated the National Strength of Juche Korea," *Nodong Sinmun*, September 7, 1998.
3. "Kim Yong-ch'un Addresses Military Parade," KCNA, September 9, 1998.
4. Interview by author, September 2008.
5. Sigal, *Disarming Strangers*.
6. "Foreign Ministry Spokesman Announces Satellite Launch," KCBS, September 4, 1998.
7. "DPRK Foreign Ministry Spokesman Comments DPRK-U.S. Talks," KCBS, September 10, 1998.
8. Ibid.
9. "Uncovering the Truth About North Korea's Alleged Underground Nuclear Facility: The Kumchang-ri Controversy," North Korea Special Collection, Center for Nonproliferation Studies (CNS), http://cns.miis.edu/archive/country_north_korea/uncover.htm.
10. "DPRK Foreign Ministry Spokesman Comments DPRK-U.S. Talks," KCBS, September 10, 1998.

11. "KCNA Reviews 11 Sep Pyongyang Press," KCNA, September 11, 1998.
12. "*Nodong Sinmun* Lauds Kim Jong Il as 'Sun of Nation,'" KCNA, September 14, 1998.
13. "The Respected and Beloved General Is a Great Man Among Great Men Possessed with Outstanding Farsightedness," KCBS, October 16, 1998.
14. "U.S. Allegation on Facility Called Violation of Sovereignty," KCNA, September 19, 1998.
15. Chin Ung, "Class Consciousness of the Working Class," *Nodong Sinmun*, September 21, 1998.
16. "Anti-Reunification Multilateral Dialogue Cannot Be Realized," *Nodong Sinmun*, September 29, 1998.
17. "Do Not Make Unnecessary Rackets," *Nodong Sinmun*, September 25, 1998.
18. "U.S. Imperialists' Dark Design to Light a Fuse to a New War," KCBS, September 19, 1998.
19. "Army's Anger Over U.S. Nuclear Moves Has 'Reached Its Limit,'" KCNA, December 12, 1998, BBC Summary of World Broadcasts, December 14, 1998.
20. "The United States Will Be Held Fully Responsible," *Nodong Sinmun*, October 17, 1998.
21. Kim Chong-son, "The Imperialists' Aggressive Nature Absolutely Cannot Change," *Nodong Sinmun*, October 27, 1998, 6.
22. "KCNA on Ill-Intentioned Remarks of Ex-U.S. Secretary of Defence," KCNA, October 19, 1998.
23. Choe Song-kuk, "We, Too, Have the Right to Make Independent Choice," *Nodong Sinmun*, October 23, 1998, 6.
24. "OPlan 5027 Major Theater War—West," GlobalSecurity.org, Military, www.globalsecurity.org/military/ops/oplan-5027.htm.
25. "'Inspection' Cannot Be Allowed; KCNA Commentary," KCNA, November 27, 1998.
26. Sung Chae-sun and No Yong, "The Emerging Powerful State of Juche is a Great Socialist Ideological Power," *Nodong Sinmun*, November 30, 1998.
27. "KPA General Staff Statement," KCBS, December 2, 1998.
28. "Military Officials React to KPA Statement," KCBS, December 2, 1998. "War Veterans in DPRK Support KPA Statement," KCBS, December 2, 1998. "Intellectual Views Significance of KPA Statement," KCBS, December 4, 1998. "Young People, Students Denounce U.S. War Moves," KCNA, December 6, 1998. "Workers Resolve to Annihilate U.S. Imperialists and Their Stooges," KCNA, December 6, 1998. "Foreign Groups Hail Statement of KPA General Staff," KCNA, December 10, 1998. "'Operation Plan 5027' Under Fire," KCNA, December 13, 1998.
29. "KPA General Staff Statement," KCBS, December 2, 1998.
30. "Make the Punishment Merciless," KCBS, December 4, 1998.
31. Won Kyong-ho, "Picking Up a Wrong Object and Adopting a Wrong Method," *Nodong Sinmun*, December 22, 1998.

32. "DPRK Diplomats Have Little to Do for DPRK-U.S. Relations, Says Foreign Ministry Spokesman," KCNA, December 7, 1998. The Foreign Ministry's response is also significant in that it juxtaposes its institutional role as implementers of the Agreed Framework against the military's institutional role of conducting war.

33. Kim Chong-son, "We Cannot Afford to Be Only Counting on the Agreed Framework," *Nodong Sinmun*, October 10, 1998. Choe Song-kuk, "A Test War for a Preemptive Strike," *Nodong Sinmun*, November 22, 1998.

34. Samuel Kim, "North Korea in 1999," 152. Bradley Martin, "All the Winged Horses . . . ," *Asia Times Online*, the Koreas, January 8, 2000, www.atimes.com/koreas/BA08Dg01.html.

35. "Functionaries of the National Economic Organs Should Vigorously Shoulder the Weight of the Building of a Powerful Nation," *Minju Choson*, January 5, 1999.

36. Ibid.

37. Chong Song-il, "Activities of Functionaries," *Nodong Sinmun*, January 4, 1999.

38. Kim Chin-o, "Roar of the Cannon Signals Revolution in Potato Farming," *Nodong Sinmun*, January 3, 1999.

39. Choe Yong-tok, "Cabinet Committees and Ministries Are Carrying Out Economic Operations and Commands in a Revolutionary Way in Order to Implement the Joint Editorial," *Nodong Sinmun*, January 7, 1999.

40. Hwang Chang-man, "Great Leadership That Embodies the Socialist Principle in Economic Construction," *Nodong Sinmun*, March 1, 1999. See also M.A. Yi Yong-ho, "Our Firmest State Organizational Structure," *Minju Choson*, February 2, 1999.

41. "Party Leader's Speech on Kim Jong Il Anniversary Praises Country Turned Into Fortress," KCBS, April 9, 1999, BBC Summary of World Broadcasts, April 13, 1999.

42. Han Ung-ho, "The Great Unity of the Nation Is the Basic Cornerstone of the Reunification of the Fatherland," *Nodong Sinmun*, January 7, 1999.

43. Choe Mun-il, "The Five-Point Program for the Great Unity of the Nation Is the Great Banner for the Reunification of the Fatherland," *Nodong Sinmun*, January 3, 1999.

44. "Meeting Marks Army Anniversary," KCBS, April 24, 1999, in BBC Summary of World Broadcasts, April 26, 1999. "North Korea, Army Chief of Staff Kim Yong-Chun Gives 67th Anniversary Speech," KCBS, April 24, 1999, BBC Monitoring Asia-Pacific, Political, April 25, 1999.

45. Jae-jung Suh, *Power, Interests, and Identity*.

46. Halberstam, *The Coldest Winter*.

47. "U.S. Cannot Flee from Responsibility," KCNA, January 9, 1999.

48. Hong Hwang-ki, "Nothing Can Be Expected from DPRK-U.S. Agreed Framework," *Nodong Sinmun*, January 12, 1999.

49. Kim Chin-o, "The Cabinet Maps Out a Plan of Operation and the Ministry of Agriculture Implements It," *Nodong Sinmun*, July 4, 1999.
50. Samuel Kim, "North Korea in 1999," 160. Koreans refer to the body of water between the Korean Peninsula and China as the West Sea since it is immediately west of Korea. China and others refer to it as the Yellow Sea because of the yellow sands that flow from China. Since the focus of this book is Korea, I use the Korean name for the sea.
51. Elizabeth Olson, "North Korea and U.S. Meet on Inspection of Atom Plant," *New York Times*, January 17, 1999.
52. "North Korea Chief Making 1st Trip to China," *New York Times*, March 3, 1999. David E. Sanger, "N. Korea Consents to U.S. Inspection of a Suspect Site," *New York Times*, March 17, 1999.
53. Nicholas D. Kristof, "North Korea Unresponsive in U.S. Talks, Envoy Reports," *New York Times*, May 30, 1999.
54. "DPRK's Kang Sok-chu, U.S. Special Envoy Perry Hold Talks," KCNA, May 28, 1999.
55. "Foreign Ministry Spokesman on Kumchang-ri Facility," KCNA, June 9, 1999.
56. For a detailed evaluation of conflict surrounding the NLL, see Terence Roehrig, "Korean Dispute Over the Northern Limit Line: Security, Economics, or International Law?" *Maryland Series in Contemporary Asian Studies* 3:194 (2008).
57. Sheryl WuDunn, "South Korea Sinks Vessel from North in Disputed Waters," *New York Times*, June 15, 1999. "UN Command–DPRK Talks Begin Amidst Firing Incident," Yonhap News Agency, June 15, 1999. Song Sang-kun, "A 'Disgraced DPRK' Is Likely to Purge Its Military," *Dong-a Ilbo*, June 16, 1999.
58. David Sanger, "Korean Clash May Ruin U.S. Reconciliation Bid," *New York Times*, June 17, 1999.
59. Pak Rim-su, "KPA Delegate Comments on Sea Border," KCBS, August 26, 1999.
60. Sheryl WuDunn, "North Korea Suspends Contact with South," *New York Times*, June 17, 1999.
61. "ROK Appears to Have 'Little' Idea of How to Handle DPRK," *Choson Ilbo*, July 4, 1999. Sang-chol and Yi Yong-chong, "Exclusive Interview with North Korean Chief Delegate PakYong-su," *Chungang Ilbo*, July 2, 1999. "Erik Eckholm, "South Korea Halts Talks in Dispute on Families," *New York Times*, July 3, 1999.
62. Sanger, "Korean Clash May Ruin U.S. Reconciliation Bid," *New York Times*, June 17, 1999.
63. Kim Ho-sam, "Faith Must Be Shown in Action," KCBS, July 30, 1999.
64. "More on DPRK Warning U.S. of 'Unpredictable Consequences,'" KCBS, August 3, 1999.

65. Bill Gertz, "Pentagon Predicts N. Korea Will Test Long-Range Missile," *Washington Times*, June 18, 1999. Elizabeth Becker, "U.S. Says Photos Show North Korea Preparing for Missile," *New York Times*, June 18, 1999.

66. Kim Nam-hyok, "No Maneuver of Isolation and Suffocation Can Budge Us," *Nodong Sinmun*, September 14, 1999. Choe Hak-chol, "Absolutely No One Can Frighten Us," *Nodong Sinmun*, September 19.

67. "DPRK Not to Launch Missile," KCNA, September 24, 1999.

68. "ROK to Defend Existing Northern Limit Line," *Korea Herald*, September 4, 1999. "DPRK Repudiates Border, South Korea Rejects Change," *Kyodo*, September 2, 1999. Doug Struck, "North Korea Says Sea Border Invalid, Claims New Waters," *Washington Post*, September 3, 1999. "DPRK Declares Sea Border with South Invalid," Agence France Presse (Hong Kong), September 2, 1999.

69. Paul Shin, "North Korea Unlikely to Get Significant Economic Benefits from Easing of U.S. Sanctions," Associated Press, September 17, 1999. Keiji Urakami, "Clinton Announces Plans to Ease Sanctions on N. Korea," *Japan Economic Newswire*, September 17, 1999. John F. Harris, "Officials Defend Plan to Reward N. Korea; Missile Pledge Could End U.S. Sanctions," *Washington Post*, September 14, 1999. David E. Sanger, "Trade Sanctions on North Korea are Eased by U.S.," *New York Times*, September 18, 1999.

70. "DPRK ForMin Denounces U.S. Congress Debate on Korea," KCNA, December 8, 1999.

71. "U.S. Design to Stifle DPRK Comes Under Fire," KCNA, December 30, 1999.

72. Gaku Shibata, "Lawmakers, N. Korea to Urge Talk Resumption," *Daily Yomiuri*, December 4, 1999. "Seoul Welcomes Normalization Talks Between North Korea and Japan," Deutsche Presse-Agentur, December 3, 1999. Calvin Sims, "North Korea, Apparently Seeking to End Its Isolation, Agrees to Resume Talks with Japan," *New York Times*, December 4, 1999. Shingo Ito, "Japan, North Korea Sign Deal to Resume Rapprochement Talks," Agence France Presse (Hong Kong), December 3, 1999.

73. John Pomfret, "N. Korea Threatens to Skip Talks; Visit to U.S. Tied to Removal from List of Terrorism Sponsors," *Washington Post*, March 29, 2000. "DPRK Ambassador: U.S. Must Drop 'Terrorist State' Label," Agence France Presse (Hong Kong), March 29, 2000.

74. Howard W. French, "Suddenly, Reclusive North Korea Reaches Out to the World," *New York Times*, March 17, 2000. "N. Korea Hails Italian Visit as Start of New Chapter in Ties," Agence France Presse (Hong Kong), March 29, 2000. "2 French Cos Seek to Advance into N Korea," *Asia Pulse*, March 16, 2000. Lincoln Wright, "Downer Decision Soon on Relations with N. Korea," *Canberra Times*, March 28, 2000.

75. Economic disparities between the two Koreas far surpassed the economic disparities between West and East Germany at the time of their reunification. With the economic scars of the 1997 Asian financial crisis fresh in the minds

of most South Koreans, President Kim's conclusion held widespread appeal within his country. Bringing North Korea up to 60 percent of the living standard of South Korea—a figure noted for its assumption that it would prevent mass migration from the North to the South—would cost approximately $319 billion in 1990, but the economic disparity had grown by the time of the summit in 2000 to approximately $1.7 trillion. This disparity doubled about every five years. See Noland, *Economic Integration of the Korean Peninsula*, 192–93.

76. "DPRK Premier: DPRK People 'Fully' Support DPRK-ROK Summit," KCBS, April 10, 2000.

77. "Kim Jong-il Interrupts Own Official to Say U.S. Forces May Stay After Reunification," *Choson Ilbo* August 9, 2000, BBC Summary of World Broadcasts, August 11, 2000. "Kim Jong Il Could Accept U.S. Military Presence," *Daily Yomiuri*, August 10, 2000, Foreign Broadcast Information Service (FBIS). Don Kirk, "A North Korean Shift on Opposing U.S. Troops?" *International Herald Tribune*, August 10, 2000.

78. Hwang, *Nanun Yoksaui Chillirul Poatta.*

79. Post, "Kim Jong Il of North Korea," 239–58.

80. David E. Sanger, "U.S. Says It Will Soon Drop Its Sanctions on North Korea," *Washington Post*, June 15, 2000. Yoo Cheong-mo, "Washington Expected to Ease N.K. Sanctions by June 25," *Korea Herald*, June 15, 2000. George Gedda, "U.S. Working on Sanctions Lifting for North Korea," Associated Press, June 15, 2000.

81. "Albright to Visit Seoul 23–24 Jun to Coordinate DPRK Policy," Yonhap News Agency, June 17, 2000. Jane Perlez, "After Korean Talks, Albright Plans Seoul and Beijing Trip," *New York Times*, June 17, 2000.

82. Charles Lee, "N. Korea Pledges to Abide by Missile Test Freeze," United Press International, June 21, 2000. Jane Perlez, "North Korea's Missile Pledge Paves the Way for New Talks," *New York Times*, June 22, 2000. "U.S. Hails N. Korea's New Commitment Not to Test Missiles," *Japan Economic Newswire*, June 21, 2000.

83. Calvin Sims, "Seoul Mutes War's 50th Anniversary," *New York Times*, June 26, 2000.

84. John Burton, "Hopes of Reunion Increase for Divided Korean Families," *Financial Times*, July 1, 2000. Doug Struck, "North Korea's Diplomatic Strides Pay Off," *Washington Post*, July 27, 2000. "2 Koreas Agree to Reopen Liaison Offices," *Korea Times*, July 31, 2000. "The Two Koreas Continue to Report Progress in New Talks," *New York Times*, August 31, 2000. "New Cross-Border Railway Aims to Open Economic Exchanges Between Koreas," Associated Press, September 18, 2000.

85. Paul Shin, "Putin Raises Question of North Korean Missiles with Kim Jong Il," Associated Press, July 20, 2000. Michael R. Gordon, "North Korea Reported Open to Halting Missile Program," *New York Times*, July 20, 2000. "DPRK Leader's Comments on Missile Program Proposal Not Perceived as

Joke," *Interfax*, August 15, 2000. "Kim Chong-il Was 'Entirely Serious' About Missiles to Putin," *Nezavisimaya Gazeta*, August 15, 2000. Doug Struck and Joohee Cho, "N. Korean Dismisses Missile Idea; Offer to End Program Made 'Laughingly,'" *Washington Post*, August 15, 2000.
86. Carlin and Lewis, *Policy in Context*, 8.
87. Ibid., 43.
88. Tom Carter, "Cho, Clinton Discuss Concerns About Terrorism, Proliferation," *Washington Times*, October 11, 2000. David E. Sanger, "North Korean at White House, Continuing a Warming Trend," *New York Times*, October 11, 2000. Steven Mufson, "Clinton Might Visit N. Korea Next Month," *Washington Post*, October 13, 2000. Tom Carter, "Clinton Plans First-ever Presidential Trip to N. Korea; Albright Will Visit Pyongyang to Pave Way," *Washington Times*, October 13, 2000. "U.S., N. Korea Could Restore Diplomatic Ties During Clinton Visit," Agence France Presse (Hong Kong), October 13, 2000. Jane Perlez, "Albright Greeted with a Fanfare by North Korea," *New York Times*, October 24, 2000. "Albright Says Kim Ending Long-range Missile Launches," *Kyodo*, October 24, 2000. Hong Won-sang, "ROK Government's Response," *Taehan Maeil*, October 24, 2000. "Lee, Albright, Kono Discuss Pace of Improving Ties with N.K.," Yonhap News Agency, October 24, 2000. Jane Perlez, "Albright Reports Progress in Talks with North Korea," *New York Times*, October 25, 2000. "Clinton Will Not Visit North Korea During Asia Tour: White House," Agence France Presse (Hong Kong), November 4, 2000. Jane Perlez, "U.S.–North Korea Missile Talks Stall; Clinton Trip Is in Doubt," *New York Times*, November 4, 2000.

6. Segmenting Policy and Issue Linkages, 2001–2006

1. McEachern, "Benchmarks of Economic Reform in North Korea," 231–46.
2. Yu Sang-chol, "'Kim Chong-il 'Shocked at Shanghai,'" *Chungang Ilbo*, January 19, 2001.
3. Michael Mazarr, "Kim Jong Il: Strategy and Psychology," 1–21, *On Korea*, Academic Paper Series, 2008, www.keia.org/Publications/OnKorea/2008/08mazarr.pdf.
4. "DPRK Reports Leader Kim Jong Il's Visit to PRC," KCBS, January 20, 2001.
5. "DPRK-China Friendship Will Be Strengthened and Developed Century After Century," *Nodong Sinmun*, January 23, 2001.
6. Nam-son, "Choosing the Leading Sectors of Agriculture," 35–38.
7. "DPRK Daily on Major Economic Sectors to Be Developed in 2001," *Minju Choson*, March 13, 2001.
8. "North Korea, Russia Express Interest in Linking Railways," ITAR, March 17, 2001, BBC Summary of World Broadcasts, March 21, 2001.
9. Interviews conducted by the author May–September 2008.

10. "South Korean Paper Analyzes North's Delegation to China," KCNA, January 21, 2001, BBC Monitoring Asia Pacific-Political, January 12, 2001.
11. David E. Sanger, "Bush Tells Seoul Talks with North Won't Resume Now," *New York Times*, March 8, 2001. White House Press Release 2001, www .whitehouse.gov/news/releases/2001/03/20010307-6.html.
12. "ROK Official Says Seoul Urges U.S. to Resume Talks with DPRK 'Soon,'" *Korea Times*, March 26, 2001. "CFR Urges Bush to Support Seoul's Policy of Engaging N. Korea," Yonhap News Agency, March 26, 2001. Howard W. French, "Seoul Fears U.S. Is Chilly About Detente with North," *New York Times*, March 25, 2001.
13. "There Is Nothing to Gain from the Policy to Crush Us," *Nodong Sinmun*, March 18, 2001. "U.S. Urged to Properly Understand Its Opponent," KCNA, March 19, 2001. "Hatred," KCBS, March 21, 2001. "The Ringleaders Who Strain the International Situation," KCBS, March 22, 2001.
14. Hong Song-nam, "On Juche 89 (2000) Work and Tasks for Juche 90 (2001) of the DPRK Cabinet," KCBS, April 5, 2001.
15. "Peace Lies with Bush, says N Korean leader," *Australian*, May 4, 2001. "North Korea to Keep Ban on Missile Tests," *Globe and Mail*, May 4, 2001.
16. "'Talks Between U.S., N.K. Depend on Timing of Review': Fleischer," Yonhap News Agency, May 11, 2001. "N. Korea, U.S. May Meet on Sidelines of ARF Meeting," *Kyodo*, May 11, 2001.
17. John Pomfret, "N. Korea Said to Warn of New Missile Tests," *Washington Post*, June 4, 2001.
18. "North and South Korean Vessels Clash at Sea," *New York Times*, June 25, 2001.
19. Samuel Kim, "Introduction."
20. "Colin Powell Departs for China," Yonhap News Agency, July 28, 2001. "Bush 'Tentatively Scheduled' to Visit ROK Oct Prior to APEC," *Korea Times*, July 29, 2001. Steven Mufson, "Powell Urges Resumption of N. Korea Talks; U.S. Expresses Strong Support for S. Korean 'Sunshine Policy,'" *New York Times*, July 28, 2001.
21. "DPRK Radio to ROK Reiterates Position on Dialogue with U.S.," KCBS, August 1, 2001. Doug Struck, "Koreas' Relations Bog Down; North Recoils from Hard Line by U.S.," *New York Times*, August 14, 2001.
22. Patrick Cockburn, "Russians Warm to Korea's Trans-Siberian Kim," *Independent on Sunday*, August 5, 2001. Dave Montgomery, "Russia, N. Korea Uphold Missile Ban," *Ottawa Citizen*, August 5, 2001.
23. "The DPRK and the United States; Crisis and Prospect," KCBS, October 13, 2001. "DPRK Delegate Speaks at 56th Session of UN General Assembly," KCNA, October 24, 2001. Yi Hak-nam, "Efforts for Independence and Progression, Threat to Peace and Security," *Nodong Sinmun*, December 25, 2001.
24. "Our Republic's Firm, Independent Foreign Policy," KCBS, August 30, 2001.
25. "DPRK News Agency Carries CPRF Statement on Postponing Family Reunions," KCNA, October 12, 2001.

26. "2 Koreas Set to Resume Reconciliation Talks," *New York Times*, September 7, 2001. Don Kirk, "North Korea Cancels Reunions with the South," *New York Times*, October 13, 2001. "Korea Reconciliation Talks Break Down," *Washington Post*, November 15, 2001.

27. Yi Hak-nam, "Capitalist Market Economy Gives Rise to Serious Politico-Economic Crisis," *Nodong Sinmun*, November 6, 2001. Chang Myong-ho, "Superiority of Socialist Planned Economy," *Nodong Sinmun*, November 11, 2001.

28. "DPRK Notes ROK Group's Denunciation of Unification Ministry for Ruptured Ministerial Talks," KCBS, November 23, 2001. Hwang Jang-jin, "Seoul Lifts Security Alert, Paving Way for S-N talks," *Korea Herald*, December 22, 2001. "Seoul Ends Alert, Offers Food to North," *Globe and Mail*, December 22, 2001.

29. Elisabeth Bumiller, "Bush on Way to Asia, After Repeating Demand on North Korea," *New York Times*, February 17, 2002.

30. "N. Korea Repeats Attacks on U.S.," *Korea Times*, February 25, 2002. "North Korea Rejects Talks," *New York Times*, February 25, 2002.

31. "Mean Hidden Intent That Criticizes Our Nuclear Issue," *Nodong Sinmun*, February 4, 2002. "Why Is the United States Beating on the Worn-Out Drum of Human Rights Again?" KCBS, February 10, 2002. Kim Nam-hyok, "Foolish Delusion," *Nodong Sinmun*, February 13, 2002.

32. Don Kirk, "North Korea Denounces U.S. Nuclear Plan, Promises 'Response,'" *New York Times*, March 14, 2002. Christopher Marquis, "U.S. and North Korea Hold High-Level Discussion," *New York Times*, March 16, 2002. Peter Slevin, "North Korea to Resume Nuclear Talks; Decision Suggests Pyongyang Won't Break Ties to U.S., Allies," *Washington Post*, April 4, 2002. "See Clearly Who the Opponent Is," *Nodong Sinmun*, February 15, 2002. "War Hysteria of U.S. and Japan Criticized," KCNA, February 18, 2002.

33. "DPRK Foreign Ministry Spokesman on Bush's Slanders," KCNA, February 22, 2002.

34. "KCNA on Bush's S. Korea Visit," KCNA, February 23, 2002. "DPRK Party Organ Decries U.S. 'Bush Clan,' Rejects Dialogue Proposal," *Nodong Sinmun*, February 27, 2002.

35. "DPRK Cabinet Paper Points Out U.S., Israel, Japan as 'Axis of Evil,'" *Minju Choson*, February 28, 2002.

36. One U.S. negotiator noted that the North Koreans use the "hurt feelings" construction in talks, which comes across as odd to a U.S. audience, especially when sitting across the table from representatives of a brutally repressive regime. The construction can easily be misread in a cartoonish sense, when it is more of an effort to uphold the state's dignity. Symbolic actions that some within the regime call rude or hostile are used in internal debates with a degree of effectiveness to block some engagement efforts.

37. "DPRK Cabinet Organ Decries U.S. for Taking Issue with DPRK's WMD," *Minju Choson*, February 28, 2002.

38. "'Full Text' of DPRK Foreign Ministry Spokesman Statement," KCBS, March 13, 2002.
39. Me Kim Kyong-yol, "The Era of Information Industry and Informatization of Planning Work," *Kyongje Yongu*, February 10, 2002.
40. Me Yi Chang-hui, "Juche-Oriented Opinion on the Realm of Circulation of the Means of Production in Socialist Societies," *Kyongje Yongu*, February 10, 2002.
41. Hwang Kyong-o, "Anti-People Traits of Capitalist Market Economy," *Nodong Sinmun*, February 20, 2002.
42. Cha Ki-hwa, "Remedy-Less Incurable Disease of Modern-Day Capitalism," *Nodong Sinmun*, May 26, 2002.
43. Kim Sun-hong, "Exerting Great Efforts Into Educating Posterity—from Chong Chun-taek Wonsan University of Economics," *Nodong Sinmun*, November 14, 2002.
44. "The Korean Peninsula Issue Must Be Correctly Regarded and Dealt With," *Nodong Sinmun*, May 16, 2002.
45. Don Kirk, "More Reunions Set for Families in the 2 Koreas," *New York Times*, April 15, 2002.
46. Han Ung-ho, "North-South Joint Declaration Must Be Thoroughly Adhered to and Implemented," *Nodong Sinmun*, June 5, 2002.
47. "North, South Korean Naval Clash Leaves Four Dead, One Missing, 18 Injured," Yonhap News Agency, June 29, 2002. "S. Korean Ship Sinks After Battle with North," *Globe and Mail*, June 29, 2002.
48. "South Korean Military Authorities Should Take the Blame," KCBS, July 2, 2002.
49. "DPRK TV Blames U.S., ROK 'Conservative Elements' for Yellow Sea Naval Clash," KCTV, July 5, 2002. "KPA Mission Spokesman Calls on ROK Military to Apprise DPRK of Ship Salvage Plan 'in Advance,'" KCBS, July 8, 2002. "The Responsibility Rests on the United States," *Nodong Sinmun*, July 9, 2002.
50. Doug Struck, "Koreans Accusatory After Boat Is Sunk; Tension Threatens Efforts to Resume U.S.-Pyongyang Talks," *New York Times*, June 30, 2002. Doug Struck, "N. Korea Sends Contradictory Signals; After Naval Clash, Seoul Receives Harsh Words and Congratulations," *New York Times*, July 1, 2002. Ahn, 49.
51. "S. Korea Says U.S. to Aid Increased Surveillance of North," *Washington Post*, July 2, 2002. Vernon Loeb, "U.S. Shelves N. Korea Talks; Patrol Ship Clash 'Created Unacceptable Atmosphere,'" *Washington Post*, July 3, 2002. Christopher Torchia, "N. Korea Says It Regrets Clash with South, Proposes Talks," *Washington Post*, July 26, 2002. "White Paper by the Secretariat of the Committee for the Peaceful Reunification of the Fatherland," KCBS, August 1, 2002. "Should Have a Proper Position and Stance Regarding North-South Relation," *Nodong Sinmun*, August 1, 2002. "Insisting on the Northern

Limit Line Is Aimed at Northward Aggression," *Nodong Sinmun*, August 5, 2002.

52. "NK FMs ARF Move Draws Attention," *Korea Times*, July 27, 2002. "U.S. Welcomes NK's Apology Over Naval Clash," *Korea Times*, July 27, 2002. Karen DeYoung, "Powell May Hold Talks with N. Korean Foreign Minister; Welcoming Pyongyang's 'Positive Statements' and Overtures Toward South, Secretary Hints at Possible Meeting in Brunei," *Washington Post*, July 27, 2002. Alex Spillius, "Ice Thaws in N. Korean Meeting with Powell," *Daily Telegraph*, August 1, 2002.

53. Andrew Ward, "Ageing Officials Ousted in N Korean Reshuffle," *Financial Times*, September 4, 2003. "South Korean Official Notes Possible Economic Reforms in North," Yonhap News Agency, September 5, 2003, BBC Monitoring International Reports.

54. Ko Yong-hui, "What Has Return to Capitalism Brought?" *Nodong Sinmun*, July 13, 2002.

55. "Koreas to Hold Ministerial Talks; North to Participate in Pusan Asian Games," Yonhap News Agency, August 4, 2002. "Positive Moves from Pyongyang," *Japan Times*, August 3, 2002. James Brooke, "Inter-Korea Talks Offer Signs of Progress, and Frustration," *New York Times*, August 15, 2002.

56. Peter Slevin, "U.S. to Sanction North Korean Manufacturer; Penalty for Missile Parts Sales Comes as State Dept. Official Prepares to Visit Region," *Washington Post*, August 23, 2002.

57. "ROK Views Under Secretary Bolton's Calls for DPRK 'To Accept' IAEA Inspections, Dialogue with U.S.," Yonhap News Agency, August 29, 2002. "Civic Groups Protest About John Bolton's Visit Here," Yonhap News Agency, August 28, 2002. Ken Belson, "North Korea, Help Sought on U.S. Talks," *New York Times*, August 27, 2002. Don Kirk, "Senior U.S. Official Underscores Bush's Criticism of North Korea," *New York Times*, August 29, 2002.

58. "U.S. State Undersecretary's Anti-DPRK Remarks Under Fire," KCNA, August 31, 2002.

59. "Koreas, North Holds Ceremony for Start of Work on Railway Connection," Yonhap News Agency, September 18, 2002, BBC Worldwide Monitoring.

60. "The 2 Koreas Set a Site for Family Reunions," *New York Times*, September 9, 2002. Sohn Jang-hwan, "Sports Diplomacy Can Unify Us," September 9, 2002. "North-South Accord on Key Korean Projects," *New York Times*, September 18, 2002. Don Kirk, "2 Koreas Celebrate Decision to Reconnect a Railway," *New York Times*, September 19, 2002. "NK Unveils Shinuiju Special Law," *Korea Times*, September 27, 2002. Michael Zielenziger, "N. Korea planning capitalist enclave," *Philadelphia Inquirer*, September 27, 2002.

61. "Our Armed Forces Are a Strong Fortress for Defending Socialism and Peace," *Nodong Sinmun*, Special Article, October 4, 2002.

62. There has been a great deal of debate over whether the North Koreans actually admitted to having a uranium enrichment program. See Harrison, "Did North Korea Cheat?" Reiss and Gallucci, "Red-handed." Pritchard, *Failed Diplomacy*.

63. "DPRK FM Spokesman Decries U.S. 'Hardline Hostile Policy' Conveyed by U.S. Special Envoy," KCBS, October 7, 2002.

64. "The United States Must Be Sincere in Implementing the DPRK-U.S. Agreed Framework," KCBS, October 21, 2002.

65. "U.S. Policy Causes KPA and DPRK People to Be More Vigilant Against U.S.," KCNA, October 12, 2002. Yi Hyon-to, "Pressure and Arrogance Do Not Work on Us," *Nodong Sinmun*, October 15, 2002. Kim Chong-son, "Vigilance Against Viciousness and Wiliness of Imperialism Should Be Heightened," *Nodong Sinmun*, October 20, 2002.

66. Kim Ji-ho, "Seoul, Washington View N.K. Nuclear Issue Differently," *Korea Herald*, October 19, 2002. Hau Boon Lai, "Neighbours Say N. Korea No Nuclear Threat; Experts in Japan and China Disagree with Rumsfeld that Pyongyang Has Nuclear Weapons, Saying He Offered No Evidence," *Straits Times*, October 19, 2002. Peter S. Goodman and John Pomfret, "2 U.S. Allies Urge Engagement; S. Korea, Japan to Continue Pursuing Diplomacy with North," *Washington Post*, October 18, 2002.

67. Pak In-chol, "DPRK Cabinet Details Joint Declaration Content, Urges Expedited Implementation," *Minju Choson*, October 22, 2002.

68. "Firm Will," *Choson Sinbo*, November 6, 2002. James Dao, "KEDO Begins Fuel Oil Shipment to DPRK Despite Nuclear Row," Yonhap News Agency, November 6, 2002. "Oil Shipment to DPRK Goes Ahead Despite Nuke Crisis," Agence France Presse (Hong Kong), November 6, 2002.

69. "DPRK FM Spokesman Issues Press Statement on Nuclear Issue 25 Oct," KCBS, October 25, 2002.

70. Yi Hak-nam, "The Predatory Nature of the Imperialists' 'Aid,'" *Nodong Sinmun*, October 26, 2002.

71. "DPRK's CPRF Spokesman Urges Defense of 'Military-First Politics of Patriotism,'" KCBS, October 28, 2002.

72. "Missile-test Warning," *Gazette*, November 6, 2002.

73. "DPRK 'Should Reconsider' Missile Moratorium If Japan Talks 'Prolonged,'" KCNA, November 5, 2002.

74. "DPRK KPA, Others Rethinking Missile Moratorium Based on U.S.-Japan Isolation Moves," KCNA, November 30, 2002.

75. Don Kirk, "North Korea Softens Its Tone on Nuclear Arms Agreement," *New York Times*, November 7, 2002. Don Oberdorfer, "My Private Seat at Pyongyang's Table," *Washington Post*, November 10, 2002. "FYI, Comparison—DPRK *Nodong Sinmun* Version of 'Entitled to Have' Statement," *Nodong Sinmun*, November 17, 2002. Howard W. French, "North Korea Clarifies Statement on A-Bomb," *New York Times*, November 19, 2002.

76. Doug Struck, "Nuclear Program Not Negotiable, U.S. Told N. Korea," *New York Times*, October 20, 2002. Karen DeYoung, "U.S. Might Try to Salvage Part of N. Korean Accord," *Washington Post*, October 25, 2002.

77. "DPRK Says Pyongyang Does Not Want Aggravated Relations with U.S.," KCBS, November 20, 2002.

78. "U.S. Bellicose Forces Urged to Stop Running Amuck," *Nodong Sinmun*, November 20, 2002.

79. "DPRK's KPA Navy Command Issues Statement on 20 Nov ROK 'Provocation' on West Sea," KCNA, November 21, 2002.

80. "DPRK Government to Immediately Resume Operation and Construction of Its Nuclear Facilities," KCNA, December 12, 2002. Jonathan Watts, "North Korea Shuts Door on Nuclear Inspectors," *Guardian*, November 23, 2002. "North Korea Ups Ante," *Gazette*, December 15, 2002.

81. "N Korea Nuclear Pledge," *Sunday Herald Sun*, October 27, 2002. "Leaders Pledge to End Nuclear Crisis," *Sunday Telegraph*, October 27, 2002.

82. "Roh Projects Himself as a Kim-like Moderate," *International Herald Tribune*, December 21, 2002. "Roh to Continue Kim's Policy Toward NK, U.S.," *Korea Times*, December 21, 2002.

83. "U.S. Hindrance to Inter-Korean Economic Cooperation Assailed," KCNA, December 15, 2002. Howard W. French, "U.S. Gets Warning from North Korea," *New York Times*, December 25, 2002. "Inspectors to Quit," *Daily Star*, December 29, 2002. Michael R. Gordon, "U.S. Readies Plan to Raise Pressure on North Koreans," *New York Times*, December 29, 2002. 84. "DPRK Foreign Ministry Spokesman on 'Multi-Party Talks,'" KCNA, January 25, 2003.

85. "FM Statement Denounces State of the Union Address," KCBS, January 30, 2003. Yi Hyon-to, "Own Defense Capabilities Must Be Firmly Solidified," *Nodong Sinmun*, February 2, 2003.

86. "DPRK Ministry of Armed Forces Vows to Wage 'Life-or-Death Battle' Against U.S.," KCTV, February 5, 2003. Steven R. Weisman, "U.S., in a Shift, Is Willing to Talk with North Korea About A-Arms," *New York Times*, January 8, 2003. David E. Sanger and Julia Preston, "U.S. Assails Move by North Koreans to Reject Treaty," *New York Times*, January 11, 2003. Peter S. Goodman and Philip P. Pan, "N. Korea Threatens to Resume Missile Tests," *New York Times*, January 12, 2003. Christopher Torchia, "U.S. Hints at Energy Deal for North Korea," *South Australian Advertiser*, January 14, 2003. Stephen Lunn, "U.S. Softens on Korean Nukes," *Australian*, January 14, 2003. "2 Koreas to Resume Talks," *International Herald Tribune*, January 17, 2003. Howard LaFranchi, "U.S. Rethinks North Korea Strategy," *Christian Science Monitor*, January 16, 2003. James Brooke, "North Koreans Still Demand Direct Talks with the U.S.," *New York Times*, January 26, 2003. "Timeline: N Korea Nuclear Stand-Off," BBC News, http://news.bbc.co.uk/2/hi/asia-pacific/2604437.stm.

87. O Yong-hwan, "North May Have Started Its Reactor, Officials Say," *Chungang Ilbo*, February 7, 2003. "Threat to Tear Up War Truce," *Herald Sun*, February

19, 2003. Doug Struck, "N. Korea Fires Missile on Eve of Transition in the South," *Washington Post*, February 25, 2003. James Dao, "U.S. to Resume Food Aid to North Korea, at a Reduced Level," *New York Times*, February 26, 2003. "North Korea Restarts a Nuclear Reactor," *Birmingham (Eng.) Post*, February 27, 2003. Michael Kilian, "Big Bombers Moved Near to N Korea," *South Australian Advertiser*, March 6, 2003. Shane Green, "U.S. Sends Bombers to Deter N Korea," *Age*, March 6, 2003. "North Korea Fires Anti-ship Missile in Test Launch," *New York Times*, March 10, 2003. Doug Struck, "Citing Iraq, N. Korea Signals Hard Line on Weapons Issues," *Washington Post*, March 30, 2003. Peter Slevin, "U.S. Imposes Sanctions after Missile Sale," *Washington Post*, March 31, 2003.

88. Carlin and Lewis, *Policy in Context*, 14.

89. FM Spokesman Says DPRK 'Successfully Reprocessing' Fuel Rods in 'Final Stage,'" KCNA, April 18, 2003. "U.S., China, Koreas Agree on Nuclear Talks," *Daily Yomiuri*, April 16, 2003. David E. Sanger, "Bush Takes No-Budge Stand in Talks with North Korea," *New York Times*, April 17, 2003. Shane Green, "North Korea Threatens to Demonstrate its Nukes," *Sydney Morning Herald*, April 26, 2003. "DPRK Radio Carries Foreign Ministry's Spokesman's Comments on Beijing Talks 25 Apr," KCBS, April 25, 2003.

90. David E. Sanger, "Bush Issues Directive Describing Policy on Antimissile Defenses," *New York Times*, May 21, 2003. Bill Sammon, "Missile Shield Gains Support Across Globe," *Washington Times*, May 21, 2003. "Japan May Impose Sanctions Against North Korea if Situation Worsens," *Mainichi Shimbun*, May 21, 2003. Doug Struck, "Bush's N. Korea Efforts Stymied; Partners Reluctant to Raise Pressure," *Washington Post*, June 1, 2003.

91. Howard W. French, "Official Says U.S. Will Reposition Its Troops in South Korea," *New York Times*, June 3, 2003.

92. Alla Startseva, "Korean Rail Link a Potential Watershed," *Moscow Times*, June 10, 2003. "South-North Railway Linking Ceremony to Be Held Saturday," *Korea Times*, June 10, 2003. "Ground-breaking Ceremony of Kaesong Industrial Zone Held," KCNA, June 30, 2003. "Inter-Korean Ministerial Talks Open," KCNA, July 10, 2003.

93. "DPRK Navy Command Decries ROK, U.S. for NLL Violations," KCBS, June 3, 2003. "DPRK Notes ROK's 'Infiltrating Combat Ships' Into DPRK Waters, Warns of 'Unpredictable Crisis,'" KCBS, June 12, 2003. "'Press Statement' the Chief of the Panmunjom Mission of the Korean People's Army Issued on 1 July 2003," KCBS, July 1, 2003.

94. "DPRK Timeline of Recent Events," Nautilus Timeline, www.nautilus.org/DPRKBriefingBook/dprktimeline.html.

95. "DPRK's CPRF Issues Bulletin Assailing ROKA Exercise in Seoul," KCTV, July 9, 2003.

96. "Rodong Sinmun on Anti-U.S. Independence and Reunification," *Nodong Sinmun*, June 9, 2003.

97. Ho Yong-kil, "Proper Proposal Suitable for Set Situation," *Nodong Sinmun*, July 12, 2003.

98. "North Korean Premier Delivers Reunification Speech on National Day," KCBS, August 15, 2003, BBC Monitoring Asia Pacific-Political, August 16, 2003.

99. O Yong-hwan and Chong Yong-su, "Possibility of Five-Party Talks Is Slim; Is North Korea's Nuclear Issue Subject to UN Sanctions?" *Chungang Ilbo*, June 19, 2003. Doug Struck, "U.S. Focuses on N. Korea's Hidden Arms; Nuclear 'Bunker-Busters' Could Damage Deterrence, Some Say," *Washington Post*, June 23, 2003.

100. DPRK Foreign Ministry on Six-way Talks," KCNA, August 30, 2003. Park Chan-kyong, "Seoul Gives Upbeat Assessment to Six-Way Talks on Nuclear Crisis," Agence France Presse (Hong Kong), August 30, 2003. John Pomfret and Anthony Faiola, "U.S. Flexibility Sought on N. Korea," *Washington Post*, September 4, 2003. Cho Myong-nok, "NDC First Vice Chairman, DPRK to 'Maintain,' 'Continuously Reinforce' Nuclear Deterrent," KCBS, September 5, 2003.

101. "North Korea's New Premier Speaks at Supreme People's Assembly Session," KCBS, September 3, 2003, BBC Monitoring Asia Pacific-Political, September 4, 2003.

102. "U.S. Says N. Korea Plutonium Reprocessing Has Stopped," *Canberra Times*, September 13, 2003. "North Korean Radio Report Confirms 8,000 Spent Fuel Rods Reprocessed," KCBS, October 2, 2003.

103. "DPRK Radio Carries FM Spokesman's Comments Stressing 'Principle of Simultaneous Actions,'" KCBS, October 25, 2003. Julie Chao, "Bush Offers North Korea Guarantee," *National Post*, October 20, 2003. James Brooke and David E. Sanger, "North Korea *Nodong Sinmun*, in Shift, to Mull Security Offer," *New York Times*, October 26, 2003.

104. "'Decree' on DPRK-PRC Discussions, DPRK Will Attend Future 'Six-Party Talks,'" KCBS, October 30, 2003. "Kim Jong Il Receives Chinese State Delegation," KCNA, October 30, 2003. BBC News, http://news.bbc.co.uk/2/hi/asia-pacific/1132268.stm.

105. Rupert Cornwell and Raymond Whitaker, "N Korea: U.S. Team Saw Our Nuclear Arms," *Independent on Sunday*, January 11, 2004. Jack Pritchard, "What I Saw in North Korea," *New York Times*, January 21, 2004.

106. "U.S. Troops to Pull Out of Seoul," *Washington Post*, January 18, 2004. "USFK Relocation Will Not Weaken Defense Posture: Ambassador to U.S." Yonhap News Agency, February 4, 2004.

107. "Destroy Nuclear Program, U.S. to Tell N. Korea," *Globe and Mail*, February 20, 2004. "S. Korea to Propose Detailed Conditions for Freeze of DPRK Nuclear Program in Next Round Talks," *Xinhua*, February 20, 2004. Anthony Faiola, "Seoul Urges U.S. 'Flexibility' in Nuclear Talks with North," *Washington Post*, February 21, 2004. "N. Korea Denounces U.S. Hard-line Stance," Yonhap

News Agency, February 29, 2004. "N. Korea Voices Disappointment at U.S. Stance in 6-Way Talks," *Kyodo*, February 29, 2004.

108. "DPRK Radio Carries First Official Remarks on Six-Party Talks; Processing Plans," KCBS, February 29, 2004.

109. "DPRK Foreign Ministry Spokesman on Meeting of Working Group of Six-Way Talks," KCNA, April 29, 2004.

110. "N. Korean Leader, Chinese Aide Discuss Arms," *Washington Post*, March 25, 2004. "North Korea Rejects Complete Disarmament," *Korea Herald*, March 29, 2004. Edward Cody and Anthony Faiola, "N. Korea's Kim Reportedly in China for Talks; Meetings with Leaders Said to Focus on Nuclear Standoff," *Washington Post*, April 20, 2004. Jim Yardley, "North Korean Leader Tells China He's Committed to Nuclear Talks," *New York Times*, April 22, 2004. Anthony Faiola and Edward Cody, "North Koreans Agree to Mid-Level Talks," *Washington Post*, April 30, 2004.

111. "Japan Mulling Aid to N. Korea After Train Blast," *Jiji Press*, April 24, 2004. "Russian Envoys Visit Site of North Korean Train Disaster," *Interfax*, April 24, 2004. "North Korean Train Station 'Obliterated' by Blast, Aid Workers Say," Agence France Presse (Hong Kong), April 24, 2004. "S. Korea Receives Aid Request from N. Korea," Yonhap News Agency, April 24, 2004.

112. "North Korean Prime Minister Thanks South for Help," Yonhap News Agency, May 1, 2004, BBC Monitoring Asia Pacific-Political.

113. "North Korean Premier Delivers Report at Supreme People's Assembly Second Session," KCBS, March 25, 2004, BBC Monitoring Asia Pacific-Political, March 28, 2004.

114. "DPRK Timeline of Recent Events."

115. "Abductees' Kin Arrive in Japan," *Daily Yomiuri*, May 23, 2004. Kanako Takahara, "Koizumi Gets Four Abductees' Kids," *Japan Times*, May 23, 2004. Anthony Faiola, "New Capitalist Symbol Rises in N. Korea's Dust; Industrial Park to Broach Free Market," *Washington Post*, May 23, 2004.

116. "Korean Neighbours to Open Road Links," *Independent*, June 7, 2004. James Brooke, "Koreas Agree to Open a Cross-Border Road and Rail Links," *New York Times*, June 6, 2004.

117. "DPRK TV Carries Gist of Chief Delegate's Keynote Speech at Inter-Korean Talks 5 May," KCTV, May 5, 2004. "DPRK Radio Report on 26 May N-S Military Talks Highlights 'Reconciliation,'" KCBS, May 26, 2004.

118. Anthony Faiola and Bradley Graham, "U.S. Plans Major Cut of Forces in Korea; 12,500 Troops to Be Relocated by End of 2005," *Washington Post*, June 8, 2004.

119. Joseph Kahn and Susan Chira, "Chinese Official Challenges U.S. Stance on North Korea," *New York Times*, June 9, 2004. David E. Sanger, "U.S. to Offer North Korea Incentives in Nuclear Talks," *New York Times*, June 23, 2004. Aya Igarashi and Satoshi Saeki, "N. Korea Nuke Freeze Eyed," *Daily Yomiuri*, June 27, 2004. Philip P. Pan, "N. Korea Says It Can 'Show Flexibility';

Possible Dismantling of Nuclear Arms Programs Tied to Broader Aid Package," *Washington Post*, June 26, 2004.

120. James Brooke, "North Korea to Wait Out Election in U.S., Then Talk, Diplomat Says," *New York Times*, September 15, 2004.

121. "Japan, ROK, U.S. Agree to Avoid Fallout of ROK Experiments," *Jiji Press*, September 10, 2004. "Rumsfeld, Powell Back S Korean Position on Seoul's Nuke Issue," Yonhap News Agency, September 10, 2004. Anthony Faiola and Dafna Linzer, "S. Korea Admits Extracting Plutonium; Acknowledgment of '82 Test Follows Disclosure on Uranium," *Washington Post*, September 10, 2004. "ROK Official Says Seoul 'Fully Cooperating' with IAEA," *Choson Ilbo*, September 11, 2004.

122. "DPRK TV Carries FM Spokesman's Comments on ROK Uranium Enrichment; ROK 'Under U.S. 'Nuclear Umbrella,'" KCTV, September 11, 2004.

123. Kim O-song, "What Do the Nuclear-Related Experiments Show?" Tongil Sinbo, www.uriminzokkiri.com, September 18, 2004.

124. Selig S. Harrison, "Getting Around Pyongyang's Hard-Liners," *Washington Post*, June 10, 2005.

125. The U.S. used third-party sanction threats, targeting WMD and missile proliferation, to pressure the regime. The actions would have much broader economic consequences for North Korea as some U.S. officials cautioned foreign interlocutors and businesses to avoid business relationships with *any* North Korean business. "North Korea Reports It's Ready to Resume Nuclear Arms Talks," *New York Times*, January 15, 2005. David E. Sanger and William J. Broad, "U.S. Asking China to Increase Pressure on North Korea to End Its Nuclear Program," *New York Times*, February 9, 2005. James Brooke and David E. Sanger, "North Koreans Say They Hold Nuclear Arms," *New York Times*, February 11, 2005. Glenn Kessler and Philip P. Pan, "White House Dismisses Idea of Direct Talks with North Korea," *Washington Post*, February 12, 2005. Keith Bradsher and James Brooke, "China Calls on North Korea to Return to Regional Talks," *New York Times*, February 13, 2005. David E. Sanger, "U.S. Is Shaping Plan to Pressure North Koreans," *New York Times*, February 14, 2005. Joel Brinkley, "U.S. and Japan Declare Concern Over North Korea," *New York Times*, February 20, 2005.

126. Jim Yardley, "North Korean Said to Be Willing to Resume Talks," *New York Times*, February 22, 2005. Chris Buckley, "China Calls for Restarting Six-Party Talks at an Early Date," *Xinhua*, February 23, 2005. Joel Brinkley, "China Balks at Pressing the North Koreans," *New York Times*, March 22, 2005. Joel Brinkley, "North Korea Said to Reject China's Bid on Nuclear Talks," *New York Times*, April 9, 2005. "State Dept Spokesman Says U.S. Following Situation in DPRK Closely," *Xinhua*, May 6, 2005. Glenn Kessler, "China Rejected U.S. Suggestion to Cut off Oil to Pressure North Korea," *Washington Post*, May 7, 2005. Anthony Faiola and Sachiko Sakamaki, "N. Korea Suggests It Will Hold Atomic Test; Country Also Hints at Return to 6-Party Talks," *Washington Post*,

May 10, 2005. David E. Sanger, "What Are Koreans Up To? U.S. Agencies Can't Agree," *New York Times*, May 12, 2005.

127. "Seoul Woos N. Korea with Economic Aid," Korea Times, May 17, 2005. Lee Tee Jong, "Seoul Offers Pyongyang 'Substantial Proposal,'" *Straits Times*, May 17, 2005. "U.S. Halts Search for Its War Dead in North Korea," *New York Times*, May 26, 2005. "North Korea and U.S. Swap Insults," *Independent*, June 3, 2005. David E. Sanger, "North Korea Said to Offer to Rejoin Nuclear Talks," *New York Times*, June 8, 2005.

128. Choe Thae-bok, "Let Us Eternally Glorify Our Party as Revolutionary Party of Chuch'e Under Great Comrade Kim Jong Il's Leadership," *Nodong Sinmun*, June 19, 2005.

129. South Korea's electricity proposal offered to supply North Korea with 2,000 kilowatts of electricity transmitted across new power lines crossing the DMZ. The project would cost $1.4 billion in infrastructure developments and $1 billion annually to supply the energy.

    Norimitsu Onishi, "North Korea's Leader Says He's Ready to Resume Talks to End Nuclear Standoff," *New York Times*, June 18, 2005. Joel Brinkley, "Rice Has No Plans to Improve Offer to North Korea in Arms Talks," *New York Times*, July 9, 2005. Nicholas Kralev, "N. Korea Agrees to Nuke Talks," *Washington Times*, July 10, 2005. Choe Sang-hun, "Goal Is Peace Treaty with U.S., North Korea Says," *International Herald Tribune*, July 23, 2005. Anthony Faiola, "South Koreans Weigh Burden of Massive Assistance for North; Electricity Project Seen as Payment Toward Unification," *Washington Post*, July 25, 2005.

130. Jim Yardley and David E. Sanger, "U.S. Tries a New Approach in Talks with North Korea," *New York Times*, July 27, 2005. David E. Sanger and Jim Yardley, "U.S. Offers North Korea Evidence That Nuclear Secrets Came from Pakistani's Network," *New York Times*, July 29, 2005. Tschang Chi-chu, "Joint Statement to be Drafted at N-Talks," *Straits Times*, July 30, 2005. "6-Way Talks Recess for 3 Weeks," *Korea Times*, August 8, 2005. Jim Yardley, "U.S. and North Korea Blame Each Other for Stalemate in Talks," *New York Times*, August 8, 2005.

131. "NK Demand for Reactor Is Nonstarter," *Korea Times*, September 16, 2005. Edward Cody, "Talks Deadlock Over N. Korea's Demand for Reactor; U.S. Could Seek Sanctions at UN," *Washington Post*, September 16, 2005. "U.S. May Freeze N Korean Assets," *Irish Times*, September 17, 2005.

132. For a sophisticated view on the often elusive concept of face, see Ho, "On the Concept of Face," 867–84.

133. "China Presents 'New Plan' at North Korea Talks," *Kyodo*, September 18, 2005. Edward Cody, "U.S. Raises Objections to China Proposal in Talks," *Washington Post*, September 18, 2005. "Six-Party Talks Reach Agreement," *Korea Herald*, September 20, 2005. Jane Macartney, "North Korea Vows to End Nuclear Plans in Return for Aid and Oil," *Times* (London), September 20, 2005.

134. The 311 action was formally a provisional advisory issued by the U.S. Treasury Department to U.S. financial institutions to be wary of doing business with Banco Delta Asia, because its specific business with the North Korean government demonstrated a "primary money laundering concern." This in turn prompted the Macao Monetary Authority to freeze suspect accounts at the bank for investigation. The amount the Macao Authority froze was contemporaneously reported as approximately $27 million, although this figure would be modified to about $25 million by the time the complex action was reversed. More importantly, the 311action had the effect of cutting the Macao bank and related entities off from the U.S. financial sector. The Macao bank, with more than US$5 billion in assets, failed over the dispute of approximately one-half of 1 percent of its business. "Treasury Designates Banco Delta Asia as Primary Money Laundering Concern under USA PATRIOT Act," September 15, 2005, www.ustreas.gov/press/releases/js2720.htm. Delta Asia 2004 Annual Report, www.delta-asia.com/eng/files/2004annualreport.pdf. The *Wall Street Journal* published the story on its front page, and the message to the international financial community was clear. The threat of cutting off a bank's access to the U.S. financial sector was far too great to accept any business dealings with a North Korean business, person, or government entity. North Korean individuals and institutions found themselves isolated from any international banks. The Patriot Act provision requires consultation with the secretary of state, and North Korea would come to call this a pressure tactic, but the United States held that the diplomatic and legal tracks were separate. (Anthony Faiola, "N. Korea Gains Aid Despite Arms Standoff," *Washington Post*, November 16, 2005. James Brooke, "North Korea Says Bumper Crop Justifies Limits on Aid," *New York Times*, October 6, 2005. Donald Kirk, "Two Koreas' Dream: One Olympic Team," *Christian Science Monitor*, November 3, 2005.) The day after the September 19 agreement, the U.S. Treasury Department published its "311 action" in the *Federal Register*, laying out the allegation that North Korean drug trafficking and counterfeiting profits were channeled through the Macao bank.

135. During the famine, people starved waiting for the government to supply rations. Others bought food on the black market. Authorities began to turn a blind eye toward the black markets and occasionally cracked down on them, but crackdowns further disrupted the food supply. Consequently, the black markets became gray as authorities allowed private exchange of food and other consumer goods from China. See Haggard and Noland, *Famine in North Korea*. The reintroduction of the PDS removed major market incentives for agricultural production, raising the serious specter of shortages the following year as farmers lost their economic incentive to produce surplus foodstuffs.

136. "North Korea PM Says Farming, Increased Electricity, Coal Production Key in 2005," KCBS, April 11, 2005, BBC Monitoring Asia Pacific-Political, April 13, 2005. All Pak quotes in the following paragraphs are from this speech.

137. For a quantitative review of North Korean media that shows a rise in socialist and military-first slogans roughly corresponding with this policy reversal on marketization, see Frank, "Dreaming an Impossible Dream?"

138. Tim Johnson, "N. Korea's Kim Reportedly Slips into China," *Philadelphia Inquirer*, January 12, 2006. Andrew Salmon, "China Seen Unlikely to Press Nuke Issue," *Washington Times*, January 12, 2006. Philip P. Pan, "In China, Kim Vows Commitment to Talks," *Washington Post*, January 19, 2006.

139. Choe Hak-chol, "The Basic Factor That Breaks Up the Talks Should Be Removed First," *Nodong Sinmun*, January 3, 2006. "DPRK Foreign Ministry's Spokesman Urges U.S. to Lift Financial Sanctions Against DPRK," KCNA, January 9, 2006.

140. Ryu Yong-su, "Unchanging Manifestation of Attempt for Nuclear Preemptive Strike," *Minju Choson*, February 15, 2006. "DPRK Cabinet Paper Decries U.S. 'Defense Review' as Attempt at 'World Hegemony,'" KCNA, February 15, 2006. "Rodong Sinmun on Main Obstacle to Peaceful Reunification," KCNA, February 21, 2006. "DPRK FM Spokesman Says U.S. 'Forced' ROK to Agree to U.S.FK 'Strategic Flexibility,'" KCBS, February 21, 2006. "DPRK Foreign Ministry Spokesman Urges U.S. to Lift Financial Sanctions," KCNA, February 28, 2006.

141. The overall U.S. strategy remained controversial even within the president's own party. Chairman of the Senate Foreign Relations Committee, Richard Lugar (R-Ind.), had legislation prepared that would force the White House to open a liaison office in North Korea, pending progress on the nuclear issue, according to a press leak.

142. Nicholas Kralev, "U.S. Rules Out Visit by Hill to Capital, but State Keeps Possibility Alive," *Washington Times*, June 2, 2006.

143. Glenn Kessler, "N. Korea Warned on Testing Missile; Act Would Spur Penalties, Rice Says," *Washington Post*, June 20, 2006. Dana Priest and Anthony Faiola, "North Korea Tests Long-Range Missile; Controversial Rocket Fails as Other Types Are Fired; UN Session Set After U.S., Japan Condemn Action," *Washington Post*, July 5, 2006. Norimitsu Onishi, "U.S. Wants North Korea to Return to Talks," *New York Times*, July 10, 2006. Anthony Faiola, "S. Korea Suspends Food Aid to North; Push for Renewal of Nuclear Talks Brings Meeting to Bitter End," *Washington Post*, July 14, 2006. Colum Lynch, "Security Council Rebukes N. Korea; Nations Agree to Demand End of Missile Program," *Washington Post*, July 16, 2006. Anthony Faiola, "U.S., Japan to Start Deploying Missile Interceptors," *Washington Post*, July 21, 2006. "Floods Claim Huge Toll in North Korea, Group Says," *New York Times*, August 17, 2006. Anthony Faiola, "Seoul's Push to Regain Wartime Control from U.S. Divides South Koreans," *Washington Post*, August 29, 2006.

144. "Text of North Defence Minister's Korean War 'Victory' Anniversary Address," Pyongyang, July 26, 2006, BBC Monitoring Asia Pacific-Political, July 29, 2006, Uriminzokkiri.com.

145. "Pyongyang Taking It to the Brink?" *Japan Times*, September 2, 2006.
146. "DPRK FM Statement Reveals New Measures for War Deterrent; Warns of 'Nuclear Test,'" KCBS, October 3, 2006.
147. "DPRK Successfully Conducts Underground Nuclear Test," KCNA, October 9, 2006.
148. "Become Talents of the Fatherland," *Nodong Sinmun*, October 13, 2006.
149. Glenn Kessler, "N. Korean Move Comes Amid Bid for Talks; with Plan to Conduct Nuclear Test, Pyongyang Again Dismisses U.S. Peace Feelers," *Washington Post*, October 4, 2006. Anthony Faiola, Glenn Kessler, and Dafna Linzer, "N. Korea Claims Nuclear Test; Geologists in the South Detect Man-Made Blast," *Washington Post*, October 9, 2006. "Text of North Korea Announcement," *New York Times*, October 9, 2006. Simon Saradzhyan, "N. Korean Test Will Have Global Fallout," *Moscow Times*, October 10, 2006. Ewen MacAskill, "North Korea: United Nations: Punitive Measures on the Agenda," *Guardian*, October 10, 2006. Anthony Faiola, "N. Korea's No. 2 Official Warns of Further Tests," *Washington Post*, October 12, 2006. Thom Shanker and Martin Fackler, "South Korea Tells Rice It Won't Abandon Industrial and Tourist Ventures with North," *New York Times*, October 20, 2006. Jim Yardley, "Sanctions Don't Dent North Korea–China Trade," *New York Times*, October 27, 2006. Joseph Kahn, "China May Be Using Oil to Press North Korea," *New York Times*, October 31, 2006.
150. "DPRK FM Statement, DPRK Says Ready for 'Dialogue,' 'Confrontation' with U.S.," KCNA, October 11, 2006.

7. Policy Reversals, 2006–2008

1. The most notable pressure advocate who resigned was John Bolton, UN ambassador and former undersecretary of state for international security. He resigned after Democrats refused to approve his recess appointment. Two days after Bolton's resignation, American negotiators put forward a new proposal at the six-party talks offering aid. In January, another key official pushing confrontation with North Korea, Bob Joseph, who served as John Bolton's replacement as Undersecretary of State for International Security after a position as a senior staffer at the National Security Council focused on the same issues, also resigned. For an extensive review of the internal disagreements within the U.S. government on North Korea policy. See Chinoy, *Meltdown*.
2. Glenn Kessler, "N. Korea Agrees to Return to Talks; A Surprise Reversal in Nuclear Dispute," *Washington Post*, November 1, 2006. Norimitsu Onishi, "South Korea Won't Intercept Cargo Ships from the North," *New York Times*, November 14, 2006. Glenn Kessler, "Democrats Blast Bush Policy on N. Korea," *Washington Post*, November 16, 2006. Helene Cooper and David E. Sanger, "U.S. Offers North Korea Aid for Dropping Nuclear Plans," *New York Times*, December 6, 2006.

3. "N. Korea Reports Progress in Talks with U.S. Envoy," *Washington Post*, January 20, 2007. "U.S. Envoy Upbeat About New Korea Talks," *New York Times*, January 22, 2007.
4. "Spokesman for DPRK Foreign Ministry on Results of DPRK-U.S. Talks," KCNA, January 19, 2007.
5. Ri Sok-chol, "Timely Appeal for Reunification and Patriotism," *Nodong Sinmun*, January 19, 2007. "Revelation of the Attempt Aimed at Carrying Out Preemptive Nuclear Strike for Northward Aggression," *Nodong Sinmun*, January 20, 2007.
6. "Secretary of WPK C.C. Supports Joint Statement of DPRK Political Parties, Government, and Organizations," KCNA, January 21, 2007.
7. Paek Mun-kyu, "Dangerous Maneuvers that Run Counter to Dialogue," *Nodong Sinmun*, February 13, 2007.
8. Jim Yardley and David E. Sanger, "In Shift, a Deal Is Being Weighed by North Korea," *New York Times*, February 13, 2007.
9. Carlin and Lewis 2008, 50. "DPRK Radio Reports on 6-Party Talks, Agreement on Provision of Energy Aid to DPRK 13 Feb," KCBS, February 13, 2007.
10. The three years of fighting in the Korean War ended in 1953 with an Armistice Agreement. However, both sides remain technically at war, since no peace treaty has ever been finalized. "North Korea Calls on South to Resume Humanitarian Projects," Yonhap News Agency, February 28, 2007, BBC Monitoring Asia-Pacific, Political. Andrew Salmon, "U.S., N. Korea to Normalize Ties," *Washington Times*, February 28, 2007.
11. "North-South Ministerial Talks Open," KCNA, February 28, 2007.
12. "20th North-South Ministerial Talks Close," KCNA, March 2, 2007.
13. Despite diplomatic breakthrough, private banks were reluctant to process the North Korean funds given the state of U.S. law and the grave risks still legally associated with transferring North Korean funds. Three months would pass before the funds were returned to North Korea. Glenn Kessler and Edward Cody, "U.S. Ends Bank Probe; Possible Step Toward N. Korean Reactor Closure," *Washington Post*, March 15, 2007.
14. "North Korean Agency Reports on Army Day 'Grand Military Parade,'" KCBS, April 25, 2007, in BBC Monitoring Asia-Pacific, Political.
15. Yi Kyo-kwan, "DPRK Vice Trade Minister Kim Mun-song Executed by Shooting," *Choson Ilbo*, January 8, 2002, BBC Monitoring Asia-Pacific, Political, January 8, 2002. "Report, N. Korea Wants to Join International Fund Groups," *Korea Times*, January 21, 2000.
16. "Let Us Even More Thoroughly Implement the Party's Economic Policy with the Taechon Spirit—Cabinet Enlarged Plenary Meeting Was Held," *Minju Choson*, April 18, 2007, DPRKmedia.com.
17. "DPRK Premier Kim Yong Il Delivers Report Marking DPRK's 59th Founding Anniversary," KCBS, September 8, 2007.
18. "North Korean Radio Reports on Assembly Session," KCBS, April 11, 2006, BBC Monitoring Asia-Pacific, Political, April 12, 2006.

19. Norimitsu Onishi, "In Surprise Move, U.S. Envoy Visits North Korea," *New York Times*, June 22, 2007.

20. "Foreign Ministry Spokesman on DPRK Visit by U.S. Assistant Secretary of State," KCNA, June 23, 2007.

21. "Foreign Ministry Spokesman Emphasizes We, Too, Will Enter Into 13 February Agreement Implementation Under Condition Where the Frozen Funds Issue Has Been Resolved," KCNA, June 25, 2007. Edward Cody, "N. Korea Says Funds Issue Is Resolved," *New York Times*, June 26, 2007. Choe Sang-Hun, "North Korea Receives Funds and Says It Will Shut Down Its Main Nuclear Reactor," *New York Times*, June 26, 2007.

22. "DPRK FM Spokesman, DPRK Ready to Implement 13 Feb Agreement 'Earlier Than Promised Time, Order,'" KCNA, July 6, 2007.

23. "DPRK KPA Panmunjom's Mission Chief Proposes DPRK-U.S. Military Talks," KCBS, July 13, 2007.

24. "DPRK FM Spokesman on Suspension of Yongbyon Operation, Six-Party 'Obligations,'" KCNA, July 15, 2007. Choe Sang-Hun, "U.N. Inspectors Confirm Shutdown of North Korean Reactor," *New York Times*, July 17, 2007.

25. "DPRK-U.S. Talks and Meeting of Heads of Delegations to Six-Party Talks Held," KCNA, July 20, 2007.

26. Norimitsu Onishi, "Leaders of 2 Koreas Will Meet in the North," *New York Times*, August 8, 2007. Choe Sang-Hun, "South Korean Visits North, Offering Aid For Arms Cuts," *New York Times*, October 3, 2007.

27. "DPRK FM Spokesman Responds to Question on 1–2 Sep DPRK-U.S. Talks in Geneva," KCNA, September 3, 2007. "North Korea and U.S. Discuss Steps to End Nuclear Program," *New York Times*, September 2, 2007.

28. "DPRK Radio Carries FM Spokesman's 'Grateful' Remarks on International Aid 5 Sep," KCNA, September 5, 2007.

29. "U.S. and S. Korean Bellicose Forces' War Exercises Against DPRK Assailed," *Nodong Sinmun*, September 3, 2007. "Lesson of History," *Nodong Sinmun*, September 6, 2007.

30. "North Korean Radio Reports on First Round of Inter-Korean Premiers' Talks," KCBS, November 14, 2007, BBC Monitoring Asia-Pacific, Political, November 15, 2007.

31. "DPRK Radio Details First Round of N-S Premier Talks in Seoul on 14 Nov," Korean Central Satellite Television, FBIS, November 14, 2007.

32. Choe Sang-Hun, "Inter-Korean Talks Focus on Expanding Economic Cooperation," *New York Times*, November 15, 2007. Choe Sang-Hun, "2 Koreas Agree on Aid to North and Trains Across Border," *New York Times*, November 18, 2007.

33. Choe Sang-Hun, "Regular Freight Rail Service Starts Between the Koreas," December 12, 2007. Norimitsu Onishi, "Conservative Wins Presidential Election in South Korea," *New York Times*, December 20, 2007.

34. Ri Hyo-chin, "What Is the Promise for 'Nuclear Umbrella Provision' Aimed at," *Nodong Sinmun*, January 19, 2008.

35. Choe Song-kuk, "Political Dwarf's Silly Talk," *Nodong Sinmun*, January 21, 2008.
36. Paek Mun-kyu, "Reckless Acts That Bring About Fire Clouds of War," *Nodong Sinmun*, February 23, 2008.
37. Cho Tong-chol, "Dangerous Military Commotion Suggestive of the Eve of War," KCBS, March 1, 2008.
38. "War Maniacs Stirring up Fiery Cloud of War," KCBS, March 2, 2008.
39. "DPRK CPRF Decries ROK, U.S. for Signing MOU on Establishing New Marine Forces Command," KCBS, February 26, 2008.
40. "Repeated Babble About 'Alliance' Which Calls for the Era of Confrontation," *Nodong Sinmun*, March 17, 2008.
41. Ri Hyo-chin, "Product of Following Outside Forces—Maneuver to Establish Interceptor Missile System," *Nodong Sinmun*, March 25, 2008.
42. Pak In-chol, "Shameless Act of a Thief Holding up a Whip of Punishment," *Minju Joson*, March 27, 2008.
43. Kwon Kum-ryong, "Ridiculous Assertion," *Tongil Sinbo*, March 29, 2008.
44. "DPRK Military Official Responds to ROK JCS Chairman's Remarks on 'Preemptive Strike,'" KCBS, March 29, 2008.
45. "Ruin Is the Only Thing That the South Korean Authorities Will Gain Through Their Anti-North Confrontation," *Nodong Sinmun*, April 1, 2008.
46. Sim Chol-yong, "We Can Never Bury Past Crimes Against Humanity," *Nodong Sinmun*, April 2, 2008. Sin Hung-kuk, "Bulldozer of Pragmatism," April 3, 2008, www.uriminzokkiri.com. Chong Son-myong, "Anti-North Confrontation Is the Road to Destruction," April 4, 2008, www.uriminzokkiri.com.
47. "Lee Myung Bak and His Gentries' Treacherous Outbursts Under Fire in S. Korea," KCNA, April 2, 2008. Pak Chol-chun, "Establishing a True National View Is a Primary Demand in Developing North-South Relations," *Nodong Sinmun*, April 5, 2008. Pak In-chol, "Why Act Irrationally?" *Minju Choson*, April 6, 2008. Kim Chong-ok, "Traitorous Gang Ushering in a Nuclear Disaster," *Nodong Sinmun*, April 7, 2008.
48. Pak In-chol, "Will the Shallow-Minded Trickery Work?" *Minju Choson*, April 8, 2008. Song Yong-sok, "A Reckless Acts of a Crook Who Does Not Know Where to Draw the Line," *Nodong Sinmun*, April 9, 2008. Ri Kyong-chol, "Should Not Recklessly Behave," *Minju Choson*, April 27, 2008. Choe Chol-sun, "Expression of Consciousness of Pro-U.S. Flunkeyism and Following Outside Forces," *Nodong Sinmun*, April 16, 2008. "The Ringleader Who Pushes North-South Relations to Ruin," *Nodong Sinmun*, April 30, 2008. "Lee Myung Bak's Junket to Japan Branded as Treacherous," KCNA, May 5, 2008. "Un Chong-chol, "Harping on About the Ludicrous 'Successful Diplomacy,'" *Nodong Sinmun*, May 3, 2008. "Pak In-chol, "'Pragmatic Government' Gone Mad with Mad Cow–Infected Beef," *Minju Choson*, May 7, 2008. "Villainous Splittist Maniac," *Minju Choson*, May 10, 2008. "DPRK Radio Decries ROK's Plan to Purchase Additional F-15K, Cruise Missiles," KCBS, May 10, 2008.

"DPRK Party Organ Notes ROK Efforts to Stop 'Rumors' on ROK Administration," *Nodong Sinmun*, May 12, 2008. "DPRK Organization's White Paper Recounts Lee Myung-bak's 100 Days in Power," KCNA, June 1, 2008. Ri Kyong-chol, "Plunging 'Approval Ratings,' Increasing Sense of Distrust," *Minju Choson*, June 1, 2008. Kim Chong-son, "Must Heighten Vigilance Against Imperialists' Tactics for Internal Collapse," *Nodong Sinmun*, Special Article, May 31, 2008. "Condemn South Korean Authorities' Anti-National 'Pragmatism,'" *Nodong Sinmun*, May 30, 2008. Song Yong-sok, "Military Confrontation Racket Is a Grave Obstacle to Implementation of the 4 October Declaration," *Nodong Sinmun*, Special Article, May 27, 2008. "DPRK's CPRF Issues Bulletin on Seoul's 'Anti-Reunification' Education Guidelines," KCNA, May 24, 2008. Pak In-chol, "Crafty Stratagem Aimed at Having Fellow Countrymen Fight Among Themselves," *Minju Choson*, May 24, 2008. "DPRK Group on ROK President's 'Confrontational Moves' Affecting North-South Ties," KCBS, June 30, 2008. "Lee Myung Bak's 'Policy Speech' Under Fire," KCNA, July 13, 2008. Choe Kwang-hyok, "Anti-Unification 'Explanatory Document' in Pursuit of Confrontation and War," *Tongil Sinbo*, August 9, 2008.

49. "'Ministry of Unification' Which Turned into 'Ministry of Division,'" *Minju Choson*, August 19, 2008. Cho Nam-su, "Anti-Reunification Confrontation Theory Driving North-South Relations to Ruin," *Nodong Sinmun*, August 20, 2008. Ri Hyo-chin, "Military Warmongers Crazy About Confrontation with the Republic," *Nodong Sinmun*, September 29, 2008. Kim Chong-ok, "Strengthening 'Alliance' with Outside Forces Is the Anachronistic Act of Treason," *Nodong Sinmun*, October 7, 2008. "[We] Will Fight to the End and Settle with Those Who Are Seeking to Realize a Foolish Fantasy," *Nodong Sinmun*, October 16, 2008. Chong Son-myong, "Blatant Declaration of Confrontation Against the Fellow Countrymen," October 18, 2008, www.uriminzokkiri.com. "Anti-DPRK Psychological Campaign Under Fire," KCNA, October 21, 2008. Choe Chol-sun, "The Lame Excuse of Those Who Are Destroying the North-South Relations," *Nodong Sinmun*, November 17, 2008. Song Yong-sok, "Political Provocation Inciting Aggravation of Situation," *Nodong Sinmun*, November 18, 2008. "KPA Notifies S. Korean Puppet Authorities of Crucial Measure to Be Enforced by It," KCNA, November 24, 2008. "DPRK State Security Spokesman on ROK's 'Sabotage' Against DPRK," KCBS, December 18, 2008. "Koreans Called Upon to Meet Anti-Reunification Forces' Challenge," KCNA, December 23, 2008.

50. "DPRK Foreign Ministry Spokesman on Issue of Implementation of October 3 Agreement," KCNA, January 4, 2008.

51. Nam Chon-ung, "Taking the Position of Resolving the Issue?" *Minju Choson*, January 4, 2008.

52. Ri Hyon-to, "Petty Tricks by Nuclear War Fanatics," *Nodong Sinmun*, January 4, 2008.

53. Sim Chol-yong, "Absurd Remark on 'Permanent Presence,' Which Lays Bare Wicked Intention," *Nodong Sinmun*, January 25, 2008.

54. Un Chong-chol, "Extremely Dangerous Fighter Build-up Commotion," *Nodong Sinmun*, January 26, 2008. Kim Chong-son, "Nonsensical, Self-Righteous Speculation," *Nodong Sinmun*, January 28, 2008.

55. "DPRK FM Spokesman 'Press Statement' of 28 March on 6-Party Talks 'Stalemate,'" KCNA, March 28, 2008.

56. Keith Luse, "North Korea Trip Report," Memo to the Senate Foreign Relations Committee Members, March 6, 2008, www.ncnk.org/resolveuid/3fi8cbcaf6c 9e3ebd9ob870012ae24f8.

57. Ibid.

58. Siegfried Hecker, "Report of Visit to the DPRK, March 14, 2008," National Committee on North Korea, www.ncnk.org/resources/publications/Hecker DPRKreport.pdf/file_view.

59. Kim Chong-ok, "Peace and Prosperity Are the Nation's Aspiration and Intention," *Nodong Sinmun*, March 29, 2008.

60. Robin Wright, "U.S. Details Reactor in Syria; Americans Push Damascus, N. Korea to Admit Collusion," *Washington Post*, April 25, 2008.

61. "Disgraceful Conduct in the Manner of the Thief Raising the Whip," KCBS, April 28, 2008. "Foreign Ministry Spokesman Denounces the United States for Taking Issue with and Slandering Our-Style Socialist System," KCNA, May 31, 2008.

62. Paek Mun-kyu, "Provocative Act of Putting a Wet Blanket Over Improvement in DPRK-U.S. Relations," *Nodong Sinmun*, June 4, 2008. "KCNA Denounces U.S. Conservative Hardliners for Their Reckless Remarks," KCNA, June 7, 2008. Kim Chong-son, "We Should Raise Vigilance Against Imperialists' Cunning Art of Disguise," *Nodong Sinmun*, June 18, 2008. Cho Taek-pom, "Must Smash the Imperialists' Vicious Psychological Smear Campaign," *Nodong Sinmun*, June 21, 2008.

63. "DPRK Foreign Ministry's Spokesman on DPRK-U.S. Experts Negotiations," KCNA, June 12, 2008. "DPRK FM Spokesman's Response to U.S. Lifting Major Economic Sanctions Against DPRK," KCNA, June 27, 2008. "DPRK FM Spokesman on Removal from U.S. Terror Sponsor List, Nuclear Declaration," KCBS, June 27, 2008.

64. Kim Hye-song, "Ringleader of Nuclear Threats and Arms Race," *Nodong Sinmun*, June 24, 2008.

65. Cho Nam-su, "Eliminating the Root Cause of War Is the Basic Way of Guaranteeing Peace," *Nodong Sinmun*, Special Article, June 30, 2008.

66. "South Korean Puppet Military's 'Human Rights' Racket Which Cannot Escape the Gun Barrel's Grave Judgment," *Nodong Sinmun* Military Commentator Article, June 28, 2008. "S Korean Puppet Military's Anti-DPRK 'Human Rights' Racket Blasted," KCNA, June 27, 2008.

67. Blaine Harden, "U.S. Wheat Begins New Aid to N. Korea; U.N. Agreement Aims to Feed Millions More, with Unprecedented Monitoring," *Washington Post*, July 1, 2008.

68. "Press Statement by a Spokesman for the DPRK Foreign Ministry," KCNA, July 4, 2008. "Intentional Act Aimed at Rupturing Realization of Denuclearization," KCNA, July 10, 2008. Paek Mun-kyu, "Aggression and War, the Imperialist Ways of Survival," *Nodong Sinmun*, Special Article, July 12, 2008.

69. Kim Hye-song, "Provocative Reckless Act Against Dialogue Partner," *Nodong Sinmun*, July 16, 2008. Ri Hyon-to, "Arms Buildup Policy Is the Source of Fostering Arms Race and Nuclear Threat," *Nodong Sinmun*, July 17, 2008. "DPRK Radio Reports U.S. Deploys Nuclear-Powered Aircraft Carrier Group in ROK," KCBS, July 17, 2008. Hong Pyong-u, "Today's General Onward March Is General Onward March of Ideology," *Nodong Sinmun*, July 18, 2008. "U.S. and S Korean Warmongers' Projected War Exercises Assailed," KCNA, July 18, 2008.

70. Kim Chong-son, "Imperialists' Economic Infiltration Is a Means of Aggression and Plunder," *Nodong Sinmun*, July 20, 2008.

71. Nam Chon-ung, "How Can One Try to Shake Hands, While Holding a Dagger?" *Minju Choson*, July 22, 2008.

72. Nam Chon-ung, "Why Do [They] Distort the Situation?" *Minju Choson*, July 29, 2008.

73. "Imperialism Bound to Go to Decline and Ruin," KCNA, August 11, 2008. Ser Myo-ja, "North Breaks Its Silence, Decries U.S. Blacklist Delay," *JoongAng Ilbo*, August 18, 2008. "Who Is the Provoker," *Nodong Sinmun*, August 29, 2008 "DPRK FM Spokesman on Ongoing U.S.-ROK Ulchi Freedom Guardian Military Exercise," KCNA, August 20, 2008.

74. "DPRK FM Spokesman on Nuclear Facilities Restoration, Removal from U.S. Terrorism Sponsor List," KCBS, September 19, 2008.

75. "The Republic's Government Will Make Every Possible Effort for Permanent Peace and Stability on the Korean Peninsula," *Minju Choson*, September 30, 2008. "Foreign Ministry Spokesman on DPRK's Will to Cooperate in Verification of Objects of Nuclear Disablement," KCNA, October 12, 2008. "DPRK FM Spokesman on 'Forces' Blaming DPRK for Delay in Implementation of Agreement," KCNA, November 12, 2008.

76. Ri Hyon-to, "Belligerent Forces That Unchangingly Pursue a Nuclear War," *Nodong Sinmun*, October 15, 2008. Ri Hyon-to, "Our Republic's Ideology on Foreign Policy Is Firm and Unwavering," *Nodong Sinmun*, October 18, 2008.

77. Glenn Kessler, "N. Korea Doesn't Agree to Written Nuclear Pact; Earlier Assurances Contradicted, U.S. Says," *Washington Post*, December 12, 2008.

78. Kim Un-chu, "The First National Power of Military-First DPRK," *Nodong Sinmun*, January 12, 2008.

79. "Let Functionaries Become Persistent Doers Who Implement the Party Policy to the End," *Nodong Sinmun*, February 20, 2008.

80. "Full Text of DPRK's 2008 New Year's Joint Editorial," KCBS, January 1, 2008.
81. M. A. Pak Sang-chol, "Immortal Revolutionary Accomplishments That Great Leader Comrade Kim Jong Il Has Achieved in the Construction of an Economically Powerful Socialist State," *Kyongje Yongu*, January 10, 2008. Writing in the government newspaper, the party makes sure to identify itself as the institution calling for the defense-led socialist economic line. Hwang Chol-u, "The Leading Sectors and the Basic Industrial Sectors of the National Economy Are the Lifeline of Economic Construction," *Minju Choson*, January 27, 2008.
82. "Adhering to the Chuch'e Character and National Character Is an Essential Demand in Carrying Out the Socialist Cause," KCBS, May 10, 2008.
83. Cho Yong-nam, "Superiority of the Socialist Planned Economy," *Nodong Sinmun*, March 5, 2008.
84. Chang Chol-san, "Adhering to and Developing Socialist Ownership Is the Fundamental Principle of Socialism," April 26, 2008, www.uriminzokkiri.com. Choe Chol-sun, "The Talk About 'Opening Up' Is [an] Insult to and Provocation Against Us," *Nodong Sinmun*, April 8, 2008.
85. "Price Index," *Minju Joson*, April 1, 2008.
86. "The DPRK Government Is Consistently Pursuing the Policy of Encouraging Joint Venture," *Foreign Trade of the Democratic People's Republic of Korea* (August 5, 2008). Available online at www.kcckp.net/ko/periodic/f_trade/index.php?contents+1198+2008-03+35+17.
87. Kim Pyong-chin, "Thorough Embodiment of Collectivist Principles and Methods in Economy Management," *Nodong Sinmun*, Special Article, August 7, 2008.
88. "Superiority of Planned Socialist Economy," *Minju Choson*, August 17, 2008.
89. Though North Korean officials told Sig Harrison in January 2009 that the regime had "weaponized" some of its fissile material, this claim is ultimately not verifiable. The "unknown number of nuclear weapons" includes zero as a distinct possibility.

8. Conclusion

1. This does not suggest that Kim Dae Jung's engagement policy was a failure. Such a conclusion can only be reached rationally if one determines that the costs of the policy exceed its gains. Gains are not limited to those diplomatic concessions that the North Korean regime explicitly gives to the South; they also include the difficult-to-measure long-term impact of the engagement policy on the North Korean economy and society.
2. One observer took this argument a step further with a simple but memorable line: "The North Korean system is built to withstand pressure, but it has no defense against friendly behavior." See Frank, "Dreaming an Impossible Dream?"

3. See, for example, "Foolish Delusion," *Rodong Sinmun*, February 26, 2009.

4. CRS Report for Congress, *Congress and U.S. Policy on North Korean Human Rights and Refugees: Recent Legislation and Implementation* (Washington, D.C.: Congressional Research Service, October 22, 2008). CRS Report for Congress, *North Korean Refugees in China and Human Rights Issues: International Response and U.S. Policy Issues* (Washington, D.C.: Congressional Research Service, September 26, 2007).

5. Such informational programs are largely accepted outside of North Korea and a handful of like-minded states as legitimate informational programs, not a punishment for a regime's behavior. Enhancing such information programs should not be articulated as a punishment for regime behavior but part of a long-term commitment to democracy and human rights.

6. Such policy options are not cost free, given the extreme punishments the regime can impose on those found with an illicit radio, cell phone, or even foreign videos, though these "crimes" have become sufficiently common that bribes often settle the problem.

7. "N. Korea's 1st Uni Delayed," *Straits Times*, December 30, 2008. Powell, "The Capitalist Who Loves North Korea."

8. Regime reversals of marketization over the last four years in favor of administrative controls over the economy seemed to be intensifying at the time of publication, but the cabinet's more vocal recognition of corruption and social ills that accompany this reversal may presage yet another shift back toward marketization and economic reform in the medium term.

9. Choi Jinwook, "Why Is North Korea So Aggressive? Kim Jong-il's Illness and North Korea's Changing Governing Style," July 30, 2003, www.nautilus.org/fora/security/09062Choi.html.

10. "Japan's Move to Tighten Sanctions Against DPRK Blasted," KCBS, December 2, 2008. "DPRK FM Spokesperson: DPRK Opposed to Japan's 6-Party Talks Participation," KCBS, December 6, 2008. Ri Hyon-to, "Hampering Act of Those Who Do Not Know Where They Stand," *Rodong Sinmun*, December 16, 2008. Kim Ung-chol, "Impudent Complaints by Those Who Do Not Even Know Their Places," *T'ongil Sinbo*, December 20, 2008.

11. "For the Peaceful Use of Space," *Minju Joson*, December 11, 2008.

12. "Lively Response to U.S. Recognition of DPRK as Nuclear Weapons State," KCNA, December 17, 2008. Choe Chol-sun, "Indiscreet Words and Actions by the Fanatics of Confrontation," *Rodong Sinmun*, December 23, 2008. Pak In-chol, "Perverseness by Those Who Do Not Even Know Their Place," *Minju Joson*, December 25, 2008.

13. "DPRK Foreign Ministry Spokesman's Press Statement," KCNA, January 13, 2009.

14. Spokesman for the General Staff of the Korean People's Army, KCTV, February 2, 2009. Spokesman for the General Staff of the Korean People's Army, KCBS, February 18, 2009.

15. "Our Revolutionary Armed Forces Will Mercilessly Crush the Anti-Republic Confrontation Maneuver of Lee Myung-bak Gang of Rebels," KCBS, January 17, 2009. "DPRK Media Carry People's Reaction to 17 January KPA General Staff Spokesman's Statement," KCTV, January 18–24, 2009. Choe Chol-sun, "Our Answer Is Merciless Punishment—Moving Toward North-South Confrontation and Fascism Is a Foolish Act of Self-Destruction," *Rodong Sinmun*, January 19, 2009. Chu Chong-kyong, "'Let Us Mercilessly Crush with the Military-First Gun Barrel Those Fellows Who Try to Toy with Us'—There Is No Limit to Our Army's Striking Capabilities," *Minju Joson*, January 20, 2009. Pak In-chol, "Our Gun Barrel Knows No Mercy," *Minju Joson*, January 20, 2009.

16. Pak In-chol, "Criminal Act Aimed at Further Escalating the Maneuver of Confronting Fellow Countrymen," *Minju Joson*, January 25, 2009.

17. Committee for the Peaceful Reunification of the Fatherland Statement, KCBS, January 29, 2009. Sim Chol-yong, "History and the Nation Will Not Forgive the Traitors," KCBS, January 31, 2009.

18. "National Defense Commission," GlobalSecurity.org, Military, www.globalsecurity.org/military/world/dprk/ndc.htm. "DPRK Chart of NDC, Cabinet, SPA, April 2009," National Committee on North Korea, www.ncnk.org/resources/briefing-papers/dprk-chart-of-ndc-cabinet-spa-april-2009.

19. "Spokesman for DPRK Foreign Ministry Slams Anti-DPRK Campaign Over Its Projected Satellite Launch," KCNA, March 24, 2009. Central Committee of the Democratic Front for the Reunification of Fatherland Statement, KCBS, March 26, 2009. Choe Chol-sun, "Extremely Dangerous Walking on Tightrope of War," *Rodong Sinmun*, April 1, 2009. Ri Kyong-chol, "The Maneuver of Confronting Fellow Countrymen, Which Is Becoming Blatant," *Minju Joson*, April 2, 2009. "DPRK Foreign Ministry Statement," KCNA, April 14, 2009. "KPA General Staff Spokesman Blasts Hostile Forces' Anti-DPRK Racket" KCNA, April 18, 2009.

20. Foreign Ministry Spokesman, KCBS, May 8, 2009. Kim Hye-song, "We Will Bring Under Control Maneuvers of Sanctions and Smear Against DPRK by Seizing Principle of Independence," *Rodong Sinmun*, May 12, 2009. Sim Chol-yong, "U.S. Policy Toward DPRK Is Anti-Peace, Anti-Reunification Policy," *Rodong Sinmun*, May 14, 2009. "International Space Law," *Minju Joson*, May 15, 2009.

21. Pak In-chol, "Does It Feel That Good to Be a Poodle to the United States?" *Minju Joson*, May 17, 2009. Om Il-kyu, "Reckless Remarks by Spiritless Nation-Selling Traitors," *Rodong Sinmun*, May 18, 2009.

22. "Let Us More Fiercely Wage the Great Battle to Build a Powerful State While Holding High the Great Military-First Banner—A Grand Pyongyang Municipal Mass Rally to Celebrate the Success in the Second Nuclear Test Was Held," *Minju Joson*, May 27, 2009.

23. DPRK Foreign Ministry Statement, KCBS, June 13, 2009.

24. Pak Chae-kyong, KCBS, June 15, 2009.

25. James Jones, interview on *Meet the Press*, "'Meet the Press' Transcript for August 9, 2009," www.msnbc.msn.com/id/32341570/ns/meet_the_press/. See also Mark Landler and Mark Mazzetti, "In North Korea, Clinton Helped Unveil a Mystery," *New York Times*, August 18, 2009.

26. "Press Statement by a Spokesperson for the DPRK Ministry of Foreign Affairs," KCBS, July 27, 2009.

27. "Report on Bill Clinton's Visit to DPRK Made Public," KCNA, August 5, 2009, www.kcna.co.jp/item/2009/200908/news05/20090805-01ee.html.

28. Victor Cha, interview by Bernard Gertzman, "UN Sanctions Pushing N. Korea to 'Smile Diplomacy,'" September 3, 2009, www.cfr.org/publication/20120/un_sanctions_pushing_n_korea_to_smile_diplomacy.html.

29. Tong Kim, "The Significance of Clinton's Visit to North Korea," *Policy Forum Online* 09-065A, August 11, 2009, www.nautilus.org/fora/security/09065Kim.html.

30. Moon Sung-hwee, "North Korean Succession May Have Hit a Road-block," *Daily NK*, August 27, 2009, http://worldmeets.us/dailynk000027.shtml. Andrei Lankov, "North Korea's Succession Gets Twisted," *East Asia Forum*, September 17, 2009, www.eastasiaforum.org/2009/09/17/north-koreas-succession-gets-twisted/.

31. Pyongyang's public threat also included an oblique reference to uranium enrichment, though its activities in this area are not directly observable.

32. Julia Cunico, "The Sun Shines On: Inter-Korea Relations Warm in August," *Korea Insight*, September 1, 2009. For another view of the turnaround in inter-Korean ties, see Donald Kirk, "Pyongyang Plays 'Funeral Diplomacy,'" *Asia Times*, August 25, 2009.

33. "N. Korea Backs Positive Hatoyama Relations," United Press International, September 10, 2009, www.upi.com/Top_News/2009/09/10/N-Korea-backs-positive-Hatoyama-relations/UPI-46131252597835/. David Fedman, "Yukio Hatoyama's Big Gamble," *Asia Chronicle*, October 2, 2009.

34. For separate analyses of the new constitution, see "Revised N. Korea Constitution Legally Makes Kim Jong Il Leader," Kyodo World Service, September 25, 2009. "DPRK's Revised Constitution Gives More Power to Kim Jong Il, Assert Human Rights," Yonhap News Agency, September 28, 2009. "North Korea Modifies its Constitution to Reflect Kim Jong-il System, *Hankyoreh*, September 29, 2009.

35. Gause, *North Korean Civil-Military Trends*, 43–44.

36. Philippa Fogarty, "Profile: Chang Song Taek," BBC News, April 21, 2009, http://news.bbc.co.uk/2/hi/americas/8002562.stm.

Bibliography

Ahn, Byung-joon. "The Man Who Would Be Kim." *Foreign Affairs* 73, no. 6 (November–December 1994): 94–108.

——. "North Korean Foreign Policy: An Overview." In *The Foreign Relations of North Korea: New Perspectives*, ed. Jae Kyu Park, B. C. Koh, and Tae-hwan Kwak, 15–38. Boulder, Colo.: Westview Press, 1987.

Ahn, Choong-yong, Nicholas Eberstadt, and Lee Young-sun. *A New International Engagement Framework for North Korea? Contending Perspectives.* Washington, D.C.: Korea Economic Institute, 2005.

An, Tai Sung. *North Korea: A Political Handbook.* Wilmington, Del.: Scholarly Resource, 1983.

——. *North Korea in Transition: From Dictatorship to Dynasty.* Westport, Conn.: Greenwood Press, 1983.

Arendt, Hannah. *The Origins of Totalitarianism.* New York: Harcourt, Brace, 1950.

Armstrong, Charles. "The Nature, Origins, and Development of the North Korean State." In *The North Korean System in the Post–Cold War Era*, ed. Samuel Kim, 39–63. New York: Palgrave, 2001.

——. *The North Korean Revolution, 1945–1950.* Ithaca, N.Y.: Cornell University Press, 2004.

Barghoorn, Frederick C. "The Security Police." In *Interest Groups in Soviet Politics*, ed. H. Gordon Skilling and Franklyn Griffiths, 78–90. Princeton: Princeton University Press, 1971.

Bermudez, Joseph, Jr. *The Armed Forces of North Korea.* London: I. B. Tauris, 2001.

——. "Information and the DPRK's Military and Power-Holding Elite." In *North Korean Policy Elites*, ed. Kongdan Oh Hassig et al., I-1–I-30. Alexandria, Va.: Institute for Defense Analyses, 2004.

Bueno de Mesquita, Bruce, and Jongryn Mo. *North Korean Economic Reform and Political Stability*. Stanford, Calif.: Hoover Institution, 1996.

Buzo, Adrian. *The Guerilla Dynasty: Politics and Leadership in North Korea*. Boulder, Colo.: Westview Press, 1999.

Carlin, Robert, and Joel S. Wit. *North Korean Reform: Politics, Economics, and Security*. Adelphi Paper 382. London: International Institute for Strategic Studies, 2006.

Carlin, Robert, and John Lewis. *Policy in Context: Negotiating with North Korea, 1992–2007*. Stanford, Calif.: Center for International Security and Cooperation, 2008.

Chehabi, Houchang, and Juan Linz. *Sultanistic Regimes*. Baltimore: Johns Hopkins University Press, 1998.

Chen, Cheng, and Ji-yong Lee. "Making Sense of North Korea: 'National Stalinism' in Comparative-Historical Perspective." *Communist and Post-Communist Studies* 40 (2007): 459–75.

Chinoy, Mike. *Meltdown: The Inside Story of the North Korean Nuclear Crisis*. New York: St. Martin's, 2008.

Cho, Han-beom. "The Characteristics of the North Korean Political System: A Comparative Socialist Perspective." *Vantage Point* (April 2003): 44–54.

Choi, Jinwook. "Changing Relations Between Party, Military, and Government in North Korea and Their Impact on Policy Direction." Stanford, Calif.: Shorenstein Asia/Pacific Research Center, 1999. Available at http://iis-db.stanford.edu/pubs/10018/ChoiPM.pdf.

Chong, Bong-uk. "Changes in North Korea's Hierarchy." *Vantage Point* (February 2007): 16–21.

Cohen, Warren. *East Asia at the Center*. New York: Columbia University Press, 2001.

Cumings, Bruce. "Corporatism in North Korea." *Journal of Korean Studies* 4 (1982–83): 269–94.

——. *Korea's Place in the Sun*. New York: W. W. Norton, 1997.

——. *North Korea: Another Country*. New York: New Press, 2004.

Eberstadt, Nicholas. *The End of North Korea*. Washington, D.C.: AEI Press, 1999.

Eckert, Carter, Ki-baik Lee, Young Ick Lew, Michael Robinson, and Edward W. Wagner. *Korea Old and New: A History*. Seoul: Korea Institute, Harvard University, 1990.

Foster-Carter, Aidan. "North Korea: Development and Self-Reliance, a Critical Appraisal." In *Korea, North and South: The Deepening Crisis*, ed. Gavan McCormack and Mark Selden, 115–20. New York: Monthly Review Press, 1972.

Frank, Rüdiger. "Dreaming an Impossible Dream? Opening, Reform, and the Future of the North Korean Economy." *Global Asia* 4, no. 2 (Summer 2009).

Available at www.globalasia.org/Current_Issues/V4N2_2009/Ruediger_Frank
.html.

———. "Economic Reforms in North Korea, 1998–2004: Systemic Restrictions,
Quantitative Analysis, Ideological Background." *Journal of the Asia Pacific Economy* 10, no. 3 (August 2005): 278–311.

Gause, Ken. *North Korean Civil-Military Trends: Military-First Politics to a Point.* Carlisle, Pa.: Strategic Studies Institute, 2006.

———. "The North Korean Leadership: System Dynamics and Fault Lines." In *North Korean Policy Elites*, ed. Kongdan Oh Hassig et al., II-1–II-44. Alexandria, Va.: Institute for Defense Analyses, 2004.

Geddes, Barbara. *Paradigms and Sand Castles: Theory Building and Research Design in Comparative Politics.* Ann Arbor: University of Michigan Press, 2003.

Gleason, Abbott. *Totalitarianism: The Inner History of the Cold War.* New York: Oxford University Press, 1995.

Goldfarb, Jeffrey. "Post-Totalitarian Politics: Ideology Ends Again." *Social Research* 57, no. 3 (Fall 1990): 533–54.

Groth, Alexander J. "USSR: Pluralist Monolith?" *British Journal of Political Science* 9, no. 4 (1979): 445–64.

Gwak, In-su. "Guiding Role of North Korean Workers' Party." *Vantage Point* (May 2004): 43–53.

Haggard, Stephan, and Marcus Noland. *Famine in North Korea: Markets, Aid, and Reform.* New York: Columbia University Press, 2007.

Halberstam, David. *The Coldest Winter: America and the Korean War.* New York: Hyperion, 2007.

Harrison, Selig S. "Did North Korea Cheat?" *Foreign Affairs* 84, no. 1 (January–February 2005).

Hassig, Ralph. "The Well-Informed Cadre." In *North Korean Policy Elites*, ed. Kongdan Oh Hassig et al., III-1–III-39. Alexandria, Va.: Institute for Defense Analyses, 2004.

Ho, David Yau-fai. "On the Concept of Face." *American Journal of Sociology* 81, no. 4 (1976): 867–84.

Hoare, James, and Susan Pares. *North Korea in the Twenty-First Century.* Folkestone, UK: Global Oriental, 2005.

Hough, Jerry. *The Soviet Union and Social Science Theory.* Cambridge, Mass.: Harvard University Press, 1977.

Hwang, Jang Yop. *Nanun Yoksaui Chillirul Poatta* [I Saw the Truth of History]. Seoul: Hanul, 1999.

Kihl, Young Whan. "Emergence of the Second Republic: The Kim Regime Adapts to the Challenge of Modernity," In *North Korea: The Politics of Regime Survival*, ed. Young Whan Kihl and Hong Nack Kim, 37-58. Armonk, N.Y.: M. E. Sharpe, 2006.

Kihl, Young Whan, and Hong Nack Kim. *North Korea: The Politics of Regime Survival.* Armonk, N.Y.: M. E. Sharpe, 2006.

Kim, Dough Joong. *Foreign Relations of North Korea During Kim Il Sung's Last Days.* Seoul: Sejong Institute, 1994.

Kim, Hak-chun. *North and South Korea: Internal Politics and External Relations Since 1988.* [Mississauga, Ont.:] Society for Korean and Related Studies, 2006.

Kim, Ilpyong J. *Communist Politics in North Korea.* New York: Praeger, 1975.

Kim, Samuel S. "Introduction: A Systems Analysis." In *The North Korean System in the Post–Cold War Era,* ed. Samuel Kim, 1–37. New York: Palgrave, 2001.

——. "North Korea in 1999, Bringing the Grand Chollima March Back In." *Asian Survey* 40, no. 1 (2000): 151–63.

——, ed. *The North Korean System in the Post–Cold War Era.* New York: Palgrave, 2001.

Kim, Sung Chull. *North Korea Under Kim Jong Il: From Consolidation to Systemic Dissonance.* Albany: State University of New York Press, 2006.

Kim, Young-yoon, and Soo-young Choi. *Understanding North Korea's Economic Reforms.* Seoul: Center for the North Korean Economy, 2005.

Koh, Byung Chul. "Ideology and Political Control in North Korea." *Journal of Politics* 32, no. 3 (1970): 655–74.

——. "North Korea's Foreign Policymaking Process." In *The Foreign Relations of North Korea: New Perspectives,* ed. Jae Kyu Park, Byung Chul Koh, and Tae-Hwan Kwak, 49–55. Boulder, Colo.: Westview Press, 1987.

Kwon, Soyoung. "State Building in North Korea: From a 'Self-Reliant' to a 'Military-First' State." *Asian Affairs* 34, no. 3 (2003): 286 – 96.

Lankov, Andrei. "The Natural Death of North Korean Stalinism." *Asia Policy* 1 (January 2006): 95–121.

——. "North Korea: De-Stalinization from Below and the Advent of New Social Forces." *Harvard Asia Quarterly* 10, no. 2 (Spring 2006): 4–14.

Lee, Chong-sik. *Korean Workers' Party: A Short History.* Stanford, Calif.: Hoover Institution Press, 1978.

——. "The 1972 Constitution and Top Communist Leaders." In *Political Leadership in Korea,* ed. Dae-sook Suh and Chae-jin Lee, 192–222. Seattle: University of Washington Press, 1976.

Linz, Juan. *Totalitarian and Authoritarian Regimes.* Boulder, Colo.: Lynne Rienner Publishers, 2000.

Linz, Juan J., and Alfred Stepan. *Problems of Democratic Transition and Consolidation: Southern Europe, South America, and Post-Communist Europe.* Baltimore: Johns Hopkins University Press, 1996.

Mansourov, Alexandre. "Disaster Management and Institutional Change in the DPRK: Trends in the Songun Era." *KEI Academic Paper Series* 2, no. 9 (September 2007): 1–19.

——. "Kim Jong Il's Military-First Politics." In *North Korea: The Politics of Regime Survival,* ed. Young Whan Kihl and Hong Nack Kim, 37–58. Armonk, N.Y.: M. E. Sharpe, 2006.

Martin, Bradley. *Under the Loving Care of the Fatherly Leader: North Korea and the Kim Dynasty.* New York: St. Martin's Press, 2006.

McCormack, Gavan, and Mark Selden, eds. *Korea, North and South: The Deepening Crisis.* New York: Monthly Review Press, 1972.

McEachern, Patrick. "Benchmarks of Economic Reform in North Korea." In *Korea Yearbook,* ed. Rüdiger Frank, James E. Hoare, Patrick Köllner, and Susan Pares, 231–46. Leiden: Brill, 2008.

Molina, Oscar, and Martin Rhodes. "Corporatism: The Past, Present, and Future of a Concept." *Annual Review of Political Science* 5 (2002): 305–31.

Moon, Chung In, and Yongho Kim. "The Future of the North Korean System," In *The North Korean System in the Post–Cold War Era,* ed. Samuel Kim, 221–57. New York: Palgrave, 2001.

Nam-son, Yi. "Choosing the Leading Sectors of Agriculture in Keeping with the Characteristics of the Area and Concentrating Effort in Those Sectors Is an Important Way of Resolving the Issue of the People's Livelihood." *Kyongje Yongu* (February 10, 2001): 35–38.

Neumann, Franz. *The Democratic and the Authoritarian State.* Glencoe, Ill.: Free Press, 1957.

Neumann, Sigmund. *Permanent Revolution: The Total State in a World at War.* New York: Harper and Brothers, 1942.

Noland, Marcus, ed. *Economic Integration of the Korean Peninsula.* Washington, D.C.: Institute for International Economics, 2000.

Odom, William E. "A Dissenting View on the Group Approach to Soviet Politics." *World Politics* 28, no. 4 (1976): 542–67.

Oh, Kongdan, and Ralph C. Hassig. *North Korea Through the Looking Glass.* Washington, D.C.: Brookings Institution Press, 2000.

Oh Hassig, Kongdan, Joseph S. Bermudez Jr., Kenneth E. Gause, Ralph C. Hassig, Alexandre Y. Mansourov, and David J. Smith. *North Korean Policy Elites.* Alexandria: Va.: Institute for Defense Analyses, 2004.

Paik, Haksoon. "North Korea's Choices for Survival and Prosperity Since 1990s: Interplay between Politics and Economics." *Sejong Policy Studies* 3, no. 2 (2007): 249–92.

——. "North Korea's Pursuit of Security and Economic Interests: Chasing Two Rabbits with One Stone." In *North Korea in Distress: Confronting Domestic and External Challenges,* ed. Haksoon Paik and Seong-Chang Cheong, 95–126. Seoul: Sejong Institute, 2008.

Paik, Haksoon, and Seong-Chang Cheong. *North Korea in Distress: Confronting Domestic and External Challenges.* Seoul: Sejong Institute, 2008.

Park, Jae Kyu. Introduction. In *The Foreign Relations of North Korea: New Perspectives,* ed. Jae Kyu Park, Byung Chul Koh, and Tae-Hwan Kwak, 3–14. Boulder, Colo.: Westview Press, 1987.

——. "Power Structure in North Korea." In *The Politics of North Korea,* ed. Jae Kyu Park and Jung Gun Kim, 111–42. Seoul, Korea: Institute for Far Eastern Studies, Kyungnam University, 1979.

Park, Jae Kyu, and Jung Gun Kim. *The Politics of North Korea.* Seoul, Korea: The Institute for Far Eastern Studies, 1979.

Park, Jae Kyu, Byung Chul Koh, and Tae-Hwan Kwak, eds. *The Foreign Relations of North Korea: New Perspectives*. Boulder, Colo.: Westview Press, 1987.

Post, Jerrold. "Kim Jong Il of North Korea: In the Shadow of His Father." In *Leaders and Their Followers in a Dangerous World: The Psychology of Political Behavior*, 239–58. Ithaca, N.Y.: Cornell University Press, 2004.

Powell, Bill. "The Capitalist Who Loves North Korea." *Fortune*, September 15, 2009.

Pritchard, Charles L. *Failed Diplomacy: The Tragic Story of How North Korea Got the Bomb*. Washington, D.C.: Brookings Institution Press, 2007.

Reiss, Mitchell B., and Robert L. Gallucci. "Red-handed." *Foreign Affairs* 84, no. 2 (March–April 2005).

Roehrig, Terence. "Korean Dispute Over the Northern Limit Line: Security, Economics, or International Law?" *Maryland Series in Contemporary Asian Studies* 3, no. 194 (2008).

Scalapino, Robert. "In Search of Peace and Stability in the Region Surrounding the Korean Peninsula: Challenges and Opportunities." *American Foreign Policy Interests* 28 (2006): 367–78.

——. Introduction. In *North Korea in a Regional and Global Context*, ed. Robert Scalapino and Hongkoo Lee, ix–xviii. Berkeley: Institute of East Asian Studies, University of California, 1986.

Scalapino, Robert, and Chong-sik Lee. *Communism in Korea*. Berkeley: University of California Press, 1972.

Scobell, Andrew. *Kim Jong Il and North Korea: The Leader and the System*. Carlisle, Pa.: Strategic Studies Institute, 2006.

——. "Making Sense of North Korea: Pyongyang and Comparative Communism." *Asian Security* 1, no. 3 (2005): 245–66.

Sigal, Leon. *Disarming Strangers: Nuclear Diplomacy with North Korea*. Princeton: Princeton University Press, 1998.

Skilling, H. Gordon. "Interest Groups and Communist Politics Revisited." *World Politics* 36, no. 1 (1983): 1–27.

Skilling, H. Gordon, and Franklyn Griffiths. *Interest Groups in Soviet Politics*. Princeton: Princeton University Press, 1971.

Suh, Dae-sook. "Communist Party Leadership." In *Political Leadership in Korea*, ed. Dae-sook Suh and Chae-jin Lee, 159–91. Seattle: University of Washington Press, 1976.

——. *Kim Il Sung: The North Korean Leader*. New York: Columbia University Press, 1988.

——. *Korean Communism, 1945–1980: A Reference Guide to the Political System*. Honolulu: University of Hawaii Press, 1981.

——. "The Organization and Administration of North Korean Foreign Policy." In *North Korea in a Regional and Global Context*, ed. Robert Scalapino and Hongkoo Lee, 1–19. Berkeley: Institute of East Asian Studies, University of California, 1986.

Suh, Dae-sook, and Chae-jin Lee. *Political Leadership in Korea*. Seattle: University of Washington Press, 1976.

Suh, Jae-jung. *Power, Interests, and Identity in Military Alliances*. New York: Palgrave, 2007.

Thompson, Mark. "To Shoot or Not to Shoot: Post-Totalitarianism in China and Eastern Europe." *Comparative Politics* 34, no. 1 (2001): 63–83.

Tilly, Charles. "Why and How History Matters." In *The Oxford Handbook of Contextual Political Analysis*, ed. Robert Goodwin and Charles Tilly, 417–37. Oxford: Oxford University Press, 2006.

Truman, David B. *The Governmental Process: Political Interests and Public Opinion*. New York: Alfred A. Knopf, 1971.

Vorontsov, Alexander. "Current Russia–North Korea Relations: Challenges and Achievements." Center for Northeast Asian Policy Studies Research Papers. Washington, D.C.: Brookings Institution Press, February 2007. Available at www.brookings.edu/papers/2007/02northkorea_vorontsov.aspx.

Weber, Max. *Economy and Society*. New York: Bedminster Press, 1968 (1914).

Wit, Joel, Daniel B. Poneman, and Robert L. Gallucci. *Going Critical: The First North Korean Nuclear Crisis*. Washington, D.C.: Brookings Institution Press, 2004.

Wu, Anne. "What China Whispers to North Korea." *Washington Quarterly* 28 no. 2 (Spring 2005): 42.

Yang, Sung Chull. *The North and South Korean Political Systems: A Comparative Analysis*. Boulder, Colo.: Westview Press, 1994.

Yonhap News Agency. *North Korea Handbook*. Seoul: M. E. Sharpe, 2003.

Yoo, Se Hee. "Change and Continuity in North Korea's Foreign Policy." *Foreign Relations of North Korea During Kim Il Sung's Last Days*, ed. Dough Joong Kim, 1–22. Seoul: Sejong Institute, 1994.

Index